HAZEL MEYER'S
FREEZER
COOK BOOK

by Hazel Meyer

HAZEL MEYER'S FREEZER COOK BOOK
THE COMPLETE BOOK OF HOME FREEZING

HAZEL MEYER'S
FREEZER
COOK BOOK

by Hazel Meyer

J. B. LIPPINCOTT COMPANY
Philadelphia/New York

For Alicia Armida Theresa Bartoli,

fabulous cook and faithful friend, who helped

immeasurably during the three long years it

required to collect, winnow, prepare, and

freezer-test recipes contained

in this book

Contents

Foreword

Science fiction writers promise robot machines in well-appointed homes of the future, displacing such primitive furnishings as kitchen equipment. Dial the meal you want, and it will materialize. Unfortunately, most of the food will be synthetic because earth can no longer supply natural nutriments.

Fantastic? Maybe. Certainly life as we know it now has changed markedly from life as it was not long ago. This is as true of food products as it is of the electronic marvels we learned so quickly to take for granted. Frozen foods have been available only since the middle of the present century, around the time American rooftops began to sprout antennas. The food industry has recently introduced freeze-dried foods and "boilable bag" packaging that permits the housewife to cook without having to wash a pot. In testing laboratories as this is written—and possibly in existence by the time you read it—are at least two related packaging products. One is an edible wrap which will provide the food it contains with an appropriate sauce. Another is a container which will self-destruct according to programed intelligence.

Well, all right. As skimming through this book will demonstrate, I am no decrier of convenience, timesaving devices, or short-cut methods. On the other hand, as long as real earth-grown food is still available I am going to eat it, with or without its package. And because to me food and freezing are almost synonymous, most of what I eat I am going to freeze—raw to be cooked later, or in recipes to be com-

pleted and served later. These are the two concerns that led
to the writing of a cookbook companion to *The Complete
Book of Home Freezing.**

HAZEL MEYER

* Published by J. B. Lippincott Company. First edition, 1953. Revised
editions, 1959 and 1964. Paperback Library edition, 1967.

HAZEL MEYER'S
FREEZER
COOK BOOK

1.

The Ins (and Outs) of Freezer Stockpiling

If you felt like it, you could spend a couple of weeks cooking nearly all the recipes your family likes and freezing them for later use. You'd need a pretty big freezer to accommodate them, especially if you insisted on freezing them in serving casseroles. You'd need a heck of a lot of casseroles, too. But you could do it. You could take a month's vacation after stacking up 30 meals for your family to eat at whim, or you could label them according to the days of the weeks and tape a corresponding calendar on the freezer door. Your stay-at-homes might compliantly follow your schedule of nutrition, but on the other hand they might eat all the Sundays first.

Cooking for the freezer is a fine thing. Cooking from it can be equally important.

Over the years, since the first printing of *The Complete Book of Home Freezing*, experience and familiarity with my subject have taught me a lot. Among other lessons, I've learned that even my comparatively generous shelf space is precious and should never be allowed to become cluttered

3

with bulky packages of raw foods seldom used routinely, or with too many precooked recipes of the "heat and eat" type. I find it preferable, although not necessarily always, to leave one or two simple finishing touches to add at serving time.

This home education has guided me to many spacesaving strategies and some character-strengthening resolutions. I now sternly resist the almost uncontrollable impulse to buy several turkeys when they are, as they often are, so very cheap. Unless, of course, it's close to the holidays. Or unless they're pretty small. The third time I come across a package of something it seemed such good economy to put tenderly away (such as a pretty small turkey) I mark it for immediate use and place it where it will look at me expectantly the next time I open the freezer door. It then becomes a good idea to invite people for dinner. You'd be surprised at how many Thanksgiving dinners I have served in March and August.

Living year-round in a fishing and summer resort town used to put strange and wonderful forage in my freezer until I developed self-restraint. Anglers' pride and parties, parties, parties are a seasonlong source of inevitable and sometimes glamorous loot which has a way of crowding out of my freezer the homelier basic foodstuffs needed for nourishment.

You won't hear me saying no to the skin diver who surfaces triumphantly with a lobster in each hand, or to my friends with Wellfleet oyster licenses. There will always be room for a dozen tinker mackerel or the center cut of a well-hooked striper, but I long ago accepted my last brimming basket of whiting.

Party-givers who forget to set a rain date for the beach barbecue after ordering a huge sirloin steak won't be refused, but please don't count on my storing 6 loaves of yard-long bread. Never again will I squander a cubic foot of space on a batch of perfectly good potato salad that didn't get served because of a last-minute decision to entertain at brunch, instead of supper, on the deck; and who wants potato salad with eye-opening Bloody Marys?

My iron *won't* applies also to highly stylized cocktail dips whose containers I can't label because I don't know what's in them and I'm too polite to ask, and it includes the un-eaten dozens of darling canapés on fancy crackers garnished with squiggles of cream cheese blended with green and red food colorings (for Christmas-in-July parties, naturally). Re-gretfully, it also embraces the nineteen 2-pound packages of wholesale chicken livers a restaurateur friend overordered. Two or three packages, yes. Nineteen, no.

Whenever I see a summer visitor walking barefoot down my path to the kitchen door or climbing up from the beach with a foil-covered mixing bowl cradled in sunburned arms, I hastily reach into my refrigerator for the big canned ham I usually have on hand in summer and stand in front of the freezer saying, "Now I wonder if I have room in the freezer for this?"

What I have learned to keep out of the freezer lets me keep in it, along with raw ingredients and a variable assort-ment of precooked one-for-the-freezer courses, the many scaled-to-recipe menu aids I use so often. These include: containers of beef, chicken, fish, mushroom, veal, and vege-table stock; purées of individual or mixed vegetables; rich gravies and heavy white sauces (which can always be thinned); fairly large containers of special Italian sauces; packages of combined diced green peppers, onions, and cel-ery for stew-starters; whole, sliced, and button mushrooms bagged separately for their intended uses; tightly rolled cab-bage leaves—the dark outer ones—to add flavor to soups, stews, pot roasts, and some casseroles.

When I buy several chickens for storage, I render the fat

and freeze it in baby-food jars. It keeps a very long time. I freeze the livers separately. I make stock from the giblets, or freeze them uncooked for use in stuffings.

There are no lunchbox toters in my family, but if there were you may be sure I would keep in my freezer at least a week's supply of sandwiches and other appropriate box fillers. As it is, the day before a picnic or a shore party finds me shopping in my freezer for the makings. Thinly sliced meat loaf, each slice wrapped separately and gathered into a bag weeks ago, can be slipped onto one slice of bread, garnished with pickle chips or relish, topped with another slice of bread, popped into a sandwich bag, and returned to the freezer ready for tomorrow's outing without shedding one tiny drop of thaw. The same procedure applies to frozen sliced turkey, chicken, ham, roast beef, luncheon meats, and cheese.

Although I practically live out of my freezer, I do find it wise to keep on a separate shelf in a room-temperature cupboard a number of condiments and ingredients I use when preparing certain recipes either for the freezer or from it. This is a long list, starting with a complete inventory of seasonings, herbs, and spices, continuing to cans of tuna and salmon and a few condensed soups I don't bother to make, and concluding with a miscellany of somewhat more exotic stuff—water chestnuts, bamboo shoots, soy and duck sauces, grated coconut for curries, caviar, smoked oysters and mussels for cocktail dips, and canned tortillas for Mexican meals in case I run out of fresh ones bought in quantity whenever I'm near a Spanish bodega, and frozen in packages of a dozen.

The commercial food processors supply us with a continually growing list of excellent food products, many of them intended for use just as they come in their colorful packages. I've found, however, that even the best of these take kindly to a little encouragement and imagination before being brought to the table. I have no wish to quarrel with the food companies' wonderful testing kitchens, but I really do prefer to add my own sauces and embellishments to frozen vegetables. Frozen Chinese products welcome the additions I keep in freezer and cupboard. When I'm too busy—or lazy—to make my own pizza and rely instead on an advertised frozen brand, I automatically reach into my freezer for a small package of Italian sausage stored for just this purpose. While the door is open, I also take out extra mozzarella and Romano cheese.

Thus, my basic freezer stockpile of menu aids is built on a foundation of stocks, gravies, plain and fancy sauces, planned leftovers, and a few oddments of my own preference. Your personal cooking routines and meal planning for family and company will ultimately dictate your stockpile, and the contents of your freezer will not necessarily resemble mine. A freezer is good-natured about anything within reason entrusted to it by whim or calculation. Mine usually holds several small containers of stirred whole eggs, quantities of packages of snack-proportioned cheeses, and always a large plastic bagful of seasoned bread crumbs made by electric blender out of day-old Italian bread.

But if you should ask for a vote for the single most valuable classification in my freezer stockpile, Stock would win in a walk.

Stock is the foundation for practically all the gravy and sauce recipes in this book. It is added to dozens of my from-the-freezer main courses. When I make pot roast or any kind of stew, the liquid used is stock, not water. When meat is basted, it is basted with stock related to it by a former marriage. When my stock harvest has been bountiful and the freezer is crowded, I'm very likely to combine 2 or 3 containers of different kinds of stock and use it instead of water for soaking dried beans, lentils, or peas for a hearty soup. (Of course, my method of cooking legumes never discards the liquid in which they were soaked.) Corn meal for Tamale Pie (page 322) is cooked in stock. Stock from mild vegetables and sometimes from the chicken pot is used for making yeast breads and rolls.

In the Chinese restaurant with which I was once involved —the involvement is described briefly on page 34—I almost went out of my frugal mind because of egg rolls. Egg rolls worthy of their honorable name require for their construction a remarkable machine called an egg roll press. It bears a vague resemblance to a wine press but is identified as, and used exclusively for, one of the intricate maneuvers performed by the high-salaried egg roll chef which lead ultimately to placing before an expectant diner that popular Chinese hors d'oeuvre, the American egg roll.

What the egg roll chef does is press until almost dry the chopped and shredded vegetables to be combined with the chopped and shredded pork and shrimp or lobster. You have no *idea* how much liquid there is in the raw vegetables used for egg rolls. It is, in Chinese restaurants, collected in buckets and thrown away. This never failed to astonish as well as grieve me, for Chinese chefs have great respect for food and abhor waste. To the amusement of the kitchen staff, I would hang around the egg roll press at milking time and fill containers with vegetable juices to be taken home for freezing. Stock!

HOW TO FREEZE STOCK: GENERAL INSTRUCTIONS

Some of the stock recipes to follow suggest special freezing methods. In general, however, strain the stock and allow it to cool before pouring it into containers. Label and seal the containers, chill them thoroughly in the refrigerator, then freeze.

If fat-free meat or poultry stock is desired, refrigerate after straining until excess fat congeals on the surface for easy removal.

Limited freezer space or limited stores of freezer containers may be a factor in deciding how much stock to put away, no matter how useful it is. There are ways of conserving both space and containers.

1. For large amounts of stock, pour it when chilled into bread pans and freeze it quickly. When solid, submerge the pans to within ½-inch of their tops in lukewarm water until the stock can be released as "bricks." Wrap each separately in Saran or other film and put as many as you have into a large plastic bag before returning them to the freezer.

2. For smaller amounts of stock—or for small freezers —pour the chilled stock into muffin tins or ice-cube trays and follow the preceding instructions.

VEGETABLE STOCKS

Vegetable Stock I

Keep a quart jar in the refrigerator. Add to the jar the small amounts of water remaining when you cook fresh *or frozen* vegetables for the table. Pour a week's collection into containers and freeze.

Vegetable Stock II

Keep a large plastic bag in the refrigerator. Put into it the outer leaves of artichokes, cabbage, lettuce; the unused stalks of celery; the tops of celery and beets; the cut-away parts of carrots, cauliflower, onions, parsnips, tomatoes, turnips; the trimmings of broccoli and mushrooms; the not-quite-perfect leaves of kale or spinach; a few of the prettier pea pods. When the bag is full—or once a week—pick over this potpourri for obvious defects and wash the salvage.

Chop the combination or put it all through the coarse blade of your meat grinder. Add 2 cups of chopped vegetables to 1 quart of lightly salted water. Bring rapidly to a boil, lower the heat to moderate, and simmer for 20 minutes.

For clear stock, strain the liquid. For a more nutritious

stock, force the simmered vegetables and liquid through a coarse sieve or a Foley mill, or blend at high speed until liquefied.

Vegetable Stock III

If quantities of fresh vegetables are yours for the gathering in your garden, or if they are inexpensively come by, or if you become so addicted to freezing lots of stock that you find yourself snitching baby carrots, celery hearts, and other table-quality vegetables from the stew you're preparing for the evening meal, this is your procedure for a thick stock which can be thinned as desired when it is removed from the freezer:

4 to 6 cups chopped fresh vegetables
4 cups water with 1 teaspoon salt

Add the vegetables to the salted water in a large saucepan, bring rapidly to a boil, and cook over moderate heat until all are tender. Force through a sieve or a food mill.

Alternative blender method: Put 1 cup of salted water at a time into an electric blender, add chopped *uncooked* vegetables 1 cup at a time, and blend at high speed until emulsified. This mixed vegetable purée can be frozen immediately for periods of up to 3 months, or it can be brought slowly to the boiling point, cooled, chilled, frozen, and stored up to a year.

Mushroom Stock

There is a brief period during the year when mushrooms, sometimes as expensive as steak, are offered at prices so low it's hard to resist bringing them home by the basketful for freezing.

Preparing a large quantity of mushrooms for the freezer leaves a residue of mushroom stems and broken pieces, and these become the basis of a simple, rich, dark, savory stock which does wonders for on-the-spur recipes.

To each cup of chopped stems and pieces, add 1 cup of lightly salted boiling water. Simmer for 15 minutes. Half-fill small containers with the mushroom bits and cover with their own liquid. Or buzz in a blender until puréed.

MEAT STOCKS

Thrifty Meat Stock
(From trimmings and meaty bones)

Use almost any kind of meat—beef, lamb, pork, veal. If the bones are large, crack them with a clean hammer. In a little fat from the meat, or in any shortening, brown the meat trimming and then the bones. Put both meat and bones into a large-bottomed heavy pot and cover to twice their depth with boiling water. Simmer for 2 hours, or until the liquid is reduced by half. Vegetable parings, outer leaves, etc., may be added for the last half-hour of simmering. Strain the stock and cool it in the refrigerator. Remove excess fat. Be sure to label the container as to the meat base.

Rich Meat Stock
(Best made with beef or veal)

2 pounds meat plus bones
1½ teaspoons salt
2 quarts cold water
½ cup chopped or sliced onions
1½ to 2 cups chopped mixed raw vegetables (optional)
½ cup raw or canned tomatoes for beef stock (omit for veal stock)

Cut the meat into small chunks and crack the bones. Put about half the meat into a large soup pot and sprinkle it with the salt. Let this stand while you brown the rest of the meat in a large skillet in a little of its own fat, or in any shortening. Brown the bones. Remove the meat and bones to the soup pot and let stand for 40 minutes. Add the water and bring to a boil. Lower the heat and simmer, covered, for 3 hours. In the fat remaining in the skillet sauté the onions until limp and remove them with a slotted spoon to the simmering stock. Add any other vegetables you are including and simmer for ½ hour. Strain and chill the stock and remove most of the congealed fat.

POULTRY STOCKS

Please, what are they doing with all the chicken feet? Done up in those nice reusable plastic bags, the cleaned and eviscerated birds one gets nowadays from most supermarkets are footless, although paper-wrapped packages of edible innards are usually tucked modestly out of sight in the body cavities. Sometimes a chicken has 2 livers, no heart. Sometimes it has 2 hearts, no gizzard. Sometimes a tiny broiler has an eagle-sized liver, but a hummingbird's heart.

Can't you just see a group of white-aproned packers at a long table laughing wildly as they grab assorted oddments from a line-up of containers and wrap the proper number without regard to their function in the body? If any one immaculate chicken ever gets back its very own vital organs, it must be the absolutely unique exception to all the laws of mathematical probability.

Thrifty Chicken Stock I
(Made with necks, giblets, backs, wings—and feet, if any)

A good time to make this stock is when you bring home an armful of chickens for the freezer. (Remove all but one of the livers and freeze them in a heavy plastic bag for a separate meal—storage time up to 3 months.)

If the chickens came equipped with feet, cover these with boiling water and cook briskly for 5 minutes. Pour off the water and when the feet are cool enough to handle, remove and discard the skin but not the jellylike substance.

Put the hearts, gizzards, 1 liver, necks, backs, and wings into a large soup pot. Add the prepared feet, if you have them. Cover with water to twice their depth, add a little salt (about ¼ teaspoon per pound of parts), bring to a boil, lower the heat, and simmer, covered, for 2 hours. If you have any stock vegetables in your refrigerator (page 9), add a cupful at the end of the 2 hours and simmer for another 30 minutes.

Strain and cool the stock and stir it before putting it into containers. There won't be much fat, and what there is will improve the flavor. If you had chicken feet, you'll find that when this stock comes out of the freezer and is thawed slowly in the refrigerator instead of being heated immediately, it is very like a jellied consommé and can be served cold.

Thrifty Chicken Stock II
(Made with a roaster's carcass and cooked skin)

When you've done everything you can about the edible portions of a roasted chicken—eaten them, made sandwiches, frozen some slices—there's still some nourishment left for the freezer.

Break up the carcass and put it into a saucepan along with the cooked skin and any shreds of meat that cling to the bones. To what was a 4-pound roaster, add 3 or 4 cups of water and ¼ teaspoon of salt. Simmer, covered, for 1 hour. Add vegetables, if you like, as in the preceding recipe. Simmer for 30 minutes longer. Strain, cool, stir, and freeze.

Rich Chicken Stock
(Made with a stewing fowl)

Unless your family insists on soup, the day you make fricassee, chicken stew, or salad is a good day to put a few containers of prime chicken stock into the freezer.

4½ - to 5½ -pound stewing fowl cut into serving pieces
5 cups water
1½ cups coarsely cut celery, with leaves
1 large carrot, sliced
1 medium onion, sliced or chopped
1 tablespoon chopped fresh parsley (or 1 teaspoon parsley flakes)
1 outer cabbage leaf
1 teaspoon salt

Cover the fowl with the water, bring it to a boil, lower the heat, and simmer, covered, for 2 to 2½ hours. Add the vegetables and salt and continue to simmer gently until the chicken is tender (about 30 minutes). Allow the chicken to remain in the broth until it is cool enough to handle, then remove it. Strain and chill the broth for freezing, saving out enough for your fricassee or stew recipe.

Turkey Stock

Because of its stronger taste, this cannot always be used interchangeably with chicken stock, but you'll find plenty of uses for it in some gravies or sauces, or in mingling its flavor with hearty soups and stews. I usually freeze turkey stock in small containers—the 8- or 12-ounce sizes.

To make turkey stock, follow the recipe for Thrifty Chicken Stock II (page 13), but increase the water to 8 cups.

FISH STOCK

Fish Stock
(Made with fresh or frozen fish parts)

Save the head, fins, and tail of a large fresh fish brought home for baking, or those of smaller ones used in other recipes. Add to these trimmings the skin and bones of the cooked fish. If you don't feel like making the stock the day you cook the fish, gather these parts in a double plastic bag and refrigerate them overnight or freeze them for a few days until you have the time.

It is a very good idea to have a container or so of fish stock in the freezer. It adds strength and savor to fish or shellfish chowders. It can be diluted and spiced for use as a quick court bouillon for cooking shrimp. Very bland fish like to be simmered in it, and it can be used instead of water if you ever decide to make your own gefüllte fish (page 143).

Very simply, put the contributing fishy parts into a saucepan, barely cover them with water, and simmer, covered, for 10 minutes. Add about a cupful of mixed vegetables—celery with leaves, onion, carrot, cabbage—and simmer for 20 minutes longer. Season lightly with salt and pepper, strain, chill, and freeze.

2.

What's Sauce for the Freezer Is Sauce for the Gourmet Cook

I have no way of knowing what kind of cook you are—casual or flustered, plain or fancy. It doesn't matter. Superb meals are prepared by all temperaments. I knew a woman who never approached her stove until she'd had several belts of strong beverage, and she approached it unsteadily. Nevertheless, and almost before anyone could say, "On the rocks," she could clear a space on the cocktail table and set down a casserole of such supreme savor and beauty that we who ate it marveled at what was surely genius. And unlike some cooks who persuade you of their superior culinary accomplishments by making you wait until you're so hungry anything at all edible would taste divine, she always seemed to know the precise moment our appetites quickened.

Another gourmet cook of my acquaintance gets hysterics if anyone comes within 10 feet of her kitchen while, cold sober, she is suffering over one of her incomparable meals. (There may be a nasty little moral to all of this, but we'd better let it go.)

No matter what kind of cook you are, it is apparent that

you occasionally look at cookbooks or you wouldn't be reading this. Until you've acquired the habit of stockpiling in
your freezer a wardrobe of sauces—basic, mix-or-match, or
high style—you won't know the magical effect it can have
on your menus, even the prosaic short-order broiled or fried
courses you rush to table after an afternoon of work, shopping, or bridge.

It may seem odd to keep simple sauces in the freezer
when they are not too difficult to prepare from scratch and
when so many canned and dehydrated varieties are available on store shelves. Maybe so, but a cup or a pint of white
sauce in the freezer means that you can bring your choice of
a long list of recipes to the table quickly and casually without the necessity of melting the butter, working in the flour,
scalding the milk, and standing at attention to stir and season, taste, and stir again.

When it comes to some of the special sauces, you might
do very well to consider stockpiling those you use with some
degree of frequency. The saving in future time can be enormous.

Italian sauces are a case in point. After I've spent several
hours with chopping block, meat grinder, garlic press, mortar and pestle and hot stove, cooking sauce the way I like it
—slowly and lengthily, seasoned just so, and without a ves-
tige of residue oil or grease—I don't care to repeat the time-
consuming process any sooner than I have to. And, despite
the flattering insistence of some guests who seem satisfied to
eat Italian food every time they come to the house, I'm not
stuck in the kitchen while they clink glasses merrily in the
living room. The sauce I take out of my freezer months after
I've entrusted it to zero storage is every bit as good as the
sauce served the day it was made. Maybe better.

Another time to think of your freezer is when you make a
very special sauce for a company dinner or for the good of
your creative soul. Some examples: puréed oysters to glorify

bland fish fillets, Chinese lobster sauce for shrimp, sweet-and-sour sauce for pork or chicken, and any of the rarer sauces calling for ingredients you don't necessarily have on hand at all times, such as shallots or fresh mint.

RULES FOR FREEZING AND USING SAUCES

Freezing: After the meal's requirements have been satisfied, permit the sauce intended for freezing to cool. Stir and pour into rigid containers. It is usually a good idea to choose small rather than large containers for all except some of the more generously served Italian sauces. Leave a margin of space at the top for expansion. Cover the containers, label and date the contents, and chill in the refrigerator. When cold, remove to the freezer.

Using frozen sauces: Open the container and remove any surface crystals with a spoon (they're practically all water). Replace the lid and put the covered container into a shallow pan of warm, not hot, water until the contents can easily be released into the top of a double boiler over simmering water. The sauce may appear lumpy and separated, but as it heats you can break it up with a fork, and when hot it will recombine as you stir briskly. If the sauce seems too thick, thin it with a little scalded milk, heated stock, or other liquid, depending on the sauce base.

Special note about wine sauces: If you have leftover wine sauce, by all means freeze it. In general, however, it is better to add wine to an appropriate sauce after it comes out of the freezer and is heated, allowing the wine to simmer in the sauce for 2 to 3 minutes.

How long to store sauces: Properly contained and at zero temperature, any sauce recipe in this book, unless otherwise noted, will retain its integrity for as long as you would ordinarily entrust a container of soup to your freezer for safekeeping. This is said on the assumption that you will be reasonable. Don't be a squirrel, hoarding exotic sauces until a month after next Christmas. On the other hand, don't feel that you have to rotate your sauce stockpile every few weeks. I have on occasion found a "lost" container of sauce hiding in the freezer, wondered about it, heated it, tasted it, reconstituted it with liquid if necessary—and eaten it with relish—as long as 6 to 8 months after it was labeled and put away.

BASIC WHITE SAUCES FOR THE FREEZER

The following recipes yield a minimum of 2 cups, on the assumption that even small-freezer owners are going to freeze at least one 8-ounce container each time they make the sauce.

Average White Sauce
(For soup bases, casseroles, vegetables, creamed courses)

1 pint		*1 quart*
4 tablespoons	butter	¼ pound
4 tablespoons	flour	½ cup
1 pint	milk	1 quart
¼ teaspoon	salt	½ teaspoon
⅛ teaspoon	pepper	¼ teaspoon

Heavy White Sauce
(For soufflés, croquettes, cutlets, or as base for thinning with stock or wine)

1 pint		*1 quart*
6 tablespoons	butter	¼ pound plus 2 tablespoons
6 tablespoons	flour	¾ cup
1 pint	milk, cream, or half each	1 quart
¼ teaspoon	salt	½ teaspoon
⅛ teaspoon	pepper	¼ teaspoon

See "Rules for Freezing and Using Sauces" (page 18).

Note: Salt and other seasonings can always be added when you take the sauce out of the freezer. Sometimes it is better to freeze a basic white sauce unseasoned, as in its later use it may be combined with salty or spicy foods or seasoned stocks.

Method I (*Roux*): Melt the butter in the top of a double boiler over simmering water. Add the flour a little at a time, blending thoroughly. Let this cook a few minutes while you scald the milk—slowly—until bubbles form around the outer edges. Add a little of the milk, enough to blend into a smooth, thick paste, then add the rest of the milk, stirring with a wire whisk or fork. Continue to cook and stir over simmering water until the sauce thickens smoothly.

Method II (*Shaker*): Melt the butter as in the preceding directions. In a jar with a tight screw cap put half the milk, then half the flour. Shake vigorously to mix. Add this to the melted butter and stir. Shake the rest of the milk with the flour and add to the mixture in the top of a double boiler. Blend with a wire whisk or fork over simmering water until the sauce thickens smoothly.

Method III (*Blender*): Put into your blender container the milk, then the flour, then the butter cut into small pieces. Cover and blend at high speed for 10 to 15 seconds, until thoroughly mixed. Pour into the top of a double boiler and stir over simmering water until thickened.

USING BASIC WHITE SAUCE
TO MAKE OTHER SAUCES

Note: Use *freshly made* white sauce for other sauces you wish to freeze. Use *frozen* white sauce for other sauces to be served when made.

See "Rules for Freezing and Using Sauces" (page 18).

Cheese Sauce
About 1 cup

To each scant cup of heated Average White Sauce add ¼ cup grated Cheddar or Swiss cheese. Stir over simmering water in the top of a double boiler until the cheese melts.

Curried Cream Sauce
About 1 cup

To each cup of heated Average White Sauce add 1 or 2 teaspoons of curry powder which you have first blended to a paste with a little milk. Stir over simmering water in the top of a double boiler until piping hot.

Poultry Sauce
2 cups

To each cup of heated Heavy White Sauce add 1 cup of rich chicken stock or 1 cup of undiluted condensed chicken broth. A little yellow coloring may be added.

Sauce Mornay
About 1 cup

To each cup of heated Average White Sauce add 1 tablespoon of grated Romano or Parmesan cheese and 1 tablespoon of grated Swiss or Gruyère cheese—or use 2 tablespoons of any one. Blend in the top of a double boiler over simmering water, then add a few grains of cayenne pepper. Before serving, stir in 1 or more tablespoons of butter.

Mustard Cream Sauce
About 1 cup

To each cup of heated Average White Sauce add 1 or 2 teaspoons of prepared table mustard and a pinch of sugar. If

See "Rules for Freezing and Using Sauces" (page 18).

a sharper taste is desired, combine ½ teaspoon of powdered mustard with a little cold water and mix to a creamy consistency before stirring it into the sauce.

Horse-Radish Cream Sauce
About 1 cup

To each cup of heated Average White Sauce add 2 or 3 tablespoons of prepared horse-radish, white or red. Stir until well distributed.

Hot Mayonnaise Cream Sauce
2 cups

To each cup of heated Average White Sauce add 1 cup of mayonnaise.

White Anchovy Sauce
About 1 cup

To each cup of heated Average White Sauce add 1 teaspoon of anchovy paste, or 3 or 4 mashed anchovy fillets. Blend thoroughly.

Oyster Sauce
About 2½ cups

1 cup whole fresh, frozen, or canned oysters
½ cup strained oyster liquid
1 tablespoon finely minced shallots or scallions
2 tablespoons butter
1 teaspoon minced chives
1 teaspoon minced fresh parsley
1 teaspoon Worcestershire sauce (optional)
1 cup Heavy White Sauce

Poach the oysters in their liquid in a flat pan until their edges curl slightly. Grind or chop the oysters—or buzz both

See "Rules for Freezing and Using Sauces" (page 18).

oysters and juice in the blender—and set aside. Sauté the shallots or scallions in the butter for 2 minutes. Add the oysters, liquid, shallots or scallions, and remaining ingredients to the sauce and stir in the top of a double boiler over simmering water until well blended.

White Clam Sauce
About 2½ cups

Follow the recipe for Oyster Sauce, substituting whole clams and adding a pinch of thyme. Or use canned minced clams, which need not be poached.

Shrimp Sauce I
1½ cups

To one cup of Average White Sauce add ½ cup of chopped cooked shrimp.

Shrimp Sauce II
2 cups

To one cup of Heavy White Sauce add ½ cup of fish stock and ½ cup of chopped cooked shrimp. For a richer sauce, just before serving add 2 or 3 tablespoons of heavy sweet or sour cream and stir in 1 tablespoon of butter. Do not let it boil.

Shrimp Sauce III
About 2½ cups

To one cup of Heavy White Sauce add ½ cup of seasoned tomato juice, ½ cup of sautéed sliced mushrooms, 1 teaspoon of minced parsley, ¼ cup of slivered celery, 2 or 3 tablespoons of chopped green or stuffed olives, 1 tablespoon of drained capers, and ½ cup of chopped cooked shrimp. Stir over simmering water until well mixed.

See "Rules for Freezing and Using Sauces" (page 18).

BASIC BROWN SAUCES FOR THE FREEZER

Basic Brown Sauce I

1 pint		*1 quart*
4 tablespoons	butter	¼ pound
4 tablespoons	flour	½ cup
2 cups	meat stock	1 quart

Melt the butter in a heavy saucepan over low heat. Stir and cook until it is light brown while you heat the stock in a separate pan. Add and stir the flour into the butter and cook, stirring, until it is brown. Add the heated stock slowly, stir to the boiling point, and remove from heat.

Basic Brown Sauce II
(Made with onions and tomato paste)

1 pint		*1 quart*
4 tablespoons	butter	¼ pound
2 thin slices	onion	1 small, sliced
4 tablespoons	flour	½ cup
1½ cups	meat stock	3½ cups
½ cup	tomato paste	6-ounce can

Melt the butter in a heavy saucepan over low heat. Sauté the onion in the butter until it is brown, but not dark, then remove. Stir in the flour and cook, stirring, until it is brown. Heat and add the stock with the tomato paste. Stir and let boil gently for 10 minutes.

Basic Brown Sauce III
1 pint

Make this the day you cook a stew, pot roast, braised beef, or basted meat loaf. With a bulb baster, remove some of the meat gravy or bastings and reserve.

See "Rules for Freezing and Using Sauces" (page 18).

2 tablespoons butter
3 tablespoons flour
Enough meat stock added to meat gravy or bastings to yield 2
    cups

Brown the butter, add and brown the flour, stir in the liquid, and bring to the boiling point. Remove from the heat and, when cool, refrigerate until the fat rises to the surface and can be removed.

USING BASIC BROWN SAUCE
TO MAKE OTHER SAUCES

Mushroom Sauce I

To each cup of heated Basic Brown Sauce add ¼ pound of fresh or frozen mushrooms, sliced and sautéed in 2 tablespoons of butter.

Mushroom Sauce II

To each cup of heated Basic Brown Sauce add 1 small can of drained mushroom buttons, slices, or pieces.

Mushroom Sauce III

Shake ½ cup of cold liquid drained from canned mushrooms with 1 tablespoon of flour. Add to ½ cup of heated Basic Brown Sauce and stir over low heat until well blended. Add and heat the drained mushrooms.

Caper Sauce

To each cup of heated Basic Brown Sauce add ¼ cup of drained capers.

Olive Sauce

To each cup of heated Basic Brown Sauce add ½ cup of sliced pitted green or ripe olives, or sliced stuffed olives, or cut salad olives.

See "Rules for Freezing and Using Sauces" (page 18).

Creole Sauce I
About 2 cups

2 tablespoons butter
⅓ cup chopped fresh or frozen onions
2 tablespoons chopped fresh or frozen green peppers
2 raw tomatoes, peeled and chopped (or ¼ cup drained canned tomatoes)
½ teaspoon parsley flakes
½ teaspoon celery flakes
½ teaspoon sugar
Pinch each, thyme and sage
Few grains cayenne pepper
1½ cups Basic Brown Sauce
Salt and pepper to taste

Melt the butter and sauté the onions until pale yellow. Add all the remaining ingredients except the Brown Sauce and salt and pepper and simmer for 10 minutes. Stir this into the heated sauce and blend thoroughly. Season to taste with salt and pepper.

Creole Sauce II
(Richer, using garlic and more tomatoes)
About 2½ cups

4 tablespoons butter
4 tablespoons chopped fresh or frozen onions
1 small clove garlic, minced
4 tablespoons chopped fresh or frozen green peppers
1 small bay leaf
Pinch each, thyme and sage
Few grains cayenne pepper
1 cup drained canned tomatoes
1 cup Basic Brown Sauce
Salt and pepper to taste

Melt the butter and sauté the onions, garlic, and green peppers together until the onions are yellow. Add the sea-

See "Rules for Freezing and Using Sauces" (page 18).

sonings and simmer for 10 minutes. Combine the tomatoes with the thawed or heated Brown Sauce and add. Stir to blend thoroughly. Season to taste with salt and pepper.

Piquant Sauce
About 2 cups

2 cups Basic Brown Sauce
2 tablespoons minced fresh or frozen onions
2 tablespoons slivered fresh or frozen green peppers
2 tablespoons lemon juice or salad vinegar
1 tablespoon each chopped sour, dill, or sweet pickles, and drained capers
Few grains cayenne pepper

Heat the Brown Sauce, then add all the other ingredients. Stir thoroughly.

Sweet and Sour Sauce I
1 cup

To each cup of heated Basic Brown Sauce add 1 tablespoon of sugar and 1 tablespoon of vinegar. Stir over low heat until the sugar melts.

Sweet and Sour Sauce II
(Sweeter and sourer)
About 2 cups

To 1½ cups of heated Basic Brown Sauce add ½ cup of sugar and ¼ cup of wine vinegar. Stir over low heat until the sugar melts.

Jelly Sauce
Consult your menu plans before you decide on the jelly. Some suggestions: mint jelly for lamb; currant or beach plum for beef roasts; apple, berry, or grape for pork or poultry.

See "Rules for Freezing and Using Sauces" (page 18).

To each cup of heated Basic Brown Sauce add ¼ to ⅓ cup of jelly. Stir over low heat until thoroughly combined. If you like a tarter taste, add 1 or 2 teaspoons of lemon juice.

Rich Steak Sauce
About 2 cups

To 1½ cups of heated Basic Brown Sauce, add up to ¼ pound of butter, 1 tablespoon of lemon juice, ½ teaspoon of onion powder, and ¼ teaspoon of celery salt. Before serving, add ¼ cup of sherry or dry red wine. Stir over low heat for 5 minutes.

Onion Sauce I
2 cups

To 1 cup of heated Basic Brown Sauce, add 1 cup of condensed canned onion soup, using more of the onions than the liquid.

Onion Sauce II
Put 1 cup of thawed Basic Brown Sauce into your blender container. Add ½ to ¾ cup of sliced or chopped fresh or frozen onions and blend at high speed for 10 seconds. Pour into a saucepan and stir over low heat.

Onion Sauce III
Steam or cook slowly in 2 cups of boiling water 2 or 3 large *unpeeled* onions. When soft, let cool in the water until they can be handled. Pop them out of their skins and mash them through a coarse sieve or food mill, or buzz in the blender. Add to the purée enough heated Basic Brown Sauce to yield 2 cups. The sauce may be seasoned with a pinch of your favorite herb or spice.

See "Rules for Freezing and Using Sauces" (page 18).

Hollandaise Sauce
2 cups

½ pound butter
Juice of 1 large lemon (strained)—more, if you like this sauce
    tart
¼ teaspoon salt
Yolks of 6 extra large or 8 medium eggs
1 tablespoon light cream

Put the butter into the top of a double boiler set over hot
water until it is melted. Stir lightly, remove from the heat,
and add the remaining ingredients in turn, stirring to mix
well with a wire whisk or wooden spoon. Return the pan to
its perch over hot water and continue to stir until thickened,
smooth, and well blended.

ITALIAN SAUCES

Pizzaiola Sauce
(For steaks, chops, or fish)
3 cups

4 tablespoons olive oil
2 cloves garlic, minced
3 cups canned Italian-style tomatoes
½ teaspoon salt
½ teaspoon black pepper
1½ teaspoons oregano
1 tablespoon chopped parsley

Heat the oil and brown the garlic. Add the tomatoes, salt,
and pepper and cook over fairly high heat for 10 minutes.
Stir in the oregano and parsley, lower the heat, and simmer
for 5 minutes longer.

See "Rules for Freezing and Using Sauces" (page 18).

Green Anchovy Sauce Made in a Blender

(To serve cold on fish or sliced meat)

2 cups

4 tablespoons olive oil
3 tablespoons vinegar
4 tablespoons cold water
6 to 8 flat anchovy fillets, cut into pieces
2 tablespoons chopped parsley
1 tablespoon drained capers
3 or 4 tiny vinegar pickles
1 large clove garlic, quartered
2 tablespoons chopped onion
Yolks only of 4 hard-cooked eggs

Put all these ingredients into the container of your blender and buzz at low speed for 10 seconds.

Special instructions: Take this sauce from the freezer early on the day you plan to serve it, as it is not cooked. When it is almost completely thawed, either stir it briskly to recombine the ingredients or put it back into the blender for a few seconds.

Tuna Fish Sauce

About 4 cups

1 7-ounce can grated, flake, or chunk tuna fish packed in oil
Olive oil
¼ cup finely chopped onions
1 large clove garlic, minced
1 tablespoon chopped fresh parsley (or ½ teaspoon parsley flakes)
1 large can (about 2 cups) Italian tomato purée
6-ounce can Italian tomato paste mixed with 1 can water
⅛ teaspoon ground black pepper
¼ teaspoon dry basil
¼ teaspoon oregano

See "Rules for Freezing and Using Sauces" (page 18).

Drain the tuna fish over a skillet to collect the oil and add enough olive oil to yield 4 tablespoons. Heat the oil and stir into it the tuna, onions, garlic, and parsley. Stir and cook over low heat for 10 minutes. Add the tomato ingredients, pulverize and add the seasonings, and simmer over low heat for 1 hour.

Tomato Sauce
About 6 cups

3 tablespoons olive oil
½ cup finely chopped onions
½ cup finely chopped celery with leaves
1 large clove garlic, minced
¼ cup chopped green peppers
½ teaspoon parsley flakes
1 large can (about 3½ cups) Italian whole tomatoes
1 large can (about 2 cups) Italian tomato purée
6-ounce can Italian tomato paste mixed with 4 tablespoons water
1 teaspoon sugar
¾ teaspoon salt
Scant ½ teaspoon ground black pepper
¼ teaspoon dry basil
¼ teaspoon oregano
1 small bay leaf (optional)

Heat the oil in a deep, heavy saucepan. Add the onions, celery, garlic, and green peppers and cook over moderate heat until the garlic is golden brown. Add the parsley flakes, tomatoes, purée, paste, sugar, salt, and pepper, stir, and simmer over low heat for 1 hour or more. Add the basil and oregano, and the bay leaf if desired, and continue to cook over low heat for 10 minutes.

Meat Sauce
At least 8 cups

1½ pounds chopped beef (¼ of this amount may be chopped pork)

See "Rules for Freezing and Using Sauces" (page 18).

1 large onion, chopped
1 large green pepper, chopped
2 cloves garlic, minced
2 large cans (about 4 cups) Italian tomato purée
2 6-ounce cans Italian tomato paste mixed with 2 cans water
1 tablespoon minced fresh parsley (or 1 teaspoon parsley flakes)
1 tablespoon grated Romano or Parmesan cheese
½ teaspoon pulverized basil
¼ teaspoon pulverized oregano
1 teaspoon salt
¼ teaspoon ground black pepper
Dry red wine (up to ¼ cup per cup of sauce when served)

Slowly brown the chopped meat in a heavy skillet, separating it with a fork until it crumbles and is evenly brown. With a slotted spoon, drain and remove the meat to a large saucepan. In the skillet drippings sauté the onions, green peppers, and garlic until the onions begin to get transparent. For greaseless sauce, remove them to the saucepan with a slotted spoon. Add the remaining ingredients, stir thoroughly, and simmer over very low heat for at least 1 hour, preferably 2 or more. If the sauce reduces and thickens too much, add unseasoned stock.

Before serving, add the wine and simmer for 10 minutes.

Chunky Meat Sauce (with Mushrooms Added)
About 8 cups

This is a thick, stewlike sauce that simmers for a long time, absorbing its first liquid. It can be used to dress up pasta, and is fine on a bun for a child's meal—or an adult's, for that matter.

¼ pound salt pork, finely diced
1 large onion, chopped
1 large clove garlic, minced
1 large green pepper, chopped

See "Rules for Freezing and Using Sauces" (page 18).

2 stalks celery, slivered
1 carrot, chopped
1½ pounds lean beef cut into ½-inch dice
3 cups boiling water
6-ounce can Italian tomato paste mixed with 1 can water
1 teaspoon sugar
½ teaspoon salt
⅛ teaspoon ground black pepper
1 teaspoon minced fresh parsley (or ½ teaspoon parsley flakes)
¼ teaspoon dry basil
1 quart hot beef stock
Sliced mushrooms (¼ cup per cup of sauce when served)

In a large heavy skillet render the chopped salt pork very slowly until the bits are crisp. Remove them to a large heavy saucepan. In the rendered fat sauté the onion, garlic, green pepper, celery, and carrot for 3 minutes. With a slotted spoon, remove these vegetables to the saucepan. The bottom of the skillet should be lightly covered with pork drippings. If it isn't, add a little oil, heat, and brown the beef dice over moderate heat, stirring and turning them to brown all sides evenly. Remove the meat to the saucepan and add the boiling water 1 cup at a time, simmering each time over low heat until the liquid is absorbed. Now add the diluted tomato paste, sugar, and seasonings and mix well. Finally, add the hot stock, bring to a bubble over low heat, and let simmer very gently for 3 or 4 hours. Stir from time to time. Add the mushrooms (fresh or frozen, sautéed briefly in butter, or canned) just before serving.

CHINESE SAUCES

Aside from brief stir-frying in conical vessels (woks) surrounded on all sides by high, even heat, the ingredient which gives a Chinese dish its savory, exotic flavor is the sauce.

See "Rules for Freezing and Using Sauces" (page 18).

For one short season I was part owner of a Chinese restaurant in the land's-end resort town where I live. During that strange season I worked closely with a parade of Chinese chefs. This experience does not make me an expert on Chinese cooking. I have neither the kitchen equipment nor the ancestors. Chen Bing, our Number One and only continuous chef, confided to me that Chinese recipes are family trusts, handed down from father to eldest son. When the son marries, not even his wife is told all the details. Grandsons, yes, but not girl children. The secrets must remain with the family name.

Bing was a romantic elf, and I'm not at all sure I believed him even though he was King of the Kitchen and his word supreme law. Besides, my observations associated many of his heirloom mysteries with Chinese cookbooks in my collection.

For a few months after severing my connection with the now defunct establishment, my freezer was a treasury of wonderful food. Almost all Chinese dishes freeze beautifully, although their sauces may tend to become absorbed during long freezer storage. That's why it's a good idea for devotees to have on hand in the freezer a container or so of an authentic-tasting Chinese sauce to serve with dishes carried home from Chinatown in paperboard pails and frozen for later use, or bravely made at home, or purchased from the supermarket freezer cabinet.

Simple Chinese Sauce I (with Beef Stock Base)

To each cup of rich unseasoned beef stock (page 11) add 2 tablespoons of cornstarch, 2 tablespoons of soy sauce, and ½ teaspoon of Chinese (black sorghum) molasses. Stir over low heat until thickened.

See "Rules for Freezing and Using Sauces" (page 18).

Simple Chinese Sauce II (with Chicken Stock Base)

To each cup of rich unseasoned chicken stock (page 13) add 2 tablespoons of cornstarch and 1 tablespoon of soy sauce. Stir over low heat until thickened. Before serving, stir in 1 tablespoon of dry or medium sherry per cup—or, if you have it, the Japanese wine sake.

Simple Chinese Sauce III (with Fish Stock Base)

Follow the preceding recipe, substituting any fish stock for chicken.

Note: After freezer storage, these simple sauces may be enhanced by adding your choice of one or more of the following:

Drained canned water chestnuts, sliced or chopped
Drained canned mushrooms, sliced or chopped
Drained canned bamboo shoots
Drained canned bean sprouts
Whole or slivered blanched almonds, plain or toasted

Almond Sauce with Mushrooms
(For pan-broiled fish)
About 3 cups

4 or 5 large dried black mushrooms (or ¾ cup diced fresh mushrooms)
3 tablespoons peanut oil
½ cup blanched whole almonds
½ cup onion sliced with the grain
½ cup diagonally slivered celery
1 can water chestnuts, drained and sliced
2 cups Simple Chinese Sauce II or III

See "Rules for Freezing and Using Sauces" (page 18).

If you use dried black mushrooms, soak them for ½ hour or more in a cup of cold water, then drain, dry on paper toweling, and cut into small pieces. Fry the almonds in the very hot oil until they are lightly toasted. Reduce the heat to moderate and add the onions, celery, mushrooms, and water chestnuts and stir for 3 minutes. Add this mixture to the simmering sauce and mix well.

Sweet and Pungent Sauce
(For batter-fried shrimp, pork, or chicken)

Freezer portion about 3 cups, enough for 4 servings when combined with fresh and batter-fried ingredients

1 cup sugar
1 cup vinegar
1 cup water
½ teaspoon salt
Dash of white pepper
3 tablespoons cornstarch
3 tablespoons catchup
1 teaspoon minced garlic sautéed until golden in 1 tablespoon peanut oil

Mix all these ingredients together and bring to the boiling point. Lower the heat and simmer, stirring, until smooth and thickened.

When this sauce comes out of the freezer and is reheated, have ready:

2 or 3 large green peppers with seeds removed, cut into about 8 pieces each
2 large firm tomatoes, cut into wedges
1 cup canned or frozen pineapple chunks, drained
½ cup mixed sweet pickles, emphasizing cauliflower

Add these ingredients to the simmering sauce, mix thoroughly, and cook for 3 minutes. Stir in 1 pound of hot batter-fried shrimp, pork, or chicken meat. See the Index.

See "Rules for Freezing and Using Sauces" (page 18).

Lobster Sauce

(For Lobster Cantonese or Boiled Shrimp; see the Index)
About 3 cups, enough for 4 servings

2 tablespoons cornstarch
1 teaspoon sugar
3 tablespoons soy sauce
¼ cup cold water
4 tablespoons peanut oil
½ teaspoon salt
Dash of white pepper
1 teaspoon slivered ginger root (or ½ teaspoon ground ginger)
2 small cloves garlic, minced
½ cup finely ground raw lean pork
1½ cups chicken stock or consommé

Dissolve the cornstarch, sugar, and soy sauce in the water and set aside. Heat the oil in a large heavy skillet, add the salt, pepper, ginger, and garlic, and stir. Add the chopped pork and stir over moderate heat for 3 minutes. Add the stock or consommé, cover, and simmer for 10 minutes. Add the reserved cornstarch mixture, blend thoroughly, and continue to cook, stirring, until the mixture is thickened.

When this comes out of the freezer for heating, to be served with lobster pieces in the shell or with boiled shrimp, have ready:

3 or 4 scallions, peeled of their outermost skin and slivered
2 whole eggs (not beaten, just broken into a saucer)

Add the slivered scallions to the simmering sauce. Add the whole eggs in one swoop, then very quickly stir them into the sauce until they are evenly distributed and the whites are just beginning to coagulate. Work fast. Remove from the heat immediately and combine with lobster or shrimp.

See "Rules for Freezing and Using Sauces" (page 18).

3.

Gravy Train

One of the joys of having a freezer is that gravy need not be made for tonight's dinner while you are *cooking* tonight's dinner. For this blessing there are not enough hosannas. Ask any cook who has tried to maintain heat and perfection in a roasted-to perfection roast while she pours off pan-dripping fat, collects and extends pan juices, browns flour, and yearns over a skillet with wire whisk and bated breath.

Of course, to stockpile gravy in the freezer you have to start some place. What about the roast from which you collect the drippings in order to begin? Well, why not serve it without gravy this once, or with one of the sauces you froze last month? The idea of freezer living is not necessarily to be proper at all times, just free to mobilize a decent meal— even a noble one—from the ranks of calculated miscellany.

There's no law that says you have to make the gravy while the drippings are virginally hot from the roasting pan. Collect them before you do the dishes. Put them into the refrigerator. They'll be ready for you tomorrow or the next day, with an additional advantage—the fat will have risen to the surface, making it easier to work with.

Your freezer itself can provide you with rich juices for gravy making. You'll automatically collect them if you thaw frozen raw meat and poultry as you should, in a large bowl or pan, preferably in the refrigerator but optionally at room temperature.

Owners of small freezers, especially those with only one or two places to set, might be well advised to keep a cup or two of good gravy in the precious space. Many a packaged heat-and-serve frozen dinner will taste better for it. Frozen chicken croquettes are tremendously popular, judging by the numbers of packages sold annually. Little wonder— they're so easily brought home from the store (even by me) but so time-consuming to make from scratch. They come with cream gravies thoughtfully provided by the frozen food processors, but these may be too bland for some palates or too sparse for some appetites. A small container of chicken-base gravy can change a hurry-up oven-heated meal into a hurry-up meal warmed by the taste of home.

THIN MEAT GRAVIES

Possibly because it represents relief from the more usual thickened gravy with its multitude of calories, a thin but meaty-tasting gravy is frequently hailed as something special. Many people, especially men, seem to prefer it. They like it on whipped potatoes or fluffy rice, and they dote on it when they get hot bread to dunk—and to heck with the calories.

Thin Meat Gravy I
(Made with pan drippings)

Remove from its pan meat which has been roasted, broiled, pan-broiled, braised, or sautéed without flour. If the

See "Rules for Freezing and Using Sauces" (page 18).

meat was fatty (pork, lamb, short ribs of beef), skim off all but 3 or 4 tablespoons of the excess fat. Add an amount of hot water or stock approximately equal to the liquid and fat in the pan and scrape the pan well with a spatula. If these extended drippings are meager and more gravy is desired, add up to ½ cup more of stock. The meat taste will still predominate if you have scraped the pan well.

When your container of this gravy comes out of the freezer, you will note that the fat has risen to the top and is congealed. Much of the flavor is in this fat, so don't discard it. It will emulsify with the liquid as it heats and you stir.

Thin Meat Gravy II
(Made with trimmings of lean beef or veal)

Before cooking (or freezing) raw meat, trim from it about ¼ cup of the lean and about 2 or 3 tablespoons of the fat. Chop the fat and render it slowly in a heavy skillet until the bits are crisp. Mince the meat trimmings and brown them in the rendered fat. When the meat is well browned, add ½ cup of hot stock, consommé, bouillon, or water and simmer for 10 minutes, stirring occasionally. Strain. You need not discard the crisp bits of fat and meat. When they are cool, freeze them in a twist of film or foil and add them for flavor to your next pot of soup.

Thin Meat Gravy III
(Made with juice collected from thawed meat or poultry)

Brown 2 tablespoons of butter in a saucepan. Add the juices, ¼ cup of chopped onions, ¼ cup of diced celery, and a pinch of an appropriate herb: sage or thyme for poultry; savory, rosemary, or marjoram for beef; thyme, sage, or turmeric for veal; mint, basil, or dill for lamb. Simmer for 10 minutes. Strain.

See "Rules for Freezing and Using Sauces" (page 18).

THICKENED GRAVIES

Even in this day and age of oversimplification, with gravies of all kinds offered to you in cans you need only open or packets to whose contents you need only add water, there is something to be said for the flour gravy you whisk together with your own two hands. It does take two hands to make good gravy, but the process is neither complicated nor difficult if you try to remember the rule of *never more than 1 for 1*. This means never use more than 1 tablespoon of fat to 1 tablespoon of flour. You may use *less* than 1 tablespoon of fat to 1 tablespoon of flour and still produce fine, lumpless, rich gravy.

MAKING GRAVY WITH BROWNED FLOUR

When you brown the flour for gravy (it looks and tastes better), the proportion will be about twice as much flour as fat, because the breakdown in the flour's starch reduces its thickening efficiency.

If your family likes thickened brown gravy and you serve it often and you have a freezer of a size that will permit the storage of another package, you can save yourself some time and effort by prebrowning as much flour as you like, to keep on hand for gravy days. There are two ways to do it:

1. Cover the bottom of a large dry skillet with flour and stir it over the lowest surface heat your range permits until the flour is brown. Remove all the flour to a large container and follow the same procedure until the container is full.

2. Spread flour evenly over the bottom of your largest flat roasting pan and put the pan into a 250° oven. Stir from time to time. When the flour is evenly brown, pour it

See "Rules for Freezing and Using Sauces" (page 18).

into a large container. Repeat until the container is full.

If you prefer, the flour you brown for stockpiling can be stored in a heavy plastic bag, its top secured with a strip of covered wire.

Brown Gravy I
(Made with browned flour and pan drippings)

For each cupful of gravy desired, add 4 tablespoons of browned flour to 2 tablespoons of hot fat dripped by cooking meat. Blend to a smooth paste. If the meat you are cooking has released juices along with the fat, stir them into this paste before slowly adding up to 1 cup of hot stock, consommé, or bouillon. Stir briskly with a wire whisk. Season to taste lightly if the gravy is to be frozen.

Brown Gravy II
(Made with browned flour and juices collected from thawed meat)
1½ cups

In a jar with a tight lid, put ½ cup of collected meat juices, then 4 tablespoons of browned flour. Shake vigorously. Stir this mixture into 2 tablespoons of hot pan drippings, butter, or melted suet and add 1 cup of heated stock, tomato juice, or any clear broth. Stir briskly with a wire whisk and cook over moderate heat for about 5 minutes. Season lightly to taste.

Country Gravy
(Made with unbrowned flour and pan drippings, meat or poultry)

For each cupful of gravy desired, remove to a saucepan, using a bulb baster, 2 tablespoons of the fatty pan drippings

See "Rules for Freezing and Using Sauces" (page 18).

from roasting meat or poultry. Stir into this 2 tablespoons of regular flour or 4 tablespoons of quick-dissolving flour. When the roast is done, pour off excess fat and swish a little hot water around in the pan. Add this to the fat and flour mixture and whisk until smooth. Add either 1 cup of warm milk or ½ cup of warm milk combined with ½ cup of warm meat or poultry stock.

Giblet Gravy

(Based on the preceding recipe made with poultry)

Sauté the *liver only* on both sides in a little chicken fat or butter until it is just tender—a matter of a few minutes. Set this aside. Place the rest of the giblets plus the neck in a saucepan. Add 1 or 2 stalks of celery with leaves, ½ cup of diced carrots, ¼ cup of chopped onions, a sprig of fresh parsley, 2 cups of water, and ½ teaspoon of salt. Cover the saucepan, bring to a boil, lower the heat, and simmer until the gizzard is fork-tender. Strain and reserve the stock. Put the giblets and sautéed liver through a meat grinder.

To make 1½ cups of giblet gravy, stir ½ cup of chopped giblets into 1 cup of simmering Country Gravy made with poultry base.

Freeze the rest of the chopped giblets for use within 1 month. Freeze the giblet stock for as long as you like, to enrich stews, pot roasts, or soups.

See "Rules for Freezing and Using Sauces" (page 18).

4.

Soup

Any favorite or standard cookbook soup recipe can be made
by the bucketful for the freezer, and leftover soup can be
frozen for future meals. Cool it, stir it, pour it into meal-
sized containers, date and identify the soup, chill the containers in the refrigerator, and remove them to the freezer
when cold. Use them within 6 months. To serve, place an
unopened container in a pan of warm, not hot, water until
the contents can be released into a heavy saucepan. Bring to
serving temperature over low heat. Heat cream soups in the
top of a double boiler over simmering water.

Homemade soup can be a daylong labor of love with meat
bones and trimmings, a poultry carcass or ham bone, and a
mound of freshly pared vegetables or a potful of cooked dry
legumes. With a freezer in the family, however, homemade
soup can be a spur-of-the-moment impulse drawn from a variety of handy ingredients and put together with no less
love.

The soup recipes in this book may be unorthodox, but they
are adapted for orderly freezer management which not only

44

respects space limitations but also utilizes to best advantage the frozen raw or leftover foods stored at home. While this is true of any recipe prepared for or from the freezer, it is especially true of soup. Soup is bulky.

Some recipes to follow omit from their initial preparation as much liquid as it is possible to omit and still ensure proper blending of flavors. Some omit a few essential ingredients entirely. Both the liquid and the essential ingredients are added to the base when the group is heated for serving.

Whenever possible, from-the-freezer versions are given. These dip into the freezer stockpile and also put to use many of the packaged frozen foods so readily available from stores.

While we're on the subject of convenience, let's not be stuffy about the commercial soups, bisques, and chowders in store freezer cabinets and on store shelves. While these are necessarily designed to please a common-denominator palate, improvisations from your freezer stockpile mark them with your personal signature. Open a can or package and thin it—not with water, but with an 8-ounce container of meat, poultry, fish, or vegetable stock from the freezer. Thin cream soups with half milk, half stock. Additional suggestions for using frozen, canned, or dehydrated condensed soups are given for appropriate recipes. See the Index.

SOUP BASES MADE WITH DRIED BEANS, LENTILS, OR SPLIT PEAS

The time to make these, for an upcoming meal and for the freezer, is when you have a ham bone with or without a collar of rind, a turkey carcass, or the root end of a smoked tongue.

All the bases are made according to a general formula, with liquid volume and individual distinctions added at serving time.

To complete recipes for serving, you may use either freshly made base or base which has been frozen.

To freeze base, cool slightly and spoon into containers, leaving expansion space. Mark the containers to identify contents (black beans, lentils, etc.) and add the word "Base." Chill in the refrigerator and remove to the freezer when cold.

Note: A pint container of base will serve from 4 to 6 when extended with liquid and other additions. For 2 or 3 servings, freeze the base in 8-ounce containers.

To use frozen base, place the covered container in a pan of warm, not hot, water until the contents are easily released. It is not necessary to thaw before combining with stock or other liquid. Refer to the recipe when completing the soup.

Formula for Legume Base
2 pints (4 cups)*

1 pound dried beans, lentils, peas
½ cup chopped onions
½ cup chopped celery
½ cup chopped carrots
½ small bay leaf
½ teaspoon salt
Dash pepper
Ham bone (with rind), turkey carcass, or tongue root trimmed
    of excess fat

Wash the legumes quickly and pick them over, discarding defects. Put them into a large, heavy pot, add cold water to cover, and bring to a rapid boil. Boil for 2 minutes, remove from the heat, and let stand for 1 hour. Stir in the vegetables and seasonings. Push the bones into the center. Cover with boiling water. Simmer, covered, over low heat until the leg-

---

* For a double recipe, double all ingredients.

umes are soft. Some take longer to cook than others, so test from time to time, adding boiling water to cover as it becomes absorbed. Stir occasionally.

When soft, cool slightly and discard the bones or rind. Force through a sieve or food mill, or purée about 2 cupfuls at a time in an electric blender.

See page 46 for freezing instructions.

Black Bean Soup

2 or 3 servings		*4 to 6 servings*
1 cup (8-ounce container)	black bean base (page 46)	2 cups (pint container)
1 cup (8-ounce container)	beef, chicken, or vegetable stock or consommé	2 cups (pint container)
few grains each	cayenne, thyme, oregano	dash each
to taste	salt and pepper	to taste
1 teaspoon	wine vinegar	1 tablespoon
1 or 2 tablespoons	butter	3 tablespoons
2 or 3 tablespoons	sherry	up to ¼ cup
	thin lemon slices	
	thin slices of hard-cooked eggs	
	fresh parsley, sprigs or chopped	

Put the black bean base and stock into a saucepan over low heat. If either or both were frozen, melt completely. Stir briskly, lower the heat, add the seasonings and vinegar, and simmer for 10 minutes. Add the butter and sherry, stir, pour into a tureen or individual soup plates, and garnish with lemon and egg slices and parsley.

Lima Bean Soup

2 or 3 servings		4 to 6 servings
1 cup (8-ounce container)	lima bean base (page 46)	2 cups (pint container)
1 cup (8-ounce container)	vegetable stock	1½ cups (12-ounce container)
1 cup	frozen baby lima beans	1 package
½ cup	boiling water, lightly salted	½ cup
to taste	pepper, added salt	to taste
1 tablespoon	butter	2 tablespoons
1 tablespoon	grated Cheddar or Swiss cheese	2 tablespoons

Put the lima bean base and stock into a saucepan over low heat. If either or both were frozen, melt completely. Drop the frozen lima beans into the lightly salted water in another saucepan. When the water returns to a boil, separate the beans with a fork, lower the heat, and cook for 2 minutes. Add the beans and their water to the soup, correct the seasonings, add the butter, and simmer for 10 minutes. Serve garnished with the grated cheese.

Navy Bean Soup

2 or 3 servings		4 to 6 servings
1 cup (8-ounce container)	navy bean base (page 46)	2 cups (pint container)
1 cup (8-ounce container)	any stock except fish	2 cups (pint container)
to taste	salt and pepper	to taste
up to ½ cup	fresh or frozen leftover ham, corned beef, or tongue OR	up to 1 cup
2 slices	crisply sautéed bacon	3 slices

Put the navy bean base and stock into a saucepan over low heat. If either or both were frozen, melt completely.

Add the seasonings and stir to blend well. Add shreds of left-over meat and simmer for 5 minutes, or serve the soup when hot garnished with crumbled bacon.

USING CANNED OR DEHYDRATED BEAN SOUPS WITH INGREDIENTS SUPPLIED BY THE FREEZER STOCKPILE

1. Follow the package directions for reconstituting soup, but instead of water use either thawed and heated stock, or the liquid decanted (and frozen) from canned kidney or lima beans.

2. After reconstituting with stock or water, add the contents of any size container (depending on the number of servings required) of any soup base or vegetable purée your freezer yields—or of your own Italian sauce. Taste and correct seasonings when hot. Sounds casual, and is—but the results are often surprisingly homemade good.

3. Follow either of the preceding directions. Add to simmering soup up to a cupful of frozen leftover cooked poultry or meat, diced or shredded while still frozen. Continue to simmer, stirring, until piping hot. Or, if extended with Italian sauce, add a 4-inch link or two of frozen hot sausage (Italian, Polish, Portuguese) partially thawed, thinly sliced, and sautéed.

Lentil Soup

2 or 3 servings		4 to 6 servings
1 cup (8-ounce container)	lentil base (page 46)	2 cups (pint container)
1 cup (8-ounce container)	beef or chicken stock *	2 cups (pint container)
1 tablespoon	butter	2 tablespoons
2 teaspoons	lemon juice	1 tablespoon
to taste	salt and pepper	to taste

* If desired, half the amount of stock may be canned tomatoes, strained through a coarse sieve to remove seeds.

Put the lentil base and stock (with strained tomatoes, if desired) into a saucepan over low heat. If the base or stock was frozen, melt completely. Add the butter, lemon juice, and seasonings and stir to blend well. When piping hot, serve with croutons or dumplings. For a hearty one-dish meal, serve with dumplings and diced or sliced cooked frankfurters.

Split Pea Soup

Follow the directions for Lentil Soup in the preceding recipe. Omit the lemon juice, optionally substituting sherry. If desired, omit the dumplings and add up to ½ cupful per serving of cooked fresh or frozen peas.

5.

Freezing Concentrates of Special Soups

As noted in a previous discussion, any soup can be made according to any standard cookbook recipe and frozen newly made or as a leftover.

The concentrated adaptations to follow originated with the author's reluctance to go through time-consuming preparations for recipes without editing them for the freezer. A concentrate—measured by the cupful—is used to finish a soup for the meal at hand. The remaining concentrate, when cool, is processed for freezing, to be combined at later will or whim with liquid and other ingredients deliberately omitted from its original preparation. This method, I have found, not only conserves freezer space; it also provides fresher, just-cooked flavor after freezer storage.

The liquid used to reconstitute a frozen soup concentrate may be the stock from a later cooking (and freezing) session, or from appropriate vegetables prepared for the evening meal, or a good canned consommé or bouillon. Life in the age of convenience foods is flexible enough to permit even the small-freezer owner a foundation for soup-on-impulse which nevertheless relates to her own kitchen talents. This philosophy is inherent also in the alternate recipes given for making soup from the freezer stockpile—yours, the store's, or a combination of both.

Some soups which do not lend themselves readily to concentrates because of their bulky ingredients (such as minestrone and Portuguese couvres) are included here in somewhat abbreviated form for freezing because of their popularity and the time required for their composition.

HOW TO USE SOUP CONCENTRATES, BEFORE OR AFTER FREEZING

To use a soup concentrate before freezing, see the serving directions which follow the recipes for concentrates.

To freeze a soup concentrate, stir the remaining concentrate again to distribute the ingredients evenly and spoon into containers, leaving expansion space. Keep family or entertaining requirements in mind when choosing containers. *A pint container of concentrate will serve from 4 to 6 when combined with liquid and other additions.* (For smaller amounts use 8-ounce containers and divide number-of-serving ingredients in half.) Identify and date contents, adding the word "Concentrate." Chill in the refrigerator and remove to the freezer when cold. Soup concentrates may be stored for up to 6 months in freezers maintaining zero temperature or below.

To use a soup concentrate from the freezer, place a covered container in a pan of warm, not hot, water until the contents are easily released. Unless otherwise specified, it is not necessary to thaw the concentrate before combining it with a liquid.* Refer to recipe directions expressed in the

---

* *Personal note:* When I combine a frozen concentrate with a frozen stock, I am very likely to release both into a saucepan or double boiler over low heat. As they melt, I probe with a heavy fork to break up lumps and hasten thawing. When completely liquefied, they can be blended by brisk stirring.

number of servings (not cups) when completing the soup. As a general rule, do not refreeze soups made with previously frozen concentrate.

Borsch Concentrate
About 6 cups of concentrate

6 to 8 good-sized beets, peeled and grated or chopped
3 or 4 carrots, peeled and grated or chopped
2 cups shredded cabbage
1 medium onion, chopped
½ cup chopped celery
2 tablespoons butter
3 cups canned tomatoes
2 tablespoons lemon juice
2 teaspoons sugar

Cook the prepared beets, carrots, and cabbage until tender in just enough water to prevent sticking, adding boiling water if necessary. Sauté the onions and celery in the butter until the onions are limp and golden. Combine the vegetables and add them to the simmering tomatoes. Raise the heat and cook for 15 minutes, stirring often. Add the lemon juice and sugar and simmer for 10 minutes. (This may be puréed in an electric blender, if desired.)
See page 52 for freezing instructions.

Borsch
4 servings

2 cups (1-pint container) borsch concentrate
2 cups (1-pint container) stock, consommé, beet juice, or bouillon
Salt and pepper to taste
Sour cream

Combine the first two ingredients in a saucepan over moderate heat. When boiling, stir, reduce the heat, then taste and correct seasonings. Simmer for 10 minutes. Top each serving with sour cream.

Borsch from the Freezer Stockpile
8 to 10 servings, hot

8-ounce container frozen beef, chicken, or vegetable stock
2 cups canned tomatoes
½ cup fresh or frozen chopped onions
½ cup fresh or frozen chopped celery
1 tablespoon fresh or frozen diced green peppers
3 or 4 fresh or frozen outer cabbage leaves, shredded
1 cup (½ package frozen) diced carrots
2 cans diced beets and juice
2 tablespoons lemon juice
1 teaspoon sugar
Salt and pepper to taste
Sour cream

Release the stock into the simmering tomatoes in a large saucepan and set over low heat. In a smaller saucepan add the frozen onion, celery, green peppers, cabbage shreds, and carrots to 1 cup of boiling beet juice. When this returns to a boil, lower the heat and cook for 7 minutes. Add these vegetables to the larger saucepan along with the diced beets, remaining beet juice, lemon juice, and sugar. Taste and correct seasonings and simmer for 10 minutes. Serve topped with sour cream.

Cold Creamy Borsch (Alternate Blender Recipe)
4 to 6 servings

8-ounce container frozen beef or chicken stock
¼ cup fresh or frozen diced carrots
2 tablespoons fresh or frozen chopped onions or chopped fresh scallions
¼ cup chopped peeled cucumber
2 cans diced beets and juice
1 teaspoon sugar
½ teaspoon salt
2 tablespoons lemon juice
1 cup sour cream

Discard accumulated fat, if any, before releasing the stock into your blender container. Let thaw until slushy. Add the carrots, onions or scallions, and cucumber and blend at high speed for 15 seconds. Add the *drained* beets (reserving the juice), sugar, salt, lemon juice, and ½ cup of the sour cream. Blend at high speed for 10 seconds. Pour into a chilled tureen, mix well with the reserved beet juice, top with spoonfuls of the remaining sour cream. Or mix in a chilled bowl and serve in individual soup plates or cups topped with sour cream.

Broccoli Soup Concentrate
About 6 cups of concentrate

1 large bunch fresh broccoli (about 2 pounds)
½ cup minced or finely chopped sweet onions
2 tablespoons chopped fresh parsley
2 cups water with ½ teaspoon salt
Dash of white pepper
Pinch of sweet basil, nutmeg, or powdered allspice

Separate the broccoli into 1-inch stalks, removing the outer leaves, discolored buds, and fibrous ends. Soak the stalks in a pan of heavily salted cold water for 15 minutes, drain, then rinse thoroughly with cold water. Cut the stalks into small pieces. Drop the broccoli, onions, and parsley in the 2 cups of boiling salted water and cook until the stalks are very tender—up to 10 minutes, depending on the age of the broccoli. Do not drain, but force with the liquid through a sieve or food mill, or purée 2 cupfuls at a time in an electric blender. Stir in the seasonings.

See page 52 for freezing instructions.

Broccoli Soup
4 servings

2 cups (1-pint container) chicken stock or consommé
2 cups (1-pint container) Broccoli Soup Concentrate

Additional salt and pepper to taste
Croutons
Grated cheese (Cheddar, Swiss, Romano, Parmesan)

Bring the stock or consommé to a rolling boil. Add the concentrate. When the liquid resumes its boil, reduce the heat, stir well, taste and correct the seasonings, and simmer for 10 minutes. Serve with croutons sprinkled with grated cheese.

Cream of Broccoli Soup from the Freezer Stockpile
4 to 6 servings

8-ounce container frozen Average or Heavy White Sauce (page 19)
2 packages frozen chopped broccoli *
8-ounce container (1 cup) chicken stock or consommé, brought to a rolling boil
½ teaspoon salt
Dash of white pepper
Pinch of basil or nutmeg
Grated Cheddar or Swiss cheese (optional)

Release the white sauce into the top of a double boiler over simmering water. As it melts, break up lumps with a fork. Drop the frozen chopped broccoli into the boiling stock or consommé. When the boil resumes, break up lumps with a fork, lower the heat, and cook only until no lumps remain. The mixture need not be hot. Force it through a course sieve or food mill, or purée in an electric blender. When the white sauce is completely melted, stir briskly before adding it to the puréed broccoli mixture. Add the seasonings and stir. Continue to heat, stirring, for 5 or 10 minutes, until piping hot. Do not boil; do not refreeze. Serve with sprinklings of grated cheese, if desired.

* A pint container of frozen broccoli concentrate (page 55) may be used in place of frozen chopped broccoli. Release the concentrate into the boiling stock, stir briskly when melted, then combine with the hot white sauce. Taste for seasonings; additions may not be necessary. Heat to a serving temperature without boiling. Do not refreeze.

Fresh Fruit Soup Concentrate
About 8 cups of concentrate

When summer fruits are abundant, this is fine to freeze for winter surprises.

2 quarts mixed fresh sweet berries, cherries, any juicy fruits
Up to 1 cup sugar, depending on tartness of fruits
3 tablespoons cornstarch stirred into 1 cup cold water

Wash the berries and cherries. Slice the larger berries and pit and slice the cherries. Peel and cut the fruit into small dice, collecting their juices in a bowl. Combine the fruits, juice, sugar, and cornstarch mixture, stirring well to distribute evenly.

See page 52 for freezing instructions.

Fresh Fruit Soup, Hot
4 to 6 servings

2 cups (1-pint container) Fresh Fruit Soup Concentrate
1 cup water
1 cup fruit juice (orange, apple, pineapple, etc.)
Stick cinnamon (about 3 inches)
3 or 4 whole cloves
1 teaspoon lemon juice (optional)
2 egg yolks, beaten to a froth

Release the concentrate into the mixed water and fruit juice in a saucepan. Add the cinnamon and cloves, and lemon juice if desired. Bring to a boil slowly. Simmer for 10 minutes and remove from the heat. Slowly add the beaten egg yolks, stir, and serve.

To serve cold: Thaw the concentrate and combine with the water and fruit juice. Stir in ½ teaspoon of ground cinnamon and ¼ teaspoon of ground cloves. Add 1 whole egg, beaten, if desired.

Fruit Soup from the Freezer Stockpile
6 to 8 servings

1 package frozen sliced strawberries or raspberries
1 package frozen mixed fruits
1 can frozen fruit juice concentrate (orange, grape) diluted with
    3 cans water
2 tablespoons cornstarch stirred into ½ cup of the fruit juice
Sugar to taste, if fruit needs it
1 piece stick cinnamon (about 3 inches)
3 or 4 whole cloves
2 egg yolks (if frozen, thaw completely)

Partially thaw the frozen berries and fruits according to package directions, being sure to collect the juices; or open them directly into the diluted fruit juice in a saucepan. Add the cornstarch mixture, sugar if desired, and spices. Stir and bring slowly to the boiling point. Pour over the beaten egg yolks. Serve hot or cold.

Green Soup Concentrate
(An example of freezing the "unfreezable")

5 to 7 cups of concentrate

1 medium head of lettuce, solid type
1 small bunch of scallions
1 cup chopped or slivered celery
2 tablespoons butter
½ pound fresh leaf spinach or mixed greens (beet tops, kale,
    Swiss chard, etc.)
2 cups stock or consommé

Shred the lettuce and mince the scallions. Sauté the scallions and celery in the butter for 3 minutes. Add and "frizzle" the washed greens for 3 minutes more. Combine with the lettuce and add to the simmering stock or consommé. Cook for 10 minutes.

See page 52 for freezing instructions.

Green Soup
4 servings

2 cups (1-pint container) stock
2 cups (1-pint container) Green Soup Concentrate (page 58)
Salt and pepper to taste
Fresh parsley, sprigs or chopped

Bring the stock to a rolling boil. Add the concentrate. When the liquid resumes its boil, reduce the heat, stir well to combine, taste and correct seasonings, and simmer for 15 minutes.

This may be puréed in a blender or forced through a food mill and reheated to serving temperature. It may also be extended with 1 or 2 cups of Average White Sauce (page 19) for serving as a cream soup.

Serve garnished with fresh parsley.

French Onion Soup
4 servings

2 cups prepared onion soup rings (see recipe below)
3 cups boiling beef stock or consommé
Salt to taste
Toasted French bread slices
Grated Gruyère or Swiss cheese

Add the rings to the boiling stock or consommé. When the boil resumes, stir to separate the rings, lower the heat, and simmer gently for 15 minutes. Taste and correct for salt. Serve in heated soup plates. Float in each plate a round or two of toasted French bread covered generously with grated cheese, which has been melted under the broiler, if desired. Pass additional grated cheese.

French Onion Soup Rings
Enough for about 10 to 12 eventual servings

6 to 8 large, sweet onions
6 tablespoons butter

Light sprinkling of salt and pepper
3 tablespoons flour
2 cups beef stock, consommé, or water

Peel the onions and cut across the grain into very thin slices. Separate the rings. Melt the butter to bubbling, but do not let it brown, in a large heavy skillet (a chicken fryer is useful). Sauté the rings over your range's lowest heat, stirring constantly with a wooden spoon, until they start to turn transparent. Cover the skillet and continue to cook over lowest heat until they are evenly golden brown. (Raise the cover occasionally to stir.) Sprinkle with salt and pepper and then with the flour, lifting the rings with a wooden spoon to coat evenly. Add the liquid, raise the heat slightly, and cook until bubbles form around the sides of the skillet. Lower the heat, cover, and simmer very gently for 10 minutes.

Special freezing instructions: Remove to a bowl the amount you wish to freeze, allowing ½ cupful or more per serving. Refrigerate. When cold, pack either in containers or in heavy plastic bags.

Onion Soup from the Freezer Stockpile
4 servings

4 tablespoons butter
2 cups frozen chopped onions
2 tablespoons flour
Quart container (4 cups) beef or chicken stock
Salt and pepper to taste

Melt the butter in a Dutch oven and remove from heat. Add and stir in the frozen chopped onions. Return the pot to very low heat and sauté the onions, stirring, until they are evenly golden brown. Sprinkle with the flour and stir well to blend. Release the stock directly into the pot to melt. Raise the heat to moderate, and stir from time to time. When the soup reaches the boiling point, lower the heat and simmer until ready to serve. Correct seasonings and serve topped with cheese-sprinkled toast slices.

Mushroom Soup Concentrate

(For that brief period each year in most sections of the country when mushrooms are in such abundant supply that their low price makes them irresistible to freezer owners)

Enough concentrate for at least 12 eventual servings

2 pounds fresh mushrooms (or the stems and broken pieces from
    two 3-pound baskets; see Index for mushroom recipes)
¼ cup minced onion
½ cup finely slivered celery
6 tablespoons butter
2 or 3 tablespoons minced parsley
1 teaspoon salt
½ teaspoon paprika
4 tablespoons flour
2 cups beef, chicken, or vegetable stock

Slice the mushroom caps, chop the stems and pieces, and set aside while you sauté the minced onions and slivered celery in butter in a large, heavy skillet or Dutch oven for 3 minutes. Add the mushrooms and sauté for 3 minutes, stirring with a wooden spoon. Add the parsley, stir, sprinkle with the salt, paprika, and flour and continue to stir until well blended. Add the stock, bring to a boil, lower the heat, and simmer for 10 minutes.

See page 52 for freezing instructions.

Mushroom Soup
4 servings

2 cups (1-pint container) Mushroom Soup Concentrate
2 cups (1-pint container) beef stock
Salt to taste
2 to 4 tablespoons sherry

Combine the mushroom concentrate with the stock over moderate heat. When boiling, reduce the heat to low, stir, add salt to taste, and simmer for 30 minutes. Add the sherry and simmer for 5 minutes.

Cream of Mushroom Soup
4 to 6 servings

1 cup (8-ounce container) Average or Heavy White Sauce (page 19)
2 cups (1-pint container) Mushroom Soup Concentrate (page 61)
2 cups (1-pint container) beef stock

Heat the white sauce in the top of a double boiler over simmering water. In a separate saucepan, simmer the mushroom concentrate and stock together for 30 minutes, stirring occasionally. When both are hot, combine, stir, and serve.

Mushroom and Barley Soup from the Freezer Stockpile
6 to 8 servings

¼ cup barley
1 quart boiling salted water
1-quart container (4 cups) beef or chicken stock
1-pint container (2 cups) Mushroom Soup Concentrate (page 61)
Up to 2 cups frozen cooked beef, chicken, or turkey, diced or shredded while still frosty

Wash the barley and drop it into the boiling salted water. When the boil resumes, lower the heat to moderate and boil gently for 1 hour (or, if you are using quick-cooking barley, for half the time specified in the package directions). Add boiling water as or if necessary. While the barley cooks, combine in a separate large pot the stock and mushroom concentrate and let them thaw over very low heat. Stir when both are completely melted. Add the half-cooked barley to this mixture, stir, and simmer gently for 40 minutes. Add the diced or shredded meat or poultry and continue to simmer until you're ready to serve.

Minestrone
Tonight's soup course for 4 to 6, plus leftovers for the freezer

There are more variations on this robust theme than there are provinces in Italy. The following version is a composite which divides its heritage among Genoa, Florence, Milan, Cape Cod, and Aunt Alicia.

1 cup dried red kidney beans
1 cup dried chick-peas
4 quarts boiling water with 1 tablespoon salt
4 tablespoons olive oil
1 cup chopped onions
1 cup chopped celery
2 cloves garlic, minced
2 cups shredded cabbage
1 cup diced carrots
2 cups chopped fresh tomatoes or canned Italian tomatoes
¼ cup chopped fresh parsley (or 1 tablespoon parsley flakes)
½ teaspoon basil
½ teaspoon oregano
½ teaspoon pepper
Cooked diced potatoes and pasta added at serving time

Wash the beans and chick-peas, picking them over for defects, and add them slowly to the boiling salted water in a large soup pot. When the boil resumes, lower the heat and simmer until tender. This may take more than an hour. Heat the olive oil in a skillet, lower the heat, and sauté the onions, celery, and garlic for 5 minutes, stirring. Add these to the soup pot along with the cabbage, carrots, and tomatoes, raise the heat, and cook at a fairly rapid boil for 10 minutes. Reduce the heat to a steady simmer, and stir in the parsley and seasonings.

To serve 4–6: Remove about 6 or 7 cupfuls of the soup

(seconds will be called for) to a smaller pot over very low heat. Peel and dice a large potato and boil rapidly in lightly salted water for 10 minutes. At the same time, cook 1 cup of pasta (tubetti, tubettini, ditalini, elbow macaroni) according to package directions. Drain both and stir them into the soup. Serve in large soup plates and pass a bowlful of grated Romano or Parmesan cheese. If desired, shredded cooked meat may be added to the soup before serving.

To freeze leftover minestrone, see the instructions on page 52.

To serve after freezer storage, release into a saucepan over low heat. As it thaws, cook diced potatoes and pasta, allowing a cupful of each for 4 servings (quart container). If the soup has thickened during freezer storage, add a little boiling stock, consommé, or bouillon.

Note: Although this soup is frozen without potatoes, which may become mushy during storage, or pasta, which may absorb too much liquid, I think it only fair to tell you that any pasta cooked *al dente* (firm) freezes like a charm. It's one of the bonus leftovers of freezer housekeeping. When you've overestimated appetites and cooked too much spaghetti or any other similar product, freeze it—with or without sauce—for use in soups, or to be served again as a side dish.

The best way I've found to freeze leftover cooked pasta is to coax it into a plastic bag, secure the bag with a strip, and put it in plain view on the same shelf where containers of soup concentrates and Italian sauces are stored: small bags for soup garnishes, larger ones for side dishes.

Frozen pasta can be released directly into simmering soup. To heat it for a side dish, turn the bag inside out, release the pasta into a lightly oiled casserole of correct size, cover the casserole, and put it into a 350° oven until piping hot. It can also be heated in the top of a double boiler over simmering water.

Minestrone from the Freezer (and Pantry) Stockpile
8 to 10 servings

1-quart container any frozen stock except fish
⅔ cup fresh or frozen chopped onions
⅔ cup fresh or frozen chopped celery
3 tablespoons olive oil
½ package fresh or frozen diced or sliced carrots
½ package fresh or frozen baby lima beans
3 to 6 fresh or frozen outer cabbage leaves, shredded
1-pound can red kidney beans
1-pound can chick-peas
1-pound can tomatoes
1 cup or more cooked pasta (see the preceding note)
Garlic salt and pepper to taste
Basil and/or oregano (optional)
1 cup (½ small package) frozen French fried potatoes

Release the stock to thaw in a large heavy soup pot over low heat. Sauté the onions and celery in the olive oil in a skillet until the onions are light golden brown and add them to the thawing stock. Cook the frozen carrots, lima beans, and shredded cabbage together in a separate saucepan according to the package directions and time given for the lima beans, but use 1 cup of boiling slightly salty water. Add these ingredients, including their liquid, to the soup pot. Add to the pot the contents of the cans of beans, chick-peas, and tomatoes, and the cooked pasta. Stir and bring the soup to a simmer over moderate heat. Taste for seasonings, and add garlic salt and pepper if necessary and a pinch of basil and/or oregano if desired. Cut the frozen French fried potatoes into half-inch pieces and add. Simmer the soup for 10 minutes. Serve with grated Romano or Parmesan cheese.

If desired, add a cupful or more of shredded or diced frozen leftover meat to the simmering soup at the same time you add the potatoes.

Portuguese Couvres (Kale Soup)

Tomorrow's soup course for 4 to 6, with leftovers for the freezer

1 pound dried yellow-eye or pea beans
2 pounds fresh kale
1 pound linguica or chorico (a hot sausage available in many Spanish-speaking neighborhood stores)
2 teaspoons salt
½ teaspoon pepper
1 tablespoon vinegar

Wash the beans, picking them over for defects, and cover with cold water. Soak overnight. The next day, drain the beans, reserving the water. Wash the kale and cut or break the leaves into small pieces. Slice or chop the sausage. Add to the reserved bean water enough cold water to yield 3 quarts. Put everything into a large soup pot and mix well. Bring to a boil, lower the heat, and simmer for 2 hours.

To serve 4 to 6: Remove 4 or 5 cupfuls to a smaller saucepan to simmer. Add 1 cup of diced or sliced raw potatoes and 1 cup of water. Continue to simmer until the potatoes are tender.

To freeze leftover couvres (without potatoes): See the instructions on page 52.

To serve 4 to 6 after freezer storage: Release a quart container of couvres into a saucepan over low heat. When thawed, raise the heat moderately until the soup simmers gently. Add to the saucepan 1 cup of diced or sliced raw potatoes and 1 cup of water. Continue to simmer until the potatoes are tender.

CREAM SOUPS

Like all other soups, cream soups freeze and store well. Whenever you make a favorite recipe, by all means freeze the leftovers, even if less than a cupful remains in the bottom of the pot. If it's not enough for a serving, it's enough to use as the base of a cream sauce, or to add to a new soup you're making for the evening meal, or to a can or package of condensed soup.

The first time you take leftover cream soup from your freezer, you may be disconcerted when, released from its container, it seems to be curdled, the ice crystals separated from the mass and the whole thing looking like a lump of congealed library paste. Don't be alarmed. When it is thawed, melted, heated, and briskly stirred, it will soon regain the same smooth, creamy, appetizing texture you were proud of when you poured it into the container.

Always start heating frozen cream soups in the top of a double boiler over hot, never boiling, water. This prevents too rapid heating of the milk proteins, which tend to coagulate if subjected to high, sudden heat.

Cream soups can be composed quickly from packaged frozen vegetables—those you buy, or those from your own harvest—with the addition of frozen (or newly prepared) stock and frozen (or newly prepared) white sauce:

Basic Recipe for Cream Soups
From the Freezer Stockpile
4 to 6 servings

1-pint container (2 cups) meat or poultry stock (pages 11–14)
8-ounce container (1 cup) Heavy White Sauce (page 19)
1 package or 1-pint container frozen vegetable (asparagus,* Brussels sprouts, carrots, cauliflower, kale, lima beans, mixed vegetables, spinach)

* *Special freezer note about asparagus:* In early spring, when local or nearby farm-grown asparagus appears in big, low-cost bunches in the markets, any quantity you buy for the table or the freezer provides a bonus. Never discard the more fibrous stalk ends you normally cut or snap from the spears. Trim them of scales and peel the outer layer toward the bottom, but not those which are green. Slice them fairly thin and boil them rapidly until soft in just enough lightly salted water to prevent sticking. Force the asparagus and remaining water through a food mill, or purée in an electric blender. When cool, freeze it in labeled containers.

This bonus asparagus purée is useful in a number of ways: It adds flavor

Release the stock into the bottom half of a double boiler and bring it to a slow but steady simmer. Release (or make) the white sauce in the top half of the double boiler. Using a separate saucepan, drop the vegetable into 1 cup of lightly salted boiling water. When the boil resumes, reduce the heat and continue to cook until tender. Force the vegetable and liquid through a food mill, or purée in an electric blender. Combine the purée with the simmering stock and add the now smooth, hot white sauce, stirring briskly. Season to taste and serve with or without garnishes.

If you have frozen soup purée concentrates, the process is even easier and quicker. Heat together a frozen concentrate and frozen stock and let them simmer while you heat separately (or make) a cup of white sauce. Combine by stirring briskly.

---

and bulk to your own cream soup made with fresh asparagus. It freshens and extends canned and frozen condensed asparagus soup. It combines with a variety of other stockpiled concentrates, even canned or dehydrated products, to please and sometimes mystify a soup connoisseur when you add a small container of frozen rich beef, turkey, or chicken stock.

6.

Sea-Food Bisque and Chowder Concentrates

Like any cream or hearty soup, sea-food bisques and chowders may be prepared in their entirety and frozen in bulk. It does seem wasteful of freezer space to do this, however, when the main sea-food ingredient can be frozen and stored so much more compactly and for a great deal longer—or when a *concentrated* form of the recipe can be prepared and frozen, with the milk or cream added at serving time.

PREPARING LIVE LOBSTERS

When you buy live lobsters, be sure that they have both claws—and be doubly sure that these are plugged with wooden pegs.

Steam them in a very large pot with a close-fitting lid in 1 inch of boiling water for 20 minutes. With kitchen tongs remove the lobsters from the water and drain them, bellies down, in a clean sink.

When they are cool enough to handle, split or break the

shells. Remove all the meat from the tail and claws and pick out the meat from the joints. Dice the meat. Discard the feelers and remove the intestinal vein from the tail meat. Remove the hard sac in the head. If you have a female lobster, reserve the coral. Reserve also the soft green substance (tomalley) which in a lobster of either sex is its liver. The coral will be used in the bisque. The liver makes a delicious—and freezable—canapé spread.

LOBSTER BISQUES

Lobster Bisque Concentrate
About 4 pints

Lobster shells
3 cups chicken or fish stock, or chicken consommé
½ cup sliced or chopped onions
3 or 4 stalks of celery with leaves
8 peppercorns
2 whole cloves
3 or 4 whole allspice
1 small bay leaf
Diced lobster meat (and coral, if a female) from a 4- or 5-pound
    lobster, or two smaller ones

Break the lobster shells and claws into small pieces. If it's a large fellow with a tough shell, use a clean hammer. The shells can then be crushed in a sturdy old-fashioned food grinder—not a blender.

Put the crushed shells into a saucepan with the stock, onions, celery, and spices. Bring to the boiling point, lower the heat, and simmer for 30 minutes. Strain this stock through fine mesh.

Divide the diced lobster meat (and coral, if you have it) among your containers and cover with the stock to within ½ inch of the tops. Cover the containers, chill in the refrigerator, label, and freeze.

Lobster Bisque
4 to 6 servings

1-pint container frozen Lobster Bisque Concentrate
1-pint container frozen Heavy White Sauce (or 2 cups sauce,
    page 19)
Grating of whole nutmeg (or ¼ teaspoon powdered nutmeg)
Salt to taste
Chopped parsley
Paprika

Heat the concentrate in a heavy saucepan. Heat the white
sauce in the top of a double boiler. When the white sauce is
completely melted and hot, but not boiling, stir briskly to
blend. Add the heated lobster concentrate and stir thoroughly again. Season with nutmeg, and with salt if necessary. Serve garnished with parsley and paprika. Do not refreeze.

Lobster Bisque from the Freezer Stockpile I
4 to 6 servings

1 can commercially frozen cooked lobster meat
8-ounce container frozen chicken or fish stock
8-ounce container frozen Heavy White Sauce
Nutmeg
Paprika
Salt
Chopped parsley

Thaw the lobster meat in the refrigerator. Combine the
stock and white sauce in the top of a double boiler and melt.
When you can, break lumps with a fork. Heat to (but not
beyond) the boiling point and stir briskly to blend. Add the
diced thawed lobster meat, stir, and heat to a serving temperature. Season with nutmeg, paprika, and salt and serve
with parsley garnish. Do not refreeze.

Lobster Bisque from the Freezer Stockpile II
4 to 6 servings

1 can commercially frozen lobster bisque
8-ounce container frozen chicken or fish stock
8-ounce container frozen Average White Sauce (page 19)
8-ounce container frozen cooked lobster meat (1 cup, commercial)

Thaw everything in the refrigerator. When slushy, blend the bisque, stock, and white sauce in an electric blender at low or medium speed. Heat this purée without boiling it in the top of a double boiler over simmering water. Stir frequently. Add the diced lobster meat and season to taste. Do not refreeze.

HOW TO OPEN OYSTERS

Of course, you can always buy shucked oysters.

There are, however, several ways to open an oyster without depleting your reserve of Band-Aids—and one which requires skill, determination, and physical fitness. This last is the method used by Cape Cod oystermen, those salty farmers who seed their watery gardens and reap their succulent harvests on exclusive and very limited franchises. One such, with what looks like effortless ease, reaches into a barrel with his left hand and comes up with an oyster invariably turned right side up; that is, with the flatter shell on top and the wider end facing him. With his right hand he inserts a heavy oyster knife into the one tiny spot below the hinge where a knife can be inserted, twists both strong wrists, and empties the meat and juice into a container as he carelessly drops the shells on the floor. I've seen Francis standing calf-deep in shells without losing a single oyster. He wears heavy gloves, however.

Oyster knives are easily and inexpensively purchased, but my best oyster opener is a boy who lives up the street.

A simpler way, scorned by Francis and the boy who lives

up the street, is to use a clean hammer or pliers to knock off the underhang of the wide end of the shell, insert the oyster knife, and force the shells apart by cutting upward through the hinges.

Another way is described by Chef Louis P. De Gouy in *The Oyster Book*, published in 1951 by Greenberg: "Get an oyster intoxicated and you can get him out of his shell more easily than a professional opener can! Experiments have shown that oysters immersed for five minutes in carbonated water become intoxicated by the carbon dioxide and then relax the muscle holding the shell closed. When oysters are in this state, a mere novice can shuck over one hundred oysters in twenty minutes, which is fair going for a professional with sober oysters."

Oven and Ice-Water Method: Preheat the oven to 400°. Put scrubbed oysters into a flat pan on a middle shelf for 5 minutes. Don't go away. Oysters are protein, and protein toughens if subjected to long, high heat. Have ready a dishpan or a sinkful of icy ice water. When the 5 minutes of oven time are up, dump the oysters immediately into the ice water. The rapid and extreme temperature changes apparently confuse them, for they are then easily opened at the hinges.

Freezer Method: Put as many well-scrubbed oysters as you are going to open into a heavy plastic bag without holes, or into a large bowl, and set them in the coldest part of your freezer. In 2 or 3 hours the shells will have parted slightly and the bag or bowl will contain some juice. Work fast with an oyster opener.

OYSTER BISQUES

Oyster Bisque Concentrate
About 4 pint containers, depending on size of oysters

6 dozen shucked oysters with their juice
2 tablespoons minced onion

¼ cup chopped celery
⅛ teaspoon ground white pepper
4 tablespoons butter

Wash the oysters in their own juice. Strain the juice into a tall, narrow pitcher or jar. Refrigerate both oysters and juice. When the sand has settled to the bottom of the pitcher or jar, remove the juice with a bulb baster to a somewhat broad-bottomed pan. Simmer the oysters until they are plump and their edges begin to curl. They don't require long cooking. Remove from the heat. Sauté the onions, celery, and pepper in the butter for 5 minutes, then combine with the oysters and juice. Force through a sieve, or purée in an electric blender. Stir, divide among containers, refrigerate, and freeze.

Oyster Bisque
4 to 6 generous servings

1-pint container frozen Oyster Bisque Concentrate (page 73)
8-ounce container frozen chicken stock (or 1 cup chicken bouillon)
8-ounce container Heavy White Sauce (page 19)
1 cup rich milk
1 cup light cream
Grating of whole nutmeg (or ¼ teaspoon powdered nutmeg)
Salt and white pepper to taste
1 tablespoon sherry per serving (optional)
2 egg yolks beaten with 2 tablespoons water (optional)
Butter

(You may, if you have planned your menu in advance, thaw all frozen ingredients for several hours *in the refrigerator*.) Heat the concentrate slowly in the simmering stock or bouillon. Stir and remove from the heat when completely melted. Heat the white sauce in the top of a double boiler over simmering water, breaking up lumps as it melts. Stir briskly to blend. Add in turn the oyster concentrate, milk, and cream. Stir again. Season to taste. Stir in the sherry and beaten egg yolk, if desired. Dot each serving with butter. Do not refreeze.

Oyster Bisque from the Freezer Stockpile I
4 to 6 servings

8-ounce can commercially frozen or canned oysters
8-ounce container frozen Heavy White Sauce (page 19)
8-ounce container frozen chicken stock (or 1 cup chicken bouillon)
1½ cups rich milk or light cream
Salt and white pepper to taste
Sherry (optional)
Butter

Purée the oysters, with their juice, in an electric blender, or heat slightly and force through a sieve. Combine the white sauce and stock or bouillon in the top of a double boiler over simmering water. As they melt, break up lumps with a fork. Stir briskly to blend. Add the oyster purée and stir. Stir in the milk or cream. Season to taste, adding a little sherry if you like, and dot with butter.

Oyster Bisque from the Freezer Stockpile II
4 servings

10-ounce can frozen condensed oyster stew
1 cup rich milk or light cream
4 tablespoons butter
1 cup thinly sliced or diced raw white potato
Salt and white pepper to taste
Grating of nutmeg
1 tablespoon sherry per serving (optional)

Combine the oyster stew, milk or cream, and butter in the top of a double boiler over simmering water. As it heats, break up lumps with a fork. Meanwhile, cook the potatoes rapidly in boiling water to cover until tender, then drain, combine with the stew mixture, and purée in an electric blender or through a food mill or sieve. Reheat if necessary, correct seasonings, and serve with sherry, if desired.

SHRIMP BISQUES

Shrimp Bisque Concentrate
About 3 pint containers

2 pounds fresh or frozen green shrimp in shells
2 cups strained court bouillon (page 215) (if you are making
    court bouillon for the first time, strain, chill, and freeze the
    remainder in 8-ounce or 1-pint containers for future rec-
    ipes)

Drop the shrimp into the boiling court bouillon. Cook fresh shrimp 2 minutes, frozen green shrimp 3 minutes after the boil resumes. Let stand in the liquid until cool. Peel and devein the shrimp and divide into equal parts. Chop half the shrimp and reserve. Purée the other half with 2 cups of the strained court bouillon in an electric blender, or force through a food mill. Combine the chopped shrimp with the purée, stir, and divide among your containers. Chill and freeze.

Shrimp Bisque
4 to 6 servings

1-pint container frozen Shrimp Bisque Concentrate
8-ounce container frozen Heavy or Average White Sauce (or
    1 cup sauce, page 19)
1 cup rich milk or light cream
Salt and pepper (or paprika) to taste
½ teaspoon curry powder (optional)
1 tablespoon sherry per serving (optional)

Thaw the frozen concentrate and white sauce in the refrigerator until slushy. Combine them in the top of a double boiler over simmering water and heat slowly. Stir briskly. Add the milk or cream, stirring. Add the seasonings and cook only until thoroughly heated. Add sherry, if desired.

Shrimp Bisque from the Freezer Stockpile I
4 to 6 servings

1 pound frozen peeled, deveined, cooked shrimp
8-ounce container frozen chicken stock
8-ounce container Average or Heavy White Sauce (or 1 cup
    sauce, page 19)
1 cup rich milk or light cream
Seasonings to taste (salt, pepper, nutmeg, curry)
1 tablespoon sherry per serving (optional)

Partially thaw the shrimp, stock, and white sauce in the refrigerator. Chop or grind half the shrimp and reserve. Purée together in an electric blender the rest of the shrimp, the stock, and the white sauce. If you have no blender, heat these three ingredients together until completely thawed and force them through a food mill or sieve. Put the purée into the top of a double boiler over simmering water. Stir in the milk or cream and heat. When hot, add the reserved chopped shrimp and bring again to a serving temperature. Season to taste and serve with sherry, if desired.

Shrimp Bisque from the Freezer Stockpile II
4 to 6 servings

10-ounce can frozen condensed shrimp bisque
8-ounce container frozen chicken or fish stock
8-ounce container frozen Average White Sauce (or 1 cup sauce,
    page 19)
1 cup frozen peeled, deveined, cooked shrimp
1 tablespoon sherry per serving (optional)

Thaw or partially thaw the bisque, stock, white sauce, and shrimp in the refrigerator. Combine the first three in an electric blender and purée, or heat these ingredients in the top of a double boiler over simmering water, breaking up lumps with a fork and stirring briskly to blend. Chop the cooked shrimp and add to the purée. Taste for seasonings, bring to a serving temperature, and serve with sherry if desired.

SEA-FOOD CHOWDERS

When a Cape Codder says "clams," he means soft-shelled steamers. If he means the hard-shelled variety, from cherry stone size upward, he says "quahogs" or "round clams." For the sake of semantic simplicity and inland cooks, the clams used in the following chowder recipes are the round, hard-shelled quahogs. The delicate steamers can also be used, but these are usually more profitably served with melted butter, as in shore dinners, or batter-fried, as in Howard Johnson.

To desand clams easily, scrub them thoroughly with a stiff brush or abrasive cloth and put them into a large vessel. An old-fashioned dishpan does very nicely; or use one basin of a double sink, or a large roasting pan. Cover the clams with very cold salted water, and sprinkle on the water a handful of any corn meal (about ¼ to ⅓ cup). Leave them alone for 3 or 4 hours, or overnight. While rejecting the alien corn meal, they will also cleanse themselves of ingested sand. Rinse with cold water.

To open clams easily, put somewhat less than an inch of boiling water in a tall pot with a tight lid over low to moderate heat. A Dutch oven with a rack or a spaghetti pot with an inner strainer is good for the purpose but not essential; any large pot will do. Add the clams. Cover the pot tightly and let the clams steam gently until the hinge muscles relax and they gape open. They don't all open simultaneously or uniformly, so uncover the pot frequently to peek and stand ready with kitchen tongs to remove immediately those which do. When all are open, strain and save the juice collected in the bottom of the pot.

Clams are also opened more impressively with a strong knife or special clam-opener. Hold the clams over a bowl to catch the juice. Insert the blade in the soft spot at the hinge and force the shells apart with a twist of the wrist.

After opening clams by either method, put the juice into a

tall, narrow jar or bottle and refrigerate both juice and clams. When the sand has settled to the bottom of the juice jar, siphon off the liquid with a bulb baster and reserve it.

CLAM CHOWDERS

Clam Chowder Concentrate
About 3 pint containers

1 quart shucked clams
¼ cup finely chopped salt pork
2 large onions, thinly sliced or chopped
2 cups strained clam juice (extended with water or stock if necessary)

Chop or grind the hard parts of the clams. Render the chopped salt pork very slowly in a large, heavy skillet or Dutch oven until crisp and golden. Remove the pork bits with a slotted spoon and reserve. Over lowest heat, sauté the onions and hard parts of the clams in the rendered pork fat until the onions begin to look transparent. Add to the skillet the soft parts of the clams (you can cut them into smaller pieces if they are large), reserved clam juice, and crisp bits of pork. Simmer for 5 minutes, remove from heat, let cool, and stir. Divide among your containers, chill in the refrigerator, then freeze.

Creamy New England-Style Clam Chowder
4 to 6 hearty servings

1-pint container frozen Clam Chowder Concentrate
8-ounce container frozen Heavy White Sauce (or 1 cup sauce, page 19)
2 large or 3 medium white potatoes *
3 cups rich milk, light cream, or half-and-half
Salt and pepper to taste
Butter (up to 1 tablespoon per serving)

---

* Since this is a freezer cookbook, there's no reason why you can't use commercially available frozen whole white potatoes. Parboil, then slice or dice them and proceed with the recipe.

Thaw the chowder concentrate and white sauce overnight in the refrigerator, or heat the concentrate slowly, directly from the freezer, in a heavy saucepan or Dutch oven. Let it simmer gently while you heat the frozen white sauce in the top of a double boiler over simmering water, breaking up lumps with a fork. When this is melted, add a little of the milk, cream, or half-and-half and beat briskly with a fork to blend. Meanwhile, peel and thinly slice or dice the potatoes. Parboil them for 5 minutes in enough boiling salted water to cover, then drain and stir them into the simmering clams. Add the rest of the milk or cream to the blended white sauce, stir briskly, and add to the chowder. Season, heat without boiling, and serve in bowls, adding butter.

Manhattan-Style (or Philadelphia-Style) Clam Chowder
4 to 6 servings

1-pint container frozen Clam Chowder Concentrate (page 79)
8-ounce container frozen (or 1 cup) any stock, or bouillon
1 large can (2½ to 3 cups) stewed tomatoes
2 large or 3 medium white potatoes (see footnote to preceding recipe)
⅛ teaspoon cayenne
⅛ teaspoon powdered sage
¼ teaspoon thyme
¼ cup chopped green pepper or frozen diced peppers
¼ cup chopped celery
2 tablespoons oil
Salt to taste

Thaw the concentrate and stock or bouillon overnight in the refrigerator, or release them directly from the freezer into the tomatoes in a large, heavy pot or Dutch oven set over low heat. Stir from time to time, and let simmer while you peel, thinly slice or dice, and parboil the potatoes for 5 minutes. Add the drained potatoes and seasonings to the simmering chowder. Stir. Sauté the green peppers and celery in the hot oil for 3 minutes and add to the chowder. Taste for salt.

MUSSELS

Mussel-gathering is a joyous occupation on sunny days when the tides are right. We stand thigh-deep in the tidal pools, for we scorn mussels exposed too long to the sun and seagulls, and pluck them from the Provincetown breakwater rocks. Then comes a session of barnacle scraping, debearding, and washing—in the patio, usually, close by a garden hose connection. It's hard work, best done with good companions. Everyone carries home a bucketful of clean, beardless mussels—the poor man's oysters—for whatever recipes are old favorites or new inventions: mussels meunière; chopped mussels mixed with bread crumbs and seasonings and returned to their graceful shells; mussel fritters; mussels steamed in Italian sauce and served over rice (fingers get messy, but can be licked clean); mussels used to replace or augment clams in paella, cioppino, a version of bouillabaisse. They are a neglected fruit of the sea, although recently they have—or seem to have—grown in popularity.

The possibly unorthodox recipes which follow came into being a few months after we had gathered more mussels than even we could eat, and I froze the excess for future use exactly as I would freeze clams.

MUSSEL CHOWDERS

Mussel Chowder
4 to 6 servings

Follow the recipe for Creamy New England-Style Clam Chowder (page 79), substituting 1 pint container of frozen mussels.

Mussel-Mushroom Chowder with Wine
4 to 6 servings

1 large onion, sliced (or 1 cup frozen chopped onions)
2 or 3 stalks of celery with leaves
2 or 3 cloves garlic
1 small bay leaf
½ teaspoon peppercorns
½ teaspoon whole allspice
½ teaspoon salt
4 cups boiling water
1-pint container frozen mussels
12-ounce (or 8-ounce) container frozen Mushroom Soup Concentrate (page 61) or a can of condensed mushroom soup from freezer or pantry
8-ounce container frozen Average White Sauce (or 1 cup sauce, page 19)
1 cup any dry white table wine
Up to 1 tablespoon butter per serving (optional)

Add the onions, celery, and seasonings to the boiling water and simmer for 15 minutes. Strain the liquid into a heavy saucepan or Dutch oven and set over low heat to continue simmering. Add the mussels directly from the freezer. They will thaw and separate. Heat the mushroom and white sauce concentrates together in the top of a double boiler over simmering water, breaking up lumps with a fork until the mixture can be stirred into a thick paste. Add some (about 2 cups) of the mussel *liquor* gradually, stirring briskly until the paste thins to the consistency of heavy cream soup. Stir in the wine. Remove the mussels with a slotted spoon and add. Simmer for 5 minutes. Save, chill, and freeze the remaining mussel liquor for a future recipe. Serve the chowder in bowls. Add butter if desired.

FISH CHOWDERS

Haddock is traditional, but almost any of the lean varieties of fish may be substituted. The preference for haddock is its consideration for delicate palates, but many people do not object to a fishier taste. On Cape Cod haddock is still the favorite, but flounder, hake, whiting—and cod, naturally —are also used.

Haddock Chowder Concentrate
2 or 3 pint containers, depending on size of fish

1 fresh whole cleaned haddock (4 pounds or more)
1 quart water
½ teaspoon whole allspice
½ teaspoon peppercorns
½ teaspoon salt
½ cup finely diced salt pork
2 large onions, sliced
2 tablespoons chopped celery

Cut the haddock into 3 or 4 large chunks and put them into the bottom of a large pot. Cover with the water, add the seasonings, bring slowly to a boil, lower the heat, and simmer for 10 to 15 minutes. Remove the fish, drain, and reserve the liquid. Rinse the pot and slowly render the salt pork in it. Remove and reserve the crisp bits when they are golden. Sauté the onions and celery in the pork fat for 5 minutes. Carefully remove and discard the skin and all bones from the fish, handling it gently to keep it in fairly large pieces. Divide the fish among your containers, add equal portions of the onions, celery, and pork crisps, and cover to within ½ inch of the container tops with the strained fish stock (freeze the remaining stock). Refrigerate, then freeze.

Haddock Chowder
4 to 6 servings

1-pint container Haddock Chowder Concentrate
2 cups diced or sliced white potatoes
1 quart warm milk
Salt and pepper to taste

Grating of nutmeg
1 tablespoon butter per serving
Pilot or common crackers

Release the concentrate directly into the top of a double boiler over simmering water to thaw. Cook the potatoes until tender in just enough lightly salted water to prevent sticking. Drain the potatoes, put them into a large pot, and cover with the warm milk. Add the heated fish concentrate, season, and stir carefully with a wooden spoon to prevent the fish from crumbling. Pour into bowls, add the butter, and float crackers in each bowl.

Fish Fillet Chowder from the Freezer Stockpile
4 to 6 servings

1 pound any frozen raw fish fillets (commercial, or your own product)
¼ cup finely diced salt pork
¼ cup chopped fresh or frozen onions
2 cups diced or sliced fresh or frozen white potatoes
1-pint container frozen fish or vegetable stock (or 2 cups bouillon)
1 pint warm milk
Salt and pepper to taste
Grating of nutmeg
1 tablespoon butter per serving
Pilot or common crackers

Cut the fillets while still frozen into 1-inch pieces and let stand. Use a large, heavy saucepan to render the salt pork slowly until crisp and golden. Remove and reserve the pork bits. Add the onions and potatoes to the pork fat, stir to coat evenly, and sauté for 5 minutes. Add the stock (even if still frozen), bring slowly to a boil, and cook for 5 minutes. Lower the heat to a simmer, add the fillets (even if still frozen), and cook for 15 minutes after the liquid resumes its simmer. Add the warm milk and seasonings, stir carefully, and heat to a serving temperature. Serve in bowls with reserved pork crisps, butter, and crackers.

VEGETABLE CHOWDERS

Vegetable Chowders from the Freezer Stockpile

No point in giving freezer-concentrate versions of these. They are too easily composed, especially if you get into the economical habit of buying and storing the large bags of frozen individual or mixed vegetables—also the foresighted habit of freezing white sauce.

Corn Chowder

4 to 6 servings

½ cup finely diced salt pork
¼ cup fresh or frozen onions
¼ cup diced fresh or frozen green peppers
1 to 1½ cups diced fresh or frozen white potatoes
2 cups boiling water
2 cups canned or frozen whole kernel corn
8-ounce container frozen Average or Heavy White Sauce (or 1
      cup sauce, page 19)
2 cups warm milk
Salt and pepper to taste
Up to 1 tablespoon butter per serving
Chopped parsley or chives

In a heavy saucepan or Dutch oven, render the diced salt pork slowly until golden brown. Remove and reserve the pork bits. Add to the fat the onions and green peppers and sauté for 5 minutes. Add the potatoes, cover with the boiling water, and cook for 10 minutes. Add the corn. When the liquid resumes its boil, lower the heat and cook for 5 minutes. Heat the white sauce separately in a double boiler over simmering water, breaking up lumps with a fork. When melted, add the milk and stir briskly to blend. Add this mixture to the simmering vegetables, season, and heat without boiling until the corn is tender but not soft. Serve in bowls, adding butter and garnishing with parsley or chives and the reserved pork bits.

Succotash Chowder
4 to 6 servings

Substitute 2 cups of frozen baby or Fordhook lima beans for the potatoes in the preceding recipe.

Vegetable Chowder
Your choice is limited only by the packages of frozen vegetables in your freezer—presumably, your family's favorites. Use up to 3 cups of vegetables in combination, for example:

¼ cup chopped frozen onions
3 tablespoons butter
1 cup diced frozen carrots or carrots and peas
1 cup diced frozen green, Italian-cut, or wax beans
½ cup chopped frozen turnips
½ cup chopped frozen asparagus
1 cup boiling salted water
8-ounce container Heavy or Average White Sauce (or 1 cup sauce, page 19)
3 cups warm milk
Salt and pepper to taste
½ to 1 teaspoon curry powder (optional)

In a large, heavy saucepan or Dutch oven sauté the onions for 3 minutes in the hot melted butter. Add the frozen vegetables—all of them—and pour in the boiling water. Cover the pan, bring the water again to a boil, separate the vegetables with a fork, lower the heat, and simmer for 7 or 8 minutes. Heat the white sauce separately in the top of a double boiler over simmering water, breaking up lumps with a fork. When melted, add the warm milk and seasonings and stir briskly to blend. Combine with the vegetables, stir, and heat without boiling.

7.

Gumbos

These thick main-course soups take their name from a Bantu-derived word, softened by French-speaking Louisiana cooks. The word describes the okra plant, whose pods are one of the main ingredients of any gumbo. In Louisiana (and other places) filé powder is also used to thicken the soup. This, available in most herb departments, is ground young sassafras leaves.

As with any soup, gumbos may be made as completed recipes and frozen. Like chowders, however, much of their bulk can be omitted from the original cooking and added after freezer storage of the concentrate.

MEAT GUMBOS

Beef Gumbo Concentrate
About 4 pint containers

2 pounds lean beef (chuck, round, rump) cut into tiny cubes
    or strips *

* 2 pounds of lean chopped beef may be substituted. Brown it quickly over moderate heat, crumbling it with a fork as it cooks. Or up to 1 pound of the meat may be diced smoked ham, in which case use less salt.

5 tablespoons butter
4 cups canned tomatoes
1 pound okra pods cut into ½-inch pieces
1 cup chopped onion
1 or 2 cloves garlic, minced
1 cup chopped celery
1 cup diced green peppers
4 tablespoons chopped fresh parsley
1 tablespoon sugar
1 teaspoon salt
¼ teaspoon paprika
Pinch each, cayenne and thyme

Brown the beef quickly in a heavy skillet in 1 tablespoon of the butter, turning often. Remove the beef to a Dutch oven, add the tomatoes and okra, and start these ingredients simmering over low heat. Melt the remaining butter in the skillet and sauté the onions and garlic until limp. Add and sauté the celery and green peppers for 3 minutes. Combine these ingredients with the simmering beef, add the parsley, sugar, and seasonings, stir, cover, and continue to simmer slowly for 30 minutes. Chill, stir, divide among containers, and freeze.

Beef Gumbo
4 to 6 servings

2 1-pint containers rich beef stock (or 4 cups consommé)
2 tablespoons barley or tapioca
1-pint container Beef Gumbo Concentrate
Salt to taste if necessary
Dash of tabasco (optional)
1 teaspoon filé powder (if available)

Heat the stock or consommé to boiling, add the barley or tapioca, and cook over reduced heat for 20 minutes. Add the concentrate (directly from the freezer, or thawed in the refrigerator) and simmer for 1 hour after the boil resumes. Taste for seasonings. Add the filé powder, if you have it, and stir just before serving.

Beef Gumbo from the Freezer Stockpile
4 to 6 servings

Freezer package of boneless chuck, round, or braising beef
   (about 1 pound) *
½ teaspoon instant meat tenderizer
1 cup boiling water
1-pint container rich beef stock (or 2 cups consommé)
12-ounce store package frozen okra pods
½ cup frozen chopped onions
½ cup frozen diced green peppers
3 tablespoons butter
2 cups canned tomatoes
½ teaspoon parsley flakes
1 teaspoon sugar
⅛ teaspoon paprika
1 tablespoon barley or tapioca (or ¼ cup leftover cooked rice)
Dash of tabasco (or pinch of cayenne)
Salt and pepper to taste
1 teaspoon filé powder (if available)

Partially thaw the beef in its wrap, preferably in the refrigerator. While it is still somewhat frosty, slice it thinly
and cut into small strips or dice. Put the meat into a Dutch
oven and sprinkle it with the instant tenderizer, turning the
pieces to coat them as much as possible. Let stand for 20
minutes. Cover the meat with the boiling water, add the
stock (even if frozen), and set over very low heat. When
this is simmering, slice the okra pods while still frosty and
add. Sauté the onions and green peppers in the butter for 5
minutes. Add these ingredients to the simmering gumbo
with all the remaining ingredients except the filé powder.
Stir well and continue to simmer for 1 hour or more. Just before serving, stir in the filé, if you have it.

* A version of gumbo can be made with appropriate frozen leftovers.
Use up to 2 cups of diced frozen cooked pot roast or roast beef, or 1 cup
of beef and 1 cup of ham or pork. Trim the meat of fat and dice it while it
is still frosty. Add the meat to the simmering stock (omitting the water)
and follow the preceding recipe for the remaining ingredients. Simmer this
gumbo for ½ hour.

POULTRY GUMBOS

Chicken Gumbo Concentrate
About 4 pint containers

3½- to 4-pound chicken, or 3 pounds chicken parts (if from your
    freezer, thaw in the refrigerator)
3 tablespoons rendered chicken fat
4 cups boiling water
3 or 4 large ripe tomatoes, peeled and chopped (or 2 cups
    canned tomatoes)
½ cup chopped onion
½ cup chopped celery
1 pound okra pods cut into ½-inch pieces

Cut the chicken into frying pieces and brown them
quickly in a Dutch oven in the chicken fat, turning often.
When brown on all sides, add the boiling water, cover, and
simmer until the chicken is tender—up to 2 hours, depending on the age of the chicken. Remove the chicken to a platter to cool. Strain the stock, add to it all the other ingredients, and simmer for 30 minutes. When the chicken is cool
enough to handle, discard the skin and carefully remove the
meat from the bones. You may chop it or leave it in fairly
large pieces. Divide the chicken among your containers,
using equal parts of dark and light meat, and cover it to
within ½ inch of the tops with the stock and vegetables.
Chill in the refrigerator, then freeze.

Chicken Gumbo
4 to 6 servings

1-pint container Chicken Gumbo Concentrate
1-pint container frozen chicken stock (or 2 cups consommé or
    bouillon)
Salt and pepper to taste
1 teaspoon filé powder (if available)

Combine the concentrate and stock in a Dutch oven and set over low heat to melt. Stir when you can and simmer for 30 minutes. Add the seasonings. Stir in the filé powder, if used, just before serving.

Poultry Gumbo from the Freezer Stockpile
3 or 4 servings

This is a good way to use frozen cooked turkey and/or chicken when either has been stored for the recommended time limit: 1 month at 5°, 3 months at 0°.

1-pint container frozen chicken stock (or 2 cups bouillon)
1 cup canned whole tomatoes
1 cup frozen sliced okra
1 tablespoon tapioca (or ¼ cup leftover cooked rice)
2 tablespoons frozen chopped onions
2 tablespoons frozen diced green peppers
1 tablespoon butter
Up to 2 cups cooked turkey and/or chicken, diced while still frosty
Salt and paprika to taste
½ teaspoon filé powder (if available)

Simmer together the stock or bouillon, tomatoes, okra, and tapioca or rice. Sauté the onions and green peppers in the butter for 5 minutes and add. Continue to simmer until the liquid begins to thicken. Add the diced poultry. When the liquid resumes its simmer, cook for 20 minutes. Add the seasonings. Stir in the filé powder, if used, just before serving.

SEA-FOOD GUMBOS

Shrimp Gumbo with Oysters
4 to 8 servings, depending on additions

You may use 2 or 3 pounds of fresh or frozen *raw* shrimp, cooking it according to the directions on page 215 and freezing any elaborate multiple-serving sea-food gumbo recipe in

large containers for a party supper, if you like. But a more
space-economical and let's-have-that-again way, using the
freezer liberally, is to make gumbo for serving whenever
your stockpile boasts packages or containers of frozen
peeled, deveined *cooked* shrimp (yours or the store's), a
container of court bouillon from an earlier shrimp session,
and one of the chicken stock you've been squirreling away.
Oysters may be frozen or freshly shucked. Vegetables may
be fresh or from freezer packages. For extended servings,
other fresh or frozen ingredients may be added at whim and
availability (see the note at the end of the recipe).

1-pound package peeled, deveined cooked shrimp
8-ounce container frozen court bouillon (or 1 cup bottled clam
    juice)
1-pint container frozen chicken stock (or 2 cups consommé)
2 cups chopped fresh, frozen, or whole canned tomatoes
12-ounce package frozen sliced okra (1½ cups fresh okra)
½ cup fresh or frozen chopped onions
1 clove garlic, minced
3 tablespoons butter
½ cup fresh or frozen diced green peppers
½ cup thinly sliced celery
8, 12, or more freshly opened oysters with juice (or frozen equiva-
    lent, thawed)
Salt and pepper to taste
Dash each, cayenne and powdered thyme
½ teaspoon filé powder (if available)

Thaw the shrimp. (To hasten thawing if you forgot to
take the package out earlier, place the shrimp in a heavy
leakproof plastic bag, fasten the top securely, and let cool
water run over it.) When the shrimp is almost completely
thawed (separated, with no ice crystals) start heating together in a Dutch oven the court bouillon or clam juice,
stock or consommé, and tomatoes. When you can, stir to
blend, add the okra, and cook for 10 minutes. Lower the
heat and let it simmer while you sauté the onions and garlic

in the butter. Add the peppers and celery after 3 minutes and sauté for 3 minutes more. Put these vegetables into the Dutch oven, stir, add the shrimp and oysters, and continue to simmer until the oysters are plump. Season to taste, and add the filé powder, if used, just before serving. Do not refreeze.

Note: For extended servings, you may add:

Up to 1 cup leftover or frozen diced cooked ham
Up to 1 cup cooked lobster or crab meat

Serve over fluffy rice, if desired.

8.

Clean-the-Freezer Soup

When a creative mood attacks, some people write poems and some people paint pictures. I make soup.

When a soup-making creative mood coincides with the prevailing phenomenon of a loaded freezer, I make clean-the-freezer soup.

These clean-the-freezer soup sessions of mine are strictly ad lib., depending on what there is too much of in the freezer and what pantry ingredients I am inspired to add. Sometimes the soup resembles the *pot au feu* of thrifty French housewives; sometimes it's more like a spicy Mexican or Portuguese chowder. Sometimes it's rich with greens; other times it's beany or creamy. I have yet to make a failure, no matter what unexpected ingredients I have combined.

How can I give you a recipe for clean-the-freezer soup? The best suggestion I can offer is that you forget recipes, call upon your own creativity, and summon up your courage. Then simmer, simmer, taste and simmer. Tasting after each addition can be a filling experience.

Following is one example of the freewheeling, pop-art way I might clean the freezer to make soup, using a big pot because I may start out with the intention of making about a quart and end up with a gallon:

A few dark cabbage leaves from the freezer
1-pint container of frozen asparagus-end or broccoli-end purée
1-pint or 12-ounce container of frozen kidney bean juice from canned kidney beans
8-ounce container of frozen leftover canned tomatoes or tomato soup
2 or 3 frozen grilled frankfurters that didn't get eaten at the beach party
A lonely hamburger as above

First, the cabbage leaves are spread over the bottom of the pot. All freezer containers are emptied together into the pot over low heat to melt at leisure. In about an hour, the soup is ready to be stirred and tasted. The frankfurters are diced or sliced, the hamburger crumbled, and both are sautéed briefly in a little oil. These are added to the soup, which is stirred and tasted again. Salt and pepper, probably. Can it use a little tang? Onion or garlic powder—or, as it happens, a few tablespoons of frozen diced onions—is in a small freezer bag and can be sautéed in the frankfurter-hamburger pan for a few minutes. If the soup looks pale, I add a small container, or can, or package mix of brown gravy. If it lacks substance, I poke in the freezer for a cupful or so of leftover spaghetti. Once, unobligingly, the freezer yielded no pasta at all and I added—are you ready?—the few remaining spoonfuls of uncooked quick-type oatmeal in a box taking up pantry shelf space. That day, even I wondered at my brashness, but I needn't have worried. It was fine. I've since added oatmeal to many a clean-the-freezer soup or casserole in place of rice or pasta.

Well, that's the idea. I wouldn't dare tell you in print some of the things I've rummaged out of the freezer for soup, but here's a hint: I found half a package of frozen commercial fish sticks, half a package of frozen fried scallops, and a small container of cooked shrimp in court bouillon. I banished everyone from the kitchen, set up the meat grinder and blender, and headed for the freezer to check supplies of stock, white sauce, and grated cheese. On the way back to the kitchen, the pantry contributed a can of smoked oysters. No law says clean-the-freezer soup can't have its element of elegance. There were raves for my unusual "sea-food bisque," with special enthusiasm for the ingenious cheese-flavored bread-crumb garnish.

9.

The Smell of
Home-baked Bread

There are no readily available statistics, but I suspect that a list of women who bake all the family's daily bread would not resemble a list of registered voters. I do know one dedicated young wife who spent every Saturday baking the week's entire supply. After the first year of marriage, however, bakery items were added to her shopping list, which now included diaper pins and pablum. By the time her marketing memos advanced to peanut butter and cereals with valuable box tops, she had acquired a freezer. Not all her small family's breadstuffs are home-baked, but enough of them are in a continuing supply (kept fresh in the freezer) to mark her as a heroine to her husband and a source of irritation to other wives who are tired of hearing about it.

The freezer may not inspire you to bake all the bread consumed in your household, but it will safeguard the loaves you do bake—for a year, if allowed to stay off the table that long.

Added in recent years to the constantly growing inventory of frozen food products calculated to pin a *cordon bleu* on casual cooks is one which encourages a bit of housewifely deception. This, of course, is frozen bread dough. The baking firm does the work; you get the glory. What woman, observed taking from her oven a crusty, aromatic loaf, is going to deny that it is handmade?

The commercial "home-bake" bread doughs come with package instructions for their use. I shall add the following suggestions: Unless your family members are so accustomed to soft, squashy white bread with a silken texture that they are suspicious of anything else, do punch the dough down after its first rising (at which time some package instructions say to bake it) and allow it to double again in bulk. An even better product is obtained by eliminating a bread pan. After the first rising, shape the dough on a lightly floured cooky sheet into a loaf, oval, circle, or braid.

FREEZING FULLY BAKED BREAD

Standard recipes for yeast bread of any kind you wish to freeze fully baked are no different in any way from recipes in standard cookbooks. I like to wrap my loaves individually in aluminum foil while they are still quite hot. The foil stays on when the loaf is removed directly from the freezer to a 350° oven to heat for half an hour or so, but is opened for the last 5 minutes. Let the bread cool on a rack before trying to cut it.

FREEZING HALF-BAKED ROLLS

Follow any recipe for making and shaping rolls. Remove them from the oven when they have risen but before they start to brown. Cool, then freeze in plastic bags. After freezer storage finish baking for about 20 minutes in a 350° oven.

FREEZING YOUR OWN YEAST DOUGH

Prepare dough according to directions in any recipe, making sure that the yeast you use has not passed its expiration date. Without letting it rise, flatten the dough into 2-inch-thick bricks, or roll it into tight cylinders of a length to fit into your bread pan. Make one brick or cylinder out of each 1-loaf recipe. If you are using a 2-loaf recipe, divide the dough in half before flattening or rolling it. Wrap the slabs or cylinders individually in freezer film or foil. Freeze the dough immediately or it will start outgrowing its wrap.

Do not freeze more dough than you will use within a 3-week period. Yeast is variable and temperamental. Subjection to long periods of frigid storage may cause it to lose its leavening vitality, and the rising process may be sabotaged.

USING YOUR FROZEN YEAST DOUGH

Method I: Five to 7 hours before baking, unwrap the dough, put it into a lightly greased bread pan or bowl, and set it in a warm place (85°–100°)—for instance, on a trivet or rack over the pilot light of a gas range. The dough will double in bulk in 4 to 6 hours. Remove it to a lightly floured bread board and punch it down, kneading lightly. Return the dough to a greased bread pan, or shape it on a lightly floured cooky sheet into any desired form. Brush the top with oil or melted butter and allow it to double in size again (about 1 hour).

Method II: Three and a half to 4 hours before baking, preheat the oven to 125°. Unwrap the dough and put it into a lightly greased bread pan or bowl. *Turn the oven heat off.* Put the dough into the oven until it doubles in bulk (about 2½ to 3 hours). Remove the dough to a lightly floured board, punch it down, and knead lightly. Continue as in Method I.

To bake bread after the second rising: Preheat the oven to 350°. Bake pan bread for 35 to 45 minutes. Bake shaped loaves on a cooky sheet for 30 to 40 minutes.

Easy Freezer Biscuit and Muffin Mix

A timesaving and economical way to impress family and guests with a never-ending supply of hot breadstuffs is to store a quantity of your own mix in the freezer. The following recipe requires 6 quart containers or plastic bags, each holding the basis for 1½ to 2 dozen biscuits or muffins.

5 pounds all-purpose flour
⅓ cup double-acting baking powder
3 tablespoons salt
3½ cups (1½ pounds) solid vegetable shortening

Combine without sifting the flour, baking powder, and salt in a large shallow pan, such as a dishpan or the bottom half of a roaster. With a pastry blender, cut in the shortening until it is fine and evenly distributed. The mixture should resemble coarse meal. Put 4 level cupfuls of the mix into each container or bag. Cover containers, secure bags with wire closures. Store in the freezer—a year or more, if you like.

Rolled Biscuits
Makes 18

Preheat the oven to 450°. Empty a quart container of mix into a bowl. Pour in not quite 1 cup of cold milk and stir until well blended into a soft dough. Knead on a lightly floured board, about 20 times. Pat or roll to the thickness of ½ inch, and cut with a floured 2½-inch biscuit cutter. Set the biscuits on an ungreased cooky sheet and bake for 12 to 15 minutes.

Drop Biscuits
Makes 18 to 24

Preheat the oven to 450°. Empty a quart container of mix into a bowl. Pour in 1½ cups of milk and stir until well blended. Drop by the spoonful onto an ungreased cooky sheet or into lightly greased muffin tins, filling them about halfway. Bake for 12 to 15 minutes.

Muffins
Makes 18 to 24

Preheat the oven to 425°. Empty a quart container into a bowl. Stir in ¼ cup of sugar, 2 well-beaten whole eggs, and 1½ cups of milk. Mix only until blended and moist. Spoon into greased muffin tins, filling the cups about ⅔ full. Bake for 15 to 20 minutes.

10.

Salads

Some salads are freezable.

If someone would give me a trading stamp for every time I have said so, I could clean out all the premium catalogs. Being a gambling woman, I've won countless wagers from friends who yell, "I don't care if you *did* write a book; you can't freeze salads!" The bets may seem a little off balance, because the stakes are usually set by the dissenters. They say, "If you can freeze salad, I'll eat it."

Losers sometimes accuse me of betting on a sure thing when I point out that except to the unbending purist not all salads are composed entirely of raw green leaves untouched by a knife blade and tossed grandly at the table with a flourish of cruets. Not lettuce, and not mixed greens combined with sliced raw carrots, cucumbers, and radishes. But what's wrong with salads made of fresh or frozen vegetables cooked briefly to retain their crispness? Canned vegetables combined without heating? Main-course salads made with cooked shellfish, chicken, ham, or veal? Any of these can be fully prepared in advance, frozen in containers or bags, and removed to the refrigerator a few hours before serving. You can jolly well *put* them onto a bed of lettuce and surround them with all the raw, unfreezable vegetables the plate or bowl will hold.

Take raw tomatoes, I say to the scoffers. Because the idea of freezing them at all had apparently been unthinkable, several of the country's newspaper and magazine food editors quoted my instructions on freezing them whole (peeled) for salads when the first edition of *The Complete Book of Home Freezing* was published.

I'll concede that it may not make total sense to freeze simple salads for simple family meals. The time to take advantage of your freezer's willingness to help out with the salad course is when you're getting ready to entertain a crowd, even a crowd of four.

For example, you've invited the girls over for luncheon and you plan to serve chicken or shrimp salad. How much simpler it is to cook the chicken or shrimp, bone the chicken or clean the shrimp, dice into salad size, and freeze all ready to go—or mixed with the dressing you're famous for. Do this at unflustered leisure some days before the party, and you'll have more time to set a pretty table and your hair. Just don't forget to transfer the containers to the refrigerator early in the morning, or even the night before. Chopped raw vegetables can be added at the last minute.

There are salads which appeal even to confirmed salad haters. People who are too polite to hit you when you put fronds of greenery in front of them (but not necessarily polite enough to eat them) will reward you with a grateful smile if you give them solid, substantial vegetables served refreshingly cool with a piquant dressing. If one of these sits at your table often along with dedicated salad buffs, he (it's usually a he) can be served his own private little bowl from containers kept at the ready in your freezer. He won't feel neglected or left out of things, and his sense of being warmly cherished won't be marred by guilty feelings that he's being a bother.

With salads as with everything else, your freezer performs double duty. It will hold a salad you make, and it will hold the ingredients for a salad you are going to make.

11.

Salads for Freezing *

VEGETABLE SALADS

Snap Bean Salad
8 servings

2 pounds fresh green or wax beans
½ cup finely chopped mild onions
¼ cup chopped pimiento
½ cup French, Italian, or spiced creamy dressing

Wash the beans and snap or cut them into 1-inch pieces. If they are small, leave them whole. Drop them into about 2 cups of boiling salted water and cook rapidly for 8 to 10 minutes. Drain. While the beans are still warm, toss them with the rest of the ingredients. Spoon into meal-proportioned containers, chill in the refrigerator, then freeze.

To serve after freezer storage: Thaw in the refrigerator.

* Recipes for salad dressings start on page 128.

Mixed Bean Salad I

12 servings

2 pounds fresh green beans
1 pound fresh wax beans
1-pound can kidney beans, drained (saving juice for freezer
    stockpile)
1 cup chopped or thinly sliced onions
½ cup salad oil
½ cup cider vinegar
½ cup sugar
½ teaspoon salt
¼ teaspoon ground black pepper

Wash, snap or cut, and cook the green and wax beans together in about 2 cups of boiling water for 8 to 10 minutes. Drain. Mix with the drained kidney beans and onions. Combine the oil, vinegar, sugar, salt, and pepper in a jar or bottle and shake until well blended. Pour the dressing over the beans and toss. Spoon into meal-proportioned containers, chill in the refrigerator, then freeze.

To serve after freezer storage: Thaw in the refrigerator.

Mixed Bean Salad II

12 to 16 servings

1-pound can kidney beans
1-pound can lima beans
1-pound can garbanzos (chick-peas)
1-pound can bean sprouts
½ cup chopped or thinly sliced onions (optional)
1 cup French or Italian dressing

Chill the cans in the refrigerator. Drain the beans and garbanzos, mixing their juices together to add to the freezer stockpile. Mix the vegetables with the drained bean sprouts, onions if desired, and dressing. Spoon into meal-proportioned containers and freeze.

To serve: Thaw in the refrigerator.

Cauliflower Salad
4 to 8 servings, depending on size of head

1 whole cauliflower
2 teaspoons lemon juice
½ to 1 cup French, creamy, or Roquefort dressing
½ to 1 cup grated Swiss or Cheddar cheese

Remove the outer leaves and hard core from the cauliflower and soak it, head down, in cold salted water for 15
minutes. Drain and break the head into flowerets of reasonably equal size. Drop them into 2 cups of boiling unsalted
water to which you have added the lemon juice. When the
water returns to a boil, cook for 7 to 9 minutes. Drain. Toss
the flowerets in your choice of dressing until all are evenly
coated. Put one layer at a time into freezer containers, sprinkling each layer with grated cheese. Chill in the refrigerator,
then freeze.

To serve: Thaw in the refrigerator.

Corn Salad
This is a good way to use sweet corn you've bought too
much of. No quantities are given, for amounts of other ingredients used will depend on how many ears of corn and how
large they are. In general, use 2 tablespoons of chopped garnish vegetables and ¼ cup of dressing for each cup of kernels cut from the cobs.

Corn on the cob
Chopped onion
Chopped pimiento
Chopped green pepper
French, Italian, or creamy dressing

Remove the husks and silk from the corn and cut off any
ends which are immature. Drop the ears into boiling unsalted water and cook until just tender (from 6 to 10 min-

utes, depending on age and size). Drain. When cool enough to handle, cut the kernels from the cobs with a sharp knife. Mix well with the chopped vegetables and dressing. Spoon into meal-proportioned containers, chill in the refrigerator, then freeze.

To serve: Thaw in the refrigerator.

Succotash Salad I

Add cooked fresh green beans to the above recipe, cup for cup.

Succotash Salad II
6 servings

1-pound can baby lima beans
1-pound can whole kernel corn
2 tablespoons minced onion
¼ cup chopped green pepper
1 or 2 canned pimientos, chopped or cut into thin strips
½ cup French, Italian, or creamy dressing
Chopped celery (optional)

Drain the lima beans (adding the juice to your stockpile) and combine with the drained corn kernels. Add the remaining ingredients and toss until well distributed. Spoon into meal-proportioned containers, chill in the refrigerator, then freeze.

To serve: Thaw in the refrigerator. If desired, add a few tablespoons of freshly chopped celery before serving.

Pea and Cheese Salad
4 servings

About 2 pounds fresh peas (2 cups when hulled)
2 tablespoons chopped green pepper
1 tablespoon chopped pimiento
1 tablespoon minced onion
2 tablespoons finely chopped sweet pickles

4 tablespoons small-dice American, Cheddar, or Swiss cheese
⅓ cup mayonnaise or boiled salad dressing

Hull the peas and cook them in just enough boiling salted water to prevent scorching. Drain. Combine with all the other ingredients, chill in the refrigerator, then freeze.

To serve: Thaw in the refrigerator. Serve topped with crumbled egg yolk.

Variations: A surprisingly delicious addition to this recipe is chopped, peeled raw mushrooms. Add them before or after freezing.

Remember this salad in your freezer the next time you have leftover veal roast. Dice the veal and add it to the thawed pea and cheese combination for a main salad course.

CHICKEN AND MEAT SALADS

Chicken Salad

Any of your favorite recipes for chicken salad, if made without hard-cooked eggs, will freeze successfully and may be stored up to 3 months even if the chicken used came from the freezer before it was cooked. Prepare the salad as usual, toss with dressing, and freeze in meal-proportioned containers. To serve, thaw in the refrigerator and heap on a bed of lettuce with a garnish of green pepper rings and sliced hard-cooked eggs.

The following variations may also be frozen:

Curried Chicken Salad
6 to 8 servings

5-pound stewing chicken
1 large carrot, sliced
1 large onion, quartered
1 or 2 stalks of celery with leaves
2 teaspoons salt
3 cups boiling water

1 cup mayonnaise or French dressing
1 teaspoon curry powder
¼ teaspoon pepper
¼ cup cream
⅔ cup diced green pepper
1 cup slivered green celery

Cut the chicken into sections and wash them quickly under running cold water. Add the carrot, onion, celery with leaves, and salt to the boiling water and simmer for 5 minutes. Add the chicken pieces slowly to keep the liquid simmering, cover the pot tightly, and continue to simmer until tender (up to 2 hours). Let the chicken cool in the broth, then remove it. (Strain the broth, chill it, and freeze it as stock.) Dice the chicken meat. In a large bowl combine the dressing, curry powder, and pepper, blend well, and stir in the cream. Add the chicken and raw vegetables and mix thoroughly. Chill in the refrigerator, then freeze in meal-proportioned containers.

To serve: Thaw in the refrigerator. Serve on a bed of lettuce. Pass your choices of the following for garnishes: shredded or toasted flaked coconut; chopped peanuts or cashews, or slivered almonds; mango chutney; grated onion; hard-cooked egg whites and yolks, chopped separately; chopped ripe olives.

Chicken, Sweetbread, and Mushroom Salad
6 to 8 servings

1 pair (about 1 pound) sweetbreads
1 pound small mushrooms
4 tablespoons butter
2 cups diced cooked chicken
1 cup diced celery
1 cup mayonnaise or creamy salad dressing

Simmer the sweetbreads gently for 15 minutes in 1 cup of lightly salted water to which you have added 1 tablespoon of vinegar. Drain. When cool enough to handle, remove the membranes and cut into ½-inch cubes. Sauté the mushrooms whole in the butter for 2 minutes. Combine all the ingredients, mixing well. Chill thoroughly and freeze in meal-proportioned containers.

To serve: Thaw in the refrigerator. Garnish with walnut meats.

Leftover Meat and Vegetable Salad

This is a good way to use any cooked lean meat remaining from a roast (even one cooked after freezer storage), especially if there is not enough for another meal. To each cupful of diced cooked meat add 1 cup of briefly cooked fresh vegetables—diced carrots, cut green or wax beans, flowerets of cauliflower, green peas, etc., in any combination. Toss these ingredients with ⅓ cup of French or Italian dressing. Chill in the refrigerator, then freeze in a container.

To serve: Thaw in the refrigerator. You may extend this salad by adding about half its volume of cold diced cooked potatoes, plus a little more of its original dressing or sour cream.

SEA-FOOD SALADS

Any fish or shellfish salad recipe of your choice may be frozen (without hard-cooked eggs) and stored up to 3 months. The following are interesting variations for shrimp salad:

Oriental Shrimp Salad
6 to 8 servings

2 pounds fresh shrimp cooked according to the directions on page 215
1 cup (2 small cans) water chestnuts
1 cup small raw mushrooms (or 1 cup drained canned button mushrooms)

¼ cup minced scallions
¼ cup slivered Chinese cabbage
1 cup mayonnaise or creamy salad dressing
2 teaspoons curry powder
2 tablespoons soy sauce

Peel, devein, and cut the shrimp into small pieces. Slice the water chestnuts and combine them with the mushrooms, scallions, and cabbage. Combine the mayonnaise or dressing, curry powder, and soy sauce, blending well. Toss all the ingredients together. Chill in the refrigerator and freeze in meal-proportioned containers.

To serve: Thaw in the refrigerator. Serve on a lettuce bed and garnish with toasted almonds.

Shrimp Salad Maison
6 to 8 servings

2 pounds fresh shrimp cooked according to the directions on
    page 215
10- or 12-ounce can of artichoke hearts in brine
½ cup sliced green or stuffed olives
2 tablespoons chopped green pepper
1 cup mayonnaise or creamy salad dressing

Drain, peel, devein, and cut the shrimp into small pieces. Drain the artichokes and cut into small pieces. Combine and toss all the ingredients. Chill in the refrigerator, then freeze in meal-proportioned containers.

To serve: Thaw in the refrigerator. Serve on a bed of lettuce and garnish with chopped hard-cooked eggs.

JELLIED SALADS

It is possible to freeze aspics and other gelatin salads, but I seldom do. About the only time I spoon a quivering salad into plastic containers or metal molds for freezing is when I've made a whopping amount that proved too much for the occasion. I find that it's easier on my nerves to prepare and chill a jellied salad for dinner than to thaw a frozen one and mourn over the inevitable melting of some ice crystals.

There's another exception. I'll freeze some aspics from time to time if I want to serve them as a glacial first course on a hot summer day. I partially thaw the mold in the refrigerator, pour off the melt, chop the salad into frosty cubes, and serve them in chilled glass bowls. Very pretty and refreshing.

Molded salads which contain more solids than gelatin do somewhat better, but even these are likely to sacrifice some of their quality if held in zero storage for any length of time. Rather than risk disappointment or embarrassment (most of these fancy salads are made for company), I prefer to call on the freezer to supply some of the ingredients as required.

Just in case you intend to freeze an aspic or jellied salad, here are the basic recipe and procedure:

Aspic Made with Stock or Tomato Juice
4 to 6 servings

1 envelope (tablespoon) unflavored gelatin
½ cup cold water
·1½ cups hot stock, consommé, bouillon, or tomato juice
1 teaspoon onion juice
¼ teaspoon salt (unless stock is salty)
1 tablespoon vinegar or lemon juice
1½ cups solids (grated vegetables, shredded meat, diced poultry, flaked fish)

Soak the gelatin in the cold water for 5 minutes. Combine with the hot stock or other liquid, onion juice, salt, and vinegar or lemon juice. Stir until well blended and refrigerate until the mixture begins to thicken. Stir in the solids, distributing them evenly. Pour into plastic or metal freezer containers, or into ceramic or metal molds, allowing ½-inch expansion space at the top. If these do not have lids, cover the containers with heavy foil or plastic film secured with freezer tape. Refrigerate until well chilled, then freeze.

To serve: Set the container or mold in cool water, gradually adding warm water until the contents can be unmolded into a shallow soup plate. Refrigerate until almost completely thawed, pour off the liquid, and serve on lettuce leaves. Or refrigerate until not quite thawed, with some ice crystals remaining, and cut into large cubes for serving as a compote.

12.

Salads from the Freezer Stockpile

Almost endless are the number and variety of side-dish or main-course salads it is possible to compose from ingredients which can be stored in your freezer. Many of them may be there this minute. Some of these salads are served cold; others are served unconventionally, but interestingly, hot. Some use the meat, poultry, and sea food you routinely freeze raw. Easier ones are made of frozen cooked meat, poultry, and sea-food you stored a few weeks ago as leftovers—or from the market's freezer cabinets. Some salads use store packages of frozen fruits and vegetables, occasionally in combination with fresh or canned varieties.

Note: When a recipe calls for 1 package of a frozen product, it means the standard box found in store cabinets. Weights vary from 4 to 6 ounces (mushrooms) to 10 to 12 ounces (fruits, vegetables). "Family size" boxes are also available, and so are 2- or 2½-pound plastic bags of some frozen foods. To judge the amount of a vegetable or fruit to use from these larger sizes, follow the cup measurements given in the listings of ingredients.

Save the waters used for cooking frozen vegetables and add them to your freezer stockpile.

SIDE-DISH SALADS AND RELISHES

Antipasto Beans
4 to 6 servings

1 teaspoon mixed pickling spice
1 cup water
1 package frozen cut Italian-style green beans (1½ cups)
1-pound can red kidney beans
¼ cup frozen chopped onions
Italian dressing

Bring the pickling spice and water to a boil, lower the heat, and simmer for 10 minutes. Strain and cool. Cook the frozen beans according to the package directions, but reduce the cooking time to 3 minutes after boiling resumes. Drain them immediately to retain crispness. Add them, along with the drained kidney beans and chopped onions, to the pickling spice water. Refrigerate for at least 1 hour. Drain, toss with the dressing, and serve in small side dishes. You may garnish the salad with sliced stuffed olives or with chopped anchovy fillets. This is a fine accompaniment to pasta meals.

For a Mexican variation, good served with Chili Con Carne (page 320), add 1 teaspoon of chili powder to the pickling spice water. Omit the onions. Mix with the drained green and kidney beans 1 tablespoon of capers and 1 small can of chopped ripe olives. Garnish with minced onions and shredded lettuce.

Artichoke Hearts with Asparagus and Mushrooms
4 to 6 servings

1 package frozen artichoke hearts (1½ cups)
1 package frozen asparagus tips (1½ cups)

1 cup thinly sliced raw mushrooms
Creamy, Roquefort, bleu or vinaigrette dressing

In separate saucepans, cook the artichoke hearts and asparagus tips according to the package directions. Drain. Combine with the mushrooms and refrigerate until thoroughly chilled. Serve on lettuce topped with dressing.

Carrot–Asparagus–Mushroom Salad
4 to 6 servings

6 to 8 frozen whole baby carrots
1 package frozen asparagus tips or spears
1 cup sliced mushrooms, fresh or frozen
2 tablespoons butter
Vinaigrette dressing

Put the carrots into a saucepan with ½ cup of boiling salted water. When the water returns to a boil, lower the heat and cook for 5 minutes. Remove the carrots and, in the same water, cook the asparagus according to the package directions. Drain. Sauté the mushrooms in the butter (3 minutes for fresh, 5 for frozen). Cut the carrots into thin strips and mix with the mushrooms. Put these into a salad server or on individual plates, top with asparagus, and chill thoroughly in the refrigerator before serving. Pass the dressing.

Cauliflower-Cheese Salad
4 to 6 servings

2 packages frozen cauliflower (3 cups)
⅓ cup Roquefort, bleu, or French dressing
2 tablespoons minced fresh parsley
½ pound mellow or sharp yellow cheese, cut into small cubes
Mayonnaise (optional)

Cook the cauliflower according to the package directions, doubling the amount of water specified for 1 package. Time the cooking accurately after the water returns to a boil, as the flowerets should not be overcooked. Drain and roll the flowerets first in the dressing, then in the parsley. Refrigerate until thoroughly chilled.

To serve: Mix with the cheese cubes and top with mayonnaise if desired.

Sweet and Pungent Corn Salad
4 to 6 servings

½ cup frozen chopped onions
½ cup frozen diced green peppers
4 tablespoons chopped pimiento
3 tablespoons sugar
¾ teaspoon salt
½ teaspoon celery salt
½ teaspoon dry mustard
½ cup cider vinegar
½ cup water
2 packages frozen whole kernel corn (3 cups)

Combine all the ingredients except the corn and bring to a boil. Lower the heat, cover the pan, and simmer for 12 minutes, stirring occasionally. Add the frozen corn and raise the heat. When the boil resumes, lower the heat and simmer until the corn is just tender (2 or 3 minutes). Drain. Serve hot, or refrigerate and serve on lettuce leaves.

Mixed Vegetable Salad
6 to 8 servings

3 cups frozen mixed vegetables (2 packages)
1 cup diced cooked potatoes
½ cup diced celery
4 tablespoons sliced green or stuffed olives
1 tablespoon finely chopped chives or parsley
½ cup creamy French or bleu cheese dressing

Add the vegetables to 1 cup of boiling salted water. When the boil resumes, reduce the heat and simmer until tender but not soft. Drain and combine with all the other ingredients. Serve hot or chilled.

Hot Grilled Potato Patty Salad
4 to 6 servings

A frozen food company suggested the original version of the following recipe.

2 packages frozen potato patties or puffs
1 cup diced celery
2 tablespoons minced onion
¾ teaspoon salt
½ cup French dressing

Spread the potatoes on an 18- by 24-inch square of heavy-duty aluminum foil. Top them evenly with the celery and onion, sprinkle with the salt, and drench with the dressing. Wrap the foil tightly and place it on a grill over glowing coals, or in an electric fry pan, or on a range grill. Cook for about 30 minutes, until the potatoes are thawed and all the ingredients are thoroughly heated. Open the foil to test. If the potatoes do not seem fully cooked, rewrap tightly and continue cooking. When done, open the foil, pour the salad into a bowl, toss lightly, and serve.

MOLDED SALADS FROM THE FREEZER STOCKPILE

Jellied Spinach Ring with Salad Filling
4 to 6 servings

1 package frozen chopped spinach (1½ cups)
8-ounce container frozen stock (chicken or fish, depending on
    salad filling)
1 envelope (1 tablespoon) unflavored gelatin
¼ cup cold water
2 teaspoons lemon juice
½ teaspoon grated onion or onion juice
½ teaspoon salt (if stock is unseasoned)

1½ to 2 cups diced thawed chicken, turkey, shrimp, or fish,
  cooked before freezing
½ cup chopped celery
¼ cup chopped green pepper
Mayonnaise or French dressing

Cook the spinach in ¼ cup of boiling salted water according to the package directions. Drain and reserve the spinach. Add the stock to the spinach water. Heat to simmering, then remove from the heat. Dissolve the gelatin in the cold water, add to the hot liquid, and stir until well mixed. Add the spinach, lemon juice, onion or onion juice, and salt if needed, and stir. Pour into a wet quart ring mold and refrigerate. Mix the diced ingredient with the celery and green pepper, and toss with enough mayonnaise or French dressing to moisten. Refrigerate. When the spinach mold is firmly set, unmold it on a bed of lettuce and fill the center with the salad.

Aspic Salad from Frozen Leftovers
4 to 6 servings

1 envelope (1 tablespoon) unflavored gelatin
½ cup cold water
8-ounce container frozen stock, melted and hot
1 teaspoon onion juice
½ teaspoon salt
1 or 2 tablespoons lemon juice
1 cup chopped leftover meat, poultry, or fish from the freezer
½ cup any cooked leftover vegetables, chopped
2 tablespoons chopped celery
2 tablespoons chopped green pepper
Hard-cooked eggs, sliced (optional)

Soak the gelatin in the cold water for 10 minutes, then dissolve the mixture in the hot stock. Add the onion juice, salt, and lemon juice and stir until well mixed. Refrigerate until it begins to thicken. Stir in the remaining ingredients, pour into wet molds, and refrigerate until firm. Unmold on lettuce leaves and garnish, if desired, with the egg slices.

MAIN-COURSE SALADS
FROM THE FREEZER STOCKPILE

Curried Fish Salad
4 to 6 servings

2 or 3 pounds frozen fish fillets (cod, flounder, haddock)
2 cups salted (¾ teaspoon) water
¾ cup mayonnaise
¼ cup heavy sour cream
2 tablespoons French or Italian dressing
1 tablespoon drained capers
1 teaspoon curry powder
1 tablespoon water in which fish was cooked

It is preferable to thaw the still wrapped fillets in the refrigerator before proceeding, but they may also be cooked from the frozen state. If you choose the latter method, be sure to reserve and freeze the cooking water as stock because it will have received much of the flavor-bearing liquids the fish provided.

Add the fillets to the boiling salted water. If they were thawed, simmer for 7 to 10 minutes. If frozen, simmer for 20 to 30 minutes. Drain and reserve the liquid. Flake the fish and refrigerate it until well chilled. Mix all the remaining ingredients together, blending well. Combine with the chilled fish and serve in a lettuce-lined bowl, or spoon the salad onto lettuce leaves on individual plates and cover with the dressing. Garnish with tomato wedges and sprigs of fresh parsley. Pass lemon slices.

Scallop Salad
4 to 6 servings

2 or 3 pounds frozen raw unbreaded bay or sea scallops
1 cup boiling salted (½ teaspoon) water
1 cup thinly sliced celery
1 cup diced peeled cucumber

¼ cup sliced green or stuffed olives
3 or 4 tablespoons French dressing
Lemon juice
½ cup mayonnaise
2 or 3 tablespoons tartar sauce

If you are using the large sea scallops, cut them into small pieces. Bay scallops may be cut in half or permitted to remain whole if tiny.

It is preferable to thaw the scallops in their wraps in the refrigerator, but they may also be used from the frozen state. Simmer them in the boiling water for 7 minutes if thawed, 20 if frozen. Drain and toss with the celery, cucumber, olives, and French dressing. Refrigerate until well chilled. To serve, spoon on lettuce leaves or water cress, sprinkle with lemon juice, and top with the mayonnaise mixed with the tartar sauce.

Lobster or Crab-Meat Salad

Frozen cooked lobster or crab meat is usually at its salad best when served with a simple mayonnaise or Russian dressing as soon as all ice crystals have disappeared. You may, however, use one of the shrimp salad recipes on pages 111 and 112. Substitute lobster or crab meat for the shrimp, or mix all three of the shellfish.

SHRIMP

As owners of large freezers must know, 5-pound boxes of raw shrimp in the shell and sometimes also of peeled, deveined, cooked shrimp are frequently to be found in supermarkets at very attractive prices. Usually imported at certain peak times of harvest from shrimp-abundant coasts, both are excellent buys. *For long storage periods, however, the raw variety is preferable.* It will retain its original firmness up to a year if properly packaged.

The time to buy a 5-pound box of *cooked* shrimp is close to a season of heavy entertaining, when you are reasonably sure the whole box will be consumed within a 3-month period. After that, some texture and flavor loss may be expected.

Whichever of these bargain boxes you buy, it is wise to divide the still-frozen contents into meal-proportioned amounts, package each one separately, and return them to the freezer at once. This requires the use of a frozen food saw—or you can, as I do, place a heavy meat cleaver blade down across the frozen block and pound it with a hammer. Please don't let the shrimp thaw for easier handling unless you are going to use the whole amount as soon as defrosted. The saw or cleaver method will chop some of the shrimp into small pieces, but does it really matter? If you want whole jumbo shrimp for scampi, tempura, or another picturesque recipe, buy the smaller packages.

When you use frozen raw shrimp, cook them according to the directions on page 216. When you use frozen peeled, deveined, cooked shrimp, thaw them in the refrigerator until only a few ice crystals remain before proceeding with a recipe. They are best served as soon as they are thawed.

SHRIMP SALADS

Shrimp and Asparagus Salad
4 to 6 servings

2 or 3 cups cooked shrimp
½ cup chopped celery
½ to ⅔ cup French dressing
1 package frozen asparagus tips or spears
2 or 3 hard-cooked eggs
Mayonnaise

Cut the shrimp into small pieces, toss with the celery and dressing, and refrigerate. Cook the asparagus according to the package directions, drain, then cool in the refrigerator. Arrange the chilled asparagus on lettuce leaves, add the shrimp, and garnish with quarters or slices of the hard-cooked eggs. Top with mayonnaise.

Shrimp and Citrus Fruit Salad
4 to 6 servings

2 to 2½ cups cooked small whole shrimp
1 package frozen grapefruit sections, thawed (or 1 can drained grapefruit or tangerine sections, or any table citrus fruits in combination)
¼ cup mayonnaise
¼ cup sour cream

Combine the shrimp with the citrus fruits on lettuce leaves. Mix the mayonnaise and sour cream together and spoon over the salad.

SALADS MADE WITH FROZEN COOKED LEFTOVERS

Those small packages of miscellaneous cooked leftovers you tucked away and didn't get around to using have a talent for getting shoved into the back or bottom of a freezer, reappearing suddenly during a defrosting or inventory program. I usually find myself making turkey salad in January, the main ingredient contributed by holiday guests whose appetites vanished before the turkey did. Into the salad, sometimes, go little cubes of leftover stuffing which was wrapped in foil and frozen the day after Thanksgiving. Dipped in beaten egg, rolled in crumbs, dipped in egg again, and deep-fried until golden brown, they are a very good salad addition.

To make a salad whose recommendations are palatability, heft, and economy, look into your freezer's recesses for packages of leftover cooked poultry, beef, corned beef, tongue, ham, veal, lamb, or cooked fish fillets. While still frosty, trim off any skin or fat and dice the poultry or meat, and flake the fish. If you don't have enough of a single variety, combine it with one or more of the others: chicken or turkey with ham, smoked meat, or pork; beef with veal. Fish can be extended with a can of chunk or flaked tuna. A few suggested recipes follow. Your own ingenuity—and the contents of your freezer—will invent others.

Leftover Chicken or Turkey Salad
About 4 servings

1½ to 2 cups diced leftover poultry
Creamy French dressing
⅔ to 1 cup diced celery
¼ cup diced green peppers
¼ cup sliced green or stuffed olives
Salt and pepper (if needed)
Mayonnaise (optional)
Tomatoes
Hard-cooked eggs

While the poultry is still a little frosty, dice it and toss it with a few spoonfuls of French dressing and let it marinate in the refrigerator for an hour or more. Combine it with the celery, peppers, and olives, taste for seasonings, and mix with mayonnaise or more French dressing. Serve on lettuce leaves garnished with quartered tomatoes and hard-cooked eggs.

Leftover Meat Salad
About 4 servings

2 cups diced cooked leftover meat
1 cup diced cooked potatoes
1 tablespoon minced chives or mild onion
2 tablespoons chopped celery
½ cup cooked green beans, peas, or beets
½ cup herb, tarragon, or wine vinegar
¾ cup chili sauce

A few drops of tabasco
Salt (if needed)
Parsley sprigs

Combine all the solid ingredients and toss with the vinegar mixed with the chili sauce and tabasco. Taste before adding salt. Refrigerate for 1 hour or more. Serve on lettuce leaves and garnish with parsley sprigs.

Leftover Smoked Meat Salad
About 4 servings

2 cups diced leftover cooked ham, tongue, or corned beef (or any combination)
1 cup shredded cabbage
¼ cup chopped or grated raw carrots
¼ cup chopped celery
½ cup heart of lettuce broken into small pieces (or ½ cup cubed cucumber)
½ cup mayonnaise
1 tablespoon horse-radish
1 tablespoon prepared mustard
1 tablespoon lemon juice

Combine the meat with the cabbage, carrots, celery, and lettuce or cucumber. Mix the mayonnaise with the horse-radish, mustard, and lemon juice. Toss the two mixtures together and refrigerate for 1 hour or more.

Leftover Fish Salad *
About 4 servings

2 cups flaked leftover fish (or 1 cup fish, 1 can chunk or flaked tuna)
2 hard-cooked eggs, coarsely chopped
1 cup chopped firm tomatoes
¼ cup chopped sweet or dill pickles

* This is one of the salads which are interesting when served warm. Have all the ingredients at room temperature before combining with hot, freshly cooked rice.

½ cup mayonnaise
1 cup (or more) cooked rice (dry and fluffy)
Salt and pepper (if needed)

Combine all the ingredients except seasonings, add salt and pepper if necessary, refrigerate for 1 hour or more, and serve on lettuce leaves.

13.

Salad Dressings

Recipes for an assortment of salad dressings are included for convenience. They are not intended for bulk freezer storage, for they are best either freshly made when used—as for salads you freeze—or kept in tightly capped bottles in a cool place. Dressings made with cream, eggs, or cheese should always be refrigerated.

FRENCH-TYPE DRESSINGS

Basic French Dressing
2 cups

¼ cup vinegar
¾ teaspoon salt
¼ teaspoon ground white pepper
1 teaspoon to 1 tablespoon sugar
1½ cups refined olive oil

Combine the vinegar with the salt and pepper, add sugar as desired, and stir well. Add the oil. Beat with a fork or wire whisk, or shake vigorously in a capped bottle, or buzz for 1 minute in an electric blender. Shake again before each use.

A variety of excellent salad dressings can be made by adding other ingredients to this Basic French Dressing.

Chiffonade Dressing

1 cup Basic French Dressing
3 hard-cooked eggs, finely chopped
1 tablespoon minced or grated onion, or finely chopped chives
1 tablespoon minced fresh parsley
2 tablespoons minced green or stuffed olives

Stir all the ingredients together to distribute evenly.

Creamy French Dressing

½ cup sweet cream
1 cup Basic French Dressing

Add the cream to the dressing gradually and beat well.

Caper Dressing

1 cup Basic French Dressing
1 tablespoon chopped drained capers
1 clove garlic, minced or put through garlic press
1 yolk of hard-cooked egg, crumbled
¼ teaspoon anchovy paste (optional)
Few drops of tabasco

Combine the ingredients and mix well.

Chutney Dressing

1 cup Basic French Dressing
3 tablespoons mango chutney or chut-nut
1 teaspoon minced fresh parsley

Combine all the ingredients and mix well.

Cottage Cheese Dressing

1 cup Basic French Dressing
3 tablespoons small-curd creamy cottage cheese
1 tablespoon minced fresh parsley
1 tablespoon finely chopped sweet pickles (optional)

Combine the ingredients and mix well.

Curry Dressing

1 cup Basic French Dressing
1 teaspoon curry powder
1 tablespoon minced or grated onion or shallots

Make a paste of a little dressing and the curry powder. Blend well and add to the rest of the dressing with the onion or shallots.

Horse-Radish Dressing (with French Dressing)

1 cup Basic French Dressing
3 tablespoons horse-radish
½ teaspoon paprika
Few drops of tabasco

Combine all the ingredients and mix well.

Roquefort or Bleu Cheese Dressing

1 cup Basic French Dressing
4 tablespoons (more or less) crumbled Roquefort or bleu cheese

Combine and mix well.

Creamy Roquefort or Bleu Cheese Dressing

½ cup sweet or sour cream
½ cup Basic French Dressing
4 tablespoons crumbled Roquefort or bleu cheese

Add the cream slowly to the French dressing, beating well. Combine with the cheese.

Vinaigrette Dressing

1 cup Basic French Dressing
Yolk of 1 hard-cooked egg, crumbled
1 teaspoon each: finely chopped green or stuffed olives, chopped
   capers, chopped chives, chopped fresh parsley, chopped
   sweet pickle

Combine all the ingredients and mix well.

ITALIAN DRESSINGS

Basic Italian Dressing
1½ cups

1 large clove garlic (minced, or put through garlic press)
½ teaspoon salt
½ teaspoon dry mustard
½ cup wine vinegar
1 cup pure olive oil, superrefined

Mix the garlic with the salt and mustard. Add the vinegar
and stir. Add the oil and beat briskly with a fork or wire
whisk, or shake in a capped bottle, or buzz in an electric
blender.

Variations: Several hours before serving, add to ½ cup
of Basic Italian Dressing *one* of the following:

2 tablespoons chopped fresh sweet basil (or ¾ teaspoon dried
   basil)
½ teaspoon oregano
2 or 3 tablespoons crumbled Gorgonzola cheese
½ teaspoon rosemary

MAYONNAISE-TYPE DRESSINGS

Basic Mayonnaise
2 cups

Does anybody really make this nowadays?

2 egg yolks
¾ teaspoon dry mustard

¾ teaspoon salt
1 teaspoon sugar
⅛ teaspoon ground white pepper
¼ cup lemon juice or white vinegar (or 2 tablespoons of each)
1½ cups olive or salad oil

Method 1 (by hand, or in an electric mixer)

Use a chilled bowl and cold ingredients. The eggs should remain in the refrigerator until you are ready to start. Separate the eggs and beat the yolks thoroughly (freeze the egg whites). Add and beat in the dry ingredients until well blended. Add—alternately and slowly—the lemon juice and/or vinegar and oil. Continue beating until thickened. If the mayonnaise tends to separate or curdle, beat another chilled egg yolk in a cold bowl and slowly stir it into the dressing. If the mayonnaise seems too thick, thin to the desired consistency with sweet or sour cream.

Method 2 (blender)

Combine in the blender container the eggs, dry ingredients, and half the lemon juice and/or vinegar. Cover and blend for 10 seconds at high speed. Add 1 cup of the oil, blend for a few seconds, then add the remaining lemon juice and/or vinegar and the remaining ½ cup of oil. Blend for 2 or 3 seconds longer until smooth and thickened.

A variety of excellent salad dressings can be made by adding other ingredients to mayonnaise.

Creamy Mayonnaise

½ cup mayonnaise
½ cup heavy sweet or sour cream

Combine one tablespoonful at a time until smooth and well blended.

Tangy Cheese Dressing

½ cup mayonnaise
½ cup crumbled Roquefort, bleu, or Gorgonzola cheese
½ cup heavy sour cream
Few drops of tabasco

Combine and blend well.

Horse-Radish Dressing (with Mayonnaise)

½ cup mayonnaise
¼ cup heavy sweet or sour cream
1 tablespoon or more of horse-radish
½ teaspoon dry mustard
1 tablespoon red or black caviar (optional)

Combine and blend well.

Russian Dressing

1 cup mayonnaise
¼ cup chili sauce
1 teaspoon chopped pimientos
1 teaspoon chopped chives

Combine and blend well.

Remoulade Dressing

1 tablespoon finely chopped anchovy fillets
1 teaspoon dry mustard or curry powder
1 tablespoon chopped fresh parsley
1 tablespoon chopped capers or sweet pickles
1 tablespoon chopped green pepper or pimientos
1 cup mayonnaise

Combine all the ingredients and mix well.

Thousand Island Dressing

1 cup mayonnaise
2 tablespoons chili sauce or catchup

1 tablespoon minced onions or chives
1 tablespoon minced green peppers
1 tablespoon minced pimientos
1 tablespoon minced sweet or dill pickle
1 tablespoon chopped ripe or green olives

Combine all the ingredients and mix well. You may substitute heavy sweet or sour cream for up to half the amount of mayonnaise.

14.

Fish and Shellfish

Properly packaged raw fish stays stream or ocean fresh for a long time in the freezer (up to a year for lean varieties, 6 months for fatty ones). It is very easy to work with frozen raw fish after freezer storage. The home freezing of pre-cooked fish courses—except terribly fancy ones—is, therefore, largely a matter of choice. My personal choice is not to do it very often—but then, I live in a seashore community. When freshly caught fish comes my way, it usually comes in bunches during the busy summer season. I process and freeze it as quickly as possible to preserve delicate flavor, texture, and freshness. Come winter, there it is—and there are also several containers of stocks and sauces to transform it into a festive dish with a pretty name.

Large, elaborate fish recipes take up more freezer space than I'm willing to spare, and besides they tie up the serving dishes they will be heated in. A few of these recipes for family or company are indicated for freezing in the pages to follow, and so are a number of more prosaic fish courses such as croquettes, loaves, pies, and the like. For the most part, however, the recipes in this large section will concentrate heavily on what to do with frozen fish. So many women have written so many questions about the handling of frozen fish that careful and definitive answers would seem required. In the section on Fish from the Freezer, starting on page 150, I have tried to answer all of them.

It's another story with shellfish, as the recipes for freezing will demonstrate. For many of these some real timesaving is realized, and I don't begrudge the casseroles' lying fallow for a while. They will come out of the freezer soon enough for "impromptu" meals when company drops in, or for planned luncheons or dinners.

A special note about salt in fish cookery: Many of the recipes in this section either omit salt as an ingredient or specify what may seem to be very little of it. The reason for this is that most fish—even fresh-water varieties—are naturally salty, although not all to the same degree. When fish is properly cooked, the natural salt remains in the flesh. Too much salt in a recipe tends to draw out juices and flavors. Even when a recipe is cooked in a sauce which receives the juices, a heavy hand with a shaker may make the sauce itself too salty. It is better to season to individual taste when served. The only exception is when fish is prepared with an effective barrier against the leakage of juices, as with batter or egg and crumbs for recipes to be deep-fried.

Freezer containers for fish recipes: The containers you use for freezing fish recipes should be nonporous. While they may be any of your freezer-to-heat-to-table casseroles, a very handy way to freeze some individual, twosome, or family fish courses is to prepare them in the heavy foil containers—square, rectangular, round—so many commercial frozen foods come in. Wash and save these for the purpose. Cover all open baking dishes or containers with foil. Seal the covered casseroles with freezer tape.

15.

Fish Recipes for the Freezer

Fish Sticks *

18 sticks (4 to 6 servings)		3 dozen sticks (9 to 12 servings)
2 cups	flaked cooked fish	4 cups
1 cup	Heavy White Sauce (page 19)	2 cups
2 teaspoons	lemon juice	1 tablespoon
1 tablespoon	minced onion	2 tablespoons
1 tablespoon	minced parsley	2 tablespoons
½ teaspoon	salt	1 teaspoon
⅛ teaspoon	pepper	¼ teaspoon
½ teaspoon	curry, basil, or oregano (optional)	⅔ teaspoon
2	eggs, beaten in measuring cup	4
2 tablespoons	cold water or milk bread crumbs	2 tablespoons

* This recipe can be made with canned salmon or tuna fish—drained and flaked—in place of cooked fish. You may substitute cold mashed potatoes for half the quantity of white sauce. The mixture may be shaped into croquettes instead of sticks, or into marble-sized balls for hot hors d'oeuvres.

Add the fish to the hot white sauce and stir in the lemon juice, onion, parsley, and seasonings. Remove from heat and add half the beaten eggs, mixing well. Let cool. With moistened hands or a wide spatula spread the mixture on a platter to a depth of ½ inch (use 2 platters for the larger quantity), cover with waxed paper, and refrigerate until well chilled. Cut into 3- by 1½-inch sticks. Stir the 2 tablespoons of water or milk into the remaining eggs. Roll the sticks first in the bread crumbs, then in egg, and again in crumbs until completely coated on all sides. Refrigerate for 2 hours. Package carefully in rigid boxes, slip-sheeting layers with double thicknesses of waxed paper or freezer film. Freeze.

To serve: Without thawing, fry in hot deep fat (375° to 385°) until golden brown.

Fish au Gratin Ramekins
4 to 6 servings °

2 cups flaked cooked fish, or drained, flaked canned salmon or
    tuna
2 cups Cheese Sauce (page 21)
2 tablespoons chopped pimiento
2 tablespoons chopped green pepper
1 tablespoon minced parsley
1 tablespoon chopped green or ripe olives
4 tablespoons bread crumbs
2 tablespoons grated Cheddar or American cheese

Combine the fish, sauce, pimiento, green pepper, parsley, and olives. Mix well. Spoon into ovenproof ramekins (custard cups will do) that you can spare for the freezer, or into small heavy foil containers. Top with the crumbs mixed with cheese, cover with foil or freezer film, refrigerate until chilled, then freeze.

To serve: Preheat the oven to 400°. Unwrap and place the ramekins on a cooky sheet and bake for 35 to 40 minutes, until piping hot. Brown the topping under the broiler, if desired.

° For larger quantities, all recipe ingredients may be doubled or tripled.

Fish à la King
4 servings (1 quart or 2 pint containers)

1 cup sliced raw mushrooms
2 tablespoons butter
2 cups flaked or shredded cooked fish
2 tablespoons chopped pimiento
2 tablespoons chopped green pepper
2 well-beaten egg yolks
2 teaspoons lemon juice
2 cups Heavy White Sauce (page 19)

Sauté the mushrooms in the butter for 2 minutes, then combine with the other ingredients in the top of a double boiler over simmering water. Stir until well blended and thickened. Pour into rigid plastic containers, chill in the refrigerator, then freeze.

To serve: Place the unopened container in a pan of cool water, gradually adding warmer water until the contents can be released into the top of a double boiler over simmering water. Break up lumps with a fork during the melting and stir when you can. When hot (not boiling), add 2 or 3 tablespoons of sherry or dry white wine.

Fish Pie
4 to 6 servings

1 cup diced raw white potatoes
½ cup diced carrots
½ cup second vegetable (peas, lima beans, cut green or wax beans)
2 cups flaked cooked fish
2 cups Heavy or Average White Sauce (page 19) or Cheese Sauce (page 21)
½ teaspoon salt
⅛ teaspoon pepper
1 tablespoon chopped parsley
1 recipe any pie crust (your own, or a package mix)

Combine the vegetables and parboil them for 5 minutes in 1 cup of boiling salted water. Drain and combine them with the fish, sauce, and seasonings. Mix well. Chill the mixture in the refrigerator. When cold, pour it into a lightly buttered, fairly deep pie pan or baking dish and cover it with pastry. Wrap in foil or freezer film, or secure in a large plastic bag and freeze.

To serve: Preheat the oven to 400°. Unwrap the pie and put it, still frozen, onto a cooky sheet. Bake for 10 minutes, cut a few vent gashes in the crust, and continue baking for 40 minutes until the crust is golden brown. Or thaw the pie in the refrigerator, cut vent gashes, and bake at 400° for 30 to 35 minutes.

Fish Loaf
4 to 6 servings

2 cups flaked cooked fish
2 cups Average White Sauce (page 19)
1 cup soft bread crumbs
1 beaten egg
½ teaspoon salt
⅛ teaspoon pepper
1 tablespoon minced onion
1 tablespoon minced green pepper
1 tablespoon slivered celery
2 teaspoons lemon juice

Combine the fish with the white sauce, mixing well. Soak the bread crumbs in beaten egg and add to the fish mixture with all the other ingredients. Stir well. Pour into a lightly oiled bread pan and bake in a preheated 400° oven for 20 minutes. Chill in the refrigerator, wrap, and freeze.

To serve cold: Thaw in the refrigerator and frost the loaf with mayonnaise.

To serve hot: Unwrap the loaf and bake in a preheated 400° oven for 35 to 40 minutes. Serve with or without any appropriate sauce.

Tuna-Noodle Casserole

There are boxes of noodles and cans of tuna on the pantry shelf. Why bother to freeze this humble recipe? I can't count the times I've congratulated myself on having in the freezer a 1- or 2-quart stainless steel container holding the second half of the recipe I cleverly doubled the day I served the first half. It takes little additional time to make 2 casseroles instead of one, no time at all to freeze the spare, and it's a ready meal any day up to 3 months later when I don't feel like cooking. Not *haute cuisine*, certainly, but a great homespun favorite.

This recipe will make about 8 servings—4 for tonight, 4 for the freezer. If you like, the freezer portion may be layered in smaller containers for individual or twosome meals.

1-pound box broad noodles
3 7-ounce or 2 family-size cans tuna fish, drained
1 cup or more sliced stuffed green olives
2 cups Average White Sauce (page 19) or 1 can condensed
  cream-style soup (mushroom, celery, chicken) diluted with
  about ⅔ can milk
1 cup grated Cheddar or American cheese
⅔ cup fine crumbs (bread, cracker, cornflake) mixed with 3
  tablespoons melted butter

Pour the noodles gradually into at least 3 quarts of boiling water to which 1 tablespoon of salt has been added. Cook briskly for 8 minutes until barely tender, stirring occasionally, then drain. Make a production line of all the ingredients and start building up layers in 2 (or more) lightly buttered ovenproof casseroles or deep baking dishes: first a layer of noodles, next tuna, next olives, next sauce, next a sprinkling of cheese. Repeat 3 times. The topmost layer should be noodles sprinkled first with cheese, then with buttered crumbs.

Bake tonight's casserole in a preheated 350° oven for 30 minutes. Brown the topping under the broiler.

To freeze the extra casserole(s): Cover, refrigerate, bag, then freeze.

To serve after freezer storage: Thaw at room temperature for 1 hour or more. Preheat the oven to 425°. Put the covered casserole onto a middle rack for 30 to 40 minutes. Uncover, reduce the oven temperature to 350°, and heat until bubbly. Brown the topping under the broiler.

Cabbage Rolls Stuffed with Tuna or Salmon
4 servings now, 4 in the freezer with a container of sauce

8 very large cabbage leaves
15-ounce can tuna fish, or 1-pound can salmon (drained, deboned, flaked)
1½ cups cooked rice
1 cup finely chopped celery
½ cup minced onion
½ cup minced green peppers
1 tablespoon salad type mustard
1 egg, beaten lightly with a fork

2 cups chicken or fish stock, or consommé
1 tablespoon brown sugar
½ cup cream or rich milk
2 tablespoons flour
¼ teaspoon salt
⅛ teaspoon pepper
¼ teaspoon ground nutmeg
2 tablespoons horse-radish

Cut the bottom stem from a cabbage head and carefully remove 8 outer leaves. Plunge them into boiling salted water and cook for 2 or 3 minutes until they become a little limp. Drain and cool. With scissors or a sharp knife make a 2-inch lengthwise slit through the heavy bottom vein of each leaf. Mix together the drained tuna or salmon, rice, celery, onion, green pepper, mustard, and egg. Divide the mixture into 8 parts (about 2 tablespoons each) and put each portion into the center of a cabbage leaf. Fold from the bottom, tucking the sides in as you fold. Refrigerate 4 of the rolls, continuing as follows for the 4 you are going to serve:

Secure them with toothpicks, put them into a skillet, and pour the stock or consommé over them. Sprinkle with the sugar. Bring to a boil, lower the heat, and simmer, covered, for 15 minutes. Remove the rolls to a warm platter or to serving plates. Mix the milk and flour together until smooth and stir into the hot liquid in the skillet. Add all the remaining ingredients and stir over low heat until smooth and thickened.

Spoon half the sauce over the warm cabbage rolls and serve. Let the remaining sauce cool, and pour it into a freezer container.

Wrap the other 4 cabbage rolls individually in freezer film or foil and put them into a plastic bag. Refrigerate along with the container of sauce. When thoroughly chilled, freeze.

To serve after freezer storage: Unwrap the cabbage rolls and put them into the top of a double boiler over simmering water. Cover and let them heat through (about 30 minutes). Release the sauce into a small saucepan to heat. Stir with a fork to break up frosty lumps. When hot, stir briskly with a wire whisk and spoon over the cabbage rolls.

GEFÜLLTE FISH

The time to make a batch of gefüllte fish balls for freezing is when the gift or availability of the three kinds of fish requisite for this time-honored recipe coincides with the gift or availability of about 3 hours—or more—of your time.

Even with the proper ingredients, however, the recipe given here takes liberties with tradition. Gefüllte fish means *filled* fish. To be correct, you start out with one handsome large fish as well as two or more smaller ones. You peel the big one, leaving the skin intact except for a careful incision.

You scrape the flesh of all fish from skin and bones, combine the flesh, chop it in a wooden bowl with a single-blade chopper, add the remaining ingredients, chop some more, wash the reserved fish skin, stuff it with the mixture, suture the incision, and simmer it in fish-trimming stock until well done. There are many wonderful cooks who do this every spring and they don't need any instruction from me. Can a filled fish be frozen? It can. It can be thawed overnight in the refrigerator in its wrap, along with a container of the stock, sliced at the table, moistened with the stock, and served with cold cooked beets and horse-radish.

Gefüllte Fish Balls
The number of servings will depend on the size you make them. Usually this recipe yields from 12 to 16 boat-shaped patties, or up to 30 balls.

6 pounds undressed fish (2 of whitefish, 2 of pike, 2 of carp)
1 large onion
2 eggs
1 teaspoon salt
½ teaspoon ground black pepper
¾ cup ice water or cold fish stock
Up to 4 tablespoons matzoth meal

Behead the fish and separate the flesh from the skin and bones. Reserve the heads, skin, and bones. You may grind the fish with the onion in a food chopper, using the medium blade, before chopping it in a large wooden chopping bowl. Beat together the eggs, salt, pepper, and ice water or cold stock, mix with the fish, and chop until very fine. Gradually add the matzoth meal to make a stiff, well-blended mixture. Refrigerate for at least 1 hour while you make the stock; it's easier to shape when very cold.

Stock for gefüllte fish balls

Reserved fish heads, skin, bones
1 large or 2 smaller onions, quartered
1½ teaspoons salt

½ teaspoon pepper
4 cups water

Put the fish trimmings, onions, and seasonings into a large pot, cover with the water, bring to a boil, lower the heat, and simmer for 20 minutes while you shape the fish mixture into patties or balls with moistened hands. Shape them all before you start cooking any. Add the balls one at a time to the simmering stock, cover, and continue to simmer for 1 hour. Remove from the heat and let cool. Use a slotted spoon to remove the fish. Put serving portions into plastic bags and secure the tops. Strain the stock into freezer containers. Refrigerate both fish and stock, and freeze when cold.

To serve cold: Thaw the fish balls in the refrigerator. Serve with beet horse-radish.

To serve hot: Heat the stock, add the fish balls, and simmer until hot. Cook carrot slices or fingers until tender, drain, and add them to the simmering fish balls. Serve with beet horse-radish.

Fish Balls

Use 4 pounds of frozen fish fillets as available—3 pounds lean (flounder, haddock), 1 pound fatty (halibut). Thaw the fillets until they can be put through a grinder. Proceed as in the preceding recipe for gefüllte fish balls. Use bottled clam juice for the stock, or make the fish balls a day or so after you have made (and refrigerated) a court bouillon (page 215) for cooking shrimp.

Note: Either of the fish ball recipe mixtures can be rolled into marble-sized balls before cooking and freezing, and served as a toothpick appetizer or as a noble addition to fish stews and chowders.

Kedgeree

Note: For a party supper, this recipe's main ingredient may be lobster meat, fresh-boiled or canned. For a cocktail party, the smoky taste of finnan haddie is appropriate and popular. For family meals, any favorite cooked fish may be flaked—cod, haddock, salmon, flounder, etc.

Except for the last-minute addition of cream and hard-cooked eggs, the recipe may be frozen in one very large or a few smaller containers for later heating and serving, or it may be prepared in part for the midday or evening meal, in part for the freezer. A smaller quantity is given for first-timers or those with limited freezer space.

4 to 6 servings		*8 to 12 servings*
6 tablespoons	butter or margarine	½ cup
2 teaspoons	curry powder	1 tablespoon
3 cups	cooked rice	6 cups
2 cups	cooked lobster meat or	4 cups
1½ teaspoons	flaked cooked fish	1 tablespoon
Dash	lemon juice	2 dashes
½ cup	Worcestershire sauce	1 cup
	chopped parsley or water cress	

Melt the butter in a skillet and add the curry powder, stirring until well blended. Cook over low heat for 1 minute. In a large bowl, combine all the ingredients until thoroughly mixed with the curry butter.

Freezer portion: Allowing 1 scant cup per serving, spoon the mixture into freezer containers, chill in the refrigerator, and freeze.

Serving the unfrozen portion: Use 1 hard-cooked egg and 2 tablespoons of cream per serving. Chop the egg whites and stir them into the mixture. Add the cream and stir. Season to taste with salt and pepper. Heat to serving temperature in the top of a double boiler over simmering water. Serve on a hot platter or individual plates and garnish with crumbled egg yolk.

Serving the frozen portion: Partially thaw in the refrigerator or at room temperature. Empty the container into the top of a double boiler over simmering water. When completely thawed, finish the recipe for serving as in the preceding directions.

Stuffed Fillets I (with Shrimp and Mushrooms)
8 servings

8 thin, wide fresh fish fillets (flounder or sole)
Paprika
3 tablespoons butter
4 shallots or 2 small onions, minced
⅔ pound mushrooms, sliced
2 tablespoons minced parsley
⅔ pound peeled, deveined, precooked shrimp, chopped

Sprinkle the fillets with the paprika on both sides. Melt the butter in a skillet, add the shallots or onions, and sauté until limp. Add the mushrooms and stir for 2 minutes. Remove from the heat and mix with the parsley and shrimp. Place a spoonful of this stuffing toward the wider end of each fillet. Roll the fillets, starting at the wide end and tucking in the sides as you roll. Wrap individually in foil and refrigerate until chilled. Freeze. When frozen, gather into a plastic bag.

To serve: Thaw the foil-wrapped fillets in the refrigerator or at room temperature. When thawed, unwrap and arrange the fillets close together in a lightly buttered shallow baking dish. Preheat the oven to 400° while you make the sauce: *

Brandied Wine Sauce

For 4 fillets		*For 8 fillets*
2 tablespoons	butter	4 tablespoons
2 tablespoons	flour	4 tablespoons
½ teaspoon	salt	⅔ teaspoon

* Any favorite light sauce in your freezer stockpile may be substituted—one 8-ounce container for each 4 fillets. Thaw in the top of a double boiler over simmering water, breaking up lumps with a fork, and stir until smooth and hot.

For 4 fillets		*For 8 fillets*
¾ cup	warm milk or cream	1½ cups
¼ cup	stock, consommé, or bouillon	½ cup
¼ cup	dry white wine	½ cup
2 tablespoons	brandy or cognac	2-ounce jigger
2 tablespoons	grated Swiss or Gruyère cheese	¼ cup

Melt the butter and blend in the flour and salt. Add the liquids, stirring until smooth. Bring to a boil, lower the heat, and simmer for 5 minutes. Pour this sauce over the fillets, top with the grated cheese, and bake at 400° for 20 to 25 minutes, until the cheese is melted and bubbly.

Stuffed Fillets II (with Bread Dressing)
8 servings

8 long, thin fresh fillets (any kind)
½ cup melted butter
2 tablespoons minced onion
½ cup chopped celery
2½ cups soft bread crumbs
2 tablespoons minced parsley
½ teaspoon salt
¼ teaspoon sage, thyme, basil, or fennel

Line an 8-cup deep muffin tin with oiled, buttered, or greased foil. Line each cup with a fillet, leaving a hole for the stuffing. In 2 tablespoons of the melted butter, sauté the onions until limp, then add and sauté the celery for 2 or 3 minutes. Combine with the remaining butter, bread crumbs, parsley, and seasonings. Fill each rolled fillet with this mixture, cover with foil or freezer film, refrigerate until chilled, then freeze. When solid, release the fillets and wrap them individually in foil. Gather in a plastic bag for storage.

To serve: Remove the serving portion from the freezer and replace in the muffin tin to thaw in the refrigerator or at room temperature. When thawed, place the muffin tin in a pan containing about 1 inch of hot water (half-fill the empty cups with water also). Bake at 350° for 25 to 35 minutes. Unmold on a warm platter or individual plates and serve with lemon wedges or with any sauce or light gravy of your choice.

16.

Fish from the Freezer

Among the reasons for planning this book were letters women have written asking for advice on how to handle frozen fish—home-processed, or selected from varieties displayed in store freezer cabinets. Having read my earlier book, they knew that I recommend thawing fish. They also knew that anything done with fresh-caught or bought fish can be done with frozen fish after thawing.

The letter writers were seeking information about cooking methods and timing for fish they forgot to take out of the freezer before meal preparation began, or remembered too late to allow for more than partial thawing. Many reported failures. Fish cooked from the frozen or partially thawed state turned out flat and tasteless. Or dry. Or scorched on the outside, undercooked on the inside. It was possible that they would forget thawing time requirements again. Would I please help?

This led to many sessions of kitchen-testing recipes for solidly frozen and partially thawed fish. Fortunately, I live in a fishing community. Much of the fish on my freezer shelves is summer largesse, processed and frozen as quickly as possible for winter menus. And I have a cat, a critical gourmet about canned food, to whom my own failures were delicious.

The use of a meat thermometer is a very good habit to acquire when you cook fish. As soon as the flesh can be penetrated, angle the thermometer in the thickest part. Remove the fish from the heat when the thermometer reading just passes 140° and is on its way to 145°. This is important, and here's why: Unlike meat animals who roam and romp around, fish are lazy-muscled. They glide through the water with the greatest of ease. Their flesh is tender. Their connective tissues are paper-thin. For eating enjoyment, the flesh (protein) should be firm while the tissues remain intact, for when these break down the flavorsome juices dissipate. Tissues break down at or around 150°.

If you have no meat thermometer, the test for doneness is when the flesh has lost its translucent quality and is tender but firm and moist. When it flakes too easily or falls away from the bones, it is usually overdone by all standards of appearance, taste, and nutrition. Time will vary according to the size of the fish, its temperature when you started cooking it, and the method used. But proper cooking is probably quicker than you think.

17.

Recipes for
Solidly Frozen Fish

Fillets Baked in Stock or Wine Sauce
4 servings

1½ pounds frozen fish fillets (any kind)
¼ cup flour
Scant ½ teaspoon salt
⅛ teaspoon pepper
½ pound mushrooms, sliced (or 1 package frozen sliced mush-
    rooms)
3 tablespoons butter
2 tablespoons minced onion
⅔ cup fish or vegetable stock or dry white wine (or ⅓ cup each,
    stock and wine)

Preheat the oven to 450°. Cut the frozen fillets crosswise
into 8 equal pieces. Mix together the flour, salt, and pepper
and dredge the pieces in this mixture until they are well and
evenly coated. Put them into a buttered baking dish which
has a closely fitted cover. Sauté the mushrooms in the butter
for 3 minutes, remove them with a slotted spoon to the fish
dish, and sauté the onions in the same pan until limp and
golden. Add them to the fish. Add the liquid, cover the dish,
and bake at 450° for 25 minutes.

Variations: Solidly frozen fish fillets cut into small pieces, or quartered, may be baked as above in your choice of stock-piled sauce from the freezer—cheese, curry, Mornay, etc. (see the Index). Add the sauce after melting and stirring smooth, and bake 20 to 25 minutes for small pieces, 25 to 30 minutes for quartered fillets.

Fillets in Foil
4 servings

1½ pounds frozen fish fillets (any kind)
4 tablespoons melted butter
1 tablespoon lemon juice
¼ teaspoon salt
¼ teaspoon paprika, ground ginger, or basil

Cut the frozen fillets into four equal pieces. If you can cut them lengthwise, so much the better. Roll the pieces in the melted butter mixed with the lemon juice and seasonings. Put the fillets, separated, into the center of a fairly large piece of heavy aluminum foil. Pour any remaining butter mixture over them. Make a "drugstore wrap" by bringing the opposite sides of the foil together evenly, then folding down in a series of folds. Fold the ends toward the center. The foil does not have to hug the fish tightly, but should resemble a sealed envelope.

To pancook: Put the foil-wrapped fish into a skillet over moderate heat and add 1 cup of boiling water. Simmer for 30 minutes. Add more boiling water if necessary.

To bake: Preheat the oven to 450°. Put the foil-wrapped fish into a baking dish or on a cooking sheet. Bake for 25 to 30 minutes.

Fish Steaks in Foil
The preceding method may also be used for pancooking or baking frozen but separated small fish steaks. Do not cut them. Pancook for 35 minutes, or bake for 40 minutes.

Fillets Florentine
4 to 6 servings

2 packages frozen chopped spinach
4 tablespoons butter
Water
½ cup dry white wine
Half an onion, stuck with 2 or 3 cloves
3 or 4 peppercorns
2 or 3 whole allspice
1 teaspoon parsley flakes
1 teaspoon lemon juice
4 frozen fish fillets, any kind
2 tablespoons flour
⅓ cup sweet or sour cream, warmed
Grating or pinch of nutmeg
Grated Romano or Parmesan cheese

Preheat the oven to 450° while you cook the spinach according to the package directions. Drain, reserving the water. Stir 2 tablespoons of the butter into the spinach and spread it evenly over the bottom of a baking dish. Add enough water to the reserved spinach water to make ½ cup and combine it in the spinach saucepan with the wine, cloved onion, spices, parsley, and lemon juice. Bring this to a boil, lower the heat, and simmer for 10 minutes. Raise the heat to boiling again and add the frozen fillets. When the liquid resumes its boil, lower the heat and simmer for 10 minutes. Carefully raise the fillets and place them on the spinach bed. Strain the broth. Melt the remaining 2 tablespoons of butter in a double boiler top, then add and blend in the flour. Add the strained broth a little at a time. Stir over boiling water until thickened and smooth. Add the warmed cream and nutmeg, stir, and pour over the fillets. Sprinkle with grated cheese and heat in the oven for 10 minutes.

Fillets in Shrimp or Lobster Bisque
4 servings

4 frozen fish fillets, any kind (1½ to 2 pounds)
1 or 2 tablespoons sherry (optional)
2 cans frozen concentrated shrimp or lobster bisque, thawed
2 tablespoons dry bread crumbs
2 tablespoons grated Cheddar, Swiss, Parmesan, or Romano cheese
2 tablespoons butter

Preheat the oven to 400°. Separate the fillets, brush them on both sides with sherry if desired, and arrange them in a shallow buttered casserole. The bisque must be completely thawed and smooth, but not diluted. If necessary, heat it only until it can be stirred briskly, or buzz it in a blender. Spread the bisque over the fillets, sprinkle with the combined crumbs and cheese, and dot with the butter. Bake at 400° for 10 minutes, insert a meat thermometer in one of the fillets, reduce the heat to 375°, and continue baking for 25 to 30 minutes longer, or until the thermometer reads 140°.

Portuguese "Galvanized" Fillets (in Vinha d'Ahloes)
4 to 6 servings

"Galvanizing" is the name given by Portuguese fishermen and their families to a pickling process used for fish and also for pork chops. This is not a spur-of-the-moment recipe, as the fish must marinate for at least 24 hours. However, it is suitable for frozen (as well as unfrozen) fish and is an extremely popular Cape Cod recipe. If you try and like this interesting method, do not discard the marinade (Vinha d'Ahloes). Keep it in a jar in the refrigerator, add to it if necessary, and use it for pickling other varieties of fillets from time to time.

2 pounds frozen fillets (cod, haddock, flounder, etc.)
2 cups cider vinegar
3 cups water
2 large cloves of garlic, minced
1 teaspoon salt
½ teaspoon ground black pepper
Pinch of cumin seed

The fillets may be left whole or cut into pieces. Mix together all the marinade ingredients in a glass, ceramic, or enamelware container. Do not use aluminum or steel. (Traditionally, an old-fashion red wooden firkin is used.) Add the fillets to the marinade, but do not pack them down. If possible, see to it that the garlic is more or less evenly distributed among the pieces. Cover the vessel and let it stand for 24 hours or more in the refrigerator, or in a reliably cool place.

To cook the fillets: Remove them from the marinade with kitchen tongs and allow them to drain on paper towels for about 30 minutes. Pat dry, dust with flour or dip in cracker meal, and sauté in hot oil or butter until golden brown, turning once.

Baked Fish Steaks au Gratin
4 servings

4 frozen fish steak portions (cod, halibut, salmon, swordfish, etc.)
⅔ cup thinly sliced or chopped onions
¼ cup butter
1½ cups soft bread crumbs (or ¾ cup fine bread crumbs)
½ cup grated Cheddar or Swiss cheese
½ teaspoon salt
⅛ teaspoon pepper
1 cup cream, milk, or half-and-half

Preheat the oven to 375°. Arrange the steaks separately in a buttered baking dish. Sauté the onions in the butter until limp and golden, then spread over the fish steaks. Combine the crumbs with the cheese and seasonings, tossing lightly with a fork until well mixed. Spread this mixture over the fish steaks, pour the cream, milk, or half-and-half over them, insert a meat thermometer in one steak, and bake at 375° for 40 minutes, or until the meat thermometer reads 140°.

Baked Fish Steaks with Olives
4 servings

4 frozen fish steak portions (cod, halibut, salmon, swordfish, etc.)
Paprika
½ cup chopped onions
¼ cup softened butter
1 tablespoon herb or tarragon vinegar
½ cup or more chopped, sliced, or salad olives with pimientos

Preheat the oven to 375°. Sprinkle both sides of the steaks with paprika and arrange them in a buttered baking dish. Blend the onions with the butter, vinegar, and olives and spread the mixture over the steaks. Insert a meat thermometer in one steak. Bake at 375° for 40 minutes, or until the meat thermometer reads 140°.

Fish Steak Casserole (with Anchovies and Potatoes)
4 servings

4 medium white potatoes, peeled and thinly sliced
½ cup finely chopped onions
½ teaspoon ground black pepper
1 small clove garlic, minced or put through garlic press
1 tablespoon chopped fresh parsley
4 anchovy fillets, chopped
½ cup fine olive oil
4 frozen fish steak portions (halibut or swordfish)

Preheat the oven to 375°. Oil or butter an ovenproof serving casserole and cover the bottom with half the sliced potatoes. Divide the remaining ingredients (except the fish) in half and sprinkle them over the potatoes. Arrange the fish steaks separately over this base, cover them with the rest of the potatoes, and sprinkle with the remaining half of the other ingredients. Bake for 45 to 50 minutes, or until the potatoes are tender and the meat thermometer reads 140°.

Baked Marinated Fish Steaks
(2 or 3 hours required for marinating)
4 servings

4 frozen fish steak portions (halibut or swordfish)
½ cup olive oil
1 teaspoon parsley flakes
¼ teaspoon powdered thyme
1 small bay leaf
4 whole peppercorns
¼ cup chopped fresh or frozen onions
½ cup flour
Salt and pepper
Lemon wedges

Separate the fish steaks and let stand at room temperature for 2 or 3 hours in a marinade made with the oil, seasonings, and onions. Turn the steaks occasionally, then remove, drain, and dry. Strain the marinade and heat it in an oven-proof skillet large enough to accommodate the steaks. Dredge the steaks in the flour and brown them lightly on each side in the skillet, turning once. When browned, transfer the skillet to a preheated 375° oven and bake for 20 minutes, basting often with the marinade. Season to taste at table with salt and pepper and serve with lemon wedges.

Baked Fish Steaks in Italian Sauce *
4 servings

4 frozen fish steak portions (cod, halibut, swordfish) or 1 large (2-pound) steak
2 tablespoons chopped fresh or frozen green peppers
2 tablespoons chopped fresh or frozen onions

* Your freezer may yield a stockpiled container of meatless Italian sauce (page 31). Heat it slowly in a saucepan, breaking up lumps, bring to a boil, remove from the heat, and pour over the fish for baking.

2 tablespoons chopped celery
4 tablespoons olive oil
1 tablespoon flour
1 cup canned tomatoes
1 teaspoon parsley flakes
½ teaspoon salt
Dash of ground black pepper

Arrange the fish steaks in a shallow oiled baking dish. Sauté the chopped vegetables in the oil until the onions are limp and golden. Sprinkle with the flour, stir to blend, and stir in the remaining ingredients. Bring this sauce slowly to the boiling point, lower the heat, simmer for 10 minutes, then pour it over the fish. Bake in a preheated 375° oven for 40 minutes, or until the meat thermometer reads 140°.

Baked Fish Steaks in Curry Sauce
4 servings

4 frozen fish steak portions (cod, halibut, salmon, swordfish)
2 tablespoons minced onion
2 tablespoons butter
2 tablespoons flour
1 cup fish, veal, or chicken stock (from freezer) or canned con-
    sommé
Salt to taste, depending on stock seasonings
1 to 2 teaspoons curry powder
½ cup heavy sweet or sour cream

Preheat the oven to 375°. Arrange the fish steaks separately in a buttered or oiled baking dish. Sauté the onion in the butter until light gold. Sprinkle with the flour and mix well. Add this mixture to the simmering stock or consommé, stir thoroughly, and simmer until thickened. Add the salt and curry powder, stir in the cream, and cook over very low heat until smooth. Do not let it boil. Pour the sauce over the fish and bake at 375° for 40 minutes, or until the meat thermometer reads 140°.

RECIPES FOR FROZEN SMALL INDIVIDUAL FISH

The hoard of a successful fisherman's catch in your freezer can provide more or less impromptu meals even without thawing. Of course, they were cleaned before you froze them—heads and tails removed or not, but fins cut off with a sharp knife or kitchen shears.

Choose a recipe according to the variety of the fish you are cooking. Fatty fish such as herring, tinker mackerel, whiting, mullet, and butterfish should not ordinarily be used in recipes requiring a large amount of oil. These are best baked in sauces. Leaner varieties—small flounder, porgy, yellow perch, small black or white bass, etc.—may be cooked either in a sauce or in an herbed oil dressing.

Small Lean Fish with Tomatoes and Crumbs
4 servings

4 individual frozen lean fish weighing ½ pound each
6 tablespoons olive or salad oil
½ teaspoon salt
¼ teaspoon ground black pepper
4 teaspoons minced parsley
1 small clove garlic, put through garlic press
4 to 6 tablespoons fine bread, cracker, or cereal crumbs
2 large firm tomatoes, thinly sliced
½ teaspoon oregano, basil, or powdered anise
Lemon wedges

Preheat the oven to 375°. Pat the fish as dry as possible. Put 4 tablespoons of the oil into a flat casserole and add the fish, turning once to coat both sides. Sprinkle with the salt, pepper, parsley, garlic, and bread crumbs. Bake at 375° for 20 minutes. Insert a meat thermometer in one fish, arrange the sliced tomatoes over all, and sprinkle with the remaining

2 tablespoons of oil and then with your chosen herb. Decrease the oven temperature to 350° and bake until the meat thermometer reads 140°. Serve with lemon wedges.

Small Fish with Wine and Mushrooms
4 servings

4 frozen small fish weighing ½ pound each
4 tablespoons fine bread crumbs
2 tablespoons melted butter
2 tablespoons minced onion
½ cup chopped fresh or frozen mushrooms
1 tablespoon minced parsley
½ teaspoon salt
¼ teaspoon ground black pepper
1 cup dry white wine

Preheat the oven to 350°. Pat the fish as dry as possible and place them in a well-buttered casserole. Combine all the remaining ingredients except the wine and spread the mixture over the fish. Pour the wine around (not over) the fish and bake at 350° for 20 minutes. Insert a meat thermometer in one fish, reduce the oven temperature to 300°, baste the fish with its own wine, and continue baking, basting occasionally, until the meat thermometer reads 140°.

Small Fish with Freezer Stockpile Sauce
4 servings

4 frozen small fish weighing ½ pound each
Butter
1-pint container any favorite sauce from freezer, melted, smooth, and hot

Preheat the oven to 350°. Pat the fish as dry as possible and arrange in a well-buttered baking dish. Pour the hot sauce over them and bake at 350° for 20 minutes. Insert a meat thermometer, reduce the oven temperature to 300°, and bake until the meat thermometer reads 140°.

HOW ABOUT A RECIPE FOR A
LARGE FROZEN FISH?

It is inevitable that someone will nervously riffle the index pages of this book looking for a miracle when a beautiful special large fish is still in its cold sleep toward sunset of the day it is scheduled for dinner. If it is a very special and very large fish you wouldn't let your husband have mounted on the study wall, better forget it until you have time to thaw it properly. Do something clever with cans of tuna or salmon, or heat the casserole you froze last week.

But if your forgotten fish is a 2 or 3 pounder, even a 4 pounder, something can be done to save the day and the dinner. It's a limited method and not one I recommend except as an emergency measure, but it will ward off starvation and maybe impel another sports fisherman's wife to ask for the recipe.

You won't be able to stuff this particular fish, so if stuffing is an important part of the meal prepare your favorite recipe (pages 412–415), add a little extra liquid, put it into a separate greased baking dish with a cover, and let it bake on the oven rack along with the fish for the last half-hour of cooking time.

Large Whole Fish Baked in Foil

1 whole frozen fish (up to 4 pounds)
1 meat thermometer (essential)
Stuffing if desired (½ cup per serving)
1-pint or 25-ounce container any meatless sauce from the freezer
   (optional)

Without removing its freezer wraps, put the fish into a new, heavy plastic bag. Secure the top of the bag firmly with a rubber band or plastic strip. Put the bagged fish into a large pan (such as a dishpan) in the sink and let cold water run over it, gradually turning the hot water spigot until the stream is lukewarm. Let the water run cold to cool for 15 minutes, lukewarm for 15 minutes more. This won't completely thaw the fish, but it will help shorten the cooking time.

Unwrap the fish. Open its lengthwise split on the underside, where you cleaned it before freezing, and sprinkle the cavity with salt, lemon juice, and pepper or paprika. If the fish is a bland variety, sprinkle it also with a few grains of a pungent herb—thyme, sage, basil, oregano, anise. Put a few thin pats of butter in the cavity.

Tear off a large sheet of heavy freezer foil and brush one side of it with oil. Place the fish on its back in the center of the oiled side of the foil and make a "drugstore wrap" by bringing the opposite sides of the foil together evenly, then folding down in a series of folds. Fold the ends toward the center.

Turn the oven control to 400°. Put the fish into a V-shaped rack or into a baking pan which will allow it to remain on its back, with the foil folds on top. Put the pan into the oven and watch the thermostat (or your own checking oven thermometer). When the temperature reaches 400°, start timing:

2- to 3-pound fish: Bake for 20 minutes.
4-pound fish: Bake for 30 minutes.

Insert a meat thermometer through the foil into the fleshiest part of the fish. Reduce the oven heat to 300° and continue baking until the meat thermometer reads 140° (see the discussion on page 151). Depending on the weight and thickness of the fish, the total cooking time will probably not exceed 1½ hours.

Serve with or without separately baked stuffing and sauce from the freezer, melted and hot.

18.

Basic Cooking Methods and Recipes for Thawed or Partially Thawed Fish

New freezer owners—and some veterans—are occasionally chagrined to find that the fish they removed from the freezer to thaw for dinner is still frosty at meal preparation time. Included here, therefore, are basic cooking methods and recipes which take frustrating frostiness into consideration.

The basic methods and specific recipes may also be used for completely thawed fish, or for fish that never saw the inside of a freezer. It must be remembered, however, that cooking times will necessarily depend on the fish's temperature when it is introduced to heat. Time margins are indicated, but your partially thawed fish may be frostier than mine was when I tested the recipe. Or your thawed fish may be refrigerator-cold, whereas mine may have been room-warm. Consequently, the use of a meat thermometer whenever possible is strongly recommended.

METHODS FOR COOKING THAWED OR PARTIALLY THAWED FISH

Suggested fish varieties for frying or sautéing

Fillets: haddock, halibut, flounder, sole, scrod, perch
½-inch steaks: haddock, halibut, red snapper, cod
Small whole fish: smelts, trout, perch, sunfish, tinker mackerel

Deep-fried Fish
4 servings

1½ to 2 pounds of fish, thawed or partially thawed and separated
About ½ cup flour
2 eggs, beaten with 1 tablespoon water
About ¾ cup fine bread crumbs, cracker meal, or corn meal
Oil or shortening in deep fryer

Pat the fish as dry as possible. Roll individually in the flour, dip into the beaten eggs until evenly coated, then roll in the crumbs or meal. Heat oil or shortening in a deep fryer with a basket to 370° on a frying thermometer, or until a small cube of crustless white bread browns in 20 seconds (count "one-and, two-and,' etc.). Place the fish in a single layer in the fryer basket and fry for the following times:

Thawed, room temperature: 3 to 5 minutes
Thawed, cold: 5 to 7 minutes
Partially thawed: 8 to 12 minutes

If more than one batch is to be fried, remove the first batch when done, drain on paper towels, keep warm, and reheat the fat to 370° before adding more fish to the basket.

Season to taste at the table; or dress with melted butter, paprika, and fresh parsley, with wedges of fresh lemon; or serve with prepared tartar sauce.

Batter-Fried Fish
Use a commercial fritter batter, following the package directions, or make this batter:

Sift ⅔ cup of flour with ¼ teaspoon of salt and 1 teaspoon of baking powder. Add 1 well-beaten egg and ⅓ to ½ cup of milk. The batter should be of a consistency to cling to the fish and coat it evenly. If too thin, add a little more flour; if too heavy, add a little more milk. Stir well until smooth.

Coat the fish with the batter and deep fry according to the times given in the preceding method for Deep-fried Fish.

Sauteéd Fish

4 servings

1½ to 2 pounds fish, thawed or partially thawed and separated
½ cup flour, fine bread or cereal crumbs, or cracker meal
Dash of ground white or black pepper
Grating of fresh nutmeg, or pinch of ground nutmeg
½ teaspoon your choice of basil, tarragon, rosemary, ginger, or
    anise
4 tablespoons butter, oil, or shortening

Pat the fish as dry as possible and dredge with the flour or crumbs mixed with the seasonings. Add the butter, oil, or shortening to a heated skillet, but do not let it smoke. Put the fish into the skillet in a single layer over moderate heat. Cook until the undersurface is golden brown, then turn carefully with a wide spatula, lower the heat, and cook the second side for the following times:

Thawed, room temperature: 2 to 4 minutes
Thawed, cold: 4 to 6 minutes
Partially thawed: 8 to 12 minutes

Broiled Fish

Suggested fish varieties for broiling:

1 to 1½-inch steaks: cod, haddock, halibut, salmon, snapper,
    swordfish, fresh tuna
Small whole fish: flounder, trout, tinker mackerel
Large fish: cod, mackerel, flounder, fluke, bass, pompano, mullet

For best results in broiling, fish steaks should be fairly thick (up to 1½ inches). If the steaks have skin, you do not have to remove it. Small fish may be broiled whole after cleaning. Larger whole headless and tailless fish should be split, bones removed or not at will, and spread open on the broiling pan, skin-down at the start.

Oil, grease, or butter a broiling pan, a piece of heavy aluminum foil placed on a broiling pan, or one of the heavy foil disposable broiling pans.

Preheat the pan in the broiler to 450°, placing the pan 4 inches from the flame. If yours is an electric broiler with a set high temperature, place the rack at least 6 inches from the source of heat.

Place the fish on the broiler pan and brush liberally with melted butter. Broil one side for the following times, basting occasionally with melted butter:

	Steaks or small whole fish	*Large fish*
Thawed, room temperature:	4 to 5 minutes	6 to 8 minutes
Thawed, cold:	6 to 8 minutes	8 to 10 minutes
Partially thawed:	8 to 10 minutes	10 to 12 minutes

Remove the broiler pan and, with one or two side spatulas, carefully turn the fish. Brush with melted butter. Insert a meat thermometer in the fleshiest portion and broil, basting with melted butter, until the thermometer reads 140°.

Poached Fish

Suggested fish varieties for poaching:

Fillets: halibut, haddock, red snapper, sole, whitefish
Steaks: halibut, haddock, red snapper, salmon, sea bass
Large pieces: salmon, haddock, halibut, sea bass, hake
Whole: trout, ocean perch, whitefish

Into the bottom of a pan large enough to hold the fish put the following items:

Trimmings, if any
1 quart water *
1 cup dry white wine
1 onion stock with 4 or 5 cloves
6 to 8 peppercorns
1 stalk celery with leaves
½ small bay leaf
3 or 4 whole allspice
3 or 4 sprigs parsley
1 teaspoon salt

Bring these ingredients to a boil, lower the heat, and simmer for 15 minutes. You may, but need not, strain the stock.

Wrap the fish in cheesecloth. Tie the ends loosely, allowing enough length to permit them to remain outside the cooking pan for easier removal. Insert a meat thermometer through the cheesecloth into one fillet, steak, piece, or fish. Lower the wrapped fish into the stock and continue a gentle simmer until the thermometer reads 140°. Remove the pan from the heat and allow the fish to cool slightly in the stock, but do not let its thermometer reading rise above 145°. Lift the fish by the cheesecloth handles and unwrap it on a serving platter.

Serve poached fish hot with Hollandaise or any favorite sauce, or cold with mayonnaise or similar dressing.

Steamed Fish

Suggested fish varieties for steaming:

Fillets: sea bass, cod, flounder, haddock, pompano, red snapper, lake trout
Steaks: salmon, haddock, cod, sea bass
Whole: any variety not heavier than 4 pounds

For steaming, two pieces of equipment are essential: a meat thermometer and a fish steamer. The fish must not be immersed in water, but cooked over boiling water. Lacking a

* *Note:* Quite small fish, thin steaks, or fillets may be poached in white wine or milk without the addition of water.

real fish steamer, you can fit a large pot with a shallow colander in such a way that it clears the bottom of the pot by ½ inch or more, yet permits the pot to be tightly covered. Or punch holes in an expendable pie plate and put it into the pot upside down. Or—an ingenious method suggested by a fisherman camper—save a few flat tins of the sort tuna fish comes in, remove the lids from both ends, and group the rings together to cover most of the bottom of the pot. This cannot be used with fillets, but works very well with large steaks or whole fish.

Place the fish on the steamer rack over boiling water, insert a meat thermometer into the fleshiest portion, cover the pot closely, and steam the fish until the thermometer reads 140°.

Baked Fish

Suggested fish varieties for baking:

Fillets: haddock, halibut, flounder, cod, shad, mackerel, sole
Steaks: salmon, halibut, swordfish, cod
Whole: any variety weighing up to 4 pounds

Preheat the oven to 325°, whether your fish is thawed or still somewhat frosty. Prepare the fish as for broiling (page 166). Butter or oil a baking dish and brush the fish with melted butter, using less butter for fatty fish such as mackerel and shad. Insert a meat thermometer into the fleshiest portion and bake at 325°, basting occasionally with pan drippings, until the meat thermometer reads 140°.

RECIPES FOR THAWED OR PARTIALLY THAWED FISH

Sautéed Fillets and Bananas in Wine Sauce
4 servings

4 fillets (any kind), thawed or partially thawed
½ cup flour

½ teaspoon salt
¼ teaspoon ground black pepper
¼ teaspoon paprika
¼ cup vegetable oil
½ cup dry sherry or vermouth
½ teaspoon ground ginger or anise
2 tablespoons lemon juice
2 tablespoons brown sugar
4 bananas, peeled and sliced lengthwise
¼ cup chopped walnuts, pecans, peanuts, or almonds

Pat the fillets as dry as possible and dredge them with the combined flour, salt, pepper, and paprika. Heat the oil in a large skillet, but do not let it smoke. Put the fish into a single layer in the skillet, set over moderate heat, and cook until the undersurface is golden brown. Lower the heat, turn the fish carefully, and cook the second side for the following times:

Thawed, room temperature: 2 to 4 minutes
Thawed, cold: 4 to 6 minutes
Partially thawed: 6 to 10 minutes

or until a meat thermometer, inserted in one fillet, registers 140°.

Remove the fillets from the skillet, drain on paper towels, and arrange them on a large warmed platter. To the oil in the skillet add the wine, ginger or anise, lemon juice, and sugar and stir to blend. Add the sliced bananas and simmer for 3 minutes, basting them with the skillet mixture. Surround the fillets with the banana slices, cover with pan sauce, and garnish with the chopped nuts.

Flounder or Sole Fillets Mornay
4 servings

4 thin fillets of flounder or sole, thawed or partially thawed
Ground white pepper
Cayenne
8-ounce container frozen Mornay sauce (or 1 cup sauce, page 21)
Salt

Preheat the oven to 350°. Arrange the fillets in a well-buttered baking dish and sprinkle lightly with white pepper. Add a few grains of cayenne pepper to the hot Mornay sauce, stir well, and pour over the fillets. Insert a meat thermometer in one fillet. Bake at 350° until the meat thermometer reads 140° (10 to 15 minutes if thawed, 15 to 25 minutes if partially thawed). Salt lightly before serving.

Broiled Fillets with Herbs
4 servings

4 fillets (any kind), thawed or partially thawed
1 medium onion, grated or minced
1 tablespoon lemon juice
4 tablespoons melted butter
⅛ teaspoon ground black pepper
⅛ teaspoon marjoram
⅛ teaspoon sweet basil powder
⅛ teaspoon powdered ginger or anise
¼ teaspoon paprika
1 tablespoon minced chives
1 tablespoon minced fresh parsley (or 1 teaspoon parsley flakes)
Salt
Parsley sprigs
Lemon wedges

Preheat the broiler to 450°.* Arrange the fillets on a piece of heavy freezer foil on the broiler rack, or on a foil broiling pan. Insert a meat thermometer in one fillet. Blend together all the remaining ingredients and spread over the fillets. Place the rack 4 inches from the flame.* Broil until the meat thermometer reads 140° (about 6 to 10 minutes if thawed, 10 to 15 minutes if partially thawed). Remove the fillets to a heated platter or individual serving plates, pour pan drippings over them, sprinkle lightly with salt, garnish with parsley sprigs, and serve with lemon wedges.

* If yours is a preset high-heat broiler, place rack 6 inches from heating element.

Rolled Fillets Creole
4 servings

4 long, thin fillets (any kind), thawed or partially thawed but
    pliable
4 tablespoons melted butter
1 tablespoon lemon juice
3 tablespoons chopped onions
1 tablespoon chopped fresh parsley (or 1 teaspoon parsley flakes)
4-ounce package frozen sliced mushrooms
8-ounce container frozen tomatoes (or 1 cup canned tomatoes)
8-ounce container frozen fish, chicken, or veal stock (or 1 cup
    consommé or bouillon)
1 teaspoon sugar
¼ teaspoon oregano
Grated Romano, Parmesan, or Cheddar cheese

Pat the fillets as dry as possible and brush on both sides
with 2 tablespoons of the melted butter mixed with the
lemon juice. Roll the fillets, fastening them securely with
toothpicks. In a large skillet or heavy 2-quart saucepan sauté
the onions and parsley in the remaining 2 tablespoons of
melted butter for 3 minutes. Add the mushrooms and sauté
for 2 minutes longer. Add the tomatoes, stock or other liquid, and sugar, stir, bring to a boil (breaking up lumps with
a fork if the tomatoes and stock were frozen), stir, reduce
the heat, and simmer for 10 minutes. Stir again, add the
rolled fillets, and continue to simmer over low heat for 8
minutes if thawed, 10 to 12 minutes if partially thawed. Add
the oregano and simmer for 2 or 3 minutes longer. Serve on
a heated platter or individual plates, covered with sauce and
sprinkled with grated cheese.

Baked Fillets in Wine-seasoned White Sauce
4 servings

4 fillets (any kind), thawed or partially thawed
1-pint container (2 cups) Average White Sauce (page 19)

1 teaspoon Worcestershire sauce
Dash of tabasco
¼ cup dry or medium sherry
2 tablespoons chopped fresh parsley, chives, or dill

Preheat the oven to 325°. Arrange the fillets in a lightly buttered baking dish and insert a meat thermometer in one. To hot, smooth white sauce (break up lumps with a fork as it melts, if frozen) add the Worcestershire sauce, tabasco, and sherry. Stir to blend well. Pour this sauce over the fillets and bake at 325° until the meat thermometer reads 140° (about 15 to 20 minutes for thawed fillets, 25 to 35 minutes for partially thawed fillets). Serve on heated plates covered with sauce and garnished with the chopped greens.

Oyster-Stuffed Baked Fillets
6 servings

6 fillets (any kind), thawed or partially thawed
1 cup fresh or frozen shucked oysters
1 tablespoon minced chives
1 tablespoon minced parsley
½ cup fresh or frozen chopped mushrooms
½ teaspoon salt
⅛ teaspoon ground black pepper
½ cup fine bread crumbs
2 tablespoons melted butter

Preheat the oven to 325°. Pat the fillets as dry as possible and arrange in a well-buttered baking dish. Chop the oysters and combine them with the chives, parsley, mushrooms, salt, and pepper. Spread this mixture over the fillets, top with the crumbs, sprinkle with the melted butter, and insert a meat thermometer in one fillet. Bake the fillets at 325° until the thermometer reads 140° (about 15 to 20 minutes if thawed, 25 to 35 minutes if partially thawed).

Serve with or without your favorite sauce (see the Index).

Chinese Panned Fillets
4 servings

1½ to 2 pounds fish fillets (any kind), thawed or partially thawed
3 tablespoons vegetable oil (preferably peanut oil)
⅓ cup soy sauce
1 large clove garlic, minced or put through garlic press
½ teaspoon powdered ginger
1 tablespoon lemon juice

Cut the fillets across into 2-inch pieces. In a heavy skillet or saucepan, brown the pieces in the oil over moderate heat, turning to brown evenly. Remove the pan from the heat and siphon off excess oil with a bulb baster. Blend together all the remaining ingredients and add to the fish. Return the pan to low heat, cover it tightly, and simmer for 5 minutes. Turn the pieces to coat evenly with the sauce, cover the pan again, and simmer for 5 minutes if thawed, 8 to 10 minutes if partially thawed.

Chinese Sweet and Sour Fillets
4 to 6 servings

1½ pounds fish fillets (any kind), thawed or partially thawed
2 eggs, beaten with 1 tablespoon water
½ cup flour
2 inches vegetable oil (preferably peanut oil) in deep fryer with basket
1 cup chicken stock or consommé
½ cup white vinegar
½ cup French vermouth or pale dry sherry
½ cup sugar
1 cup frozen carrots, lattice-cut or thin rounds
1 tablespoon soy sauce
1 level tablespoon cornstarch
2 or 3 firm tomatoes, quartered
2 green peppers, seeds removed, cut coarsely
½ cup drained canned or frozen pineapple chunks
3 to 5 cups hot fluffy rice

Cut the fillets into pieces about the size of large shrimp. Blend the beaten eggs with the flour into a smooth batter. Dip the fish pieces into the batter, coating evenly, and deep-fry in the hot oil until golden brown. Remove the fish and drain on paper towels. In a large saucepan combine the stock or consommé, vinegar, wine, and sugar, bring to a brisk boil, add the carrots, and boil for 5 minutes. Lower the heat to a simmer. Combine the soy sauce and cornstarch and stir this mixture into the simmering carrots. Add the quartered tomatoes, cut peppers, and pineapple chunks and stir. Add the fried fish pieces and stir carefully with a wooden spoon to distribute all the ingredients evenly. Simmer until the sauce clears somewhat and is thickened (about 8 to 10 minutes). If more liquid seems to be needed, stir in your choice of stock or sherry.

Serve in a footed bowl for self-service, with individual small bowls of rice.

Chinese Panned Fish Steak with Bean Sprouts
4 to 6 servings

1 large fish steak (2 or 3 pounds) or 4 to 6 smaller steaks (cod, halibut, swordfish), thawed or partially thawed
½ teaspoon paprika
5 tablespoons vegetable oil (preferably peanut oil)
4 or 5 shallots or scallions, minced
1 clove garlic, minced or put through garlic press
4 tablespoons soy sauce
¼ cup dry white wine (sherry or vermouth)
1 tablespoon chopped preserved (candied) ginger
1 cup water
1-pound can bean sprouts, drained

Sprinkle the fish with the paprika. Heat 3 tablespoons of the oil in a very large skillet and brown the shallots or scallions and garlic until they are pale gold. Add 3 tablespoons of the soy sauce, also the wine, ginger, water, and fish steaks. Cover the skillet and bring the liquid quickly to a brisk boil. Lower the heat immediately and simmer for 15 minutes if thawed, 20 to 25 minutes if partially thawed. In a separate saucepan, cook the drained bean sprouts with the remaining 2 tablespoons of oil and 1 tablespoon of soy sauce for 5 minutes. With a bulb baster, remove ½ cup of liquid from the fish skillet and stir it into the bean sprouts. Simmer the bean sprouts for 5 minutes longer, then drain them. Arrange the bean sprouts on a serving platter, place the fish on top of them, and pour over all the remaining sauce from the skillet.

Baked Fish Steak with Danish Bleu Cheese
4 to 6 servings

1 large (2- or 3-pound) fish steak (cod, halibut, salmon, sword-
    fish), thawed or partially thawed
½ teaspoon paprika
6 tablespoons softened butter
½ cup crumbled Danish bleu cheese
1 tablespoon lemon juice

Preheat the oven to 325°. Sprinkle the fish with the paprika and place it in a lightly oiled baking dish. Combine the butter with the cheese and lemon juice, blending well. Spread this mixture over the steak, insert a meat thermometer in the fleshiest part, and bake at 325° until the thermometer reads 140°. The cooking time will depend on the thickness of the steak and whether or not it was thawed, but is usually 25 to 30 minutes if thawed, 35 to 50 minutes if partially frozen.

Baked Fish Steak, Spanish Style
4 to 6 servings

1 large (about 2- or 3-pound) fish steak (swordfish, tuna),
    thawed or partially thawed
Paprika
1 large sweet red pepper or 2 pimientos, minced

½ cup dry white wine
½ cup hot water
1 cup Average White Sauce (page 19)
4 to 6 tablespoons fine bread crumbs
4 tablespoons melted butter
4 to 6 tablespoons grated Cheddar or sharp American cheese

Preheat the oven to 325°. Sprinkle the steak with paprika and place it in a lightly oiled baking dish. Sprinkle with the minced pepper or pimientos, pour over it the combined wine and hot water, insert a meat thermometer in the fleshiest part, and bake until the thermometer reads 135°. Heat the white sauce. Remove the dish from the oven, cover the fish with the white sauce, sprinkle with the bread crumbs, melted butter, and grated cheese, and place 6 inches from the broiler flame until the cheese browns.

Baked Fish Steak, Greek Style
4 to 6 servings

1 large (about 2- or 3-pound) fish steak (halibut, swordfish, tuna), thawed or partially thawed
2 or 3 tablespoons lemon juice
¼ teaspoon ground white pepper
1 cup chopped onions
1 large clove garlic, minced or put through garlic press
⅓ cup minced fresh parsley
⅓ cup fine olive oil
3 large tomatoes, chopped (or 1½ cups drained canned tomatoes)
½ teaspoon salt
¼ teaspoon oregano or basil
½ cup dry white wine

Preheat the oven to 325°. Sprinkle the steak with the lemon juice and pepper and let it stand at room temperature while you prepare the vegetables. Sauté the onions, garlic, and parsley in the oil until the onions are golden. Add the tomatoes and seasonings and simmer over low heat for 5 minutes. Stir in the wine and simmer for 5 minutes longer. Pour half this sauce into a large, shallow baking dish and add the fish. Insert a meat thermometer in the fleshiest part. Pour the remainder of the sauce over the fish and bake until the thermometer reads 140°.

19.

Shellfish Recipes

CLAMS

See the discussion and instructions for preparing clams (pages 78–79).

When clam juice is not used in a recipe, strain and freeze it in small containers for later use.

Deviled Clams I

Note: In general, 4 to 6 clams will provide enough meat to fill one shell when combined with other recipe ingredients. The following two recipes will yield from 4 to 8 deviled clams, depending on their size. To make larger quantities for freezer storage up to 3 or 4 months, measure the chopped clams in pints. Use the recipe amounts given below for each pint of chopped clams.

About 24 good-sized clams (quahogs), well scrubbed
6 tablespoons softened butter
3 tablespoons minced onion
1 clove garlic, minced or put through garlic press

1 tablespoon minced parsley
2 tablespoons strained clam juice
4 slices bacon, fried to a crisp and crumbled
½ cup fine bread crumbs

Open the clams by any method described on page 78, reserving the juice. Save several of the scrubbed shells, scraping all clinging bits of clam from the insides. The shells may be further processed by boiling them for 10 minutes in water to which you have added a tablespoon of cream of tartar. Rinse them well.

Chop the clams coarsely. Combine the butter with the onion, garlic, and parsley and blend well with the clam juice. Add the clams and bacon crisps and mix thoroughly. Mound this mixture in the clean clam shells and sprinkle with the bread crumbs.

Freezer portion: Wrap each filled clam shell individually and snugly in freezer foil, with the seam of the foil at the bottom. Freeze the clams in a single layer on the contact shelf of your freezer, or in the fast-freeze compartment, then gather into a strong plastic bag. Store up to 4 months.

Serving the unfrozen portion: Preheat the oven to 375°. Without wrapping, bake the filled clams on a cooky sheet for 10 minutes. Brown the bread crumbs under the broiler.

Serving the freezer portion: Preheat the oven to 400°. Remove from the freezer as many wrapped clams as you plan to serve. Loosen the foil so that it forms an easily removed cover. Place the clams on a cooky sheet and bake for 20 minutes. Remove the foil and top each clam with a small, thin pat of butter. Place the sheet under the broiler until the butter melts and the crumbs are brown.

Spacesaving suggestion: Prepare the foregoing clam mixture without using bread crumbs. Pack it into freezer containers for freezer storage after refrigeration. To serve, thaw the container overnight in the refrigerator. Pack the mixture into sea-food shells or ramekins, sprinkle with bread crumbs, and dot with butter. Place on a cooky sheet in a 375° oven for 10 minutes, then brown the crumbs under the broiler.

Deviled Clams II

For larger amounts, refer to the note in the recipe for Deviled Clams I.

About 24 good-sized clams (quahogs), well scrubbed
2 tablespoons minced shallots
3 tablespoons finely chopped mushrooms
2 tablespoons butter
1 tablespoon minced chives
1 tablespoon minced parsley
6 tablespoons fine bread crumbs
1 or 2 tablespoons sherry

Shuck and chop the clams. Sauté the shallots and mushrooms in the butter for 1 minute. Combine this mixture with the chopped clams, chives, parsley, and 2 tablespoons of the bread crumbs. Moisten with the sherry. If more moistening seems needed, add a little strained clam juice. Mound this mixture in scrubbed clam shells and sprinkle with the remaining bread crumbs.

Freezer portion: Wrap each filled clam shell individually and snugly in freezer foil, with the seam of the foil at the bottom. Freeze the clams in a single layer on the contact shelf of your freezer, or in the fast-freeze compartment, then gather into a strong plastic bag. Store up to 4 months.

Serving the unfrozen portion: Preheat the oven to 350°. Without wrapping, bake the clams on a cooky sheet for 10 minutes. Brown the bread crumbs under the broiler.

Serving the freezer portion: Preheat the oven to 375°. Remove from the freezer as many wrapped clams as you plan to serve. Loosen the foil so that it forms an easily removed cover. Place the clams on a cooky sheet and bake for 25 minutes. Remove the foil and top each clam with a small, thin pat of butter. Brown the crumbs under the broiler.

Spacesaving suggestion: Prepare the foregoing clam mixture, using only 2 tablespoons of the bread crumbs. Refrigerate, then pack in freezer containers and freeze. To serve, thaw the container overnight in the refrigerator. Mound the mixture in sea-food shells or ramekins, sprinkle with bread crumbs, and dot with butter. Place on a cooky sheet in a 350° oven for 15 minutes, then brown the crumbs under the broiler.

Deviled Clams from the Freezer Stockpile

The summer's cache of chopped or whole shucked clams in the freezer may be used for either of the two preceding recipes. Thaw in containers overnight in the refrigerator and follow the recipe directions. Do not refreeze.

Lazy Baked Stuffed Clams

Commercially packaged poultry stuffing
Chopped clams

Following the package directions, make enough of the stuffing to yield one loosely packed cupful for each cupful of chopped clams (fresh, canned, or frozen). If you wish (I do), add a few tablespoons of chopped fresh or frozen mushrooms, celery, and additional onions. For further zest, add also a few tablespoons of finely chopped sautéed linguica or other spicy sausage. Toss all the ingredients together lightly, moistening them with sherry if desired. Mound the mixture in shells or ramekins. Follow the freezing and serving directions in the recipes for Deviled Clams I or II. Do not refreeze if made with frozen clams.

Clam Fritters

8 to 16 fritters, depending on size

2 cups chopped sea clams or quahogs
1 cup flour

1 teaspoon baking powder
¼ teaspoon salt
⅛ teaspoon paprika
2 eggs, beaten
¼ cup milk
¼ cup clam juice
4 tablespoons butter

Drain the clams. Sift the dry ingredients together, add the eggs, milk, and clam juice, and beat to a smooth batter. Add the chopped clams, stir to distribute well, and drop by the spoonful into the hot butter in a skillet.

Freezer portion: Cook one side until lightly browned, then turn and cook the other side only until the fritters hold together. Cool, chill in the refrigerator, then place the fritters in a single layer on a large cooky sheet and freeze. When the fritters are solidly frozen, put several of them in a double row on a piece of freezer film, foil, or paper. Fold both long sides of the material over the rows, then fold one row of fritters over the other, making them two deep. Accordion-fold into a compact stack. Do this for all the fritters you are going to freeze, then gather the stacks into a freezer bag. Store up to 3 months.

Serving the unfrozen portion: Brown the fritters thoroughly on both sides.

Serving the freezer portion: Heat on a cooky sheet in a 425° oven for 15 to 20 minutes, or sauté slowly in hot oil or grease until brown on one side, then turn and brown the other side.

Clam Pie
2 deep-dish pies, each serving 4 to 6

2 quarts shucked sea clams or quahogs
⅓ pound salt pork, finely chopped
½ cup chopped onions
2 tablespoons flour
2 eggs, well beaten

1 cup milk
½ cup strained clam juice
1½ cups broken unsalted crackers
Salt and pepper (optional)
2 packages pie crust mix, each making 2 crusts (or your own
    favorite plain recipe)

Drain the clams, reserving and straining the juice, and
chop or grind them. Try out the chopped salt pork slowly in
a large heavy skillet until the bits are crisp and light golden
brown. Remove the bits with a slotted spoon and reserve
them. Add the chopped clams to the hot pork fat, cover, and
simmer over very low heat for 20 minutes. Add the onions
and continue simmering for 5 minutes. Sprinkle with the
flour and stir. Combine the eggs with the milk and clam
juice and add to the skillet, mixing well. Stir in the crackers
and pork crisps. Taste for seasonings, and add salt and pepper if needed. Follow the package directions on the pie
crust mix to make 4 pie crusts. Line 2 deep-dish pie plates
with crusts.

Freezer portion: Let the clam mixture cool. Fill the crust,
top with a second crust, and chill in the refrigerator. Slip the
pie into a plastic bag and store it in a section of the freezer
where it won't be crushed. *Hint:* Next time you buy frozen
pies, save the cartons. Be sure to label this one "Clam Pie."

Serving the unfrozen portion: Preheat the oven to 350°.
Without chilling the clam mixture, make the pie according
to the preceding instructions. Brush the top crust with milk,
cut steam vents in the crust, and bake for 35 to 45 minutes,
until golden brown.

Serving the freezer portion: Thaw the pie at room temperature for 1 hour. Preheat the oven to 400°. Cut steam
vents in the top crust and brush with milk. Place the pie on
a cooky sheet and bake for 30 to 35 minutes, until golden
brown.

Spacesaving suggestion: If you have quantities of sea

clams or large quahogs and you like clam pie, it is uneco-
nomical of freezer space to store a lot of made-up pies. Instead, follow (or double) the preceding recipe for the filling, chill it in the refrigerator, and freeze it in quart containers. Each will make a 4-serving pie, or 4 individual pies
baked in the foil containers you wash and save when you
buy commercial frozen meat pies. To complete the pie, thaw
a container of filling overnight in the refrigerator. Release
into a saucepan and heat it slightly. Prepare a double pie
crust recipe, make the pie, brush the top crust with milk, cut
steam vents in it, and bake at 350° until golden brown.

Batter-fried (Soft-Shell) Clams
For each pint of shucked clams (serving 4 to 6):

⅔ cup flour
¼ teaspoon salt
1 egg, beaten with 1 teaspoon water
½ teaspoon lemon juice
½ cup milk or light cream
Deep fat in French-fryer with basket

For this recipe, use soft-shelled steamer clams. They are
easily opened with a strong sharp knife, or by steaming over
boiling water just until the shells part. Drain the clams, reserving the juice. Remove and discard the dark tough skin
which covers the necks. Wash the clams in their own juice
to remove sand. Drain again.

Sift the flour with the salt. Mix the beaten egg, lemon
juice, and milk or cream and add to the flour, beating until
smooth. Drop the clams into this batter and coat them
evenly.

Freezer portion: Drop about a cupful of clams at a time
into hot deep fat (375°) and fry until light golden brown.
Drain on paper towels, chill in the refrigerator, then freeze
in heavy plastic bags or waxboard cartons. Store up to 6
months.

Serving the unfrozen portion: Fry the clams as above until they are deep golden brown. Serve with lemon wedges and tartar sauce.

Serving the freezer portion: Heat in a 425° oven for 15 to 20 minutes, or drop into hot deep fat (375°) until deep golden brown.

OYSTERS

Your friendly freezer loves to take care of oysters. It will store for a year the frozen ones you can buy. It will freeze the shucked ones you pack in containers covered with their own liquor. Also, it will hold in readiness the simple or elaborate recipe you prepare at leisure to serve for a special occasion. The oyster is such a delicately textured fellow, however, that my personal preference is to store him (or her— it's hard to tell with oysters) in the freezer, and make the simple or elaborate recipe the day of the occasion. I sometimes do freeze recipes which can be composed of raw or almost raw—not cooked—oysters, as in the examples to follow. This is not because the freezer will do other recipes any real harm. It is because oysters, which require only the briefest of cooking, may shrink and toughen if cooked both before and after freezing.

RECIPES USING OYSTERS

Creamed Oysters
4 servings

1 pint shucked oysters with liquor
3 tablespoons butter
3 tablespoons flour
Milk or cream to extend oyster liquor to 2 cups
½ teaspoon salt
Dash of pepper
Dash of paprika

Drain the oysters, straining and reserving the liquor. In the top of a double boiler over low heat, melt the butter, blend in the flour, and stir in the combined liquids and seasonings. Simmer, stirring, until thickened and smooth. Remove from the heat and allow to cool. Stir again to smoothness and add the oysters. Pour into a freezer container, chill in the refrigerator, then freeze. Store up to 6 months.

To serve: Set the container in a pan of cool water until the contents can be released into the top of a double boiler over simmering water. Heat until the sauce is smooth and the oysters curl. Beat 2 egg yolks, add a little of the sauce to them, beat again, and stir into the oysters. If desired, add 1 or 2 tablespoons of sherry. Serve on hot toast points or in patty shells.

Creamed Oysters from the Freezer Stockpile I
4 servings

1 pint frozen oysters with liquor
1 can frozen condensed oyster stew
½ can milk or cream
½ can oyster liquor
1 tablespoon flour
2 beaten egg yolks
Salt, pepper, paprika
1 or 2 tablespoons sherry (optional)

Release the oysters into the top of a double boiler over simmering water and heat until their edges curl. Remove from the heat and drain, reserving ½ cup of the liquor. Follow the directions on the can of oyster stew for heating. Combine the milk or cream with the oyster liquor, shake or stir with the flour, and add this to the heating stew. Break up lumps with a fork and continue to heat until smooth. Add a little of the sauce to the beaten egg yolks, beat again, and add to the stew along with the oysters. Season to taste, stir in sherry if desired, and heat without boiling. Serve on hot toast points or in patty shells.

Creamed Oysters from the Freezer Stockpile II
4 servings

1 pint frozen oysters with liquor
8-ounce container (1 cup) Heavy White Sauce (page 19)
Salt and pepper to taste

Partially thaw the container of oysters in cool water while you heat the white sauce in the top of a double boiler over simmering water. Break up lumps with a fork and heat until smooth. Add the contents of the oyster container and heat, stirring occasionally, until the oysters curl. Season to taste. See the preceding recipe for additions of egg yolks and sherry, if desired.

Variations: Either of the foregoing recipes for Creamed Oysters may be extended to serve larger groups by adding one or more of the following:

1 cup sliced mushrooms, fresh or frozen, sautéed in butter for 2
    minutes
1 cup diced cooked shrimp or lobster
1 cup canned, fresh, or frozen (thawed) crab meat
1 cup cooked flaked fish
1 cup diced cooked white meat of chicken

Combine one or more of these ingredients with the creamed oysters and pour into a lightly buttered serving casserole. Mix together ½ cup of fine bread crumbs and 2 tablespoons of grated Swiss, Gruyère, or mild Cheddar cheese and sprinkle over the top. Broil to brown the topping.

Deviled Oyster Casserole
6 to 8 servings

1 quart shucked oysters with liquor
1 cup broken unsalted crackers
2 tablespoons Worcestershire sauce
2 tablespoons catchup

3 or 4 drops tabasco sauce
1 teaspoon lemon juice
2 tablespoons minced parsley
½ cup slivered celery
4 tablespoons minced onion
2 tablespoons melted butter
½ cup fine bread crumbs

Simmer the oysters in their own liquor until the edges curl slightly. Remove them with a slotted spoon. Add the cracker crumbs to the liquor, stir, and add the Worcestershire sauce, catchup, tabasco sauce, lemon juice, and parsley. In a separate skillet sauté the celery and onion in the hot butter until the onions are light golden brown and add them, with the oysters, to the liquid. Remove from the heat, pour into a well-buttered casserole, sprinkle with the bread crumbs, refrigerate until well chilled, then slip the casserole into a plastic bag or cover with foil and freeze. Store up to 6 months.

To serve: Thaw the casserole in the refrigerator overnight, or at room temperature for 2 hours. Preheat the oven to 350°. Place the casserole in the oven and heat for 30 to 35 minutes. Brown the crumbs under the broiler, if desired.

Scalloped Oyster Casserole
6 to 8 servings

2 cups fine unseasoned bread crumbs
⅔ cup melted butter
1 quart shucked oysters with liquor
Salt, pepper, cayenne

Combine the crumbs with the melted butter and divide the mixture into 5 equal parts. Spread one part in the bottom of a buttered freezer-to-oven casserole or baking dish. Cover with 1 cup of the oysters and their liquor, then sprinkle lightly with seasonings. Continue this build-up with the remaining crumb mixture and oysters, seasoning each layer lightly and finishing with a topping of the buttered crumbs. Refrigerate, cover the casserole with foil or slip it into a freezer bag, then freeze. Store up to 6 months.

To serve: Preheat the oven to 400°. Put the freezer-to-oven casserole on the middle shelf for 15 minutes. Pour ½ cup of sherry over the top, dot with thin pats of butter, lower the oven heat to 350°, and continue to bake for 35 to 40 minutes. Or thaw the casserole in the refrigerator, pour sherry over the top, dot with butter, and bake in a 350° oven for 30 to 35 minutes.

Freezer Stockpile Variations with Oysters
8 servings

1 quart frozen oysters, thawed in refrigerator
3 tablespoons butter
2 tablespoons minced frozen onions or chives
3 tablespoons minced frozen carrots
4-ounce package frozen sliced mushrooms
1-pint container frozen brown gravy, Heavy White Sauce (page
    19), or any other appropriate sauce
2 egg yolks
1 teaspoon lemon juice

Drain the oysters, reserving the liquor. Melt the butter in a saucepan and remove from the heat. Add the frozen vegetables, return the saucepan to low heat, and sauté for 5 minutes. Add the contents of the sauce container, break up lumps with a fork, and heat until smooth. Remove from the heat. Beat the egg yolks with the lemon juice and add to the saucepan. Add the oysters and a little of their liquor. Taste for seasonings (you might like a dash of cayenne) and heat until the oysters curl and plump, or until they are cooked the way you like them. Serve on hot toast points or in pastry shells, or pour into a buttered casserole, top with bread crumbs (and grated cheese), and heat to bubbling. Do not refreeze.

SCALLOPS

Inside their pretty fluted shells, the American scallop comes in two sizes: the small, sweet bay (Cape Cod) variety and the larger but equally delicious sea scallop. Unlike other edible bivalves (clams, mussels, oysters), scallops are not eaten whole. What we eat are the firm adductor muscles, small or large, and these are frequently billed on French-cuisine restaurant menus as "Coquilles St. Jacques." The true coquille lives abroad, however.

If fried scallops with French fried potatoes, cole slaw, and tartar sauce are all you've ever eaten, try some of the other methods—for the freezer, or from it—on later pages. Don't hesitate to tackle recipes called Coquilles St. Jacques à la Something. They are as simple to prepare and freeze as they are a delight to eat.

Stockpiling Your Own Sautéed or Fried Scallops for the Freezer

Deservedly, fried scallops are among the most popular prepared main dishes offered in store freezer cabinets. An 8- to 12-ounce package, however, can cost quite a bit more than a pound of raw fresh or frozen scallops during the season of plentiful supply. Why not freeze your own?

For each 4-serving portion you wish to freeze:

1 to 1½ pounds fresh or frozen raw scallops (if frozen, thaw in refrigerator before using)
2 small eggs beaten with shaking of salt and pepper
About 1 cup fine bread crumbs
Shallow oil for sautéing (or deep fat in French fryer)

Drain the scallops and pat them dry between paper towels. Sea scallops may be halved or quartered, if you like. Dip them into the seasoned egg, then roll in the bread crumbs.

Sauté in oil, turning once, or fry in deep fat, until light golden brown (about 3 minutes). Drain on paper towels, cool, chill in the refrigerator, then freeze in waxed paperboard boxes, plastic bags, or containers. Store up to 6 months.

To serve: Do not thaw. Heat on a cooky sheet in a 425° oven for 15 to 20 minutes, or sauté in shallow oil or fat, or fry in deep hot fat until golden brown. Serve with tartar sauce and lemon wedges.

Scallops au Gratin
6 to 8 servings

2 to 2½ pounds fresh or frozen raw scallops
2 cups fine bread crumbs
4 tablespoons melted butter
¾ cup diced green pepper
¾ cup diced celery
Salt and pepper
⅓ cup grated Cheddar cheese
1½ cups light cream or half-and-half

Barely cover the scallops with cold water in a saucepan and bring them slowly to the boiling point. Remove from the heat and drain. Mix 1½ cups of the bread crumbs with 2 tablespoons of the melted butter, divide the mixture into thirds, and spread one-third in a thin layer over the bottom of a buttered freezer-to-oven casserole. If the scallops are large, they may be cut into smaller pieces. Build up alternate layers of scallops, green pepper combined with celery, and bread crumbs, seasoning lightly as you go. The top layer should be the remaining bread crumbs mixed with the remaining butter and all the grated cheese. Slowly pour in the cream or half-and-half, distributing it evenly. Cover the casserole with freezer foil or film, slip it into a plastic bag, chill in the refrigerator, then freeze. Store up to 3 months.

To serve: Put the freezer-to-oven casserole directly into a preheated 425° oven for 35 to 45 minutes. Or thaw in the refrigerator and bake in a preheated 350° oven for 25 to 30 minutes.

Scallops à La Newburg
4 to 6 servings

1½ to 2 pounds fresh or frozen raw scallops
3 tablespoons butter
1 tablespoon flour
⅔ cup light cream or half-and-half
2 egg yolks, lightly beaten
½ teaspoon salt
Dash of tabasco sauce

Barely cover the scallops with water in a saucepan and bring slowly to a boil. Remove from the heat and drain. Large scallops may be cut into smaller pieces. Heat the butter in the same saucepan, blend in the flour and cream or half-and-half, and cook over very low heat until slightly thickened. Add the egg yolks, salt, and tabasco sauce and remove from the heat. Combine with the scallops, refrigerate until chilled, pour into freezer container(s), and freeze. Store up to 3 months.

To serve: Place the container in a pan of cool to lukewarm water until the contents can be released into the top of a double boiler over gently boiling water. Heat without boiling. When piping hot, add 2 or 3 tablespoons of sherry and continue to heat for 10 minutes. Serve on hot toast points or in patty shells.

Coquilles St. Jacques Provençal
4 to 6 servings

1½ to 2 pounds scallops
Salt and pepper
2 tablespoons minced onion
6 tablespoons butter

½ pound sliced fresh or frozen mushrooms
2 large tomatoes, peeled and chopped
½ cup dry white wine
1 tablespoon minced chives
1 clove garlic, minced or put through garlic press

Pat the scallops dry. If they are large, cut them into smaller pieces. Sprinkle them lightly with salt and pepper and sauté them along with the minced onion in 4 tablespoons of the butter until the onions look transparent (about 5 minutes), turning the scallops to brown all sides lightly. Remove the scallops and onions. Add the remaining butter to the pan and sauté the mushrooms for 2 minutes. Add the tomatoes, wine, chives, and garlic and simmer for 5 minutes.

To freeze: Combine the scallops with the sauce, cool, pour into containers, refrigerate until chilled, then freeze. Store up to 3 months.

To serve: Set the container in a pan of cool to warm water until the contents can be released into a saucepan. Heat until piping hot. Serve on toast points or in patty shells. Or, when hot, pour the scallop mixture over crustless toast or fried bread in a shallow buttered baking dish. Sprinkle with grated Parmesan, Romano, or Cheddar cheese and heat in a 350° oven until the cheese bubbles.

Coquilles St. Jacques Parisienne
4 to 6 servings

1½ to 2 pounds scallops
1½ cups dry white wine
½ teaspoon salt
¼ teaspoon white pepper
4 tablespoons butter
2 tablespoons flour
1 cup milk
½ cup (or more) chopped mushrooms

3 tablespoons grated Swiss or Gruyère cheese
Fine bread crumbs

Combine the scallops, wine, and seasonings in a large heavy saucepan, bring slowly to a boil, lower the heat, and simmer gently for 5 minutes. Drain the scallops, reserving the liquid in a bowl. Cut the scallops into small pieces and reserve. In the same saucepan melt the butter and blend in the flour. Combine the wine liquid with the milk and add slowly, stirring constantly. Simmer until somewhat thickened. Add the scallops and mushrooms, cook for 2 minutes, remove from the heat, and stir in the grated cheese, distributing it evenly. Let cool slightly.

To freeze: Spoon the mixture into a buttered casserole, sprinkle with bread crumbs, cover with foil, refrigerate until chilled, then freeze. Store up to 3 months.

To serve: Heat in a 425° oven for 30 to 35 minutes. Dot with butter and place under the broiler until the topping is browned.

RECIPES USING FROZEN RAW OR PRECOOKED SCALLOPS

Ménagère (Using Frozen Large Sea Scallops)
4 servings

¼ cup white wine
¼ cup water
8 to 12 large frozen sea scallops
8-ounce container (1 cup) frozen sauce (Mornay, cheese, curry, etc.)
4 tablespoons butter
Garlic salt
Paprika

Combine the wine and water in a saucepan and bring to a boil. Drop in the frozen scallops. When the water resumes its boil, lower the heat and simmer for 5 minutes. Meantime, release the contents of the sauce container into the top of a double boiler over simmering water. Break up lumps with a fork. When melted, stir briskly and heat without boiling.

Drain the scallops (adding a little of the liquid to the sauce, if it's thick) and sauté them in the hot butter, turning once, until golden brown on both sides.

These may be served on crustless toast triangles, unsweet waffles, pancakes, or crepes, sprinkled lightly with garlic salt and paprika and covered with hot sauce.

En Brochette (Using Frozen Small Raw Scallops)
6 to 8 servings

2 to 2½ pounds (about a quart) small frozen scallops
½ cup fine olive oil
2 tablespoons lemon juice
1 clove garlic, minced or put through garlic press
½ teaspoon salt
¼ teaspoon pepper
¼ teaspoon each, marjoram and thyme
Sliced bacon (about 1 pound)
Large mushroom caps

Partially thaw the scallops until they can be separated, or drop, frozen, into a small amount of boiling water until they separate by themselves. Drain and pat dry. Combine the olive oil, lemon juice, garlic, and seasonings and stir to blend well. Marinate the scallops in this mixture for at least 1 hour, then drain, reserving the marinade. Accordion-fold each slice of bacon into a scallop-sized square and thread alternately with the scallops on long skewers. Cut the stems of the mushrooms close to the caps and put one cap on the end of each skewer. Line a broiler pan with foil and broil 4 to 6 inches away from the heat source, turning often and basting occasionally with the marinade. Or rotate over charcoal embers. Cook until the scallops are golden brown and the bacon is crisp.

Chinoise, Sweet and Sour
(Using Frozen Precooked Scallops)
4 to 6 servings

2 regular or 1 family-sized store package frozen precooked scallops (or yours, page 191)
8-ounce container fish or chicken stock
½ cup white vinegar
½ cup pale dry sherry
½ cup sugar
1 small package frozen whole baby carrots (or 1½ cups frozen sliced carrots)
1 tablespoon soy sauce
1 tablespoon cornstarch
1 cup frozen diced green peppers
½ package (1 cup) frozen pineapple chunks
2 firm tomatoes cut into eighths

Remove the scallops from the freezer to thaw slightly while you prepare the sauce: In a large saucepan combine the stock, vinegar, wine, and sugar. Bring this to a brisk boil, stir, add the carrots, and boil for 7 minutes. (If you are using sliced carrots, boil for 5 minutes.) Lower the heat to a simmer. Combine the soy sauce and cornstarch and stir this mixture into the simmering carrots. Add the green peppers, pineapple chunks, and tomatoes and stir. Add the scallops and stir with a wooden spoon to distribute all the ingredients evenly. Simmer until the sauce clears somewhat and is thickened (about 8 to 10 minutes).

Serve in a large footed bowl with or without another bowl of hot fluffy rice.

CRABS

Hard shell or soft, hand-caught or purchased, live crabs should be vigorously active before being cooked.

The upper shells of big hard-shelled crabs make colorful,

inexpensive, logical ramekins. Scrub and scrape them clean, cover them with cold water, add a teaspoon of baking soda, cover the pot, and boil them for about half an hour. Wash in clear water, drain, and dry. Be sure they are absolutely free of organic matter.

Soft-shelled crabs (same crabs, different season) are usually cooked and eaten in their entirety.

HOW TO PREPARE HARD-SHELLED CRABS

In a tall vessel or pail, wash the crabs in several waters. They'll resent it, so wear heavy gloves or use a pair of kitchen tongs to remove them, one by one, and plunge each into rapidly boiling salted water (about 1 cup of water and 1 teaspoon of salt per crab). When the water returns to a hard boil, cook them rapidly for 5 minutes, then lower the heat and continue to simmer gently until the shells redden (10 to 15 minutes). Drain and cool. If you are not going to extract the meat immediately to use or freeze, refrigerate the crabs until you are ready.

Hold a cooked crab in both hands. It's a good idea to work on several thicknesses of newspaper. With your thumbs, pull the shells apart at the tail end. Remove and discard all spongy or waxy substances. Use a nutpick and nutcracker (you may need a hammer for big crabs) to get the meat from the claws in one piece.

Whether you are going to flake the crab meat for immediate use or freeze it for another day, be sure to remove all cartilage, membranes, and bits of shell.

It's hard to say how many crabs you'll need per serving, as they come in various sizes. Generally speaking, a cupful of flaked meat—fresh, frozen or canned—will serve two in most recipes.

For party-giving, some of the more elaborate recipes

made with fresh or canned crab meat may be frozen to be served either hot or cold, but you may prefer (as I do) to pack fresh crab meat tightly in plastic containers and freeze it for later use. It saves space, and most of the hard work has been done by the time you have extracted, flaked, and picked over the meat.

FREEZER RECIPES USING
FRESH OR CANNED CRAB MEAT

Deviled Crab Meat
6 to 8 servings

6 tablespoons butter
2 tablespoons minced onion
2 tablespoons finely cut green pepper
1 cup sliced or chopped mushrooms
½ teaspoon salt
1 teaspoon dry mustard
1 teaspoon Worcestershire sauce
Dash of cayenne pepper or tabasco sauce
3 cups soft bread crumbs
1 cup light cream or half-and-half
3 cups flaked cooked crab meat, fresh or canned
4 tablespoons sherry
½ cup fine bread crumbs
2 tablespoons melted butter

Heat the butter and sauté the onion until pale gold. Add the green peppers and mushrooms and sauté for 2 minutes. Remove from the heat, stir in the seasonings and Worcestershire sauce, and tabasco sauce if desired. Moisten the bread crumbs with the cream or half-and-half and add. Toss the crab meat with the sherry and fold into the mixture, distributing well.

To freeze: Spoon the mixture into a lightly buttered ovenproof casserole. Combine the fine bread crumbs with the melted butter and spread over the top. Chill in the refrigerator, wrap in freezer film or foil, label, and freeze. Store up to 3 months.

To serve: Preheat the oven to 400°. Uncover the casserole and heat for 15 minutes. Lower the temperature to 350° and bake for 30 minutes. Sprinkle generously with paprika for color or grated cheese for taste (or both) and place under the broiler for 5 minutes.

Spacesaving suggestion: After all ingredients to be combined are well blended, pack the mixture lightly into freezer containers according to serving proportions (a 1-pint container equals 3 or 4 servings). Omit the buttered bread crumbs. Chill and freeze. To serve, thaw in the refrigerator until the contents can be spooned into a buttered casserole or in shells or ramekins. Top with the buttered bread crumbs, sprinkle with paprika and/or grated cheese, and heat in a 350° oven for 20 minutes.

Crab Meat au Gratin
4 to 6 servings

2 cups fresh or canned crab meat
1½ cups Heavy White Sauce (page 19)
½ cup canned sliced mushrooms
½ cup grated mild Cheddar cheese
½ cup fine bread crumbs

Combine the crab meat, white sauce, mushrooms, and ¼ cup of the grated cheese, mixing well.

To freeze: Spoon into a buttered baking dish, top with the bread crumbs mixed with the remaining cheese, cover with foil or freezer film, label, and freeze.

To serve: Preheat the oven to 400°. Uncover and heat for 25 to 30 minutes.

Crab-Meat Croquettes
4 to 6 servings

2 cups flaked fresh or canned crab meat
1 cup Heavy White Sauce (page 19)

1 tablespoon minced parsley
½ teaspoon salt
Dash of pepper
1 tablespoon lemon juice
Grating of fresh nutmeg (or dash of ground nutmeg)
2 eggs, beaten
About ½ cup fine bread crumbs

Combine all the ingredients except the eggs and bread crumbs. Blend well. Spread the mixture evenly on a platter and refrigerate for 1 hour. Shape spoonfuls of the mixture into 8 to 12 balls, patties, or cones.* Roll each croquette in the egg, then in the crumbs. Refrigerate again for 1 hour.

To freeze: Without wrapping, freeze the croquettes on waxed paper in a single layer. When frozen, gather them carefully into a plastic bag or into a freezer box. Store up to 3 months.

To serve: Fry no more than 4 at a time in deep hot fat until golden brown. Drain on paper towels. Serve with any favorite sauce.

RECIPES USING FROZEN CRAB MEAT

Crab Meat Newburg
4 servings

1-pint container (2 cups) frozen crab meat
4 tablespoons butter
½ teaspoon salt
Pinch of paprika, pepper, or cayenne
Pinch of ground nutmeg
1 cup cream
2 whole eggs or 3 egg yolks, beaten
2 tablespoons sherry

Set the container in cool to warm water until the contents can be released and separated with a fork. Melt the butter in the top of a double boiler over boiling water. Add the crab meat and stir from time to time until hot. Add the sea-

* For hot hors d'oeuvres, roll the mixture into marble-sized balls.

sonings and cream, lower the heat, and continue to cook, without boiling, for 5 minutes. Add the eggs and stir until thickened. Stir in the sherry. Serve on buttered toast points or in patty shells. Do not refreeze.

Crab Meat Florentine
4 to 6 servings

1-pint container (2 cups) frozen crab meat
2 packages frozen chopped spinach
½ cup grated Cheddar cheese, or half Cheddar, half Romano
2 tablespoons minced onion
2 teaspoons lemon juice
8-ounce container Italian sauce (pages 31–33), or 1 cup canned
    sauce
½ teaspoon salt
Dash each, paprika and basil
2 tablespoons sherry

Thaw the crab meat until it can be flaked with a fork. Cook the frozen spinach according to the package directions, drain, and spread it over the bottom of a buttered baking dish. Preheat the oven to 350°. Sprinkle half the cheese over the spinach and spread the crab meat evenly over this. Combine all the remaining ingredients and pour over the crab meat. Top with the remaining cheese. Bake for 30 to 35 minutes. Do not refreeze.

Crab-Meat and Cheese Soufflé
4 to 6 servings

1-pint container (2 cups) Heavy White Sauce (page 19)
1-pint container (2 cups) frozen crab meat
1 cup grated Cheddar or American cheese
½ teaspoon salt
¼ teaspoon paprika
Pinch of nutmeg
3 egg yolks, beaten
3 egg whites, stiffly beaten

If the white sauce was frozen, set the container into cool to warm water until the contents can be released into the top of a double boiler over simmering water. Break up lumps with a fork and stir briskly when melted. Similarly release the crab meat onto a cutting board. Use a sharp heavy knife to cut the block into small shreds or flakes. Preheat the oven to 375°. When the white sauce is hot and smooth, add the crab meat, cheese, and seasonings. Stir well. Add the egg yolks and stir in the egg whites. Pour this mixture into a buttered soufflé pan or deep baking dish and bake for 25 minutes. Do not refreeze.

Crab Meat Creole
4 to 6 servings

1-pint container (2 cups) frozen crab meat
8-ounce container fish stock (or 1 cup consommé)
2 tablespoons frozen chopped onions
1 tablespoon frozen chopped green pepper
2 tablespoons butter
2 tablespoons flour
4 fresh, canned, or frozen peeled whole tomatoes, diced
2 tablespoons minced parsley
¼ cup sliced or chopped stuffed green olives
Pinch of powdered thyme or sage
½ cup fine bread crumbs mixed with 1 tablespoon melted butter

Thaw the crab meat in its container until it can be released and flaked with a fork into fairly large pieces. Melt and heat the stock or consommé in a saucepan. In a large skillet sauté the onions and green pepper in the butter until the onions are transparent. Preheat the oven to 350°. Sprinkle the flour over the vegetables in the skillet, stir to blend well, and cook for 3 minutes. Add the liquid and all other ingredients except the crab meat and buttered bread crumbs. Stir to mix thoroughly and simmer gently for 10 minutes. Fold in the crab meat. Pour into a buttered casserole, sprinkle with the buttered bread crumbs, and bake for 20 minutes. Do not refreeze.

Crab Meat with Snow Peas
4 to 6 servings

1-pint container (2 cups) frozen crab meat
2 tablespoons sherry
½ teaspoon curry powder
¼ teaspoon powdered ginger
3 tablespoons vegetable oil (preferably peanut oil)
½ teaspoon salt
1 package frozen snow peas
1½ cups liquid (fish stock, clam juice, consommé, unseasoned
    vegetable stock)
1½ tablespoons cornstarch

Thaw the crab meat until it can be chunked or flaked with a fork and toss it with the sherry, curry, and ginger. Heat the oil and sauté this mixture over moderate heat for 3 minutes, stirring to complete thawing and heat evenly. Remove from the heat and sprinkle with the salt, blending well. In a separate saucepan cook the snow peas according to the package directions, then drain. Heat the fish stock or other liquid, add the cornstarch, and stir over low heat until slightly thickened. Add the prepared crab meat and stir well, then add and heat the drained peas. Serve with fluffy rice. Do not refreeze.

LOBSTERS

A recently developed commercial blast-freeze process has brought whole raw lobsters to market for home freezer storage or for immediate cooking.

Some people freeze lobsters whole, in their shells, after boiling them in salted water.

This book, however, takes the position that if lobster is going to be home-frozen it had better be cooked first and the meat extracted. I've tried the frozen-whole way in my own freezer. Except after the briefest of storage—a week or two at most—I find them good eating but not superb, and when I eat lobster I want it to be superb. Thawed or reheated after being frozen whole in the shell at zero or 5 to 10 below, which is about the best that can be expected from home freezers, the meat tends to become somewhat coarser in texture and stronger in taste.

HOW TO CHOOSE AND PREPARE
A LOBSTER FOR RECIPES

Select lively lobsters in full possession of their claws and feelers. When buying live lobsters from a market tank or pound, be sure that the claws have been plugged with wooden pegs.

There is a theory that only lobsters weighing up to 2 pounds are tender and sweet, and that "chicken" lobsters (under 1½ pounds) are best of all. I have found this to be a fallacy, having enjoyed some of monstrous size. They may have been big babies or relaxed adults of sedentary habits.

Lobsters are readied for recipes by pithing and splitting while alive for broiling or baking, or by steaming in shallow water. You may pith and split them while alive; except for Lobster Cantonese (page 211), which uses live lobster in the shell chopped into chunks, the recipes on the pages to follow are for lobster meat extracted from lobsters cooked the way they are cooked by my favorite source, the wife of a local lobsterman. When they are to be pithed and chopped, the surgery is performed by someone—anyone—other than me, and I don't inquire about the procedure.

HOW TO COOK LOBSTERS

Refrigerate live lobsters until you are ready to use them, putting them into a heavy paper bag or cloth sack.

Cook them in an enormous pot with a tight-fitting cover.

A steaming or canning kettle is useful; so is a rack roaster big enough to accommodate a 20-pound turkey.

Put no more than 1 inch of cold water into the pot, and about 1 teaspoon of salt. Set the pot over high heat and, when the water boils furiously, drop the lobsters in one by one *on their backs,* with the tails curled upward. Cover the pot immediately. If the lid is not heavy, weight it with something.

When the water returns to a boil, cook for 20 minutes only unless the recipe gives a different time. Turn the heat off and remove the lobsters with kitchen tongs. Put them into a clean sink, bellies down, to drain and cool sufficiently for handling.

Don't throw the water away. It will have increased in volume and can be used in recipes calling for liquids or to replace some of the water for making lobster stock.

To extract the meat: Place a lobster on its back on a counter or table. An underpadding of newspapers keeps things neat. Separate the head from the body with a firm twist of both hands. If you are going to use the head for making stock, remove the hard sac. Remove and reserve the claws. With a pair of kitchen shears or a heavy *stainless steel* knife (to prevent discoloration of the meat), cut through the entire length of the underside and pull the shell apart, exposing the tail meat. Remove this in one large piece and look for and discard the black intestinal vein. Don't worry if you can't find it. Your lobster may have fully digested its latest meal.

With a blunt spoon remove and reserve the green liver (tomalley) and, in a female lobster, the coral (egg-producing organ). These are considered delicacies and may be eaten as they are, or combined with buttered and seasoned bread crumbs for use as a topping on lobster casseroles. Also, they may be used as the basis of a delicious—and freezable—canapé spread by mashing them together with a little lemon juice and your choice of soft cheese, mashed avocado, and minced onion or hard-cooked egg yolks.

Crack the large front claws with a hammer or nutcracker to extract the meat, feeling for and removing any cartilage. Crack or slit the claw joints and draw out the meat. Cut all meat into large or small pieces, depending on recipe requirements.

The small claws or "legs" may be cut open and their meat —meager but sweet—extracted, but the wise freezer owner will add them to other lobster leavings for stock.

FREEZER RECIPES USING LOBSTER

Lobster Stock
3 pints

Head, shells, and legs of 2 or more lobsters
2 quarts water (including water in which lobsters were cooked)
½ cup chopped or sliced onion
½ cup chopped celery plus a handful of celery leaves
½ cup chopped carrot
1 clove garlic, halved
2 or 3 sprigs of fresh parsley (or 1 teaspoon parsley flakes)
½ teaspoon salt
1 small bay leaf
5 or 6 whole peppercorns
2 or 3 pellets of clove or allspice
¼ teaspoon whole thyme or sage

Bring these ingredients to a rolling boil, lower the heat, and simmer gently for 30 to 40 minutes. Cool, strain, and refrigerate. Pour into 1-pint (or 8-ounce) containers, leaving expansion space. Label and freeze. This stock may be used as a court bouillon for cooking shrimp (page 215), or in sauces for fish, or for bisques.

Deviled Lobster
6 to 8 servings

3 cups diced lobster meat
1 cup soft bread crumbs
2 hard-cooked eggs
1 tablespoon lemon juice
3 tablespoons butter
3 tablespoons flour
1 cup any light stock, or consommé
1 cup milk or half-and-half
½ teaspoon salt
¼ teaspoon paprika
Pinch of cayenne
2 teaspoons Worcestershire sauce
Fine bread crumbs

Lightly toss the lobster meat with the soft bread crumbs, crumbled egg yolks, and lemon juice and set aside. Melt the butter in a saucepan, blend in the flour, slowly add the stock or consommé and milk or half-and-half, and stir until thickened. Stir in the seasonings and Worcestershire sauce and cook over low heat without boiling for 3 minutes.

Freezer portion: Remove ½ cup of sauce for each cup of the lobster mixture you are going to freeze and set it aside to cool. When cool, stir the sauce and combine it with the lobster mixture. Spoon this into a lightly buttered casserole or individual ramekins. Top with fine bread crumbs, cover with foil, refrigerate, and freeze.

Serving the unfrozen portion: Preheat the oven to 375°. Add the remaining lobster mixture to the remaining sauce. Chop and add the hard-cooked egg whites. Spoon this into a casserole or individual ramekins, top with fine bread crumbs, and bake for 10 to 15 minutes.

Serving the freezer portion: Remove from the freezer one hour before heating. Preheat the oven to 375°. Uncover and bake the casserole for 1 hour, ramekins for 30 minutes.

Piquant Lobster
6 to 8 servings

4 tablespoons butter
4 tablespoons flour
2 cups milk, or half milk, half chicken stock
½ teaspoon salt
⅛ teaspoon pepper
2 tablespoons chopped chives
2 tablespoons chopped green pepper
2 tablespoons chopped pimiento
1 teaspoon capers
1 clove garlic, minced
¼ teaspoon dry mustard
⅛ teaspoon celery seed
2 hard-cooked eggs
4-ounce can button or sliced mushrooms, drained
3 cups diced lobster meat

Melt the butter in a saucepan, blend in the flour, slowly add the liquid, stir in the salt and pepper, and cook over very low heat until thickened. Add all the chopped vegetables and seasonings and continue to cook for 3 minutes. Add the crumbled egg yolks, mushrooms, and lobster meat and stir to distribute evenly.

Freezer portion: Remove to a container as much of this as you wish to freeze. Let cool, chill in refrigerator, then freeze.

Serving the unfrozen portion: For each serving remaining in the saucepan, stir in 1 tablespoon of brandy and 1 tablespoon of dry sherry. Stir, heat without boiling, and serve on toast points or in patty shells. You may chop and add the hard-cooked egg whites as a garnish, sprinkled wih paprika.

Serving the frozen portion: Set the container in cool to warm water until the contents can be released into the top of a double boiler over simmering water. When melted and hot, stir in the brandy and sherry and serve as above.

Lazy Lobster with Sea-Food Dressing
8 to 12 ramekins, depending on their size

Meat of two 2-pound lobsters (or 3 cups claw and joint meat)
3 tablespoons lemon juice
½ cup melted butter
1 tablespoon minced onion
2 tablespoons slivered celery
¾ cup chopped fresh mushrooms
½ teaspoon salt
⅛ teaspoon ground black pepper
1 cup cooked shrimp or crab meat, fresh or canned
1½ cups soft bread crumbs or dice

Cut the lobster meat into fairly large pieces. Put them into a bowl with the lemon juice and let stand for 1 hour, turning the pieces frequently. Remove the lobster meat with kitchen tongs and sauté it in a skillet in ¼ cup of the butter for 2 minutes. Add any lemon juice remaining in the bowl, stir, remove from the heat, and divide among individual ovenproof ramekins.

Add the remaining butter to the skillet and sauté the onion, celery, and mushrooms for 2 minutes. Remove from the heat and stir in the seasonings. Mince the shrimp or crab meat into fine shreds and mix with the sautéed vegetables. Toss this mixture lightly with the soft bread crumbs until thoroughly mixed and spread the dressing over the lobster.

Freezer portion: Chill in the refrigerator as many of the ramekins as you wish to freeze. Cover them with foil before freezing.

Serving the unfrozen portion: Preheat the oven to 350°. If desired, sprinkle each ramekin with a little sherry and bake until sizzling hot.

Serving the freezer portion: Thaw for 1 hour at room temperature. Preheat the oven to 375°. Bake, covered, for 25 to 30 minutes. Uncover, sprinkle with sherry if desired, and bake for 5 minutes longer, or brown under the broiler.

Lobster Cantonese

Serves up to 12 people family-style if accompanied by other
Chinese dishes, and rice; 4 to 6 people if the only course

Chinese cooks, home or restaurant, rinse living lobsters in
cold water, pat them dry, and chop them into 14 pieces
each.

The squeamish (including me) can prepare lobsters for
this recipe by plunging them headfirst into about 3 inches of
vigorously boiling water until they redden—a matter of 3 or
4 minutes. Remove them immediately from the water and,
when cool enough to handle, remove and discard the head
and head-sac. Split them into two lengthwise, cutting
through the back shell, and look for and remove the intestinal vein. Remove and discard the last 3 joints of the little
legs. Discard all spongy substances (gills). Remove the
green liver (tomalley) with a spoon and reserve it for the
sauce. For each lobster you now have 2 lengthwise pieces in
the shell, each with a claw. Remove the claws at the first
joint, separate them from the pincers, and crack them. Cut
the finlike tails from the body. Cut the body pieces into 6 or
8 parts, dividing the meat equally. The large joints where
the claw meets the body may be left whole, or cut into 2
equal parts each.

2 live lobsters, up to 2 pounds each
2 tablespoons cornstarch
½ teaspoon sugar
3 tablespoons soy sauce
½ cup cold water
4 tablespoons vegetable oil (preferably peanut oil)
½ teaspoon salt
Dash of white pepper
1 teaspoon minced ginger root (or ½ teaspoon ground ginger)
2 large cloves garlic, minced or put through garlic press
½ pound fresh lean pork, very finely ground (put through
  grinder twice)

1 tablespoon pale dry sherry
1½ cups chicken stock or consommé

Prepare the lobsters as directed, reserving the tomalley. Set aside while you combine the cornstarch, sugar, and soy sauce in the cold water. Set this aside. Heat your largest skillet and add the oil, salt, pepper, ginger, garlic, and the reserved tomalley. Stir. Add the finely ground pork and stir for 3 minutes. Add the lobster pieces and sherry and stir. Add the stock or consommé, cover the skillet, and cook over lowered heat for 5 minutes.

With kitchen tongs, remove the lobster to a platter. Stir the cornstarch mixture, add it to the skillet, and stir constantly until the sauce thickens.

Freezer portion: Put half the lobster pieces into a container, or into a heavy plastic bag, being careful that the shells don't puncture it. Pour half the sauce into a separate container. Chill both in the refrigerator, then freeze. Store up to 1 month.

Serving the unfrozen portion: Return the skillet to the heat. When the sauce bubbles, use a fork to stir in 1 beaten egg. Return the lobster pieces to the skillet, mix well, and serve when hot with hot fluffy rice and with or without other Chinese dishes (see the Index).

Serving the freezer portion: Thaw the lobster at room temperature. Release the sauce into a large saucepan to melt, breaking up lumps with a fork. When hot, stir in 1 beaten egg, add the thawed lobster, and cook until the lobster is heated through. Serve as above.

Lobster Cantonese, Boston Style

Chinese food fans from the Boston area—and possibly a great many other places—prefer their lobster sauce to be made with fermented black beans, available in Chinese grocery stores. To the foregoing recipe, add 2 or 3 tablespoons of minced black beans to the hot oil along with seasonings and garlic.

Lazy Lobster Cantonese
Made with Frozen Rock Lobster Tails
6 servings

6 frozen rock lobster tails (6 to 8 ounces each)
3 tablespoons vegetable oil (preferably peanut oil)
1 clove garlic, minced or put through garlic press
6 ounces fresh lean pork, put through grinder twice
2 tablespoons cornstarch
¼ cup cold water
2 tablespoons soy sauce
½ teaspoon sugar
½ teaspoon salt
Dash of white pepper
1½ cups boiling stock, consommé, or water
1 can water chestnuts, chopped
2 eggs
½ cup slivered scallions

When the lobster tails are thawed enough to permit, cut the shells away with kitchen shears and remove the meat in one piece. Cut it across into 1-inch pieces. Heat the oil in a large skillet with a cover. Add the garlic and pork and stir over moderate heat until the pork loses its pinkness (about 5 minutes). Combine the cornstarch with the water. Stir into the skillet the soy sauce, sugar, salt, pepper, boiling liquid, and the cornstarch mixture. Stir to blend, bring rapidly to a boil, reduce the heat, and simmer, stirring, until the sauce thickens. Add the lobster and water chestnuts, cover the skillet, and cook over low heat for 8 to 10 minutes. In a small bowl or measuring cup beat the eggs lightly with a fork. Add to this a little of the hot sauce, stir, then add all at once to the skillet. Remove from the heat, stir, and add the scallions.

This recipe, like the previous one, may be frozen in whole

or part. Use a rigid container and chill in the refrigerator before freezing. To serve, release into a saucepan and heat.

A note about cornstarch in frozen Chinese recipes: Chinese foods you prepare in your kitchen or take home from a favorite restaurant tend to become a little watery after freezer storage. When you heat these recipes, or when you heat commercially packaged Chinese food, mix a little cornstarch (about 1 tablespoon) in 2 tablespoons of cold water and add it to the simmering food.

SHRIMP

Inch for inch and dollar for dollar, shrimp can represent one of the best freezer investments on the market if bought when prices are low. A 5-pound box of frozen raw shrimp can be chopped with a cleaver into 4 bricks, each weighing a little more than 1 pound, if your aim is good. The bricks, still frozen, can be wrapped in freezer film, foil, or paper and stored for up to a year.

Or when the shrimp boats have had a fine season, fresh shrimp in shells can be bought in quantity at good prices and stored in the freezer in heavy plastic bags in meal-proportioned amounts.

Or meal-sized bricks can also be made with 5-pound boxes of frozen precooked shrimp and stored for up to 6 months.

The freezer takes kindly to shrimp, cooked or raw. I prefer to store the latter. Even when I occasionally freeze precooked shrimp for use in quick recipes, I would rather do the cooking myself because then I know that the shrimp are cooked in a court bouillon (page 215) with proper restraint as to timing. Shrimp sacrifice tenderness, taste, and texture if overcooked. The cooking times given in the recipes which follow may seem incredibly short—but aren't. One reason you enjoy shrimp dishes in Oriental restaurants is that the shrimp are cooked only until they turn pink, if naked, or only until the batter is light golden brown, if coated.

USING COMMERCIALLY FROZEN PEELED, DEVEINED, PRECOOKED SHRIMP IN RECIPES

Drop the shrimp directly into simmering court bouillon, remove immediately from the heat, and let the shrimp cool in the liquid, where they will separate.

In general, for best taste and texture, do not refreeze recipes for which you use frozen precooked shrimp. The reason is only that when you take the recipe out of the freezer and heat it for serving, the shrimp will have been cooked 3 times.

Court Bouillon for Shrimp

1 medium onion, chopped or sliced
1 or 2 stalks celery with leaves, coarsely cut
1 medium carrot, chopped or sliced (with tops, if any)
1 clove garlic, halved
2 or 3 sprigs fresh parsley (or 1 teaspoon parsley flakes)
1 teaspoon salt
⅛ to ¼ teaspoon cayenne (the larger quantity for spicy recipes)
2 or 3 cloves
2 or 3 pellets whole allspice
2 or 3 thin slices lemon with peel (or 1 tablespoon lemon juice)
1 very small bay leaf
2 quarts water

Combine all the ingredients, bring rapidly to a boil, reduce the heat, and simmer for 20 to 30 minutes. Strain the liquid into a clean large saucepan, bring it to a boil, and cook the shrimp as follows:

Fresh Raw Shrimp in Shells

Drop all at once into boiling court bouillon, adjust the heat immediately to a gentle simmer, and cook for 2 minutes. Remove from the heat and allow the shrimp to cool in the liquid.

Frozen Raw Shrimp in Shells

Drop into boiling court bouillon. When the water resumes its boil and the shrimp are separated, lower the heat and simmer for 3 minutes. Remove from the heat and allow the shrimp to cool in the liquid.

Frozen Raw Peeled Shrimp

Drop into boiling court bouillon. When the water returns to a boil, lower the heat and simmer for 2 minutes. Allow the shrimp to cool in the liquid, then remove any black particles by rinsing quickly under cold water.

Note: Remember to chill and freeze as much of the court bouillon as your freezer space will permit.

RECIPES USING SHRIMP

Shrimp Jambalaya
8 to 10 servings

2½ to 3 pounds raw shrimp
2 tablespoons flour
3 tablespoons melted ham or bacon fat
1½ to 2 cups chopped, minced, or shredded lean ham
1 cup chopped onions
1 large clove garlic, minced or put through garlic press
2 cups peeled, diced fresh tomatoes, or coarsely cut canned whole
    tomatoes
2 cups uncooked long-grain white rice
1 teaspoon salt
½ teaspoon thyme
Dash of cayenne pepper
2 teaspoons chili powder
Dash of tabasco sauce

Have ready a kettle of boiling water.

Shell and devein the shrimp. If they are large, cut them into 2 or 3 pieces. If small to medium, leave them whole. In a very large heavy skillet or Dutch oven stir the flour into the fat until it is brown. Add the ham, onions, and garlic and stir until the onions are limp. Add the tomatoes, rice, and seasonings and stir. Pour in enough boiling water to moisten the mixture thoroughly, add the shrimp, stir lightly to distribute, and cook, tightly covered, over low heat. Raise the cover occasionally and add more boiling water as the rice absorbs the moisture.

Freezer portion: Cook only until the rice is barely tender. Cool, spoon the amount you wish to freeze into a casserole, chill in the refrigerator, then slip the covered casserole into a plastic bag and freeze.

Serving the unfrozen portion: Continue cooking until the rice is tender.

Serving the freezer portion: Thaw at room temperature until the ice crystals are melted. Heat, covered, in a 350° oven. As the jambalaya thaws, stir gently with a fork and, if necessary, add a little boiling water to maintain the moisture. Serve when piping hot.

Shrimp Marinara
8 servings

"Marinara"—mariner's style—implies garlic you can taste and well-blended herbs and spices. The recipe for Shrimp Marinara is given here in its entirety, but the sauce can be made separately and stored in the freezer for a number of other Marinara main courses—spaghetti or other pasta, fish fillets, mixed sea food, etc.

2½ to 3 pounds raw shrimp
2 fairly large onions, sliced or chopped
2 large cloves garlic, minced or put through garlic press

4 tablespoons fine olive oil
1 large can Italian whole peeled tomatoes (3 cups)
2 or 3 flat anchovy fillets, chopped
1 tablespoon grated Romano or Parmesan cheese
1 teaspoon sugar
½ teaspoon oregano
½ teaspoon sweet basil
¼ teaspoon pepper
Salt only if needed (anchovies are salty)

Shell and devein the shrimp and set them aside while you prepare the sauce. Sauté the onions and garlic, covered, in the hot oil over low heat until the onions are limp. Add the tomatoes, raise the heat, and cook rapidly for 3 minutes. Lower the heat and simmer for 40 minutes longer. Add the anchovies, cheese, sugar, and seasonings, stir to blend, then add the shrimp and cook for 3 minutes.

Freezer portion: Remove as much of the recipe as you wish to freeze, let it cool, pour into containers, chill in the refrigerator, then freeze.

Serving the unfrozen portion: Continue to cook over low heat for 5 to 8 minutes. Serve with pasta.

Serving the freezer portion: Place a container in cool to warm water until the contents can be released into the top of a double boiler over simmering water. Turn occasionally to hasten thawing. Heat until piping hot, and serve as above. Or thaw the container in the refrigerator and heat the contents in a chafing dish.

Spacesaving suggestion: Make the sauce only and freeze it in 2 pint containers. *To serve 4:* Melt and heat 1 pint of the sauce. Add 1 to 1½ pounds of fresh or frozen raw shrimp, shelled and deveined. Cook fresh shrimp in the simmering sauce for 8 minutes, frosty shrimp for 12 minutes, frozen shrimp for 15 to 20 minutes.

Shrimp Marinara from the Freezer Stockpile
4 servings

1-pound package frozen peeled, deveined, cooked shrimp
1-pint container any meatless Italian tomato-based sauce

Thaw the cooked shrimp until they can be separated, or thaw in court bouillon (see page 215). Heat the sauce and taste it. If it lacks piquancy, sauté in hot oil 2 tablespoons of chopped onions and 1 clove of minced garlic for 2 minutes. Add also ¼ teaspoon each of oregano and sweet basil. Let the sauce simmer with these added ingredients for 15 minutes or so before adding the cooked shrimp. Stir until well mixed, pour into a lightly oiled casserole, sprinkle with ½ cup of bread crumbs mixed with 2 teaspoons of grated Romano or Parmesan cheese, and place in a preheated 350° oven until piping hot. Just before serving, remove the casserole to the broiler section and lightly brown the bread crumbs. Do not refreeze.

Shrimp Creole
8 to 10 servings

3 pounds raw shrimp, small to medium count
1 cup chopped onions
1 cup diced green peppers
1 cup chopped celery
1 large clove garlic, minced or put through garlic press
½ cup melted butter (or ¼ cup each, butter and fine olive oil)
3 tablespoons chopped parsley
½ teaspoon salt
½ teaspoon thyme
¼ teaspoon pepper
Few grains of cayenne
Dash of tabasco sauce
2 tablespoons flour

2 cups chopped fresh tomatoes (or 2 cups drained canned tomatoes)
1 cup hot stock (fish, chicken, or consommé)

Shell and devein the shrimp. Sauté the onions, green peppers, celery, and garlic in the hot butter over very low heat until the onions are limp. Add the parsley, seasonings, and flour, stir to blend, and continue stirring over low heat for 2 minutes. Add the tomatoes and stock, stir, add the shrimp, and simmer, covered, for 3 minutes.

Freezer portion: Remove as much as you wish to freeze, let cool, pour into containers, chill in the refrigerator, then freeze.

Serving the unfrozen portion: Continue to simmer for 3 or 4 minutes longer. Serve with hot fluffy rice.

Serving the freezer portion: Thaw in the refrigerator or at room temperature. Release into a saucepan over low heat until bubbling. Serve as above.

Spacesaving suggestion: Make the sauce only and freeze it in pint containers. *To serve 4:* Melt and heat one pint of the sauce. Add 1 to 1½ pounds of fresh or frozen raw shrimp, shelled and deveined. Cook fresh shrimp in the simmering sauce for 8 minutes, frosty shrimp for 12 minutes, frozen shrimp for 15 to 20 minutes.

Baked Stuffed Shrimp
6 servings

18 raw jumbo shrimp
3 tablespoons oil
¼ cup melted butter
2 tablespoons minced onion
2 tablespoons minced celery
1 tablespoon minced green pepper
1 small clove garlic, minced or put through garlic press
2 tablespoons minced raw mushrooms
2 tablespoons minced shrimp, lobster meat, or crab meat (optional)

½ teaspoon salt
Dash of pepper
Dash of paprika
¼ teaspoon tarragon seasoning
¼ teaspoon dill seasoning
⅛ teaspoon powdered sage
1½ cups fine bread crumbs

Split the shrimp down the back and remove the veins. Remove all but the tail sections of the shells. Spread the shrimp into "wings" and flatten them with a broad spatula or the bottom of a heavy glass. Heat the oil in a heavy skillet and sauté the shrimp for 1 minute on each side, or until they turn pink. Remove the shrimp from the skillet. Add the melted butter to the skillet and sauté the onion, celery, green pepper, and garlic until the onion is transparent. Add the mushrooms, minced seafood if desired, seasonings, and bread crumbs and stir to blend thoroughly. Let this mixture stand over your lowest heat, or over the pilot light, stirring occasionally, for 3 minutes.

Freezer portion: Place the shrimp you wish to freeze on individual squares of freezer foil. Spread each one with about 1 tablespoon of the stuffing. Wrap individually, chill in the refrigerator, then freeze. When solidly frozen, gather them into a plastic bag for storage.

Serving the unfrozen portion: Allowing 3 shrimp per serving, put them into a shallow buttered baking dish or individual ramekins, tails upturned, and spread each shrimp with about 1 tablespoon of stuffing. Pour over each one a teaspoon or so of sherry, dot them with a little butter, and bake in a preheated 400° oven for 5 or 6 minutes. Brown the crumbs under the broiling unit.

Serving the freezer portion: Put the foil-wrapped shrimp into a preheated 400° oven for 15 to 20 minutes. Remove them from the oven with kitchen tongs, open the foil, place the shrimp in a shallow buttered baking dish or individual ramekins, pour over each about 1 teaspoon of sherry, dot with butter, and continue baking until the crumbs are brown.

Shrimp with Lobster Sauce, Chinese Style

Serves up to 12 people family-style if accompanied by other Chinese dishes, and rice; 4 to 6 people if the main course

2 pounds raw shrimp (any size, but large ones are more impressive)
3 tablespoons cornstarch
1 teaspoon sugar
4 tablespoons soy sauce
¼ cup cold water
4 tablespoons vegetable oil (preferably peanut oil)
½ teaspoon salt
Dash of white pepper
1 teaspoon slivered whole ginger (or ½ teaspoon ground ginger)
2 or 3 cloves garlic, minced or put through garlic press
½ pound fresh pork, very finely ground (put through grinder twice)
1½ cups chicken stock or consommé
1 small can water chestnuts, diced

Shell and devein the shrimp. If they are large, split each one along its back, being careful not to cut the shrimp through completely. Combine the cornstarch, sugar, and soy sauce with the cold water, stirring to blend well. Set this aside. In your largest skillet combine the oil, salt, pepper, ginger, and garlic. Stir well. Add the ground pork and stir for 3 minutes over fairly high heat. Add the stock or consommé, cover the skillet, and simmer over low heat for 10 minutes. Add the reserved cornstarch mixture and stir over low heat until the sauce thickens and is smooth. Add the water chestnuts and shrimp, stirring to distribute evenly.

Freezer portion: Remove as much as you wish to freeze, cool, chill in the refrigerator, then freeze in container(s).

Serving the unfrozen portion: To the remaining part, stir

in 1 beaten egg and, if desired, a little sherry. Serve in a large bowl and garnish with 1 tablespoon or so of diced scallions. Pass individual bowls of rice.

Serving the freezer portion: Set the container(s) into cool to warm water until the contents can be released into a skillet over low heat. Bring to a serving temperature. Stir in 1 beaten egg and, if desired, a little sherry. Garnish and serve as above.

Shrimp with Lobster Sauce, Boston Style
To the preceding recipe, add 2 or 3 tablespoons of minced fermented black beans (available in Chinese grocery stores) along with the seasonings.

Shrimp Sub Gum (Har Ding), Chinese
Serves up to 12 people family-style if accompanied by other Chinese dishes and rice; 4 to 6 people if the main course

2 pounds shrimp
Court bouillon
2 tablespoons cornstarch
2 tablespoons soy sauce
2 tablespoons sherry
¼ cup cold water
4 tablespoons vegetable oil (preferably peanut oil)
½ teaspoon salt
⅛ teaspoon white pepper
1 teaspoon shredded ginger root (or ½ teaspoon ground ginger)
1 large clove garlic, minced or put through garlic press
1½ cups diagonally sliced fresh green beans
2 cups diagonally sliced celery
1½ cups diced or sliced mushrooms
½ cup sliced water chestnuts
½ cup sliced bamboo shoots
2 cups sliced Chinese cabbage
1½ cups chicken stock or consommé

Cook the shrimp in court bouillon according to the directions on page 215. Peel and devein them. Combine the

cornstarch, soy sauce, and sherry with the cold water, mix
well, and set aside. Into a very large heated skillet put the
oil, salt, pepper, ginger, and garlic and stir over moderate
heat for 1 minute. Add all the vegetables, stir, add the stock
or consommé, mix well, cover, and simmer over low heat for
6 minutes. Add the shrimp, mix well, add the cornstarch mixture, and continue to stir until the sauce thickens.

Freezer portion: Remove as much as you wish to freeze,
cool, chill in the refrigerator, then freeze in container(s).

Serving the unfrozen portion: Return the skillet to heat,
bring to a serving temperature, and serve in a bowl, garnished with toasted blanched almonds. Pass individual
bowls of rice.

Serving the freezer portion: Set the container(s) in cool
to warm water until the contents can be released into a skillet for heating over low heat. Serve as above, garnished with
toasted almonds.

To toast almonds for Chinese dishes: Heat vegetable oil
(preferably peanut oil) in a skillet and stir blanched whole
almonds in the oil until golden brown.

Shrimp Florentine
6 to 8 servings

2 pounds shrimp
Court bouillon
2 cups Heavy White Sauce (page 19)
¾ cup cream
1 teaspoon lemon juice
6 tablespoons butter
3 cups (2 pounds) cooked spinach, chopped and drained
Grating of whole nutmeg (or dash of ground nutmeg)
2 tablespoons minced shallots
½ cup dry sherry
2 tablespoons grated Romano or Parmesan cheese

Cook the shrimp in court bouillon according to the directions on page 215. Peel and devein them. Keep the white

sauce hot in the top of a double boiler over simmering water as you slowly add the cream, stirring until well blended. Correct seasonings (salt, pepper, paprika) if necessary and stir in the lemon juice. Stir briskly to prevent curdling. Let the sauce continue to heat gently over simmering water, stirring from time to time, as you proceed:

Melt 2 tablespoons of the butter in a large skillet and add the drained cooked spinach. Stir over moderate heat until excess moisture evaporates. Add about ½ cup of the white sauce, sprinkle with nutmeg, lower the heat to a gentle simmer, and cook for 2 minutes.

Spread the spinach over the bottoms of 2 lightly buttered 1-quart casseroles. In the same skillet, melt 2 more tablespoons of the butter until it bubbles without darkening. Add the shrimp and shallots and stir over moderate heat for 1 minute. Add the sherry and raise the heat until the liquid boils. Lower the heat and cook, uncovered, until most of the sherry evaporates. Combine the shrimp with half the remaining white sauce and divide the mixture between the two casseroles. Top each with the remaining sauce, sprinkle with the cheese, and dot with the rest of the butter.

Freezer portion: Let cool, cover, chill in the refrigerator, then freeze.

Serving the unfrozen portion: Bake, uncovered, in a 400° oven until the sauce bubbles.

Serving the freezer portion: Remove from the freezer to a preheated 450° oven and bake, covered, for 20 minutes. Reduce the oven heat to 350°, uncover, and continue baking until the sauce bubbles.

Shrimp Florentine from the Freezer Stockpile
6 to 8 servings

2 1-pound packages frozen peeled, deveined, precooked shrimp
Court bouillon
1-pint container Heavy White Sauce (page 19)
2 packages frozen chopped spinach

Thaw the shrimp in court bouillon according to the directions on page 216. Melt and heat the white sauce in the top of a double boiler over simmering water. Cook the spinach according to package directions, then drain. Follow the preceding recipe for the remaining ingredients and directions. Do not refreeze.

Freezing Shrimp Prepared for Frying

For every 6 to 8 servings:

2 to 2½ pounds fresh raw shrimp
1½ cups milk
½ teaspoon salt
¼ teaspoon paprika
Dash of pepper
1 tablespoon lemon juice
About ¾ cup corn meal or fine cracker meal

Shell and devein the shrimp and lay them in a shallow dish. Combine the milk with the salt, paprika, and pepper and pour over the shrimp. Let this stand for half an hour. If the shrimp are not totally covered by the milk mixture, turn them at the end of 15 minutes. Drain in a colander (not on absorbent towels), sprinkle with the lemon juice, and roll in the corn or cracker meal until thoroughly coated. Put the shrimp in a single layer onto the bottom of a trunk-opening wax-coated freezer box, top with a double thickness of freezer film, and build up the layers until the box is full. If you have no trunk-opening boxes (save some, in future, when you buy prepared frozen foods), lay 6 or 8 shrimp on heavy freezer paper or foil, slip-sheet with a double thickness of freezer film, and continue to build up until all the shrimp are used. Carefully fold the paper or foil to enclose the shrimp, seal, and freeze.

To serve: Remove as many shrimp as needed. Fry in deep fat at 370° until golden brown. Drain on paper towels and serve with tartar sauce.

Batter-fried Shrimp for Freezer Storage
For every 6 to 8 servings:

3 pounds fresh raw shrimp
2 eggs
½ cup milk
¾ cup sifted flour
2 tablespoons cornstarch
1 teaspoon baking powder
1 teaspoon salt
2 teaspoons salad oil
Deep fat or oil for frying

Shell and devein the shrimp. Beat the eggs slightly. Add the milk, flour, cornstarch, baking powder, salt, and salad oil. Beat with a rotary beater or an electric mixer until the batter is smooth. Dip the shrimp in the batter and fry, a few at a time, in deep hot fat (370°) only until pale gold. Continue until all the shrimp are used, draining each batch on paper towels. Spread a piece of waxed paper on a refrigerator shelf, place shrimp in a single layer, and chill thoroughly. Gather into freezer boxes or wrap in foil and freeze.

To serve: Remove as many shrimp as are needed. Drop into deep hot fat or oil (370°) and fry until deep golden brown. Drain on paper towels. Serve with tartar or cocktail sauce.

A modest stockpile of batter-fried shrimp in the freezer can provide you with the basis for many cookbook recipes calling for this method of preparation; for example:

Batter-fried Shrimp with Apricot Sauce
4 servings

⅓ cup pineapple juice
1 tablespoon dry mustard
1 tablespoon soy sauce
¾ cup apricot jam
1 teaspoon grated lemon peel

2 tablespoons lemon juice
Frozen batter-fried shrimp (12 to 20, depending on size)
Deep fat or oil for frying

In a saucepan over low heat combine the pineapple juice with the mustard until well blended and smooth. Add all the remaining sauce ingredients, stirring after each addition, until the jam is thoroughly melted and the sauce is smooth. Turn the heat to simmer, and stir occasionally.

Fry the shrimp in deep hot fat or oil (370°) until deep golden brown. Drain on paper towels. Serve with hot apricot sauce and fluffy rice.

Sweet and Sour Shrimp, Chinese Style
Serves up to 12 people family-style if accompanied by other Chinese dishes and rice; 4 to 6 people if the main course

2 pounds frozen batter-fried shrimp (small)
Deep fat or oil for frying
1 cup vinegar
¾ cup water
2 tablespoons soy sauce
¼ cup tomato catchup
½ teaspoon salt
Dash of white pepper
1 cup sugar
1 clove garlic, crushed
3 tablespoons vegetable oil (preferably peanut oil)
2 or 3 large green peppers, seeded and cut coarsely into 8 pieces
    each
3 tablespoons cornstarch dissolved in ⅓ cup cold water
2 cups canned or frozen pineapple chunks, drained
2 large firm ripe tomatoes, cut into 6 to 8 wedges each

Fry the prepared frozen shrimp in deep hot fat or oil (370°) until golden brown. Drain well between paper towels.

In a large saucepan combine the vinegar, water, soy sauce, catchup, salt, pepper, and sugar. Mix well and bring to a boil. Lower the heat and simmer gently while you stir the crushed garlic in the hot oil in a separate skillet for 1 minute. Discard the garlic and sauté the green peppers for 3 minutes, stirring. Add the dissolved cornstarch to the saucepan, stirring constantly until the sauce thickens. Add the pineapple chunks, green peppers, and shrimp. Stir. Add the tomatoes, stir to distribute evenly, and serve when hot with fluffy rice.

MIXED SHELLFISH RECIPES FROM THE FREEZER STOCKPILE

An occasional inventory of your freezer's contents may reveal a collection of small packages of various sea-fruits tucked away as surplus when you were preparing individual recipes using lobster, crab, shrimp, scallops, oysters, clams, or mussels. Compatible in character, such hoarded treasures can be deftly combined into a number of interesting main-course specialties—once-in-a-lifetime specialties, perhaps, for you may never again find yourself with the same combinations or quantities of shellfish.

A few general recipes are given here for following in context or as a guide to your own improvisations. Lacking sufficient shellfish to yield specified amounts, you may make up the deficit with frozen cooked leftover poultry, diced and thawed.

Sea Food Newburg
4 servings

¼ cup melted butter
¼ cup flour
½ teaspoon salt
¼ teaspoon pepper or paprika
2 cups scalded milk
2 egg yolks, lightly beaten

1 cup or more frozen cooked shrimp, thawed in refrigerator
1 cup or more frozen crab or lobster meat, thawed in refrigerator
1 tablespoon lemon juice
2 tablespoons sherry
3 tablespoons bread crumbs (mixed with grated Cheddar cheese
      if desired)

Put the melted butter into a saucepan over very low heat.
Blend in the flour and seasonings. Remove from the heat
and slowly add the scalded milk, stirring constantly. Return
to moderate heat and bring to a boil, continuing to stir. Let
boil for 1 minute. Put the egg yolks into a casserole and
pour into them half the white sauce, stirring briskly. Add
and stir in the remaining white sauce. Mix the thawed sea
food with the lemon juice and sherry and fold into the
sauce. Top with the bread crumbs and keep in a preheated
350° oven until piping hot. Serve with fluffy rice or noodles,
or over toast triangles.

Note: This recipe may also be composed with stockpiled
Heavy White Sauce (page 19). Release a 1-pint container
into the top of a double boiler over bubbling water. Break
up lumps with a fork. When melted and hot, stir briskly
until smooth. Follow the preceding directions to complete
the recipe.

Curry of Mixed Seafood I
4 servings

1 small onion, chopped or minced
1 small firm apple, chopped
2 tablespoons butter
2 tablespoons flour
1 tablespoon curry powder (2 tablespoons if you like highly sea-
      soned food)
1 cup cream
3 or 4 cups mixed frozen sea food, or sea food plus diced leftover
      poultry, all thawed
¼ cup sherry
Grated or shredded coconut

Sauté the onion and the apple in the butter for 3 minutes. Sprinkle with the flour and stir to blend well. Blend in the curry powder and cream and stir over low heat for 5 minutes. Add the thawed sea food (and poultry, if needed), stir, add the sherry, and heat through. If the mixture seems dry, stir in 2 tablespoons of butter. Serve over rice cooked in bouillon or stock and top with coconut.

Curry of Mixed Sea Food II
4 servings

1-pint container frozen Average White Sauce (page 19)
1 tablespoon curry powder
¼ teaspoon salt
¼ teaspoon ground black pepper
Few grains of cayenne
¼ teaspoon ground ginger
2 egg yolks, lightly beaten
3 or 4 cups mixed frozen sea food
¼ cup bread crumbs
Grated Cheddar, Romano, or Parmesan cheese

Release the white sauce into the top of a double boiler over bubbling water. Break up lumps with a fork. When hot, stir briskly until smooth. Add all the seasonings and stir well. Blend about ¼ cup of this hot mixture into the beaten egg yolks and then add them to the sauce, stirring. Heat through without boiling. Fold in the thawed sea food, spoon the mixture into a lightly buttered casserole, sprinkle with the bread crumbs, and top with grated cheese. Bake in a preheated 450° oven until the cheese melts and the topping browns.

Baked Mixed Sea Food in Ramekins
4 servings

For this recipe, combinations of frozen raw and cooked sea food may be used.

½ cup raw or cooked peeled, deveined shrimp, diced
½ cup cooked lobster or crab meat, shredded
½ cup raw or cooked scallops, diced
½ cup cooked fish, flaked
4 tablespoons butter
Salt and pepper to taste
1-pint container (2 cups) any frozen creamy sauce (white, curry,
     velouté, etc.)
⅔ cup bread crumbs
¼ cup grated Cheddar, Romano, or Parmesan cheese

Thaw all the sea food until no ice crystals remain. Combine them and sauté in the butter for 5 minutes. Season to taste. Melt and heat the sauce and stir until smooth. Combine the hot sea food with 1½ cups of the heated sauce and pile in ramekins or pastry shells. Top with spoonfuls of the remaining sauce, sprinkle with the crumbs and grated cheese, and brown under the broiler until piping hot.

Mixed Sea Food with Pasta
4 servings

8-ounce container Heavy White Sauce (page 19)
8-ounce container any light stock
2 cups any combination of frozen cooked shellfish and fish
1 tablespoon lemon juice
8-ounce package any pasta (linguini, spaghetti, elbow macaroni,
     noodles)
1 cup grated Cheddar cheese
1 teaspoon dry mustard
½ cup sliced fresh or frozen mushrooms
¼ cup sliced stuffed olives
½ cup bread crumbs

Release the sauce and stock into the top of a double boiler over simmering water. Break up lumps with a fork. When melted and hot, stir briskly to combine. Dice the sea food, sprinkle with the lemon juice, and let stand while you cook and drain the pasta according to the package directions. Pour about ½ cup of the hot sauce over the sea food and mix. Add ¾ cup of the grated cheese to the remaining sauce and stir. Stir in the mustard and combine the sauce with the sea food. Preheat the oven to 350°. In a lightly buttered casserole build up layers of the pasta, sea-food mixture, mushrooms, and olives, ending with a thin layer of pasta. Sprinkle with the bread crumbs and remaining grated cheese and bake at 350° for 20 minutes. Brown the topping under the broiler.

20.

The Freezer's Role
in Chicken Cookery

While almost without exception any chicken recipe you know, seek, or find can be prepared in advance and entrusted to the freezer for varying storage periods *even if the raw chicken used was previously frozen,* good management recommends a befitting selectivity.

For example, I do not prescribe your making it a practice to roast a chicken deliberately for freezer storage except under special circumstances—busy holiday times, heavy entertainment schedules, impending picnics or vacation trips, or something to leave lovingly at home when you go away.

And except under similar conditions I do not ordinarily consider it profitable to use a freezer—even a big one—as the repository for bulky casseroles based on cut-up chicken parts still attached to their skeletons.

Over the years since, with wonderment, I saw the first home freezers being designed and manufactured, I have evolved a freezer-oriented program for chicken which saves time, effort, *and space* while providing the ready means for menu variety. Here is a synopsis of that program:

234

1. Frozen whole raw chickens or parts directly from the freezer for appropriate recipes to be served when cooked (pages 236–245)

2. Quickly assembled casseroles and skillet meals based on frozen prefried chicken parts (pages 246–256)

3. Recipes featuring either raw or precooked boneless chicken (pages 257–274)

21.

Recipes Using Frozen Raw Chicken

Chicken-in-a-Pot with Matzoth Balls
4 to 6 servings

This is a hearty, unpretentious, but popular one-course family meal. I also serve it to guests who appreciate the informality and simplicity of homely fare. It is astonishing—or is it?—how many gourmet sophisticates grow misty-eyed when sat down before a dinner innocent of any grandeur other than savor and, perhaps, nostalgia.

1 whole frozen 4- or 5-pound stewing fowl
1 or 2 outer leaves of cabbage (keep some in the freezer, individually rolled up in a plastic bag)
4 cups water, vegetable water, or unseasoned chicken stock (from the freezer)
½ cup chopped fresh or frozen onions
4 stalks celery with leaves
1½ teaspoons salt
¼ teaspoon white pepper
1 tablespoon chopped fresh parsley (or 1 teaspoon parsley flakes)
6 to 8 large plump carrots, scraped and coarsely cut

Choose a large pot with a tight lid. Put the chicken onto a bed of cabbage leaves and add everything else except the carrots. Bring slowly to a boil over moderate heat, then lower the heat and continue to simmer very slowly for 2½ to 3 hours. As soon as the pot has started its long simmer, prepare the recipe given below for matzoth balls. (Anytime up to half an hour before serving, parboil the carrots in a small amount of boiling salted water for 10 minutes.)

Matzoth Balls

4 whole eggs
2 tablespoons melted chicken fat (less desirably, oil or melted butter)
¼ cup chicken stock or water
½ teaspoon salt
Dash of ground black pepper
1 to 1½ cups matzoth meal (the smaller amount for lighter, fluffier matzoth balls; some people like them firm)

In a bowl beat the eggs until light and frothy and add everything else except the matzoth meal. Stir well. Gradually add the matzoth meal, stirring until well moistened. Cover the bowl and refrigerate it—the longer the better, but for at least an hour.

About 40 minutes before serving time, bring 3 or 4 quarts of water with 2 teaspoons of salt to a vigorous boil. Meantime, remove the chilled matzoth mixture from the refrigerator and form 12 to 18 balls, placing them on a plate or waxed paper until all are done. Drop them one at a time into the boiling water. When all are in and the water returns to a boil, lower the heat and simmer, covered, for 30 minutes.

Strain the chicken broth into a clean pot set over low heat, add the parboiled carrots, and simmer for 10 minutes. Cut the chicken into serving pieces—or, for fussy eaters, remove the meat from the bones in large chunks.

To serve: Put portions of chicken and carrots into large

individual bowls, ladle the broth over them, and top with the matzoth balls removed from the water with a slotted spoon. If nobody is on a diet, serve thick slabs of Jewish rye or corn bread and sweet butter.

Freezing note: The entire recipe is a little too bulky to freeze, although it can be frozen. However, matzoth balls freeze beautifully, to serve in any clear broth another time. Make a double recipe and put serving requirements of the extras, well drained, into plastic bags. Refrigerate, then freeze on a shelf or in a corner where they won't be crushed by other packages. To serve after freezing, unbag and drop them—still frozen—into boiling water or bubbling broth until they separate. Lower the heat and simmer until piping hot.

Chicken-Vegetable Stew
4 to 6 servings

This interesting recipe breaks with tradition and is in contradiction to the usual injunction to cook fresh vegetables rapidly in very little water, frozen ones according to package directions. However, it's an easy meal to cook on a long afternoon, and an occasional foray into unorthodox procedures is part of the fun of living with a freezer. The vegetables cook to softness, blending their flavors, and become a thickened gravy without the addition of processed starch.

4 to 6 frozen chicken-part servings (legs, thighs, breasts)
6 cups cold water or cold unseasoned stock
1½ teaspoons salt
¼ teaspoon black pepper
1 package frozen sliced okra
1 package frozen baby lima beans
1 cup fresh or frozen chopped onions
1-pint container frozen tomatoes (or 2 cups drained canned tomatoes)

2 cups diced fresh or frozen raw potatoes
1 package frozen corn, niblet style (or 1 can corn niblets)

In a large pot, cover the chicken parts with the cold liquid, and add the salt, pepper, and all vegetables except the potatoes and corn. Bring to a boil over moderate heat. Immediately reduce the heat to a simmer and cook, covered, for 4 hours. Add water or stock occasionally to keep the liquid content to its original level in the pot. At the end of 4 hours add the potatoes and corn and cook for 1 hour longer, stirring occasionally to prevent scorching as the liquid is absorbed.

Variation: For those who don't like to pick on bones, simmer the chicken parts alone for 1 hour in the seasoned liquid, remove with tongs, and, when cool enough to handle, cut the meat from the bones. Return the meat to the simmering liquid and continue the recipe as above.

Freezing note: The entire recipe, or leftovers, can be frozen after chilling and can be reheated without thawing in the top of a double boiler over simmering water. Store up to 2 months.

Fancy Chicken Stew
4 to 6 servings

Depending on your freezer supply, this can be made with a stewing fowl, with fryers or broilers, or with parts.

4 to 6 pounds frozen whole, halved, or disjointed chicken
6 cups boiling water, vegetable water, or stock (from the freezer)
2 teaspoons salt
¼ teaspoon ground black pepper
3 tablespoons chicken fat (rendered)
3 tablespoons flour
12 to 18 frozen whole baby carrots
12 to 18 frozen whole small onions
1½ cups frozen peas
2 egg yolks beaten with 2 tablespoons cream or milk

Cover the chicken with the boiling liquid, add the salt and pepper, cover the pot tightly, and bring to a boil over moderate heat. Lower the heat and simmer, covered, until tender (2½ to 3 hours for whole fowl, 1½ to 2 hours for parts). Remove the pot from the heat and let the chicken cool to lukewarm in the liquid. Remove and drain the chicken (reserving the liquid), discard the skin, and cut the meat from the bones into large pieces. Set the chicken aside. Melt the chicken fat in a skillet, blend with the flour, and add about a cupful of the pot liquid, stirring or beating until smooth. Add this mixture to the pot liquid, return to the heat, and simmer, stirring occasionally. In separate sauce-pans (or one saucepan, successively) cook the frozen vegetables according to the package directions. Drain them. (If enough waters remain to make it worthwhile, combine and freeze them as stock.) Add the egg yolks beaten with cream or milk to the simmering stock and stir until thickened. Finally, add the boned chicken and drained vegetables and serve piping hot with fluffy rice or cooked noodles.

Hawaiian Chicken
4 servings

4 small whole frozen chicken breasts or leg-thigh sections, or a mixture
¼ cup soy sauce
½ cup dry white wine
Juice of 1 fresh lime (or 1 tablespoon lime juice concentrate)
1 clove garlic, minced or put through garlic press
1½ teaspoons curry powder
1 teaspoon finely slivered fresh ginger root (or ½ teaspoon ground ginger)
¼ teaspoon ground white pepper
½ cup chopped onions, fresh or frozen
4 tablespoons peanut oil or melted butter
About 1 cup flour

With a cleaver or a frozen-food saw, cut the chicken breasts in half and/or disjoint the legs. Put the pieces into a large, shallow, nonmetallic bowl. Combine the soy sauce, wine, and lime juice, stir in all the seasonings, and pour over the chicken. Let this stand for 2 or 3 hours, turning the chicken from time to time to saturate all parts evenly. Drain, reserving the marinade. In a large covered skillet or chicken fryer, sauté the onions in the oil or butter until limp. Dredge the drained chicken with the flour, coating evenly, and brown in the onion skillet. Pour the reserved marinade into the skillet, cover closely, bring slowly to a gentle simmer, and cook for 1 hour, removing the cover for the last 20 minutes. While the chicken is simmering uncovered, complete the recipe:

4 slices canned pineapple, cut in half
1 tablespoon butter
2 cups hot cooked rice
½ cup slivered almonds
½ cup seedless raisins, soaked in pineapple juice until plump,
    then drained
¼ cup minced pimiento
½ cup chopped or sliced water chestnuts (1 small can)
Dry wine

Drain the pineapple and brown on both sides in the butter. Combine the rice with all the remaining ingredients, mixing well. Heap the rice mixture in the center of a warm platter, surround it with alternate pieces of chicken and pineapple, add about 4 tablespoons of dry wine to the marinade, pour a little over the rice, and pass the rest in a gravy boat.

Freezing note: If you wish to freeze the main part of this recipe for a few weeks, put the chicken and onions into a freezer-to-oven casserole after they have been browned, cover with marinade, chill in the refrigerator, and freeze. To serve, put the casserole into a preheated 375° oven for 1½ to 2 hours, uncovering for the last 15 minutes, and complete the recipe as above.

Chicken Tetrazzini
4 servings

3 or 4 whole frozen chicken breasts
4 cups cold water
1 teaspoon salt
½ cup slivered almonds
½ pound box (or a little more) linguini or thin spaghetti
½ pound fresh mushrooms, sliced (or 1 package frozen sliced
    mushrooms)
6 tablespoons butter
2 tablespoons flour
1 cup sweet or sour cream
3 tablespoons sherry
Dash of white pepper
Pinch of ground nutmeg
¼ cup grated Romano or Parmesan cheese

Cover the chicken with the cold water and bring to a boil over moderate heat. Lower the heat, add the salt, and simmer for 1 hour. Remove the pot from the heat and let the chicken cool in the broth. Drain the chicken (reserving the broth), remove the skin and bones, and cut the meat into thin strips or small dice. Mix with the slivered almonds and set aside. Add the skin and bones to the broth and simmer, uncovered, until the liquid is reduced by half. Strain and reserve the broth.

Cook linguini or spaghetti according to the package directions for firm texture, drain, rinse under hot water, and keep warm in a colander over simmering water.

Sauté the mushrooms in 3 tablespoons of the butter for 2 minutes, then combine with the pasta.

Melt the remaining 3 tablespoons of butter in the top of a double boiler over simmering water, blend in the flour, gradually add the 2 cups of strained chicken broth, and stir until thickened and smooth. Add to the sauce the cream, sherry, pepper, and nutmeg, and additional salt, if necessary. Cook for 10 minutes, stirring occasionally.

Preheat the oven to 350°. Put the pasta-mushroom mixture into a well-buttered casserole and stir into it half the sauce. Combine the chicken-almond mixture with the remaining sauce. Make a hole in the middle of the pasta and fill it with the chicken mixture. Top with the grated cheese and heat in a 350° oven for 20 minutes. Remove to the broiler section, if desired, to brown the cheese.

Freezing note: Omit oven heating. Chill the freezer-to-oven casserole when filled, then slip it into a large plastic bag for freezer storage. To serve, set the casserole in a pan of cold water and heat in a 375° oven until piping hot (about 1½ hours).

Chicken in Wine Sauce
4 servings

4 serving portions frozen chicken parts
1-pint container frozen chicken stock (or 1 can condensed clear consommé extended with water to yield 2 cups)
1 cup sliced or diced fresh or frozen carrots
½ cup chopped fresh or frozen onions
2 tablespoons minced parsley
Pinch thyme
1 small bay leaf
3 or 4 peppercorns
½ teaspoon salt
¼ pound butter
2 tablespoons flour
½ cup dry white wine
1 egg yolk, beaten with 2 tablespoons cream
½ pound small whole mushrooms (or 1 package frozen mushrooms)
Juice of 1 lemon (optional)

Put the frozen chicken parts into a large pot with the stock (even if it is still a lump of ice) or other liquid and set it over low heat until the liquid begins to boil. Add the carrots, onions, parsley, and seasonings. When boiling steadily, lower the heat and simmer for 40 to 50 minutes until the chicken is tender. Remove and drain the chicken, strain the broth, and reserve both while you make the sauce:

Melt 3 tablespoons of the butter in the top of a double boiler, blend in the flour, and cook over simmering water for 5 minutes. Add the wine and 1 cup of the strained broth, stir, bring to a boil, lower the heat, and simmer, stirring, until smooth. Add the egg beaten with cream, stir, and continue to simmer over very low heat.

In a large skillet or chicken fryer, melt the remaining butter and brown the chicken quickly, skin side down. Turn the pieces, brown them quickly, push them to one side, and sauté the mushrooms for 2 minutes.

Put the chicken into a casserole, surround with the mushrooms, and cover with half the sauce, serving the rest in a gravy boat. If desired, the juice of 1 lemon may be sprinkled over the chicken before adding the sauce.

Freezing Note: Omit the mushrooms. Put the chicken, when browned, into a freezer-to-oven casserole or in bread pans and cover with all the sauce. Chill and freeze. To serve, heat in a 400° oven while you sauté the mushrooms. When the sauce is melted, remove some with a bulb baster to a small saucepan to heat for serving in a gravy boat.

Batter-fried Chicken Wings, Chinese Style
3 or 4 servings as a main entree, or 6 servings as a side dish

¼ cup soy sauce
1 cup sherry
1 clove garlic, minced or put through garlic press
2 tablespoons minced ginger root (or 1 level teaspoon ground
 ginger)
12 chicken wings, frozen, thawed, or fresh

Combine the soy sauce, sherry, garlic, and ginger, mix well, and pour over the chicken wings in a wide bowl. Let stand at room temperature for 4 hours or more, separating the wings as they thaw, if frozen. Remove ½ cup of the marinade, strain it, and reserve for the batter. The rest of the marinade may be strained and refrigerated for future use.

Batter

1 egg
½ cup marinade
About ½ cup sifted flour or cornstarch

Beat the egg and marinade together, then stir in enough flour or cornstarch to make a smooth, thin batter. Drain the chicken wings, dust with flour or cornstarch, and dip into the batter until thoroughly coated. Drop a few at a time into deep hot oil (370°), (preferably peanut oil), and fry until golden brown. Drain on paper towels and keep warm in a 250° oven until all are done.

Freezing note: These may be stockpiled in the freezer, prepared for final frying, and stored up to 3 months. Fry only until light gold, drain on paper towels, refrigerate until chilled, and package in wax cartons or wrap in foil. To serve, thaw for 1 hour at room temperature, drop a few at a time into hot oil (preferably peanut oil), and fry until golden brown.

22.

Fried Chicken
in the Freezer

Prefried chicken parts in the freezer can provide more than fried chicken for meals or picnics. Properly fried with a protective fat barrier, then drained, chilled, wrapped, labeled, and frozen, prefried chicken parts can be stored up to 3 months, ready to be combined with any number of sauces for a variety of quickly prepared entrees in a wide range of tastes from the subtle to the exotic.

With the sauces also in the freezer it becomes a simple matter to arrange the chicken pieces in a skillet or casserole, melt and stir the sauce separately, combine it with the chicken, and bring it to serving temperature on top of the range or in the oven while the meal's accompaniments are being prepared.

True, the completed recipes can be frozen in casseroles. My reason for not doing this is dictated by several considerations—space jealousy, menus to match moods, and a creative urge to do *something* with food besides thawing it.

FRYING CHICKEN FOR THE FREEZER

Use fresh or completely thawed parts separated into half-breasts and disjointed leg sections (drumsticks and thighs). Choose any of the following methods:

Fried Chicken I (with Flour)
For every 4 pounds of chicken parts, room temperature:

½ to ⅔ cup flour
1 teaspoon salt
½ teaspoon pepper
½ cup oil or melted shortening

Dry the parts. Combine the flour with the salt and pepper and put it into a clean paper bag. Add to the bag 3 or 4 pieces of chicken at a time and shake, removing the pieces to a platter when well covered. Continue until all are floured. Let them dry for 30 minutes. Heat the oil or shortening in a large chicken fryer, heavy skillet, or Dutch oven. Shake excess flour from the chicken and place a single layer skin-side down in the pan over moderate heat. Fry until light golden brown, then turn and brown the other side. See page 248 for freezing instructions.

Fried Chicken II (with Crumbs)
For every 4 pounds of chicken parts, room temperature:

Salt and pepper
1 cup fine bread or cracker crumbs
2 eggs beaten with 1 tablespoon milk
½ cup oil or melted shortening

Sprinkle the chicken lightly with salt and pepper. Roll in the crumbs. Dip into the egg mixture, coating evenly, then roll in the crumbs again. Let dry for 30 minutes. Fry as in the preceding flour method. Drain on paper towels. See page 248 for freezing instructions.

Fried Chicken III (with Batter)

For every 4 pounds of chicken parts, room temperature:

Use a commercial fritter batter, following the package directions, or make the following batter:

1½ cups flour
1 teaspoon baking powder
½ teaspoon salt
¼ teaspoon black pepper
2 eggs
1½ cups milk

Sift all the dry ingredients together. Beat the eggs and milk together and add the flour mixture. The batter should be of a consistency to cling to the chicken and coat it evenly. If too thin, add a little more flour. If too heavy, add a little more milk. Stir until smooth.

In a French-fryer with a basket, heat deep fat or oil to a thermometer reading of 350°, or until a quarter-slice of dry bread turns golden brown in 1 minute.

Coat the chicken parts evenly with the batter and fry a few pieces at a time until light golden brown, draining them on paper towels. See below for freezing instructions.

To freeze fried chicken parts: Put the pieces onto a platter or onto waxed paper on a refrigerator shelf, slip-sheeting the layers with waxed paper, for 1 hour or more. When thoroughly chilled, wrap individual serving portions and put them in a single layer in contact with a freezing surface (an upright shelf, or a chest sidewall). When solidly frozen, gather into a large plastic bag, label, and return to the freezer for storage.

23.

Recipes Based on
Frozen Fried Chicken Parts

Unless otherwise specified, it is not necessary to thaw frozen fried chicken parts for these recipes. *Do not refreeze completed recipes when made with previously frozen fried chicken.* If you wish to follow any of the casserole recipes and freeze them up to 3 months for later serving, use fresh or thawed raw chicken and fry according to the methods on pages 247 and 248. Complete the recipe, put it into a casserole, and chill thoroughly in the refrigerator. Slip the covered casserole into a large plastic bag and put it into contact with a freezing surface. To serve, unbag the casserole and thaw it at room temperature for 1 hour or more. Bring to a serving temperature in a 350° to 375° oven.

Chicken à l'Orange I
4 servings

1 cup orange juice
½ cup chili sauce

¼ cup chopped fresh or frozen green pepper
1 small clove garlic, minced or put through garlic press
2 tablespoons soy sauce
1 tablespoon dark molasses or pancake sirup (not maple)
½ teaspoon salt
4 serving portions frozen fried chicken parts
8 half-slices peeled orange (or 1 small can mandarin sections, drained)

Combine all the ingredients except the chicken and fruit in a saucepan, bring to a boil, lower the heat, and simmer for 5 minutes. Pour the hot sauce over the frozen fried chicken parts arranged in a lightly oiled serving casserole. Cover and place in a cold oven. Turn the oven control to 375°. When the temperature reaches 375°, heat for 1 hour. Garnish with the fruit and heat, uncovered, for 15 minutes longer.

Freezing note: Do not refreeze if made with frozen fried chicken.

Chicken à l'Orange II
6 servings

1½ cups orange juice
2 tablespoons brown sugar
2 tablespoons wine vinegar
½ teaspoon ground nutmeg
¼ teaspoon basil
Few grains cayenne pepper
2 or 3 pellets whole allspice
1 clove garlic, halved
1 teaspoon salt
12 small serving pieces of frozen batter-fried chicken (page 248)
12 half-slices peeled orange

Combine all the ingredients except the chicken and orange slices in a saucepan, bring to a boil, lower the heat, and simmer for 10 minutes. Strain and pour over the frozen chicken servings arranged in a large skillet. Cover the skillet, bring to a boil over moderate heat, lower the heat, and simmer for 40 minutes. Add the orange slices and continue to simmer for 10 minutes.

Freezing note: Do not refreeze if made with frozen batter-fried chicken.

Basque Chicken
4 servings

4 serving portions frozen fried chicken parts
½ pound small whole mushrooms
4 tablespoons oil
1 cup chopped onions
1 small eggplant, peeled and diced
4 tomatoes, peeled and cut into wedges
1 cup diced green peppers
1 large clove garlic, put through garlic press
⅛ teaspoon thyme
⅛ teaspoon basil
½ teaspoon chili powder
1 teaspoon salt
¼ teaspoon pepper
1 cup dry white wine

Put the chicken into the center of a large casserole and let stand at room temperature while you prepare the vegetables:

In a large skillet, sauté the mushrooms in the hot oil for 2 minutes, then remove with a slotted spoon and reserve. Sauté the onions until limp, remove with a slotted spoon, and reserve. Combine all the remaining vegetables with the seasonings and stir them in the skillet with a wooden spoon for 3 minutes. Mix these with the mushrooms and onions and arrange them around the chicken. Rinse the skillet with the wine and pour it over the chicken and vegetables. Put the covered casserole onto an oven shelf and set the heat for

375°. When your oven thermometer reaches 350°, heat for 1 hour or until piping hot. Uncover occasionally to check for moisture. If dry, add a little wine.

Freezing note: Do not refreeze if made with frozen fried chicken.

Chicken Cuernavaca
4 servings

4 serving portions frozen fried chicken parts
¼ cup chopped fresh or frozen onions
¼ cup chopped fresh or frozen green peppers
2 tablespoons chopped pimiento
1 clove garlic, minced or put through garlic press
½ cup chopped celery
2 tablespoons oil
½ cup French-cut fresh or frozen green beans
1½ cups canned tomatoes
½ cup sliced stuffed olives

Arrange the chicken in a lightly oiled casserole. In a large skillet, sauté the onions, green peppers, pimiento, garlic, and celery in the hot oil for 3 minutes, stirring. Add the beans and tomatoes, stir, and pour this mixture over the chicken. Cover the casserole and put it onto an oven shelf set for 375°. When your oven thermometer reaches 350°, heat for 1 hour. Garnish with sliced olives.

Freezing note: Do not refreeze if made with frozen fried chicken.

Chicken Cacciatora
4 servings

½ cup chopped fresh or frozen onions
½ cup diced fresh or frozen green peppers
¼ cup chopped celery

¼ cup chopped fresh or frozen carrots
1 clove garlic, minced
3 tablespoons fine olive oil
1½ to 2 cups canned Italian tomatoes
½ cup dry white wine
⅔ teaspoon salt
¼ teaspoon basil or oregano
4 serving portions frozen fried chicken
1 cup sliced fresh or frozen mushrooms

In a chicken fryer, Dutch oven, or large skillet sauté the onions, green peppers, celery, carrots, and garlic in the hot oil for 3 minutes, stirring. Add the tomatoes, wine, and seasonings and bring to a boil. Lower the heat, add the chicken, and simmer, covered, for 45 minutes. Add the mushrooms and simmer for 10 minutes longer.

Freezing note: Do not refreeze if made with frozen fried chicken.

Coq au Vin
4 servings

4 serving portions fried chicken, thawed in the refrigerator
4 tablespoons brandy, heated (in a glass over the pilot light, or set in hot water)
1 pint dry red wine (Burgandy is traditional)
1 tablespoon minced fresh parsley
1 teaspoon marjoram
½ teaspoon thyme
1 very small bay leaf
½ teaspoon salt
Dash of black pepper
12 or more small whole peeled white onions, fresh or frozen
12 or more whole large fresh mushrooms (or 1 package frozen sliced mushrooms)
2 tablespoons butter

When the chicken is thawed enough to be pliable, put the pieces into a large skillet, skin-side up, and pour the warm brandy over them. Light the brandy. When the flames have consumed the brandy, cover the chicken with the wine and add all the seasonings. Bring to a boil quickly, lower the heat to moderate, add the onions, cover the skillet, and cook for 30 minutes. In a separate skillet sauté the mushrooms in the butter for 3 minutes, stirring. With tongs or a slotted spoon remove the onions and combine them with the mushrooms on a warm platter. Arrange the chicken on this and strain the sauce over all.

Variation: If you prefer a thickened sauce, this is the time to use an 8-ounce container of stockpiled rich brown gravy from your freezer. While the chicken is cooking, heat and stir the gravy to smoothness. Strain the wine sauce into the gravy, stir briskly over low heat, and pour it over the chicken and vegetables.

Freezing note: Do not refreeze if made with frozen fried chicken. To prepare the recipe for freezing, use fresh vegetables and see the discussion on page 249.

Chicken Singapore
4 servings

4 serving portions frozen fried chicken
½ cup orange juice
2 tablespoons soy sauce
1 teaspoon slivered ginger root (or ½ teaspoon ground ginger)
¼ teaspoon garlic salt
1 cup dry or semidry white wine
2 tablespoons cornstarch
1 small can water chestnuts, drained, sliced or chopped
12 or more pitted large ripe olives
12 or more blanched whole almonds

Arrange the chicken in a lightly oiled large skillet or fryer. Mix the orange juice with the soy sauce, ginger, garlic salt, and ¾ cup of the wine. Pour this mixture over the chicken.

Cover the skillet and cook over moderate heat for 20 minutes. With tongs, remove the chicken to a serving casserole. Stir the cornstarch into the remaining ¼ cup of wine and add it to the skillet along with the water chestnuts. Stir and simmer until thickened. Pour this sauce over the chicken, top with the olives stuffed with almonds, and heat in a 350° oven for 40 minutes.

Freezing note: Do not refreeze if made with frozen fried chicken.

Chicken and Rice with Frozen Vegetables
4 servings

½ cup frozen diced green peppers
½ cup frozen chopped onions
3 tablespoons olive oil
1 cup uncooked rice
4 serving portions frozen fried chicken
2 cups (1 pint container frozen) chicken broth or stock, heated
½ teaspoon salt (optional)
1 package frozen artichoke hearts
1 package frozen French fried eggplant sticks

In an ovenproof Dutch oven or chicken fryer, sauté the peppers and onions in hot oil on top of the range for 3 minutes. Stir in the rice. Add the chicken and broth or stock (and salt if desired) and bring to a boil over moderate heat. Lower the heat and simmer for 30 minutes. Preheat the oven to 350°. Slice the artichoke hearts and alternate with the eggplant sticks on top of the chicken. Bake, uncovered, for 45 minutes.

Freezing note: Do not freeze. This is strictly a from-the-freezer recipe which has some interesting variations:

Variations: Instead of eggplant sticks, use frozen Italian cut green beans or asparagus spears.

Instead of 2 cups of chicken broth, use 1 cup of broth and 1 cup of canned or frozen tomatoes.

To serve more people or make a fancier dish, add before baking up to 2 cups of frozen cooked shrimp and/or 1 cup or package of frozen sliced mushrooms. "Bury" the shrimp in the rice bed, to prevent hardening.

24.

Boneless Chicken Recipes

One advantage of boneless chicken recipes is that they can be frozen in casseroles of modest size. Another is that they can often be packed in freezer containers, saving a lot of shelf space. Also, they give the homemaker who has freezer foresight a way to spare herself several kitchen hours another day. Essentially the same amount of time and effort puts one meal on the table, another in the freezer.

FREEZER RECIPES USING BONELESS RAW CHICKEN

Borrowed or adapted from the native cuisine of many countries, including this one, are a number of freezer recipes which seem to be at their best when made with boneless raw rather than precooked chicken.

If the recipes you choose from this section require raw breast or leg-thigh fillets, these are most easily and economically obtained from purchases or freezer stockpiles of chicken parts. If frozen, the parts should be thawed in the refrigerator until the flesh is pliable enough to work with.

Use a sharp, slender knife to remove the flesh from the bones intact. Check carefully with your fingers to be sure that no splinters of bone remain, and make certain that the easily recognized soft cartilage and cordlike leg sinews are discarded.

Hong Kong Chicken Fillets
8 servings, total

This recipe requires overnight refrigeration before cooking.

5 tablespoons soy sauce
3 tablespoons peanut oil
1 teaspoon salt
½ teaspoon white pepper
1 large clove garlic, put through garlic press
¾ teaspoon ground ginger
8 small chicken breast fillets

Combine all the ingredients except the chicken and blend well. Rub the mixture over the fillets on both sides. Arrange them on a platter, cover with wax paper or plastic film, and refrigerate overnight or for 8 daytime hours. After refrigeration, continue as follows:

4 tablespoons peanut oil
2½ cups simmering chicken stock, broth, or consommé
3 tablespoons cornstarch
½ cup cold chicken stock, broth, or consommé
1 cup chopped or sliced mushrooms
½ cup chopped pimientos
¼ cup minced onions

Heat the oil in a chicken fryer until it sizzles, and add the cold chicken. Reduce the heat, cover, and cook for 15 minutes, turning the fillets once. Add the simmering liquid and cook for 5 minutes longer. Preheat the oven to 350°. With tongs, remove the chicken from the fryer and put 4 of the fillets into a lightly oiled freezer-to-oven casserole, the other 4 into individual ramekins. Put the ramekins into the oven while you prepare the sauce. Stir the cornstarch into the cold liquid and add this to the fryer. Stir, add the chopped vegetables, and simmer for 10 minutes.

Freezer portion: Pour half the sauce over the chicken in the casserole. Cover securely, chill thoroughly in the refrigerator, then freeze. Store up to 6 months.

Serving the unfrozen portion: Pour the remaining sauce over the chicken in the oven ramekins. Continue to heat for 20 to 25 minutes.

Serving the freezer portion: Put the casserole, covered, into a preheated 350° oven for about 1 hour, or until the sauce bubbles.

Chicken Fillets Parmigiana
8 servings, total

8 chicken fillets (breast, or leg-thigh combination)
3 whole eggs beaten with 3 tablespoons milk, ½ teaspoon salt, dash of pepper
About 1½ cups bread crumbs
2 teaspoons parsley flakes
¼ teaspoon oregano
¼ teaspoon basil
2 tablespoons grated Romano or Parmesan cheese
4 tablespoons olive oil
3 cups meatless Italian sauce, your own (see Index) or canned
8 slices mozzarella or Muenster cheese
Additional Romano or Parmesan cheese for topping

Flatten the fillets as much as possible and dip each one separately into the beaten egg-milk mixture, then into the bread crumbs mixed with the parsley flakes, oregano, basil, and grated cheese. Sauté the coated fillets in the hot oil, turning once, until lightly browned on both sides. Drain on paper towels.

Spread about 1 cup of the sauce over the bottoms of two shallow lightly oiled baking dishes, arrange 4 fillets in a single layer in each, cover both dishes with the remaining sauce, top with the sliced cheese, and sprinkle with grated cheese.

Freezer portion: Cover closely with foil, chill in the refrigerator, then freeze. Store up to 3 months.

Serving the unfrozen portion: Bake, uncovered, in a preheated 350° oven for 45 minutes.

Serving the freezer portion: Uncover a baking dish and heat in a preheated 350° oven for 1 to 1½ hours.

Chicken Breast Fillets Amandine
8 servings, total

8 chicken breast fillets
Salt, pepper, paprika
6 tablespoons butter
2 cups sliced mushrooms
3 tablespoons flour
1 cup milk, warm
1 cup chicken stock or consommé, warm
4 tablespoons sherry
Slivered almonds

Flatten the fillets and sprinkle them sparingly on both sides with salt, pepper, and paprika. Melt 3 tablespoons of the butter in a skillet and sauté the fillets until light golden brown on both sides, turning once. Arrange 4 fillets in each of 2 lightly buttered baking dishes. In the same skillet, sauté the sliced mushrooms for 2 minutes. Remove them with a slotted spoon, divide, and spread them over the chicken. Melt the remaining butter in the skillet, add the flour, stir to blend, and gradually stir in the warm milk and stock or consommé. Stir over low heat until smooth and thickened, stir in the sherry, and pour half the sauce over the fillets in each of the baking dishes. Top with slivered almonds.

Freezer portion: Cover closely with foil, chill in the refrigerator, then freeze. Store up to 3 months.

Serving the unfrozen portion: Heat in a 350° oven for 40 minutes. If desired, remove to the broiler section to brown the almonds.

Serving the freezer portion: Thaw for 1 hour at room temperature. Preheat the oven to 375°. Heat, covered, for 20 minutes. Uncover and heat for 40 to 45 minutes.

Chicken Voroshilov
8 servings, total

8 chicken breast fillets
Salt, pepper, paprika
6 tablespoons unsalted butter, melted
½ cup minced onions
1 cup slivered celery
1½ cups heavy sweet cream
½ cup tomato juice (from drained tomatoes below)
2 tablespoons chopped fresh chervil (if unobtainable, use fresh parsley)
2 cups drained canned whole tomatoes

Flatten the fillets and sprinkle them sparingly with salt, pepper, and paprika. Sauté them in the butter, turning often, until light golden brown. Remove them with kitchen tongs to 2 lightly buttered baking casseroles. In the same skillet sauté the onions and celery until the onions are limp. Add the cream and tomato juice, stir, and simmer over very low heat for 10 minutes. Do not let it boil. Add the chervil or parsley and stir. Divide and pour the sauce over the fillets. Top each with 1 cup of the drained tomatoes.

Freezer portion: Cover with foil, chill in the refrigerator, then freeze. Store up to 3 months.

Serving the unfrozen portion: Heat in a 350° oven for 45 minutes.

Serving the freezer portion: Preheat the oven to 375°. Heat, covered, for 20 minutes. Uncover and heat for 45 to 50 minutes.

Boneless Chicken Paprikash
8 servings, total

All the meat from two 3- to 3½-pound broilers
4 tablespoons chicken fat
1 clove garlic, halved
2 tablespoons butter
½ cup chopped onions
1 cup sliced or diced carrots
1 cup diced green peppers
½ teaspoon salt
3 or 4 tablespoons fresh Hungarian paprika
3 tablespoons flour
2 cups warm chicken stock or consommé
Sour cream

Cut the chicken meat into stew-size pieces. Heat the chicken fat in a large fryer and brown the garlic for 3 minutes, stirring it around. Discard the garlic. Brown the chicken slowly, turning frequently, then remove and keep warm. Add the butter to the fryer and sauté the onions, carrots, and peppers over low heat for 5 minutes. Stir in the salt and paprika and cook for 2 minutes. Stir in the flour, slowly add the warm stock or consommé, and stir over low heat. When thickened and bubbling, simmer for 10 minutes. Return the chicken and continue to simmer for 30 minutes.

Freezer portion: Remove half the recipe to a bowl to cool slightly, then pour into a freezer container. Chill in the refrigerator, then freeze. Store up to 3 months.

Serving the unfrozen portion: Continue to simmer the remaining half for 30 minutes. Add 1 cup of sour cream, stir, and heat through without boiling.

Serving the freezer portion: Set the container in cool to warm water until the contents can be released into the top of a double boiler over simmering water. When melted and hot, stir and simmer for 30 minutes. Add 1 cup of sour cream, stir, and heat through without boiling.

Russian Chicken Croquettes
12 to 16 croquettes, depending on size

All the meat from a 3- to 3½-pound chicken
8 slices white bread, crusts removed
About 1 cup milk
2 large eggs
½ teaspoon salt
4 tablespoons butter, softened with a fork
About 1 cup bread crumbs
Butter for frying

Put the chicken meat through a grinder twice, using the fine blade. Soak the crustless bread in the milk and squeeze until almost dry. Combine the ground chicken, bread, and 1 egg. Mix thoroughly, then force through a Foley mill or sieve. Add the salt and the softened butter and mix thoroughly again, using your hands. Shape the mixture into fairly thick oval cutlets, dip them into the remaining egg beaten with 1 tablespoon of cold water, and roll them in the bread crumbs.

Freezer portion: Refrigerate as many as you wish to freeze until thoroughly chilled. Place them in a single layer on wax paper in contact with a freezing surface. When solidly frozen, gather into freezer boxes. Store up to 6 months.

Serving the unfrozen portion: Fry a few at a time in a liberal amount of butter until well browned on all sides. Drain on paper towels and serve with or without a topping of chicken or mushroom gravy.

Serving the freezer portion: Thaw at room temperature for 1 hour, then fry as above.

RECIPES USING COOKED CHICKEN

Cooking Whole Chickens for Boneless Freezer Recipes
A 3-pound chicken will yield about 1 quart (4 cups) of cooked meat.

Fresh or frozen raw chickens may be used.

Put the chicken into a large pot on its back. For each pound of chicken add 1 cup of cold water. Add to the pot also 1 cabbage leaf, 1 quartered onion, a few celery stalks with leaves, 1 sliced or diced carrot, and 1 teaspoon salt. Bring to a boil over moderate heat, then lower to a simmer and cook:

Frozen whole chicken: 20 minutes per pound
Fresh or thawed whole chicken: 15 minutes per pound

Turn the chicken upside down when it has simmered for half the total time.

Remove the chicken to a cutting surface and, when cool enough to handle, remove the meat from the breasts, thighs, and drumsticks in large pieces and pick the remaining meat from the back and wings.

Break the carcass into small pieces, return them and the skin to the pot, add boiling water to cover if necessary, and simmer for 1 hour. Strain and reserve the broth for recipes, or for freezing as stock.

If you find yourself with more cooked chicken than the recipe you're using calls for, don't worry about it. You can be lavish and increase the recipe amount. Or, if there's far too much, separate the large pieces from the less attractive shreds and use the latter for croquettes, loaves, hash, and some Chinese and Mexican recipes, sandwich spreads, and soup garnishes. Freeze these "leftovers" packed in rigid containers and covered with broth. They may be stored up to 6 months. If frozen without liquid in foil or a freezer wrap, the recommended storage time is 1 month.

Chicken à La King
8 to 10 servings, total

½ cup diced green peppers
4 tablespoons melted chicken fat (half or all of this may be butter)

1½ cups sliced mushrooms (fresh, canned, or frozen)
4 tablespoons flour
3 cups seasoned chicken stock or consommé, warm (half of this
    may be cream)
2 egg yolks, beaten
4 cups diced chicken cooked according to the directions on page
    264
½ cup chopped pimiento
½ cup slivered celery
Sherry

In a large, heavy pot sauté the green peppers in the hot fat and/or butter for 3 minutes. Add the mushrooms and sauté them for 1 minute if fresh or canned, 2 minutes if frozen. Sprinkle with the flour, then stir to blend. Slowly add the warm liquid and stir until smooth. Stir a few tablespoons of the thickened liquid into the egg yolks and add to the mixture. Add and stir in the diced chicken, pimiento, and celery and cook over low heat for 5 minutes.

Freezer portion: Spoon the amount you wish to freeze into a container. Cool, chill in the refrigerator, then freeze. Store up to 3 months.

Serving the unfrozen portion: Simmer gently without boiling for 10 minutes, stirring occasionally. Stir in up to 1 tablespoon of sherry per serving. Serve on toast points or buttered split biscuits, or in pastry shells.

Serving the frozen portion: Set the container in cool to warm water until its contents can be released into the top of a double boiler over simmering water. When melted and hot, stir well and finish cooking as directed above.

Chicken or Turkey à La King
from the Freezer Stockpile
3 or 4 servings

8-ounce container frozen Heavy White Sauce (page 19)
8-ounce container frozen chicken stock (pages 12–14) or 1 cup
    canned consommé
2 cups frozen leftover cooked chicken or turkey

6-ounce package frozen sliced mushrooms or 6-ounce can of but-
    ton mushrooms
2 tablespoons butter
2 tablespoons chopped pimiento
2 tablespoons slivered celery
Yolk of 1 small egg, lightly beaten
2 tablespoons sherry

Release the sauce and stock together directly into the top
of a double boiler over simmering water. Break up lumps
with a fork as they melt. When the sauce is hot, stir briskly
with a fork or a wire whisk until smooth. Dice the leftover
poultry while it is still frosty and add to the sauce. Cook
without boiling for 15 to 20 minutes, or until the poultry is
hot. Sauté the mushrooms in the hot butter for 2 minutes
and add. Add the pimiento and celery. Add the egg yolk
and stir until thickened. Stir in the sherry. Taste and correct
seasonings if necessary. Do not refreeze.

Chicken Stroganoff
8 servings, total

Breast, thigh, and leg meat of a 3½- to 4-pound chicken cooked
    according to the directions on page 264
¼ cup minced onion
6 tablespoons butter
1 pound mushrooms, sliced
2 cups chicken or mushroom stock, or consommé
¼ teaspoon basil
¼ teaspoon ground nutmeg
Salt if needed
Sour cream (room temperature)

Slice the cooked chicken ¼ inch thick, then cut these
slices into strips about 1 inch by 2 inches. Divide into 2
equal parts and put one-half into a freezer container, reserving the rest. In a large, heavy pan or skillet, sauté the onion
in the butter for 2 minutes. Add the mushrooms and sauté

for 2 minutes longer. Add the stock or consommé and seasonings, stir, and simmer for 5 minutes.

Freezer portion: Pour half the sauce over the chicken in
the freezer container. Cool, chill in the refrigerator, then
freeze. Store up to 3 months.

Serving the unfrozen portion: Put the remaining chicken
strips into the sauce and simmer for 5 minutes. Add 1 cup of
sour cream, stir carefully with a wooden spoon, and heat
through without boiling.

Serving the freezer portion: Thaw at room temperature
until the contents of the container slip easily into the top of
a double boiler over simmering water. Heat until melted
and simmering. Stir carefully with a wooden spoon, then
simmer for 10 minutes. Add 1 cup of warm sour cream and
heat through without boiling.

Chicken Stroganoff from the Freezer Stockpile
4 servings

2 cups frozen leftover cooked chicken and/or turkey
8-ounce container frozen chicken stock
3 tablespoons butter
2 tablespoons minced onion
6-ounce package frozen sliced mushrooms
⅛ teaspoon basil
⅛ teaspoon ground nutmeg
Salt, if needed
1 cup warm sour cream

Cut the chicken while still frosty into thin slices or small
dice. Melt and heat the stock in the top of a double boiler
over simmering water. Heat the butter in a skillet and sauté
the onions for 2 minutes. Add and sauté the mushrooms for
3 minutes. Stir in the seasonings, add the heated stock, stir,
add the chicken, and heat for 10 minutes. Add the sour
cream, stir carefully with a wooden spoon, and heat through
without boiling. Do not refreeze.

Chicken Marengo
8 servings, total

4 cups diced chicken cooked according to the directions on page
    264
16 to 24 small white peeled onions
6 tablespoons butter
2 cloves garlic, put through garlic press
2 cups sliced mushrooms
4 tablespoons flour
2 cups cold chicken stock or consommé
½ teaspoon salt
Dash of pepper
Few grains cayenne
Sherry
2 firm ripe tomatoes for each of the 4-portion servings, peeled
    and diced

Divide the chicken between two lightly buttered casseroles. Simmer the onions in a small amount of lightly salted water for 10 minutes, drain, and reserve. Melt 3 tablespoons of the butter in a skillet and sauté the garlic for 2 minutes. Add the mushrooms and sauté for 2 minutes. Add the remaining butter to the skillet. Dissolve the flour in the cold stock or consommé and add to the skillet. Add the seasonings and stir over low heat until thickened. Add and stir the desired amount of sherry.

Freezer portion: Pour half the sauce over the chicken in one casserole and stir. Tuck half the onions into the mixture, cover and refrigerate the casserole, then slip it into a freezer bag and freeze. Store up to 3 months.

Serving the unfrozen portion: Pour the remaining sauce into the second casserole, stir, add the remaining onions and the tomatoes, and stir carefully with a wooden spoon. Heat in a 350° oven for 20 minutes.

Serving the freezer portion: Partially thaw in the refrigerator or at room temperature. Heat in a 375° oven until the mixture can be stirred. Reduce the heat to 350°, add 2 peeled, diced tomatoes, stir carefully with a wooden spoon, and heat through.

Chicken Marengo from the Freezer Stockpile
4 servings

2 cups or more frozen leftover cooked chicken and/or turkey
8-ounce container frozen chicken stock
5 tablespoons butter
8 to 12 frozen small white onions
1 package frozen sliced mushrooms
2 tablespoons flour
½ cup liquid from canned tomatoes
1 cup canned tomatoes, drained
Salt, pepper, cayenne to taste
2 tablespoons sherry

Dice the poultry while still frosty and put it into a lightly buttered casserole. While you melt and heat the stock in a saucepan, heat 3 tablespoons of the butter in a skillet and sauté the onions for 5 minutes, turning frequently. With a slotted spoon, remove the onions to the casserole. Sauté the mushrooms for 3 minutes. Dissolve the flour in the cold tomato liquid and add it to the skillet. Stir, then add the tomatoes and heated stock. Stir over low heat until thickened. Add the seasonings and sherry and pour the sauce into the casserole. Stir. Heat in a 350° oven until piping hot. Do not refreeze.

Chicken Piquant
8 servings, total

4 tablespoons olive oil
½ cup minced onions
Meat of a 4-pound chicken cooked according to the directions on page 264
Black pepper
2 tablespoons flour

1 cup dry white wine
2 tablespoons Italian tomato paste
2 cups chicken stock or consommé
¾ cup white or wine vinegar
4 to 6 flat anchovy fillets, minced
3 or 4 small sweet gherkins, minced
2 tablespoons capers, drained
1 clove garlic, minced or put through a garlic press
2 tablespoons minced parsley

Heat the oil in a large skillet or Dutch oven and sauté the onions for 2 minutes. Add the chicken meat, preferably in large pieces, sprinkle with pepper, and brown for 5 minutes over moderate heat, turning once. Sprinkle with the flour and add the wine. Continue to cook until the wine is almost evaporated. Stir the tomato paste into the stock or consommé and add it to the skillet. Stir and remove from the heat.

Put the vinegar into a small saucepan and cook over moderate heat, uncovered, until reduced to half its volume. Remove from the heat. Combine all the remaining ingredients and stir them into the vinegar. Combine the chicken with the sauce.

Freezer portion: Remove the amount you wish to freeze to a container, chill in the refrigerator, then freeze. Store up to 2 months.

Serving the unfrozen portion: Return the skillet to low heat, cover, and simmer for 20 minutes.

Serving the freezer portion: Set the container in cool to warm water until its contents can be released into the top of a double boiler over simmering water. When completely melted, stir carefully and simmer for 30 minutes.

Chicken Creole
8 servings, total

½ cup chopped onions
½ cup diced green peppers
3 tablespoons oil

3 tablespoons flour mixed with ½ teaspoon paprika
1½ cups canned tomatoes, or tomato purée (not paste)
1½ cups seasoned chicken stock, consommé, or bouillon
1 teaspoon lemon juice
¾ pound mushrooms, sliced
3 tablespoons butter
4 cups diced chicken cooked according to the directions on page
    271
½ cup chopped pimiento

In a Dutch oven or heavy pot, sauté the onions and peppers together in the hot oil until the onions are limp. Sprinkle with the flour mixture and stir until well blended. Add the tomatoes or purée and chicken stock or other liquid, stir, and bring to a boil over moderate heat. Stir in the lemon juice and remove from the heat.

In a separate skillet, sauté the mushrooms in the butter for 2 minutes and add them to the sauce. Add the chicken and pimientos and stir to distribute evenly.

Freezer portion: Spoon the amount you wish to freeze into a container, chill in the refrigerator, then freeze. Store up to 3 months.

Serving the unfrozen portion: Return the pot to low heat and simmer, covered, for 10 minutes.

Serving the freezer portion: Set the container in cool to warm water until its contents can be released into a heavy saucepan over low heat. Heat, covered, until the mixture can be stirred. Continue to cook over low heat for 20 minutes.

Chicken Divan
8 servings, total

4 whole fresh or frozen chicken breasts
3 cups cold water
1 cabbage leaf
1 quartered onion
1 diced carrot
1 teaspoon salt

1 large bunch broccoli
6 tablespoons butter
¼ cup flour
2 cups strained broth in which chicken was cooked
½ cup heavy cream
¼ cup sherry
About ¼ cup grated Romano or Parmesan cheese

Put the chicken breasts, skin down, into a heavy pot. Add the water, cabbage leaf, onion, carrot, and salt. Bring to a boil over moderate heat, lower to a simmer, and cook fresh or thawed breasts for 45 minutes, frozen ones for 1 hour. Turn them upside down when they have simmered for half the total time. Remove the chicken to a cutting surface and, when cool enough to handle, slice skinless meat from the bones. Add the skin and bones to the pot and simmer for 20 minutes.

While the chicken is cooking, clean the broccoli, cut it lengthwise into uniform pieces with flowerets about 1½ inches across, and remove 1 inch of the stalk bottoms. Drop the broccoli into a quart of boiling water with 1 teaspoon of salt added. When the water returns to a boil, cook for 4 minutes. With tongs remove half the broccoli, and plunge it into very cold water. Continue cooking the rest of the broccoli until the stalks are tender (about 10 minutes). Drain the chilled broccoli and arrange it over the bottom of one lightly buttered shallow baking dish. Drain and arrange the hot broccoli in a second lightly buttered baking dish.

Melt the butter in a saucepan, blend in the flour, add the 2 cups of strained chicken broth, and stir over low heat until thickened. Remove from the heat and stir in the cream and sherry.

Use about half the sauce to cover the broccoli. Arrange the chicken slices over the broccoli. Top with the remaining sauce and sprinkle equally with the cheese.

Freezer portion: Cover the chilled-broccoli baking dish

with foil and chill in the refrigerator. Slip the covered dish into a plastic bag and freeze. Store up to 3 months.

Serving the unfrozen portion: Preheat the oven to 350°. Bake for 20 to 25 minutes, then remove to the broiler section to brown the topping.

Serving the freezer portion: Partially thaw the covered casserole in the refrigerator for 4 hours or at room temperature for 1 hour. Preheat the oven to 375°. Heat, still covered, for 45 minutes. Uncover and brown the topping under the broiler.

December Divan
4 servings

This is a good way—and a good time—to use the frozen slices of Thanksgiving turkey breast you wrapped in foil or film late in November. If sliced poultry is frozen without being covered with sauce or broth, it should be used within 1 month.

Remove from your freezer stockpile the equivalent of 4 large slices of frozen cooked turkey breast and a 1-pint container of frozen chicken gravy. No frozen chicken gravy? Combine in the top of a double boiler over simmering water one 8-ounce container of frozen Heavy White Sauce (page 19) and one 8-ounce container of frozen chicken stock. Break up lumps with a fork as you can. When melted, stir briskly with a fork or wire whisk. Or use 2 cups of canned chicken gravy, or a packaged chicken gravy mix.

Continue to heat the sauce while you cook 2 packages of frozen broccoli spears according to the package directions. Drain the broccoli and arrange it in a lightly buttered baking dish, cover with half the hot sauce, top with the turkey slices, pour the remaining sauce over all, and sprinkle with grated Romano or Parmesan cheese. Heat in a 375° oven until the turkey is hot. Brown under the broiler unit.

Chicken or Turkey Pot Pie
See "Meat or Poultry Pies" (page 392–393).

ROASTING POULTRY FOR FREEZER STORAGE

When it becomes necessary or desirable to roast poultry for brief freezer storage (up to 1 month), the following procedures are recommended:

Before freezing. Use fresh or fully thawed poultry at room temperature. Do not stuff. Stuffing can, however, be prepared in advance and frozen separately in foil or a freezer bag. *Reduce the usual oven time by 10 minutes per pound.* This will help to prevent overcooking and dryness when the roasting is finished after freezer storage. At the end of the reduced oven time, remove the poultry from the oven, cool slightly, and chill in the refrigerator.

Freezing. Wrap securely in heavy freezer paper or foil,* label, date, slip the package into a freezer bag, and place in contact with a freezing surface.

Freezer to table. Thaw the still-wrapped poultry in the refrigerator, allowing 6 hours per pound. To hasten thawing, the wrapped package may stand at room temperature for 2 or 3 hours after refrigeration for 3 hours per pound. Thaw the stuffing in the refrigerator until it can be molded. Unwrap and stuff the bird. Finish the roasting in a preheated 350° oven, basting occasionally with melted butter or chicken fat. Use a meat thermometer instead of relying on clock timing. Remove for carving when the internal temperature reading is 190°.

---

* *Foil-wrapped poultry:* Thaw both the poultry and the stuffing as above. Open the foil carefully and stuff the cavity. Rewrap in the foil and insert a meat thermometer through it. Roast at 350° until the thermometer reads 170°. Open the foil to brown, and continue to roast until the thermometer reads 190°.

Roast Duck, Duckling, or Turkey for the Freezer
See "Roasting Poultry for Freezer Storage" (page 274).

Turkey Recipes
See recipes for Boneless Cooked Chicken (pages 267–269). Substitute for the chicken similar amounts of leftover roast turkey.

25.

The Name of the Game

While it is certainly possible to precook properly processed * game for freezer storage soon after the quarry is brought home in triumph, the usual practice of hunting families is to freeze most of their bag in their own large home freezers or in nearby frozen food lockers, removing the desired cuts or birds a day or so before the meal at which they plan to serve them.

Therefore, although fresh game may be used for the recipes in this book, directions are essentially for frozen game which is to be served when cooked. When time limitations or an impending company dinner make it desirable to pre-

---

* In most rural and suburban communities, there are frozen-food facilities which will process small and large game to store in your freezer or theirs at moderate cost. It is required that the game brought for processing be drawn and cleaned in the field—the hunter's responsibility.

Instructions for field care are given in a government publication, obtainable without charge by writing to the Department of Agriculture, Forest Service, Washington, D.C. Readers may also find directions for field care and home handling of game birds and small and large game, along with a chart of state game laws as they relate to freezing, by referring to Chapter 14 in any edition of *The Complete Book of Home Freezing*.

cook an elaborate recipe in whole or in part, the frozen game may be thawed or partially thawed for preparation, cooked, then frozen for a limited time. Leftover game, whether meat or poultry, may be frozen as freely as any other meat or poultry and stored in the freezer for use within a few weeks.

Game recipes using cooked frozen leftovers should not be refrozen. They won't make you ill, but the flavor and texture will have deteriorated.

WILD DUCK

To the seasoned hunter and connoisseur of game cuisine, the pungent flavor of wild duck is delicious, especially if the bird is served bloody-rare. Even the occasional fishiness of some ducks' flesh, caused by dietary habits, is admired by these stalwarts. People with more delicate palates, willingly admitting that they are in another league, do not pretend to savor the tang of wildlife in the raw—or almost raw. For the sensitive, some of the excessively strong flavors can be tempered during and after freezer storage:

Before freezing: Peel and slice a large firm apple, mix it with a generous amount of coarsely chopped fresh parsley, and stuff the cavity. Put a piece of freezer film or foil over the opening, then wrap the duck securely in heavy freezer paper. When the bird comes out of the freezer and is thawed for cooking, remove and discard this stuffing. It will have absorbed much but not all of the wild flavor.

After freezing and thawing: If the duck is to be roasted whole without additional stuffing, insert in the cavity a whole closely peeled orange or lemon, or a handful of mixed chopped carrot, parsley, celery, and onion. If it is cut into parts for stews, casseroles, or similar recipes, marinate the pieces for 1 hour or more in dry wine or orange juice.

RECIPES USING WILD DUCK

Casserole of Wild Duck
4 to 6 servings

2 large or 4 small frozen ducks
1 clove garlic, minced or put through garlic press
¼ cup olive oil, heated
Salt and pepper
1½ cups boiling water
2 cups thinly sliced raw white potatoes
2 packages frozen peas
2 onions, chopped (or ⅔ cup chopped frozen onions)
1 cup diced fresh or frozen carrots
3 or 4 slices bacon

Thaw the ducks and cut them into serving pieces. Preheat the oven to 325°. Sauté the garlic in the hot olive oil for 2 minutes. Add the duck and brown quickly on both sides. Sprinkle with salt and pepper. Pour the boiling water into a deep casserole and arrange the pieces of duck in the center, skin side up. Mix all the vegetables together and distribute them evenly around the duck. Lay strips of bacon across the top. Bake uncovered:

Small ducks, rare: 20 to 25 minutes; well done, 30 to 40 minutes
Large ducks, rare: 25 to 30 minutes; well done, 45 to 60 minutes

or insert a meat thermometer into the fleshiest part of one piece and roast until the reading is 140° (rare) or 180° (well done).

Wild Duck Stew
4 to 6 servings

2 large or 4 small frozen ducks, thawed or partially thawed
About 4 tablespoons flour
½ cup butter
2 cups boiling stock, consommé, or bouillon

½ cup chopped parsley
2 cups small peeled onions
1 cup diced potatoes or raw potato balls
1 cup diced carrots
1 small bay leaf
Pinch of sage
½ teaspoon salt (unless the liquid was seasoned)
3 or 4 peppercorns
3 or 4 pellets allspice
¼ cup dry white wine

Disjoint the duck and dredge the pieces in the flour until well coated. Cook them in the butter until nicely brown all over. Add the boiling liquid and all the other ingredients, lower the heat, cover the pot, and simmer until tender (30 to 40 minutes for thawed ducks, 40 to 50 for partially thawed ducks).

Serve immediately, or cool, chill in the refrigerator, then freeze in large containers and store up to 1 month. To serve after freezer storage, release the contents into a heavy pot over low heat and bring to a serving temperature.

Baked Stuffed Breasts of Wild Duck
4 servings

2 large frozen wild ducks, partially thawed
1 tablespoon minced onion
1 clove garlic, minced or put through garlic press
4 to 6 mushrooms with stems, minced
2 tablespoons rendered chicken fat
½ pound fresh chicken livers
4 shallots
½ teaspoon thyme or sage
½ teaspoon salt
¼ teaspoon ground black pepper
4 eggs, lightly beaten
1 tablespoon flour
½ cup dry wine (or ¼ cup brandy)
About ½ cup stock, consommé, or bouillon
Bacon slices

Split the ducks down the back, remove the skins, and carefully cut the meat away from the bones. Keep each half of the breasts in one filleted piece, and separate them from the rest of the meat.

Sauté the onion, garlic, and mushrooms in the chicken fat for 2 minutes, then add the chicken livers and sauté them for 1 minute on each side. Using the fine blade of your meat grinder, grind all but the breast meat along with the sautéed livers and the shallots. Mix well with your hands to distribute these ingredients evenly. Add the seasonings, eggs, flour, and wine or brandy. If the mixture appears dry, add enough stock, consommé, or bouillon to moisten it to the consistency of breadless turkey stuffing.

Very generously butter a shallow baking dish and spread over the bottom about half the stuffing mixture. Lay the breast fillets over this, cover them with the remaining stuffing, and top with the bacon slices.

For immediate serving: Preheat the oven to 300°. Bake, uncovered, for 2 hours.

For freezing: Preheat the oven to 300°. Bake, uncovered, for 1 hour. Remove the bacon. When cool, chill in the refrigerator, then wrap and freeze. Store up to 3 months.

To serve after freezer storage: Place the covered casserole in a preheated 350° oven and bake for ½ hour. Remove the cover, top with 6 strips of bacon, reduce the oven temperature to 300°, and continue baking for 40 minutes.

Braised Stuffed Wild Ducks

4 servings

4 small to medium frozen ducks, almost thawed
4 cups any stuffing (pages 412–414) except one using sea food
16 small white fresh or frozen onions, peeled
1 cup fresh or frozen diced or thinly sliced carrots
2 stalks celery, slivered
1 cup thinly sliced fresh or frozen mushrooms

Pinch each of ground cloves, thyme, and marjoram
1 tablespoon minced fresh parsley
2 cups boiling game or chicken stock, or consommé
½ cup sherry or orange juice

When the ducks are sufficiently thawed to open the cavities, stuff them loosely, sew or skewer the openings, and set aside. Arrange all the vegetables in the bottom of a large roasting pan or baking dish and add the seasonings, parsley, and boiling liquid. Put the stuffed ducks closely together on the vegetables, breasts up, and spoon the sherry or orange juice over them. Cover the pan tightly and cook by one of the following methods:

1. Preheat the oven to 400°. Bake for 40 minutes without raising the cover.

2. Preheat the oven to 325°. Bake for 50 minutes, remove the cover, add more liquid if necessary, and continue baking for 30 minutes.

Do not freeze.

Roast Wild Duck (Rare)
1 small to medium duck per serving

Thaw the ducks completely in the refrigerator overnight, then let them stand at room temperature for at least 1 hour. To remove some of the strong flavor, if desired, rub the cavities with a cut orange or lemon and insert in each 1 tablespoonful of coarsely cut celery, onion, or apple. You may rub the skins with gin, brandy, or orange juice. Place the ducks on a rack balanced on a shallow baking dish and wait until the oven is preheated to 475° before putting them in. Have ready a generous amount of melted butter or a mixture of half butter, half white wine. As soon as the ducks are in the hot oven, start basting them and continue to do so throughout the cooking time:

Small ducks: 15 to 20 minutes total
Larger ducks: 20 to 30 minutes total

This is traditionally served with cooked wild rice, over which some of the pan drippings are spooned.

Do not freeze, as reheating will negate the rareness.

Roast Wild Duck (Medium to Well Done)
1 small duck per serving, or 1 large duck for 2 servings

See the preceding recipe for instructions on thawing. To remove some of the strong flavor, if desired, stuff each cavity with a whole peeled orange or lemon, or a cupful of chopped peeled apples, or a cupful of coarsely chopped celery mixed with a tablespoon of parsley.

Put the ducks into a roasting pan, breasts up. Brush them generously with melted butter, or lay strips of bacon across them. Put them into a preheated 325° oven, baste frequently with pan drippings (adding more butter or some dry wine to supplement the liquid, if it is meager), and roast for the following times:

Small ducks: 30 to 45 minutes
Large ducks: 35 to 60 minutes (the larger the longer)

Remove whatever stuffing you put in before serving or freezing.

To freeze: Reduce the cooking time for small ducks by 10 minutes, large ones by 15 minutes. Cool after cooking, chill in the refrigerator, wrap in aluminum foil, and freeze. Store up to 3 months.

To serve after freezer storage: Preheat the oven to 425° and put the foil-wrapped ducks in for 10 minutes. Reduce the heat to 350°. Peel the foil away from the breasts and baste frequently with melted butter or butter mixed with dry wine. Continue to cook for 20 to 30 minutes longer.

Wine-Marinated Roast Wild Ducks
4 servings

The traditional recipe calls for a marinade of port wine, but the wild flavor is retained and intensified if Marsala is substituted.

4 small frozen ducks, thawed or partially thawed
2 tablespoons lemon juice
1 teaspoon salt
¼ teaspoon freshly ground black pepper
1 bottle (fifth) of port or Marsala wine
½ cup fresh or frozen diced carrots
¼ cup fresh or frozen chopped onions
3 or 4 whole cloves
1 small bay leaf

Sauce

1 teaspoon minced shallots or leek
Pinch of thyme
Pinch of cayenne
1 cup orange juice
1 teaspoon grated fresh orange rind (or ½ teaspoon dried peel)
1 level tablespoon flour
2 tablespoons cold water
1 cup boiling poultry stock or consommé
Salt to taste if necessary

Rub the ducks inside and out with the lemon juice combined with the salt and pepper and put them into a deep crock or enameled pot. Add the wine, vegetables, cloves, and bay leaf. Put the vessel into the refrigerator (if you have space) or in a cool place for 24 hours. Turn or baste the ducks occasionally. Remove and drain them in a colander. Preheat the oven to 450° before you start the sauce:

Strain the marinade and measure 1½ cupfuls into a saucepan. Add the shallots or leek, spices, orange juice, and rind and bring to a boil. Cook over moderate heat until the sauce evaporates to half its volume. Strain into a clean saucepan. Add the flour to the cold water, stir, and add to the boiling stock or consommé. Stir until slightly thickened and combine with the hot marinade. Bring to a boil, skim if necessary, add salt if needed, reduce the heat, and simmer for 5 minutes. Remove from the heat but keep warm.

Put the drained ducks into a roasting pan and roast for a total of 15 minutes for small ducks, up to 25 minutes for larger ones. Strain the sauce again and serve it in a gravy boat. Serve the ducks on a heated platter.

Potted Stuffed Whole Wild Ducks
4 servings

4 small frozen wild ducks, thawed
2 large onions, sliced
1 cup melted butter
Frozen giblets from 4 small ducks (or ½ pound chicken livers, fresh or frozen)
3 cups cooked white, brown, or wild rice
⅔ teaspoon salt
½ teaspoon thyme
¼ teaspoon rosemary or marjoram
1 very small bay leaf, stem removed, crushed
½ cup unsalted chopped nutmeats (walnuts, pecans)
½ cup sherry or Marsala (or ¼ cup brandy)
4 tablespoons light oil
2 long strips of bacon, cut in half
1 or 2 oranges, thinly sliced with rinds intact
1 cup dry red wine
8-ounce container frozen brown sauce (or 1 cup Brown Sauce, page 24)

When the ducks are room temperature, wipe them dry. Sauté the onion in ½ cup of the melted butter until limp, add the giblets or chicken livers, and sauté for 3 minutes, turning often. Put the giblets and onions through the fine blade of a meat chopper, or chop them by hand. Mix with the cooked rice, seasonings, nutmeats, wine or brandy, and any remaining butter in the sauté pan. Blend thoroughly and stuff the ducks loosely. Sew or skewer the openings. Preheat the oven to 300°.

Combine the oil with the remaining ½ cup of melted butter in a large heavy fryer or Dutch oven and, when very hot but not smoking, brown the ducks on all sides, taking care not to scorch the skin. Arrange them, breasts up, on a rack set in a roasting pan that has a cover and top with alternating slices of the bacon and orange, secured with toothpicks. Pour the red wine over the ducks and cover the roaster tightly. Cook in the oven for 1¼ hours, adding more red wine if necessary. Remove the ducks to a heated platter. Add 1 cupful of pan liquids (remove with a bulb baster) to the brown sauce and stir over low heat until well mixed. Serve in a gravy boat.

VENISON

Happily for venison enthusiasts and the devoted companions who cook for them, modern deerstalkers can pursue and capture their quarry without so much as loading a rifle, or even owning one. The resurgent popularity of this time-honored meat has led many neighborhood or driving-distance food suppliers to stock various cuts of the choice game animals which have been expertly eviscerated, skinned, hung, cut, packaged, and frozen.

The frozen venison you buy from market or locker is hopefully the flesh of young-as-legal deer or elk, and chops and steaks can be treated almost as if they were their counterparts of choice young beef. Because the meat is exceptionally lean, however, a generous amount of butter—alone, or mixed with an equal amount of bland oil—should be used in cooking.

Whether they are frozen purchases or processed from the

kill of a family or friendly sportsman, most roasting racks or saddles are traditionally tenderized and their flavors enhanced by being marinated for a day or longer. A frozen roast should be completely thawed before cooking; therefore it is best to start the marinating process as soon as the meat comes out of the freezer and is removed from its wrapping.

A marinade (recipes on pages 293–294) is also suggested for steaks, chops, and even braising or stew meat contributed by game animals of uncertain age.

RECIPES USING VENISON

Frozen Venison Steaks and Chops

If you are sure these were cut from properly processed young animals, thaw completely in the refrigerator, let stand at room temperature until the chill has gone, and broil or pan-fry as you would any other steak or chop. Use a lot of butter, sprinkle with minced fresh parsley, and pour the pan drippings over them when served.

Frozen venison steaks and chops from mature animals may be thawed in marinade (pages 293–294), drained, wiped dry, and cooked as above.

Venison Swiss Steak

4 servings

4 individual frozen venison steaks from round or rump (or equivalent serving for 4)
About ½ cup flour seasoned with 1 teaspoon salt and ¼ teaspoon pepper
¼ cup butter
2 large onions, sliced (or ⅔ cup frozen chopped onions)
1 large green pepper, diced (or ½ cup frozen diced green peppers)
2 stalks celery, diagonally sliced
1½ cups canned tomatoes
2 tablespoons Worcestershire sauce

Thaw the steaks completely in the refrigerator. Pound the seasoned flour into both sides with a wooden mallet or the edge of a heavy plate and brown in the hot butter, turning once, in a large, heavy skillet or Dutch oven. Add all the remaining ingredients, cover the pot tightly, and cook over low heat until tender (from 1 to 1½ hours). Or bake in a covered casserole in a preheated 275° oven from 2 to 2½ hours, until tender.

This recipe may be frozen, if desired, for not more than 3 weeks. Reduce the cooking or baking time by ½ hour, arrange in a freezer-to-oven casserole (or cook it in one), cool and chill, then slip the casserole into a large freezer bag and place in contact with a freezing surface.

To serve after freezer storage: Bake in a preheated 350° oven 1 hour or more, until piping hot.

Baked Sweet and Sour Venison
6 to 8 servings

4 or 5 pounds frozen boneless venison, partially thawed
2 cups wine vinegar
2 cups water
1 tablespoon sugar
1 cup diced fresh or frozen carrots
4 small onions, halved
2 gloves garlic, halved
1 teaspoon salt
3 or 4 whole cloves
6 peppercorns
2 or 3 sprigs fresh parsley
Flour for dredging
4 tablespoons oil
½ cup sherry

While the venison is still frosty, cut it into 2-inch cubes. Combine the vinegar, water, and sugar in a saucepan and bring it to a boil, stirring to dissolve the sugar. Pour this liquid into a large crock or a ceramic or enamel vessel with a tight-fitting cover and add the vegetables and seasonings. When the mixture is cool, add the cubed venison and allow it to marinate for 24 hours in the refrigerator, or in a very cool place. Remove the meat with a slotted spoon and drain between paper towels. Preheat the oven to 350°. Dredge the cubes thoroughly with flour until well coated and brown them on all sides in the hot oil. Transfer the seared meat to a buttered baking dish and add all the vegetables in the marinade except the garlic, along with about 1 cupful of the strained marinade. Bake for about 1 hour until the meat is tender, adding more of the marinade if necessary. When the cubes are tender, add the sherry and simmer in the oven for 10 minutes longer.

This recipe may be frozen for 3 or 4 weeks. Shorten the cooking time by 20 minutes and omit the sherry. When the cubes are cool, put them into large plastic containers with the pan liquid and vegetables, using additional strained marinade to cover. Chill and freeze. *To serve:* Release the contents into a saucepan over low heat. When bubbling, add the sherry and simmer for 10 minutes.

Pot Roast of Venison
6 to 8 servings

5- or 6-pound block of frozen boneless venison (round, chuck, rump)
1 quart marinade (page 293)
Flour for dredging
4 tablespoons oil

Put the venison, unwrapped but frozen, into an enamel, ceramic, or earthenware vessel and cover with the marinade. Let it remain in the marinade in the refrigerator or in a cool place from 2 to 10 days, depending on the maturity of the meat. If you're not sure, the longer time is advisable. Turn the meat every 24 hours.

Strain the marinade, drain and dry the meat, and dredge

it evenly with flour. Brown the meat on all sides in a Dutch oven or heavy pot in the hot oil. In a separate saucepan, bring the strained marinade to a boil and pour it over the seared meat. There should be about 1 inch of liquid in the pan. Cover and simmer over low heat until tender (from 1 to 3 hours, again depending on maturity). Add more hot marinade if necessary.

Two or more cupfuls of vegetables—carrots, potatoes, turnips, green peppers, small peeled onions, etc.—may be added for the last 30 minutes of cooking, or they may be parboiled separately and added for the last 10 minutes.

If a thickened gravy is desired, remove and cool a cupful of pot liquor, then stir in 2 or 3 tablespoons of flour and add to the pot. Stir and simmer until smooth and thickened. If you want a wine flavor, mix a cupful of dry red wine (instead of cool pot liquor) with the flour and add this to the simmering roast.

Leftovers may be frozen when chilled and warmed over low heat for serving within 3 or 4 weeks.

Spicy Venison Stew in Wine Marinade
8 servings

4 or 5 pounds frozen boneless venison, partially thawed
½ cup wine vinegar
½ cup water
2 carrots, coarsely chopped
1 large onion, sliced
2 stalks celery, coarsely cut
3 or 4 sprigs parsley
2 cloves garlic, put through garlic press
½ to 1 teaspoon each of several or all of the following, tied in cheesecloth: whole sage, whole thyme, marjoram, rosemary, allspice, cloves, peppercorns
2 cups dry red wine

About 1 cup flour seasoned with 1 teaspoon salt
½ cup oil

2 cups boiling unseasoned stock, or bouillon (omit salt above if
    bouillon is used)
1 pound small white onions, peeled
1 pound small mushrooms
6 tablespoons melted butter

While the venison is still frosty, cut it into 2-inch cubes.
Combine in a small saucepan the vinegar, water, carrots,
onion, celery, parsley, garlic, and spice bag. Bring to a boil,
lower the heat, and simmer for 2 minutes. Remove from direct heat but keep hot. Put the venison cubes into an enamel, ceramic, or earthenware vessel and pour the hot spice
mixture over it. Add the wine. The meat should be covered
with liquid. If it is not, add more wine. Put the vessel into
the refrigerator or into a cool place and let stand overnight
if the venison was young, from 2 to 6 days if mature. At the
end of the marinating time, remove and drain the meat and
discard the spice bag.

Dredge the cubes in the seasoned flour and brown them
in the hot oil in a large, heavy pot. Heat the marinade, including its vegetables. When the cubes are well browned,
pour the hot marinade over them, adding enough boiling
stock to cover them completely. Reduce the heat to a simmer and cook from 1 to 3 hours, until tender. Cook the
peeled white onions in a little salted water for 10 minutes,
then drain. Sauté the onions and mushrooms in the butter
for 2 minutes while stirring, then add them to the stew
along with the pan butter.

The stew is ready to serve when completed, but small
whole boiled potatoes or potato balls may be added to extend it.

Freezing note: This stew improves with age, and can be
frozen successfully for 4 months. Omit the potatoes until
serving time. Spoon the stew and gravy into containers,
chill, then freeze. To serve, release the contents into a heavy
pot and heat slowly. Add parboiled small whole potatoes or
potato balls for the last 20 minutes of cooking.

Venisonburgers
8 servings

2- or 3-pound piece frozen venison from mature animal, partially
    thawed
1 tablespoon minced onions
1 clove garlic, put through garlic press (optional)
1 teaspoon salt
¼ teaspoon pepper
½ teaspoon dry mustard
Dash of tabasco or Worcestershire sauce, or both
¼ cup oil and melted butter, half and half

While still a little frosty, put the venison through the fine
blade of your grinder. Combine it with all the other ingredients except the oil and butter and form into 8 flattened patties. Sauté on both sides in the hot oil and butter to your
taste—rare, medium, or well done.

Venison Chili with Beans
10 to 12 servings

2- or 3-pound piece frozen venison from mature animal, partially
    thawed
1½ cups chopped fresh or frozen onions
2 large cloves garlic, minced or put through garlic press
½ cup salad oil
2 dry chili pepper pods (or 2 or 3 tablespoons chili powder)
½ teaspoon cumin seed
½ teaspoon ground coriander
3 cups canned tomatoes
1 cup beef stock, or beer
1 teaspoon salt
1 large can red kidney beans in sauce (or 1 pound dry kidney
    beans cooked according to package directions)
Shredded lettuce
Chopped onions

While still a little frosty, put the venison through the fine
blade of your grinder. Sauté the onions and garlic in the oil
for 3 minutes in a large, heavy pot. Add the ground venison

and crumble it with a fork as it browns, turning frequently. Add all but the last three ingredients and simmer over low heat for 1 hour, stirring occasionally. Add the kidney beans and their sauce, stir, and simmer until piping hot. Serve in bowls and top with a garnish of shredded lettuce and finely chopped fresh onions.

This is another recipe which improves with age, and which may be frozen successfully for storage up to 4 months. Pour into containers, chill in the refrigerator, then freeze. *To serve:* Release the contents into a heavy pot and heat slowly.

ROAST LOIN, LEG, OR SADDLE OF VENISON

Allow approximately 1 pound per serving.

Choose one of the marinades on pages 293 and 294 and pour it over the venison as soon as it is taken from the freezer, unwrapped, and placed in an enamel roasting pan. Thaw in the marinade at room temperature, turning the roast occasionally. A 6-pounder will take a long day to thaw completely.

After the meat is thawed, roast it at once or refrigerate it in the marinade, turning occasionally, from a day to a week. Generally, it is better to keep a roast in the marinade for a few days unless you are quite certain that it came from a young animal. Loins require less marinating time than legs or saddles.

RECIPES FOR ROAST VENISON

Roast Loin of Venison

Remove the meat from the marinade and wipe dry. Preheat the oven to 450°. With a sharp, pointed knife, cut gashes about an inch apart in the meat and force small pieces of thick bacon into the slits. You may rub the bacon first with a cut garlic clove. Place the larded roast in a pan and butter it thickly. Roast at 450° for 20 minutes, reduce the oven heat to 325°, and continue to roast, basting often with pan drippings and about a cupful of the marinade. Allow 15 minutes per pound at 325°, or roast until a meat thermometer registers 120°.

See Gravies for Venison Roasts (page 294).

Roast Leg of Venison

Remove the meat from the marinade and wipe dry. Preheat the oven to 400°. Lard as for Roast Loin in the preceding recipe. Put the leg into a buttered or oiled baking pan and roast for 10 to 15 minutes per pound. See Gravies for Venison Roasts (page 294).

Roast Saddle of Venison

A saddle may be roasted by either of the 2 preceding methods.

MARINADES FOR VENISON
(STEAKS, CHOPS, ROASTS)

Uncooked Marinade

1 cup wine vinegar
1 pint dry red wine
1 large onion, sliced
1 large carrot, sliced
1 teaspoon salt
6 to 8 peppercorns, crushed
1 small bay leaf
1 teaspoon juniper berries (optional)
3 or 4 sprigs fresh parsley
¼ teaspoon thyme or sage
½ cup fine olive oil (optional)

Combine all the ingredients (except the olive oil) and pour over the meat. Add the olive oil if desired. It will rise to the top, helping to seal in the flavors of the marinade and prevent discoloration of the meat.

Cooked Marinade

3 carrots, diced
3 onions, minced
3 stalks of celery with leaves, chopped
4 tablespoons oil
1 quart wine vinegar
1 quart dry red wine
1 teaspoon chopped parsley
1 bay leaf, shredded
½ teaspoon crushed peppercorns
1 teaspoon whole allspice
1 teaspoon salt

Sauté the carrots, onions, and celery in the oil for 3 minutes. Combine all the remaining ingredients in a large saucepan, add the sautéed vegetables, and bring to a boil. Lower the heat and simmer for 30 minutes. Remove from the heat and let cool to room temperature before using with any cut of venison.

GRAVIES FOR VENISON ROASTS

(Using Marinade as an Ingredient)

Gravy for Roast Venison I
About 2 cups

Pan drippings from roast with enough added stock or consommé
     to yield 1½ cups
1½ cups strained marinade
3 tablespoons butter
3 tablespoons flour
1 tablespoon lemon juice
1 teaspoon grated lemon or orange peel

Combine the drippings and liquid with the marinade and bring to a boil in a measure-marked saucepan. Lower the heat and simmer until reduced to 2 cups. Melt the butter in the top of a double boiler over simmering water. Blend in the flour, add the simmering liquid, stir, add the lemon juice and peel, and stir until thickened.

Gravy for Roast Venison II
About 2 cups

Pan drippings from roast with enough added stock or consommé
    to yield 1 cup
1 cup strained marinade
2 tablespoons butter
2 tablespoons flour
1 cup sour cream
1 teaspoon paprika

Combine the drippings and liquid with the marinade, bring to a boil, lower the heat, and simmer until reduced to half its volume. Melt the butter in the top of a double boiler over simmering water, blend in the flour, add the simmering liquid, and stir until smooth and thickened. Combine the sour cream with the paprika and stir it into the sauce but do not let it boil. Taste for seasonings.

26.

The Freezer's Role
in Meat Cookery

It is unlikely, I hope, that you will decide some late afternoon to serve for dinner that prime large roast which is still in the freezer. Except for some specific recipes given in this section, frozen meat cooks most satisfactorily when it is thawed completely before preparations start, and the best way to thaw it is in its freezer wrap on a refrigerator shelf. Second best is to thaw it in its wrap at room temperature.

But what can be done when, inevitably, five o'clock comes and the meat for tonight's dinner is still in the freezer, darn it, and your planned menu permits no last-minute change?

Emergencies call for desperate action. Some make-do alternatives are offered here for the one occasion when you forget to allow sufficient thawing time. If the meat prepared by these methods does not taste the way you remember the very same cut tasted the last time you cooked it after proper thawing, please don't blame the butcher. And don't blame the freezer, which never promised you gourmet quality on any terms other than respectful understanding of its capabilities and limitations.

296

1. This once, you can roast, broil, or pan-broil the meat from its frozen state, or after partial thawing. Count on quite a bit of extra cooking time, the amount of increase varying with the weight and thickness of the cut. Very important: Use a meat thermometer when enough thawing has occurred to permit its insertion.

2. This once, you can rush the thawing or partial thawing process by putting the wrapped meat into a shallow metal pan and setting the pan over your gas range's pilot light. Turn the package over from time to time.

3. This once, you can put the package into an absolutely watertight plastic bag, or wrap it securely in foil, and immerse it in cool water. Add warm (never hot) water gradually.

So much for the roasts, steaks, and chops you prepare simply. There are, in addition, a number of recipes which actually do not require that the meat be thawed. These include, of course, any recipe using meat that is marinated for several hours or days, and also some stews and pot roasts. The latter are prepared without flouring or searing. If a thickened gravy is desirable, it's simple enough to make one from pot liquor and a thickening agent or to take a container of gravy out of the freezer stockpile.

27.

Meat Recipes and Variations from the Freezer Stockpile

Family Beef or Veal Stew
4 servings

Note: This may be frozen if desired. For larger-quantity recipes, see the Index.

1-pint container (2 cups) frozen stock (beef, chicken, mushroom, veal, vegetable)
½ cup chopped fresh or frozen onions
½ cup chopped fresh or frozen green peppers
2 tablespoons oil or melted shortening
2 tablespoons flour combined with ⅔ teaspoon salt and a dash of pepper
1½- to 2-pound package frozen lean stew meat (beef, veal)
8 to 12 fresh or frozen whole peeled white potatoes
1 package frozen cut carrots

Release the stock into a saucepan to melt over moderate heat. When it boils, lower to a simmer. In a heavy pot or Dutch oven, sauté the onions and green peppers in the oil or shortening over low heat for 5 minutes. Sprinkle with the seasoned flour and stir. Add the meat and cover it with the simmering stock. Bring slowly to a boil, separate the meat cubes, stir, then lower the heat immediately to a steady simmer. Cover the pot and continue simmering for 1½ to 2 hours, until a cube is easily pierced with a fork. Use the stock saucepan to parboil the potatoes for 10 minutes in 1 cup of lightly salted water. Remove them to the stewpot with a slotted spoon. In the same water, bring the carrots to a boil, lower the heat and cook for 5 minutes, and add to the pot. Continue simmering the stew for 15 to 20 minutes.

Variations: Use up to 2 cups of any suitable vegetables in your freezer—green, wax, or lima beans, peas, turnips, etc. About ½ cup of these can be frozen stockpiled mushroom stems. Add them directly to the stew for the last 30 minutes of cooking. Raise the heat until the stew bubbles, then reduce the heat to a simmer.

Substitute 1 cup of canned tomatoes for 1 cup of the stock.

Before serving, stir in up to ½ cup of dry wine (red for beef, white for veal).

Goulash of Beef or Veal (or Both)
4 to 6 servings

See the note about freezing (page 298).

8-ounce container (1 cup) frozen beef or veal stock
1 cup tomato juice
1 cup chopped fresh or frozen onions
1 cup diced fresh or frozen green peppers
½ cup diced or sliced fresh or frozen carrots
½ cup slivered celery
1 clove garlic, minced or put through garlic press
4 tablespoons oil or melted butter
4 tablespoons flour combined with 1 teaspoon salt, ¼ teaspoon
    pepper, 1 tablespoon paprika
2 pounds frozen lean stew beef or veal (or 1 pound of each,
    cubed)
1 cup sour cream

Release the stock with the tomato juice into a saucepan over moderate heat. When boiling, lower the heat to a simmer. In a heavy pot or Dutch oven, sauté all the vegetables and garlic together in the hot oil or butter for 5 minutes, stirring occasionally. Sprinkle with the flour combined with seasonings and stir to blend well. Add the meat and cover it with the simmering liquid. Cook over low heat until the cubes can be separated. Bring to a simmer, lower the heat, cover the pot, and continue to simmer for 1½ to 2 hours, until the meat is tender. (If necessary, add more stock or tomato juice.) Add the sour cream, stir, then heat until piping hot but do not boil.

Variation: If you object to bits and pieces of vegetables in your goulash, sauté them until soft enough to be forced through a Foley mill, or buzz them in a blender, then combine them with the seasoned flour before adding the meat and liquid.

Irish Lamb Stew
4 to 6 servings

See the note about freezing (page 298).

1 cup chopped fresh or frozen onions
1 small clove garlic, minced
3 tablespoons oil
3 tablespoons flour mixed with 2 teaspoons paprika, 1 teaspoon salt, ¼ teaspoon pepper
1½ to 2 pounds frozen lean lamb stew cubes (shoulder, shank, neck)
4 cups boiling water
12 to 18 fresh or frozen small whole white onions
½ cup diced or slivered celery
½ cup fresh or frozen diced or sliced carrots
¼ wedge head cabbage, cut into small pieces
1 cup canned tomatoes
2 cups diced white potatoes

In a heavy stewpot, sauté the onions and garlic in the hot oil for 5 minutes. Sprinkle with the seasoned flour and stir to blend. Add the lamb cubes, cover them with the boiling water, and bring slowly to a boil over moderate heat. Separate the cubes, lower the heat to a simmer, and cook for 1½ hours. Add all the remaining ingredients except the potatoes, bring to a fast simmer, and cook for 20 minutes. Parboil the potatoes in boiling salted water, drain, add to the stew, and cook for 20 minutes longer.

Variations: For a thicker gravy, stir 2 additional tablespoons of flour into the cold canned tomatoes before adding them to the stew.

Substitute for the cabbage 1 small eggplant cut into large cubes without peeling. Sauté the cubes in a little oil with ¼ teaspoon of thyme before adding to the stew.

Substitute for the celery and carrots 1 cup of frozen peas. Just before serving, stir in up to ¼ cup of sherry.

Quick Hamburger Stew
8 to 10 servings

This recipe may be frozen in whole or part. It's a good one to make ahead for a teen-ager party.

2 pounds frozen hamburger
2 tablespoons oil
1 cup fresh or frozen chopped onions
1 cup fresh or frozen diced green peppers
1-pound can red kidney beans with liquid
1 package frozen whole-kernel corn
4 cups peeled whole Italian tomatoes
1 cup meatless spaghetti sauce (canned or from the freezer stockpile)
1 teaspoon Worcestershire sauce
Dash each of basil and oregano
Salt and pepper to taste

Over low heat, put the frozen hamburger directly into a large, heavy pot or Dutch oven containing the heated oil. Turn the meat often until it can be broken with a fork. Add the onions and green peppers and continue stirring with a fork until the meat is crumbly. Add the kidney beans with their liquid, stir, and add all the other ingredients in turn, stirring after each addition. Cover and simmer for 15 to 20 minutes. Taste for salt and pepper.

Variation: To make this recipe into a passable chili con carne, add up to 1 tablespoon of chili powder and a few grains of cayenne before the final simmering.

Sloppy Joe Stew
4 servings (more if served on buns)

Children like this served on split biscuits, toasted English muffins, or hamburger buns.

1 pound frozen hamburger
1 tablespoon oil
½ cup fresh or frozen chopped onions
½ teaspoon salt
Dash of pepper
1½ cups canned tomatoes
2 fair-sized potatoes, peeled and sliced or diced
1 cup fresh or frozen diced or sliced carrots
½ cup chopped or slivered celery

Over low heat, put the frozen hamburger directly into a large, heavy skillet containing the hot oil. Turn the meat frequently until it can be broken with a fork. Continue breaking and stirring the meat with a fork until it is crumbly. Add the onions, salt, and pepper and stir. Add all the remaining ingredients, stir, cover the skillet, bring to a boil, lower the heat, and simmer until the potatoes are tender.

Variation: Substitute for the carrots 1 cup of any other frozen vegetable your children eat without protest—lima beans, green peas, whole-kernel corn, mixed vegetables.

"Boiled" Beef, or Family Pot Roast
6 servings

1 cup fresh or frozen chopped onions
3 tablespoons melted fat
3 pounds frozen boneless potting beef (chuck, round, brisket) (or
    4 to 4½ pounds bone-in beef)
3 cups boiling water (1 cup may be canned tomatoes)
Salt and pepper
1-pint container brown gravy from the freezer stockpile, or pack-
    aged mix

In a heavy pot or Dutch oven, sauté the onions in the hot
fat until light golden brown. Add the beef and cover it with
the boiling liquid. When the liquid returns to a boil, reduce
the heat, cover the pot tightly, and simmer very gently from
3 to 4 hours, until tender. Turn the meat once in the pot
after 1½ hours of simmering time and sprinkle it with salt
and pepper as you turn it. Slice or cut into serving pieces
and serve with the hot brown gravy.

Strain the liquid, cool and chill it, remove the fat which
rises to the top, and freeze in containers as stock.

Freezing note: Trim the leftovers of fat, then slice or cut
the meat. Combine the leftover gravy with ¼ cup of pot liquor and up to ¼ cup of horse-radish. Stir in ½ teaspoon of
lemon juice and ½ teaspoon of sugar. Arrange the slices in a
foil freezer container and cover with the gravy. Chill, cover
with foil, and freeze for a quick oven-heated meal. To serve,
heat uncovered in a 350° oven for 35 to 40 minutes.

Corned Beef, Smoked Beef Tongue,
Smoked Pork Shoulder
Approximately ½ pound per serving

This, I'm afraid, will reveal to many guests what they may
have believed to be a cherished cooking secret, although
I've never pretended it was. Whenever I serve corned beef,

smoked tongue, or smoked pork shoulder, I am asked how I cook it. I always tell the truth, giving the ingredients just as they are listed below. My guests probably don't remember between dinners that the ingredients are always the same, except for the featured meat.

2½ to 5 pounds frozen corned beef
> or

3- to 5-pound frozen smoked beef tongue
> or

4- to 7-pound frozen smoked pork shoulder

Cold water to cover
1 large peeled onion, cut in half, each half stuck with 5 whole
    cloves
2 to 4 large cloves garlic, halved
1 teaspoon peppercorns
½ teaspoon whole allspice
1 small bay leaf, broken in half
3 or 4 outer stalks of celery, coarsely cut, with leaves

Put the unwrapped meat into a large pot, cover it entirely with cold water, and let it soak for about 1 hour. Discard this water, cover the meat again with fresh cold water, and bring it slowly to the boiling point over moderate heat. As soon as the water boils, remove the surface scum and distribute all the other ingredients around the meat, adding the celery last. Cover the pot, reduce the heat until the water barely simmers, and go on about your business for a minimum of 3 hours. Additional cooking time depends on the type and weight of meat:

Corned beef: Allow 20 minutes for each pound over 3.

Smoked tongue: Allow 30 minutes for each pound over 3.

Smoked shoulder: May not need further cooking. Test with a fork in a meaty section (not fat). If not quite tender, simmer for 30 minutes longer and test again. Even a 7-pound shoulder seldom requires more than a total of 4 hours.

Special instructions:

Corned beef: Let cool to lukewarm in the cooking water. Drain, then press it under a weight before slicing.

Tongue: Remove from the pot. When cool enough to handle, cut off the root and pull off the outer rind. Return to the pot and let stay until ready to slice.

Smoked shoulder: Remove from the pot, slice off the outer rind and much of the fat, return to the pot, and let stay in the cooking water until ready to serve.

28.

Freezer Recipes Using
Fresh or Thawed Beef

Boeuf Bourguignon
8 servings, total

3 pounds lean boneless beef (chuck, round, etc.), cut into 2-inch cubes
⅔ cup flour mixed with 1 teaspoon salt and ½ teaspoon each pepper and thyme
6 slices bacon, chopped
6 tablespoons butter
1 cup chopped onions
2 cloves garlic, minced or put through garlic press
½ cup chopped carrots
2 tablespoons chopped parsley
2 tablespoons tomato paste
24 small whole peeled white onions
2 cups Burgundy wine
1 cup beef stock, consommé, or water
Mushroom caps
Lemon juice

Dredge the beef cubes in the seasoned flour. In a large skillet, sauté the chopped bacon until crisp. Add the beef and brown. Remove these ingredients with a slotted spoon and divide between two lightly buttered casseroles (one for the freezer). Add 2 tablespoons of the butter to the skillet and sauté the chopped onions, garlic, carrots, and parsley for 3 minutes. Stir in the tomato paste. Divide this mixture between the casseroles. Rinse the skillet with a little wine and add the liquid to the casseroles. Melt the remaining butter and lightly brown the whole onions. Add about ½ cup of the wine, cover the skillet, and cook over low heat for 10 minutes. Divide the onions between the casseroles. Mix the remaining wine with the stock, consommé, or water and pour over the meat. Preheat the oven to 275°, cover both casseroles, and cook for 2 hours.

Freezer portion: Remove the freezer casserole from the oven, cool, chill in the refrigerator, slip it into a large plastic bag, and freeze. Store up to 3 months.

Serving the unfrozen portion: Raise the oven temperature to 350° and continue to cook for 1 hour. Sauté 12 or more mushrooms, caps down, in 2 tablespoons of butter for 1 minute. Turn the caps, sprinkle with lemon juice, and sauté for 1 minute. Add the mushrooms to the casserole and bake, uncovered, for 20 minutes.

Serving the freezer portion: Partially thaw in the refrigerator, for several hours or at room temperature for 2 hours. Heat, covered, in a 350° oven for 1½ hours. Sauté and add mushroom caps as above and bake, uncovered, for 20 minutes.

Beef Stroganoff
8 servings, total

3 pounds tender boneless beef (fillet, sirloin, rib) *
6 tablespoons butter

---

* The tenderest of beef is usually stipulated. However, I have made successful Beef Stroganoff on fairly short notice, using whatever lean beef the freezer offered. Boneless chuck or bottom round, for example, can be sliced almost paper-thin across the grain while it is still frosty, but not solidly

½ cup minced onions
⅔ teaspoon salt
¼ teaspoon pepper
⅛ teaspoon basil
Grating or pinch of nutmeg
2 tablespoons flour
1 tablespoon tomato paste
2 cups beef stock or consommé
1 pound mushrooms, sliced
Sour cream

Slice the beef as thinly as possible and cut into strips about 1 inch by 2 inches. Melt 3 tablespoons of the butter in a Dutch oven and sauté the onions until limp. Add the beef and brown. Stir in the seasonings, flour, tomato paste, and stock or consommé. Simmer over very low heat while you melt the remaining butter in a skillet and sauté the mushrooms for 2 minutes. Combine the mushrooms and meat mixture and stir to distribute well.

Freezer portion: Spoon the amount you wish to freeze into a container. Be sure the beef is covered or well coated with sauce. Cool, chill in the refrigerator, then freeze. Store up to 4 months.

Serving the unfrozen portion: Continue to simmer gently for 20 to 30 minutes, until the beef is very tender. Stir in 4 tablespoons of sour cream per serving and heat without boiling.

Serving the freezer portion: Thaw in the refrigerator overnight, or partially at room temperature for 2 hours. Heat, covered, in the top of a double boiler over simmering water. Stir occasionally until simmering. Continue to simmer for 20 to 30 minutes. Add 4 tablespoons of sour cream per serving and heat without boiling.

---

frozen. By the time you've finished slicing, it will be thawed sufficiently to proceed. If one of these less tender cuts of beef is used, you can increase the simmering time until tender, or use a commercial tenderizer before cooking.

Braciole
8 servings, total

Two 2-pound round steaks
Salt and pepper
1 cup pine nuts or slivered almonds
½ pound *prosciutto* cut paper-thin
1 large clove garlic, quartered
3 tablespoons olive oil
3 tablespoons butter
½ cup minced onions
½ cup chopped carrots
2 cups chopped mushroom caps and stems
1 cup Italian tomato purée with basil (or ⅛ teaspoon basil added
    to plain purée)
1 tablespoon Italian tomato paste
2 cups whole peeled Italian-style canned tomatoes

Trim all fat from the steaks and pound them with a mallet or the edge of a heavy plate until they are very, very thin. Dust lightly with salt and pepper. Sprinkle the nuts over the meat, leaving about an inch of margin all around. Cover with a blanket of *prosciutto*. Roll the steaks like jelly roll and tie them securely with string. In a Dutch oven, brown the garlic in the olive oil. Discard the garlic, add the butter, and brown the beef rolls on all but one side. Add the onions, carrots, and mushrooms, turn the rolls to their unbrowned sides, and cook for 3 minutes. Combine the purée, tomato paste, and tomatoes and add. When the liquid comes to a boil, lower the heat and simmer, covered, for 1½ hours.

Freezer portion: Carefully lift one roll to the middle of a piece of heavy freezer foil and wrap it securely. Pour half the sauce into a freezer container. Label both. Cool, chill in the refrigerator, then freeze. Store up to 3 months.

Serving the unfrozen portion: Continue to simmer for 20 minutes. Put the roll onto a warm platter, remove the string, cut into serving pieces, and cover with sauce.

Serving the freezer portion: Partially thaw the wrapped braciole in the refrigerator for several hours, or at room temperature for 2 hours. Unwrap it and put it into a lightly oiled shallow baking dish. Release the sauce into a pan and heat it slowly, breaking up lumps as you can. Heat the beef in a 350° oven for 1 hour, basting occasionally with sauce. Serve as above.

Swiss Steak

8 servings, total

4 pounds top or bottom round cut into ½-inch slices (or two 2-pound round steaks)
About 1 cup flour mixed with 1 teaspoon salt, ¼ teaspoon pepper, ½ teaspoon garlic powder
4 tablespoons melted shortening
2 tablespoons butter
1 cup sliced or chopped onions
1 cup diced green peppers
½ cup slivered celery
½ cup chopped carrots
1 cup simmering beef stock or consommé
1½ cup simmering canned tomatoes

Trim all fat from the beef. With the edge of a heavy plate, pound into both sides of each slice as much of the flour mixture as the meat will hold. Cut the beef into equal serving pieces, not too small. Heat the shortening in a Dutch oven and brown the beef on both sides. Remove it to a platter. Add the butter to the pot and sauté the onions until they are limp. Add the green peppers and celery and cook for 3 minutes. Return the beef to the pot, add the carrots and the simmering liquids, cover, and cook over very low heat for 2 hours. Remove from the heat.

Freezer portion: * Remove to a lightly buttered shallow

---

* You need not divide this recipe before serving. If you prefer, cook the entire amount of beef for 2½ to 3 hours, purée the gravy as directed, and freeze leftovers. Reheat, after 1 hour thawing, for 45 minutes to 1 hour, until piping hot.

baking dish the number of pieces you wish to freeze. Force all the gravy through a Foley mill, or purée it in a blender. Pour over the freezer-intended beef a proportionate amount of the puréed gravy. Cover the dish with foil, chill it in the refrigerator, slip it into a plastic bag, and freeze. Store up to 6 months.

Serving the unfrozen portion: Return the remaining purée to the pot with the beef and simmer for 45 minutes or more, until the meat is very tender.

Serving the freezer portion: Thaw at room temperature for 1 hour and heat in a 350° oven for 1 to 1½ hours.

Beef Stew
8 servings, total

3 pounds lean boneless beef (chuck, round, etc.) cut into 1½-inch cubes
About ⅔ cup flour seasoned with 1 teaspoon salt, ¼ teaspoon pepper
1 cup sliced or chopped onions
4 tablespoons melted shortening or rendered beef suet
1 cup coarsely cut green peppers
4 cups boiling water or unseasoned stock (1 cup may be canned tomatoes)
1 teaspoon lemon juice
1 teaspoon sugar
8 to 12 small carrots, scraped and coarsely cut
24 small whole white onions, peeled

Dredge the beef on all sides in the seasoned flour. In a large skillet, sauté the sliced or chopped onions in the hot fat for 2 minutes. Add and sauté the green peppers for 3 minutes. Remove these with a slotted spoon to a large heavy pot or Dutch oven. Add the beef to the skillet and brown on all sides, removing them to the Dutch oven when browned. Cover the beef with the boiling liquid, stir in the lemon juice and sugar, and simmer, covered, for 2 hours. Add the carrots and whole onions and simmer for 10 minutes.

Freezer portion: Spoon the amount to be frozen into containers. Cool, chill in the refrigerator, then freeze. Store up to 3 months.

Serving the unfrozen portion: Parboil diced white potatoes (½ cup per serving) for 5 minutes. Drain and add them to the simmering stew. Add also, if desired, up to ½ cup per serving of frozen vegetables (peas, cut beans, mixed vegetables, etc.) Continue to simmer until the added vegetables are tender.

Serving the freezer portion: Partially thaw in the refrigerator overnight or at room temperature for 2 hours. Heat very slowly in a heavy pot. When the stew simmers steadily, make additions and finish cooking as directed above. If more gravy is desired, add flour-thickened stock, or heat and stir in a cupful of frozen, canned, or package-mix brown gravy.

29.

Space-Saver Beef Stews

Beefy stews of all kinds are greatly favored by my family and guests, but I honestly don't always have the time, energy, or desire, at the drop of a hint, to do all the necessary meat preliminaries—cubing, trimming, dredging, browning —before starting on the vegetables. So when I do have the time, energy, and desire, I prepare a big batch of beef stew base for the freezer, where it remains ready to be transformed into a number of interesting recipes. It saves freezer space, too.

Beef Stew Base
3 1-quart or 6 1-pint containers

4½ to 5 pounds lean boneless stew beef cut into 1-inch cubes
1 cup flour seasoned with 2 teaspoons salt and ½ teaspoon pepper
1½ cups chopped onions
6 tablespoons melted shortening or suet
Boiling water or unseasoned stock to cover (1 cup may be canned tomatoes)

Toss the beef cubes in a paper bag with the seasoned flour until all are well coated. In a large skillet, sauté the onions in 2 tablespoons of the fat until limp. Remove them with a slotted spoon to a large stew pot. Add the remaining fat to the skillet and brown the floured beef on all sides, one layer at a time, adding each batch to the stew pot until all are done. Cover with the boiling liquid and simmer for 1½ hours. Cool and refrigerate. Remove the fat which rises to the surface, divide among the containers, and freeze. Store up to 3 months.

RECIPES USING FROZEN BEEF STEW BASE

Harvest Beef Stew
4 to 6 servings *

1-pint container frozen Beef Stew Base (page 313)
1 cup beef stock or consommé
½ package frozen cut carrots
½ package frozen baby lima beans
½ package frozen whole kernel corn
½ package frozen sliced mushrooms

Partially thaw the stew base in its container in the refrigerator overnight or at room temperature for 2 hours. Release the contents into a heavy pot along with the stock or consommé. Heat slowly. When the meat cubes are separated, raise the heat until the liquid bubbles. Without precooking them, add all the frozen vegetables and continue to cook over moderate heat until all are thawed. Stir, reduce the heat to a simmer, and cook, covered, for 20 minutes. Taste and correct seasonings if necessary. Do not refreeze.

To extend servings, you may add sliced or diced white potatoes—up to 1 cup for every 2 servings. Parboil them in salted water for 10 minutes and add to the stew for the last 10 minutes of cooking time.

* For a larger recipe serving 8 to 10, double all ingredients.

Bavarian Beef Stew
6 servings

1 quart frozen Beef Stew Base (page 313)
1 teaspoon caraway seed
¼ cup wine or cider vinegar
1 firm, medium-sized head of cabbage
6 small gingersnaps, crushed into fine crumbs
½ cup warm water

Partially thaw the stew base in its container in the refrigerator overnight or at room temperature for 2 hours. Bring it to a slow boil over moderate heat in a heavy pot, lower to a simmer, and add the caraway seed and vinegar. Cut the cabbage into 6 wedges and add. Cover the pot and simmer for 35 to 40 minutes. With tongs, remove the cabbage to one side of a heated platter. With a slotted spoon, heap the beef cubes on the other side. Combine the crumbled gingersnaps with warm water, stir this into the stew gravy, and pour it over the meat. Do not refreeze.

East Indian Beef Stew
4 servings

1-quart container frozen Beef Stew Base (page 313)
8 small whole peeled fresh or frozen white onions
1 cup fresh or frozen diced green peppers
1 cup sour cream
1½ teaspoons curry powder
⅛ teaspoon cayenne pepper

Partially thaw the stew base in the refrigerator overnight or at room temperature for 2 hours. Bring it to a slow boil over moderate heat in a heavy pot, lower to a simmer, and add the onions and green peppers. Simmer for 30 minutes for fresh vegetables, 40 minutes for frozen vegetables. Combine the sour cream, curry powder, and cayenne with a few spoonfuls of the stew gravy, blend well, and stir this into the stew. Heat without boiling. Serve over mounds of boiled or steamed rice. Do not refreeze.

Swedish Beef Stew
4 to 6 servings

1-quart container frozen Beef Stew Base (page 313)
3 large potatoes, peeled and cut into ½-inch dice
2 cups yellow turnips, peeled and cut into ½-inch dice
¼ cup catchup
1½ cups beer

Thaw the stew base at room temperature for 3 to 4 hours, or until you can spoon half of it over the bottom of a Dutch oven. Parboil the potatoes in boiling salted water for 5 minutes, then drain. Parboil the turnips for 3 minutes and drain. Arrange these vegetables in layers over the stew in the Dutch oven, add the remaining stew, then combine the catchup with the beer and pour this into the pot. Cover and simmer over low heat until the vegetables are tender (about 30 minutes). Do not refreeze.

Spanish Beef Stew
6 to 8 servings

1-quart container frozen Beef Stew Base (page 313)
¼ cup olive oil
1 cup fresh or frozen chopped onions
1 cup fresh or frozen diced green peppers
2 cloves garlic, minced or put through garlic press
1 teaspoon salt
½ teaspoon pepper
1 cup chopped peeled tomatoes
1 can (1½ cups) garbanzos (cooked chick-peas) with liquid
½ cup chopped pimientos

Thaw the stew base in its container in the refrigerator overnight or at room temperature for 3 hours. Heat the olive oil in a Dutch oven and sauté the onions, green peppers, garlic, salt, and pepper for 5 minutes. Add the stew, tomatoes, and the juice from the canned garbanzos. Bring to a simmer over low heat. Stir, then cook for 30 minutes. Add the garbanzos and pimientos and stir. If additional thickening is needed, add 1 or 2 tablespoons of cornstarch stirred into ¼ cup of cold water and simmer until thickened. Do not refreeze.

Beef and Kidney * Stew
6 to 8 servings

1-quart container frozen Beef Stew Base (page 313)
1 pound beef kidneys
1 tablespoon vinegar or French dressing
3 tablespoons flour seasoned with ½ teaspoon salt and dash of
    pepper
3 tablespoons oil
⅛ teaspoon basil, oregano, or rosemary
1 cup fresh or frozen diced carrots
½ cup slivered celery
1½ cups boiling beef, vegetable, or mushroom stock

The stew may stand in its container at room temperature while you prepare the kidneys: Split them lengthwise and remove the tubes. Trim off fat. Wash quickly in cold water and remove the membranes. Drain, pat dry, and cut into ½-inch slices. Sprinkle both sides with the vinegar or French dressing and let stand for 2 hours. Dredge with the seasoned flour. Heat the oil in a Dutch oven, add your choice of herb to the hot oil, and brown the dredged kidneys on both sides. Add the beef stew, vegetables, and stock, stir, bring slowly to a simmer, and cook over low heat for 15 minutes. Do not refreeze.

* *Variation:* Beef heart may be substituted for the kidneys. Remove the membranes and cut into very thin slices about 1 inch square. Omit the vinegar treatment but otherwise follow the above directions for dredging and browning the kidneys. Simmer the heart slices in the boiling stock for 20 minutes. Add the stew and vegetables, stir, and simmer for 30 minutes.

30.

Grounds for Freezing

Cookbooks, magazines, and newspapers are full of recipes glorifying ground meat, notably beef. It is a wise freezer owner who takes advantage of sales to stock up, storing the thin bun-sized patties that keep her children from starvation, thick ones to serve as rare chopped steak, and bulk packages for dozens of freezable main courses ranging from the familiarly simple to the mysteriously exotic. Ground beef can be hash, and it can be haute cuisine. It can be what a young friend calls "gunk," or it can be gourmet.

There are highly opinionated philosophies about the kind of beef which should go into any ground beef recipe. Skillful cooks on limited budgets do very well indeed with the meat, unidentified as to cut or grade, that curls from the butcher's huge grinding machine. This may tend to be fatty, however, and it is often wise to choose recipes which require pre-browning. (Brown the beef in its own fat and pour off the excess.)

No less skillful cooks with expandable budgets may prefer the flavorsome chuck, the low-fat round, or the tender, expensive ground sirloin. One bachelor of my acquaintance refuses to eat ground beef in any guise unless he himself selects a prime rib roast and has the butcher trim the meat from bone and fat and grind it in his presence. So help me. We went shopping together, I observed this ritual, and he invited me home for "hamburgers." In his mahogany-paneled kitchen I watched him flatten the beef with an imported press and fry it gray, using the very best sweet butter. Onions? Don't be silly. Shallots!

The sampling of ground meat recipes given in the following pages makes no attempt at inclusiveness, for there are far too many good ones to permit that. Instead, I have adapted for the freezer a few reminiscent of the flavors associated with the native cookery of several countries. If you have a favorite recipe, by all means make an extra quantity and freeze some for a future meal. Like stews, these usually improve with age. The meat used may be fresh from the store, or it may be taken from the freezer and thawed.

RECIPES USING GROUND BEEF

Casserole Pronto
8 servings, total

½ pound any pasta (elbow macaroni, small shells, broken spaghetti, etc.)
1 cup finely chopped onions
2 cloves garlic, minced or put through garlic press
1 cup diced green peppers
1 cup slivered celery
4 tablespoons oil
2 pounds lean ground beef
3 cups prepared Italian tomato sauce (your own, or canned)
6-ounce can sliced mushrooms, not drained
1 package any frozen vegetable (Italian cut or other beans, peas, mixed vegetables, etc.)
2 teaspoons sugar

1 teaspoon salt
¼ teaspoon pepper

Cook the pasta according to the package directions for firmness. Drain and reserve. In a large heavy saucepan or Dutch oven, sauté the onions, garlic, peppers, and celery in the oil for 3 minutes. Add the beef, then stir and cook for 5 minutes, until well browned. Remove from the heat. Add all the remaining ingredients, including the cooked pasta and the frozen vegetables, and stir to mix thoroughly.

Freezer portion: Remove the amount you wish to freeze to a metal or freezer-to-oven casserole. Cover, cool, chill, slip the casserole into a plastic bag, and freeze. Store up to 3 months.

Serving the unfrozen portion: Simmer over very low heat for 1 hour. Remove to a serving casserole.

Serving the freezer portion: Unbag and place the covered casserole directly into a 325° oven and heat for 1½ to 2 hours, until piping hot.

Chili Con Carne (with Beans)
10 to 12 servings

3 cups (1½ pounds) dry kidney or pinto beans
¼ pound finely diced salt pork (or 3 tablespoons olive oil)
3 large onions, peeled and sliced or chopped
2 to 4 cloves garlic, minced or put through garlic press
3 pounds ground beef
1 teaspoon salt
⅛ teaspoon cayenne pepper
2 to 4 dry Spanish chili pepper pods (or 2 to 6 tablespoons chili
    powder)—the lesser quantities for milder taste
4 cups canned tomatoes (1 cup may be beef stock)
1 teaspoon cumin seed

Wash and pick over the beans, cover them with cold water in a very large pot, and bring rapidly to a boil. Remove from the heat and let stand for 1 hour. Add water to cover and bring again to a boil. Lower the heat and simmer slowly while you proceed:

In a very large skillet or Dutch oven, sauté the salt pork dice until crisp, or heat the oil, and sauté the onions and garlic until golden brown. Remove them with a slotted spoon and stir into the beans. Brown the meat in the same skillet, pressing and turning with a fork until crumbled and cooked through. Add the meat and skillet juice to the bean pot. Add all the other ingredients, stirring often with a long wooden spoon until thoroughly mixed. If the liquid does not cover, add a little boiling stock or water. Simmer over low heat until the beans are almost, but not quite, tender.

Freezer portion: Spoon the amount you wish to freeze into containers. Cool, chill in the refrigerator, then freeze. Store up to 6 months.

Serving the unfrozen portion: Continue to simmer, stirring occasionally, until the beans are tender. Serve in bowls, garnished with shredded lettuce and minced raw onions. Sprinkle with grated Cheddar cheese, if desired. To extend, serve over boiled or steamed rice or corn-meal mush.

Serving the freezer portion: Release into a heavy saucepan over very low heat. When thawed, add liquid—beef stock, consommé, or bouillon—if necessary. Serve as above.

Space-saver Chili Con Carne

Omit the beans. Sauté the onions and garlic as directed in the preceding recipe, then add and brown the meat. Mix the chili pods or powder with the canned tomatoes and seasonings and add. Stir, then simmer, covered, for 1 hour. Freeze as directed. *To serve after storage:* Thaw in a large heavy pot over low heat until separated. Add an equal amount of cooked or canned kidney beans with some of the bean juice and simmer for 30 to 40 minutes, stirring occasionally.

Tamale Pie (made with frozen Space-Saver Chili Con Carne)
6 to 8 servings

1-quart container frozen Chili Con Carne without beans
1 can (1½ cups) pitted whole black olives, drained
1¼ cups yellow corn meal
½ cup grated Cheddar cheese
3 cups boiling water with 1 teaspoon salt

Thaw the chili over low heat. When hot, stir in the black olives and ¼ cup of the corn meal. Simmer for 30 minutes. Add the cheese and stir until it is melted. Remove from the heat. Cook 1 cup of the corn meal in the boiling salted water until thick. Line an oiled casserole with about two-thirds of the cooked corn meal and pour in the meat mixture. Top with spoonfuls of the remaining corn meal and bake at 350° for 30 minutes. This recipe may also be combined as above in a chafing dish and kept warm over hot water. Serve with cooked kidney beans, or with one of the bean salads on pages 105 and 106.

Polish Stuffed Cabbage Leaves
8 servings, total

16 large cabbage leaves
2 pounds ground beef, fresh, not thawed (up to half may be ground pork)
½ cup minced onions
1½ cups cooked rice
1 teaspoon salt
¼ teaspoon pepper
½ teaspoon nutmeg
Juice of 1 large lemon
3 cups canned tomatoes
2 tablespoons sugar
Sour cream

Wilt the cabbage leaves until they are pliable by pouring a little boiling water over them. Remove the tough cores at the base of the leaves. Combine the meat, onions, rice, seasonings, and lemon juice and mix thoroughly. Put about 2 tablespoons of this mixture into the center of each cabbage leaf. Fold the side edges in and make compact rolls, starting at the thick ends of the leaves. Fasten with toothpicks. Put a few of the leftover cabbage leaves into the bottoms of two lightly oiled baking dishes and place the cabbage rolls on them. Combine the tomatoes and sugar and pour over the rolls. Cover the dishes tightly with foil, if they have no lids.

Freezer portion: Cool, chill in the refrigerator, slip the dish into a plastic bag, and freeze. Store up to 6 months.

Serving the unfrozen portion: Preheat the oven to 325° and bake for 1½ hours. Uncover, stir 2 generous tablespoons of sour cream per serving into the tomato sauce, spoon the sauce over the rolls, and bake for 10 minutes.

Serving the freezer portion: Thaw in the refrigerator overnight or at room temperature for 2 hours. Bake, covered, in a 350° oven for 1½ hours. Uncover, stir in sour cream as above, and follow the remaining directions.

Stuffed Cabbage Leaves Hargood House
10 to 12 servings, total

1 very large head of cabbage
3 pounds ground beef (may be thawed from the freezer stockpile)
1 jumbo or 2 medium eggs
½ cup fine unseasoned bread crumbs
1½ teaspoons salt
½ teaspoon pepper
2 tablespoons brown sugar
Juice of 1 large lemon
6 to 8 gingersnaps, crushed to crumbs
1 cup seedless raisins
2½ cups tomato purée (or 2 small bottles tomato catchup)
½ cup beef stock or broth

Remove the base of the cabbage head and steam in a colander over simmering water to loosen the leaves. Pare the tough spine to uncurl them. Combine the beef, eggs, bread crumbs, salt, and pepper and mix thoroughly. Put about 2 tablespoons of the mixture into the center of large cabbage leaves, less in small ones, until all the mixture has been used. Fold the side edges in and roll from the thick ends to make compact rolls of various sizes. Fit them together tightly in a single layer in a large, lightly oiled covered skillet (or use a 12-inch electric frypan). Sprinkle in turn with the sugar, lemon juice, gingersnap crumbs, and raisins. Cover with the purée or catchup mixed with the stock or broth. Cover the skillet and simmer over very low heat (or at "simmer" on an electric frypan) for 2 hours. Remove carefully to a platter the amount you wish to freeze. Remove carefully to a lightly oiled casserole the amount you plan to serve. Pour the pan sauce over the rolls to be served and bake at 325°, uncovered, for 1 hour. Serve.

Freezer portion: Chill in the refrigerator. Freeze in a single layer on wax paper. When solidly frozen, package meal portions in single layers in freezer boxes, or wrap securely in foil, and return them to the freezer. Store up to 3 months. Pour any sauce remaining from the dinner into a freezer container. Cool, chill, label, and freeze.

Serving the freezer portion: Put the rolls into a lightly oiled shallow baking dish in a single layer and heat in a 350° oven, covered, for 1 hour. Melt and heat the sauce. * If necessary, extend it with hot stock and/or catchup. Uncover and pour the sauce over the rolls. Heat for 20 minutes.

Stuffed Peppers I
8 servings, total

8 large, flat-bottomed green peppers
¼ cup chopped onions

---

* If no sauce was frozen, cover the rolls with frozen, canned, or package-mix brown gravy to which you may add catchup, raisins plumped in water and drained, crushed gingersnaps, brown sugar, and lemon juice. Or serve with any meatless spaghetti sauce.

3 tablespoons oil
1 pound ground beef
1½ cups cooked rice
1 teaspoon salt
¼ teaspoon pepper
½ cup grated Cheddar or American cheese
½ cup fine bread crumbs

Remove the tops, seeds, and fibers from the peppers. Drop the shells into rapidly boiling salted water and cook for 5 minutes. Drain well. Dice the raw tops, combine them with the onions, and sauté in the hot oil for 3 minutes. Add and brown the beef, breaking up lumps with a fork until crumbly. Combine this mixture with the cooked rice, add the seasonings, and mix well. Fill the drained pepper cases and top with a mixture of the cheese and bread crumbs.

Freezer portion: Wrap individual peppers in aluminum foil, cool, chill in the refrigerator, then freeze. When frozen, gather into a plastic bag. Store up to 3 months.

Serving the unfrozen portion: Put filled peppers closely together into an oiled baking dish or bread tin, standing them upright. Add a little liquid (water, stock, bouillon) to prevent scorching and bake at 350° for 15 to 20 minutes. Brown the topping under the broiler. Serve topped with brown gravy, mushroom gravy, or tomato sauce.

Serving the freezer portion: Stand the foil-wrapped peppers upright in the top of a double boiler over simmering water. When partially thawed (20 minutes), remove the foil, transfer the peppers to an oiled baking dish, and heat at 350° for 30 minutes. Or thaw, wrapped, in the refrigerator and bake at 350° for 20 minutes. Brown the topping under the broiler. Serve as above.

Stuffed Peppers II
8 servings, total

8 large flat-bottomed green peppers
1½ pounds ground beef

1 egg, beaten
1 cup fine bread crumbs
2 tablespoons grated Romano or Parmesan cheese
1 teaspoon salt
¼ teaspoon pepper
Pinch of basil or oregano
1 teaspoon parsley flakes
Olive oil or butter

Remove and reserve about 1 inch of the pepper tops. Remove the seeds and fibers from the cases. Combine the ground beef with all but the last ingredient and mix thoroughly. Fill the pepper cases, packing well, and fit the tops back into place, securing them with toothpicks. Rub olive oil or butter over the peppers and put them close together in a baking dish. Bake at 300° for 1 hour.

Freezer portion: Slightly cool those you plan to freeze. Remove the toothpicks and wrap the peppers individually in aluminum foil. Cool, chill in the refrigerator, then freeze. When frozen, gather into a plastic bag. Store up to 3 months.

Serving the unfrozen portion: Continue baking for 20 minutes, occasionally bulb-basting with water, stock, or bouillon —just enough to prevent drying. Serve with any Italian sauce.

Serving the freezer portion: Stand the foil-wrapped peppers upright, close together, in a baking dish and heat in a 400° oven for 35 to 40 minutes. Remove the foil and serve as above.

Kima (East Indian)
8 servings, total

4 tablespoons oil
1 cup chopped onions
½ cup diced green peppers
1 teaspoon salt
2 tablespoons curry powder

1½ pounds ground beef
1 cup seedless raisins, plumped in warm water and drained
1 cup beef stock or consommé
2 tablespoons cornstarch stirred into ¼ cup water
½ cup chopped pimientos
1 cup tiny chopped or slivered nuts (pine, walnuts, peanuts, almonds)
Frozen peas

Heat the oil in a large skillet or Dutch oven and sauté the onions and green peppers for 3 minutes. Work the seasonings into the beef, mix well, and add, breaking lumps with a fork until crumbly. Add the drained raisins and liquid, stir, cover, and simmer for 10 minutes. Add the cornstarch mixture and pimientos and stir until thickened. Add the nuts and mix well.

Freezer portion: Spoon into a container the amount you wish to freeze. Cool, chill in the refrigerator, then freeze. Store up to 1 month.

Serving the unfrozen portion: Continue to simmer, covered, for 8 to 10 minutes while you cook 1 package of frozen peas according to the package directions. Combine with the meat mixture and serve with steamed or boiled rice.

Serving the freezer portion: Release into the top of a double boiler over simmering water. Heat for 1 hour. Cook 1 package of frozen peas, combine with the meat, and serve as above.

Moussaka
8 to 10 servings, total

Long, narrow eggplant (about 4 or 5 pounds)
Flour
Olive oil
1 cup finely chopped onions
1 large clove garlic, minced
2 pounds ground beef or lamb, or mixture
1 cup tomato sauce

1 teaspoon salt
½ teaspoon pepper
6 tablespoons butter
6 tablespoons flour
3 cups warm milk
3 eggs, well beaten
Salt
Paprika
2 cups (loose measure) grated Greek feta cheese (or use
     Muenster or Swiss)
1½ cups fine bread crumbs

Remove the stem ends from the eggplant and cut them without peeling into ½-inch slices. Dredge both sides with flour and fry several pieces at a time in hot olive oil to the depth of ½ inch in a large skillet, turning once. Remove the browned slices to drain on paper towels. Arrange about one-third of the total slices as linings in two lightly oiled shallow casseroles or baking dishes, one for the freezer.

In the same skillet sauté the onions and garlic for 3 minutes. Add the meat and brown, crumbling it with a fork as it cooks. Stir in the tomato sauce and seasonings and simmer for 10 minutes.

In a separate saucepan melt the butter and stir in the 6 tablespoons of flour. Gradually add the warm milk and stir over low heat until bubbling. Beat this sauce slowly into the beaten eggs and add a little salt and paprika to taste.

Build up layers in both of the lined casseroles, first spooning in the meat mixture, then egg sauce, then cheese, then crumbs, then eggplant slices. Divide everything so that you have 2 or 3 layers, ending up with sauce, cheese, and crumbs.

Freezer portion: Cool, cover with foil, chill in the refrigerator, slip the casserole into a plastic bag, and freeze. Store up to 3 months.

Serving the unfrozen portion: Bake at 350° for 30 minutes. Brown the topping under the broiler section.

Serving the freezer portion: Bake, covered, at 350° for 1 hour. Remove the foil covering and bake for 30 minutes. Brown the topping as above.

Picadillo, Key West
12 servings, total

There are several versions of this tasty Cuban recipe. This one, served at parties by an artist who summers in Province-town, is especially good. Her advice: Cook the recipe a day ahead and let the flavors mingle overnight in the refrigerator before reheating for serving. The freezer portion may be stored when chilled.

6 tablespoons olive oil
2 large onions, chopped
2 large green peppers, seeds and fibers removed, diced
2½ pounds ground beef (chuck, round)
4 cups meatless spaghetti sauce with a tomato base (your own, or canned)
8-ounce jar small whole pimiento-stuffed olives, including half the juice
1 bottle (2¼ ounces) capers, drained
½ box seedless raisins
1 teaspoon garlic powder
1 teaspoon salt
1 teaspoon celery salt
½ teaspoon paprika
2 tablespoons Worcestershire sauce
3 or 4 dashes of Tabasco sauce
1 teaspoon oregano, pulverized between your palms

Heat 4 tablespoons of the olive oil in a Dutch oven and cook the onions, covered, for 20 minutes over very low heat. Add the diced peppers and cook, covered, for 20 minutes longer. Separately, in a heavy skillet, heat the remaining oil and brown the beef in it. When it is crumbly and well browned, add it to the Dutch oven along with all the re-

maining ingredients. Stir after each addition. Simmer over
low heat for 45 minutes. Let cool, then refrigerate.

Freezer portion: Spoon into containers the amount you
wish to freeze. Store up to 3 months.

Serving the unfrozen portion: Reheat slowly and simmer
for 15 minutes. Serve over yellow rice. In Key West, the coloring agent is the saffronlike herb *bijol,* but the rice may be
tinted with saffron, turmeric, or a vegetable coloring.

Serving the freezer portion: Partially thaw, release into a
heavy saucepan or chafing dish, and bring slowly to a serving temperature. Serve as above.

MEATBALLS

You can freeze a multitude of meatballs—small ones for
toothpicks at a party, * large ones for main courses, raw
ones or cooked ones, mild or highly seasoned, with or without sauces.

To freeze them raw, use meat that has not been frozen. To
save space, you can combine the ingredients and freeze the
mixture in compact meal-proportioned packages, but of
course you'll have to thaw it completely before it can be
shaped into balls. To save some time, if not space, you can
shape the raw mixture into balls and freeze them, ready to
be partially thawed and browned or dropped, still frozen,
into simmering sauce. Spread them in a single layer on wax
paper or foil in contact with a freezer surface. When solid,
gather them into plastic bags. The raw mixture or preshaped
balls can be stored in your freezer up to 6 months, if need

* *A special note about meatballs as party hors d'oeuvres:* Practically all
the meatball recipes in this section are eminently suitable as fare for a
cocktail buffet table. Servings expressed here are for dinner portions. For
parties, you can multiply the number of servings yielded by at least three.
Make the balls about ¾ inch and freeze them in containers covered with
their own sauce, or in party-proportioned plastic bags, with the sauce in
separate containers. Thaw in the refrigerator the night before the party and
start warming them in sauce in a chafing dish when the first guests arrive.

be. Partially cooked meatballs can be stored for 1 month if not in sauce, up to 3 months if sauced.

So the next time you make a favorite meatball recipe, make a lot. The recipes which follow were chosen to offer a broad sampling of flavors, both subtle and pronounced, associated with regional cooking throughout the world.

RECIPES FOR MEATBALLS

Barbecued Meatballs in Foil
8 servings, total

Sauce

1 cup chopped onions
3 tablespoons butter
1½ cups canned tomatoes
1 cup slivered celery
1 cup tomato catchup or chili sauce
2 teaspoons brown sugar
2 or 3 dashes of tabasco sauce
½ teaspoon dry mustard
1½ cups beef stock or consommé
1 teaspoon salt
⅛ teaspoon pepper

Sauté the onions in the hot butter in a Dutch oven. Add all the remaining ingredients, stir, cover tightly, and bring to a boil over moderate heat. Reduce the heat and simmer slowly for 2 hours. Remove the cover and simmer for 30 minutes longer, until the sauce is very thick. Stir frequently.

Meatballs

1½ pounds ground beef (round, chuck)
½ pound ground lean pork
3 eggs, beaten
1 teaspoon salt
⅛ teaspoon pepper
3 tablespoons flour
¼ cup oil

Combine the meat, eggs, seasonings, and flour. Mix well and shape into 24 to 32 balls. In a large, heavy skillet sauté the meatballs in the hot oil without crowding them, and remove them to a platter when well browned. When all are done, place 3 or 4 (depending on how many you made) on 8 double squares (16 sheets) of heavy aluminum foil. Spoon the sauce over the balls. Make each package into a secure envelope by folding the center edges together twice and making double folds on each end.

Freezer portion: Cool, chill in the refrigerator, then freeze. When solid, gather into a plastic bag. Store up to 3 months.

Serving the unfrozen portion: Bake at 400° for 30 minutes, or place directly on a barbecue grill over coals for 20 minutes.

Serving the freezer portion: Partially thaw at room temperature for 1 hour. Put the foil packages in a 400° oven for 1 hour, or on a barbecue grill over coals for 35 minutes.

Cheese-Filled Meatballs
8 servings, total

2 pounds ground beef
½ cup minced or grated onions
1 teaspoon salt
⅛ teaspoon pepper
¼ teaspoon garlic powder
½ cup fine unseasoned bread crumbs
1 cup coarsely grated Cheddar cheese *
¾ teaspoon powdered ginger
4 tablespoons oil or melted shortening

Combine the beef with the onions, salt, pepper, garlic powder, and bread crumbs. Mix well and divide into 16 or 24 equal parts. Toss the cheese with the ginger until well

---

* This recipe may also be made with Roquefort or bleu cheese. Omit the ginger, and mix with 2 or 3 tablespoons of minced celery.

distributed and form the same number of small balls. Flatten the meat and wrap around the cheese balls, making sure that the cheese is centered. Sauté in the hot oil or shortening, browning lightly on all sides.

Freezer portion: Cool, then chill in the refrigerator the number you wish to freeze. Gather into a plastic bag. Store up to 1 month.

Serving the unfrozen portion: Heat to bubbling a proportionate amount of any meatless spaghetti sauce with a tomato base. If bland, add a little oregano, tarragon, and ginger. Pour the sauce over the meatballs, cover the skillet tightly, and simmer very gently for 20 minutes. Do not let the sauce boil, or the cheese will run.

Serving the freezer portion: Thaw completely in the refrigerator or at room temperature. Heat and season the sauce as above in a heavy saucepan. Simmer the meatballs in the sauce for 30 to 35 minutes.

Chinese Sweet and Pungent Meatballs
8 servings, total

2 pounds ground beef
2 teaspoons salt
⅛ teaspoon black pepper
2 eggs, beaten
¼ cup flour
⅛ teaspoon white pepper
½ cup peanut oil
3 cups chicken stock, broth, or consommé
1½ cups canned pineapple chunks (or 8 pineapple slices, quartered)
24 maraschino cherries
6 tablespoons cornstarch
3 tablespoons soy sauce
⅔ cup white vinegar
1 cup light corn sirup
1 tablespoon sugar
1 cup dry white wine

Season the beef with ½ teaspoon of salt and the black pepper and shape the mixture into tiny balls. Combine the eggs, flour, 1 teaspoon of salt and the white pepper. When this batter is smooth, dip the meatballs into it and sauté a few at a time in the hot oil, using a large skillet or Dutch oven to which you have added the remaining ½ teaspoon of salt. Brown the balls on all sides, and drain on paper towels. Half-fill containers with the amount you plan to freeze. Remove the portion you plan to serve to a warm platter.

Add 1 cup of the stock or other liquid, the diced pineapple, and the cherries to the skillet or Dutch oven. Simmer for 10 minutes. Meanwhile, in a separate saucepan combine and blend together the cornstarch, soy sauce, vinegar, corn sirup, sugar, remaining 2 cups of stock or other liquid, and wine. Cook this mixture slowly, stirring until thickened, add it to the skillet, and stir.

Freezer portion: Cover the meatballs with an equal volume of fruited sauce. Cool, chill in the refrigerator, then freeze. Store up to 3 months.

Serving the unfrozen portion: For each 2 servings, coarsely cut 1 large green pepper, sauté the pieces quickly in a little oil, and add to the sauce. Return the meatballs and simmer gently for 10 minutes. Serve with rice.

Serving the freezer portion: Thaw in the refrigerator or at room temperature. Heat in a heavy skillet or pot. When simmering, prepare green peppers as above and add. Simmer for 10 minutes longer. Serve with rice.

Curried Meatballs

8 servings, total

2 pounds ground beef
1 teaspoon ground coriander
1 teaspoon ground ginger
¼ teaspoon ground cloves
¼ teaspoon ground cinnamon

2 tablespoons curry powder
½ teaspoon salt
⅛ teaspoon pepper
1 tablespoon butter
2 tablespoons oil
½ cup minced onion
2 cloves garlic, minced or put through garlic press
1 tablespoon tomato paste
2 cups beef stock or consommé

Combine the beef with the herbs, spices, and seasonings (except for 1 tablespoon of the curry) and blend well. Shape into small balls. In a large, heavy skillet heat the butter and oil and sauté the onions and garlic until the onions are limp. Add and brown the meatballs on all sides. Combine the tomato paste, 1 tablespoon of the curry powder, and stock or consommé and stir into the skillet with a wooden spoon. Cover and simmer gently for 10 minutes.

Freezer portion: Remove to containers the number of meatballs you plan to freeze and cover them with sauce. Cool, chill in the refrigerator, then freeze. Store up to 3 months.

Serving the unfrozen portion: Continue to simmer for 10 minutes. Serve with steamed or boiled rice and pass several or all of the following: chutney, separately chopped hard-cooked egg whites and yolks, shredded coconut, chopped peanuts, shredded lettuce, minced onion.

Serving the freezer portion: Partially thaw, release into a heavy saucepan, and heat through. When hot, simmer for 10 minutes and serve as above.

German Meatballs
8 servings, total

1½ pounds ground lean beef
1½ cups coarsely grated raw potatoes
1 tablespoon grated or minced onion
1 tablespoon chopped parsley

1 teaspoon salt
Pinch of black pepper
1 teaspoon lemon juice
1 egg, lightly beaten
3 cups beef stock or consommé
1 teaspoon caraway seeds
2 tablespoons cornstarch stirred into ¼ cup cold water

Combine the beef with the potatoes, onion, parsley, seasonings, lemon juice and egg. Mix thoroughly and refrigerate for 1 hour. Shape into 1-inch balls and drop them one by one into the gently simmering stock or consommé. Cover the pan and simmer for 20 minutes, never allowing the liquid to boil rapidly.

Remove all the meatballs with a slotted spoon and put into containers the amount you plan to freeze. (Keep the rest warm.) Add the caraway seeds to the liquid and simmer, uncovered, for 10 minutes. Add the cornstarch mixture and continue to simmer, stirring, until thickened.

Freezer portion: Cover the meatballs with sauce, chill in the refrigerator, then freeze. Store up to 3 months.

Serving the unfrozen portion: Return the meatballs to the remaining sauce and simmer very gently for 10 minutes.

Serving the freezer portion: Partially thaw and release into a heavy saucepan over low heat. When hot and beginning to bubble, simmer gently for 10 minutes.

Italian Meatballs I
8 servings, total

2 pounds lean ground beef
6 tablespoons minced parsley
1 cup seedless raisins, plumped in water and drained
2 cloves garlic, minced or put through garlic press
1 teaspoon oregano, pulverized between your palms
1 teaspoon basil
1 cup grated or minced onion
3 eggs, stirred but not beaten

½ cup grated Cheddar or American cheese
½ cup grated Romano or Parmesan cheese
1 tablespoon sugar
½ cup pine nuts or chopped cashews
About ⅔ cup olive oil, or half olive oil, half salad oil

Combine all the ingredients except the oil, mixing thoroughly. Refrigerate the mixture for 1 hour, then form into balls. Sauté them in the hot oil until well browned on all sides, removing them as done to drain on paper towels.

Freezer portion: Cool, then chill in the refrigerator the number you plan to freeze. Freeze in a single layer on wax paper in contact with a freezing surface. When solid, gather into a plastic bag. Store up to 1 month.

Serving the unfrozen portion: Add the meatballs to any simmering spaghetti sauce and heat for 20 minutes.

Serving the freezer portion: Thaw slightly, then add to any simmering spaghetti sauce. When the sauce returns to a simmer, heat for 20 minutes.

Italian Meatballs II
8 servings, total

1 pound ground beef
½ pound ground pork
½ pound ground veal
1 cup minced onions
1 clove garlic, minced or put through garlic press
⅓ cup minced parsley
½ cup grated Romano or Parmesan cheese
¾ cup fine dry bread crumbs
2 small eggs, lightly beaten
1 teaspoon salt
½ teaspoon pepper
Pinch each of basil and oregano
About ¼ cup olive oil

Combine all the ingredients except the oil, mixing thoroughly. If the mixture appears excessively dry, add a little stock or milk. Shape into small balls and lightly brown in the hot oil. Remove to drain on paper towels.

Freezer portion: Refrigerate, then spread the meatballs in a single layer on wax paper in contact with a freezer surface. When solid, gather them into a plastic bag. Store up to 1 month.

Serving the unfrozen portion: Continue to sauté the meatballs until well browned on all sides. Serve with spaghetti cooked according to the package directions, topped with meatballs, and covered with any spaghetti sauce.

Serving the freezer portion: Thaw the meatballs in the refrigerator, then finish browning in the hot oil. Serve as above.

Russian Meatballs Stroganoff
8 servings, total

2 pounds lean ground beef
¼ pound veal kidney fat
6 slices crustless white bread
1 large egg lightly beaten in ¼ cup milk
1 teaspoon salt
¼ teaspoon pepper
1 teaspoon lemon juice
5 tablespoons butter
¼ cup minced onion
½ pound mushrooms, sliced
2 tablespoons flour
1 cup beef stock
2 tablespoons tomato paste
1 cup sour cream
Nutmeg

Put the ground beef with the kidney fat through a meat grinder twice. The meat must be very smooth and fine. Soak the bread in the egg-milk mixture and combine this with the meat, salt, pepper, and lemon juice. Mix thoroughly and shape into an even number of balls.

Melt 3 tablespoons of the butter in a large, heavy skillet

and brown the meatballs on all sides. Remove them with a slotted spoon, draining half of them on paper towels and keeping the rest warm. Add the remaining butter to the skillet and sauté the onions for 2 minutes. Add and sauté the mushrooms for 2 minutes. Stir in the flour, add the beef stock and tomato paste, and heat to bubbling. Return the warm meatballs and simmer gently for 10 minutes. Stir in the sour cream and heat without boiling. Sprinkle with nutmeg and serve with buttered noodles or rice. This portion serves four.

Freezer portion: Chill the drained meatballs in the refrigerator and freeze them in a single layer on wax paper. When solid, gather into a plastic bag. Store up to 1 month.

Serving the freezer portion (4 servings): Partially thaw the meatballs while you sauté ¼ cup of minced onions and ½ pound of sliced mushrooms in 2 tablespoons of butter. Stir in 2 tablespoons of flour, and add 1 cup of beef stock and 2 tablespoons of tomato paste. Add the meatballs and, when the sauce simmers, stir in 1 cup of sour cream. Heat without boiling. Sprinkle with nutmeg and serve as above.

Spanish Meatballs
8 servings, total

2 pounds ground beef
1 cup uncooked rice, white or brown
½ cup minced onions
1 teaspoon salt
¼ teaspoon pepper
4 tablespoons olive oil
2 cups canned tomato sauce or purée
1 cup beef stock or consommé
2 teaspoons chili powder
¾ teaspoon ground cumin
Pinch of cayenne pepper

Combine the beef with the uncooked rice, onions, salt, and pepper and shape into balls. In a Dutch oven, brown them lightly in the hot oil. Remove them to paper towels to drain. Pour off any oil remaining in the Dutch oven and combine all the remaining ingredients. Stir and bring to a boil over moderate heat. Return the meatballs, cover, and simmer for 30 minutes.

Freezer portion: Half fill containers with the meatballs you plan to freeze and cover them with sauce. Chill in the refrigerator and freeze. Store up to 3 months.

Serving the unfrozen portion: Continue to simmer for 20 minutes.

Serving the freezer portion: Release into a heavy saucepan. When simmering, reduce the heat and continue to cook for 30 minutes.

MEAT LOAVES

I am grateful that a kindly jinni nudges me to make 2 or more meat loaves when I prepare one for a meal. A meat loaf in the freezer allows me to enjoy it when I don't enjoy making it, and the freeze-ahead practice has saved hours and pleased guests I can't count.

This seems as good a place as any to share a sneaky little secret. I try to keep in the freezer small containers of puréed mixed vegetables—green peppers, onions, carrots, celery, tomatoes. When I make certain kinds of meat loaf, I thaw this purée and blend it with the meat and seasonings. It makes a moist, fine-grained, easy-to-slice loaf for serving hot with gravy, or in cold sandwiches. It also causes a frequently repeated comment: "Now that's what I call meat loaf—made with *meat*. Anything I can't stand, it's meat loaf with vegetables in it." (I told you it was sneaky.)

Made with unfrozen meat, some loaves can be composed, shaped, and frozen raw for storage up to 6 months. Loaves made with thawed meat (or unfrozen, for that matter) may be partially or fully baked for completion or reheating after storage. These should be used within 3 months.

Because meat loaves make such nice compact packages in foil, which preserves moisture during oven heating, accompanying sauces or gravies are best frozen separately in labeled containers. However, many sauces and gravies don't have to be made at the same time you bake the meat loaves. They are easily prepared (or thawed from the freezer stockpile) while the meat is in the oven.

RECIPES FOR MEAT LOAF

Beef Loaf I
2 loaves, each serving 3 or 4

1¼ cups dry bread crumbs
1 cup milk
2 pounds ground beef
2 eggs, lightly beaten
¼ cup grated onion
1 teaspoon salt
⅛ teaspoon pepper
½ teaspoon sage, optional
Catchup, chili sauce, or canned tomatoes
1 cup beef stock or bouillon

Soak the crumbs in the milk and combine with all the ingredients except the catchup, chili sauce, or tomatoes and stock or bouillon. Shape into 2 equal loaves. Spread an undercoating of catchup, chili sauce, or tomatoes in a lightly oiled shallow baking dish and arrange the loaves on this. Bake at 325° basting occasionally with pan drippings and the stock or bouillon.

Freezer portion: Remove 1 loaf after 40 minutes of oven time. Cool, wrap securely in foil, refrigerate, then freeze. Store up to 3 months.

Serving the unfrozen portion: Continue to bake at 325° for 20 minutes. Combine 1 tablespoon of brown sugar, 2 tablespoons of catchup, ⅛ teaspoon of nutmeg, and ½ teaspoon of dry mustard. Mix thoroughly and spread this mixture over the loaf. Continue to bake for 30 minutes.

Serving the freezer portion: Place the foil-wrapped loaf in a shallow baking dish and bake at 350° for 1 hour. Push the foil away and spread with the mixture as above. Lower the oven temperature to 300° and continue to bake for 30 minutes.

Beef Loaf II
2 loaves, each serving 4

1 to 1½ cups mixed chopped raw vegetables (onion, green pepper, celery, carrots)
1 cup drained canned tomatoes (reserve the juice)
1 cup soft bread crumbs
1 egg, lightly beaten
1 teaspoon salt
¼ teaspoon pepper
2 pounds ground beef
Flour
2 slices bacon, cut in half

Mince or grind the vegetables, or purée them together in a blender. Combine all the ingredients except the flour and bacon, mixing thoroughly. Shape into 2 equal loaves. Dredge the loaves with flour and put them into a lightly oiled baking dish. Arrange the bacon over the loaves and bake at 350°, basting often with the reserved tomato juice.

Freezer portion: Remove 1 loaf at the end of 40 minutes (transfer the bacon to the second loaf). Cool, wrap securely in foil, then freeze. Store up to 3 months.

Serving the unfrozen portion: Continue to bake and baste for 1 hour. Thicken the pan drippings with flour. If there are not enough drippings to make gravy, add stock or sour cream, blend thoroughly, thicken with flour, and heat without boiling.

Serving the freezer portion: Put the foil-wrapped loaf

into a shallow baking dish and bake at 350° for 1 hour. Remove the foil and continue to bake for 30 minutes, basting often with warm stock, bouillon, or tomato juice. Thicken for gravy as above.

Bonus Meat Loaf
2 loaves, each serving 4 to 6

12-ounce can or bottle of beer
1 pound ground beef
½ pound ground lean pork
½ pound ground veal
½ cup minced onions
¼ cup minced celery
1 teaspoon salt
¼ teaspoon pepper
¼ teaspoon dry mustard
4 slices crustless white bread soaked in 1 cup milk
2 eggs, slightly beaten
1 tablespoon Worcestershire sauce
8 skinless beef or pork sausages

Pour the beer into a bowl before you start the recipe, to go slightly flat. Combine all the remaining ingredients except the sausages and mix thoroughly. Divide the mixture into 4 equal parts and shape each part into a somewhat flattened rectangle about 5 by 9 inches. Cut the ends from the sausages if necessary, so that you can line up a double column of 2 each (4 sausages) in the center of 2 meat rectangles. Press the remaining 2 meat rectangles over the sausages, enclosing them completely. Put the loaves into a lightly oiled or buttered baking dish, not touching, and bake at 325° for 1 hour, basting at 15-minute intervals with the stale beer.

Freezer portion: Remove 1 loaf to a square of foil and wrap securely with double folds. Cool, chill in the refrigerator, then freeze. Store up to 6 months.

Serving the unfrozen portion: Continue to bake and

baste for 30 minutes. Serve with a brown gravy or cheese-tomato sauce.

Serving the freezer portion: Put the foil-wrapped loaf into a shallow baking dish and bake at 375° for 1 hour. Lower the temperature to 350°, remove the foil or push it away from the loaf, and continue to bake for 30 minutes, basting occasionally with stale beer or with bouillon. Serve as above.

Rolled Stuffed Meat Loaf
2 loaves, each serving 6 to 8

Beef Mixture

4 pounds ground beef
1 cup milk
3 cups fine dry bread crumbs
2 teaspoons salt
½ teaspoon pepper
½ cup minced onions
3 eggs, lightly beaten

In a large bowl, combine all the ingredients and mix thoroughly with your hands. Divide evenly and put each half on a large double square of foil. Press and mold each half into a flattened rectangle approximately 8 by 14 inches.

Stuffing

4 tablespoons butter
2 tablespoons chopped onions
2 tablespoons slivered celery
1 large or 2 small cans mushroom pieces, drained and chopped smaller
4 cups crustless soft bread crumbs
⅔ teaspoon poultry seasoning
½ teaspoon salt
1 tablespoon chopped parsley

Melt the butter in a large heavy saucepan and sauté the onions for 2 minutes. Add and lightly sauté the celery and mushrooms. Add the remaining ingredients and toss with a fork until well mixed. The stuffing should not be moist. Divide equally and spread the stuffing over the 2 meat rectangles. Carefully roll each as for a jelly roll, finishing by pressing the ends to form compact cylinders. Bring the edges of the foil together in tight double folds, and fold in the ends.

Freezer portion: Chill in the refrigerator, then freeze. Store up to 6 months.

Serving the unfrozen portion: Put the loaf wrapped in foil on a cooky sheet or in a shallow pan and bake at 350° for 1½ hours. Open the foil and push it away from the meat to brown for 15 minutes. Slice and serve with any brown or mushroom gravy.

Serving the freezer portion: Put the foil-wrapped loaf onto a cooky sheet or into a shallow pan and bake at 400° for 1 hour. Reduce the oven temperature to 325°, open the foil, and continue to bake for 1 hour. For the first half-hour, baste occasionally with bouillon, then allow the loaf to brown. Serve as above.

Farmer's Loaf
2 loaves, each serving 4 to 6

3 large white potatoes, peeled and quartered
2 large onions, peeled and quartered
1 large green pepper, seeds removed and quartered
1 eating apple, peeled, cored, and quartered
2 pounds ground beef
½ pound bulk pork sausage meat
½ cup fine bread or cracker crumbs
1½ teaspoons salt
2 eggs, lightly beaten
½ cup heavy cream or undiluted evaporated milk

Using the medium or coarse blade, put the vegetables and apple through a meat grinder. Combine this mixture, including the juices, with all the other ingredients. Mix thoroughly. Pack into 2 buttered bread pans (9 by 5 by 3 inches) and cover both pans with foil. Bake at 350° for 1 hour.

Freezer portion: Remove 1 pan, cool, chill in the refrigerator, then freeze. Store up to 3 months.

Serving the unfrozen portion: Uncover and continue to bake for 30 minutes. Unmold, slice, and serve with tomato sauce or brown gravy.

Serving the freezer portion: Bake at 375° for 1 hour. Remove the foil and continue to bake for 40 minutes. Serve as above.

Individual Upside-Down Glazed Meat Loaves
8 servings, total

8 tablespoons dark brown sugar
1 teaspoon dry mustard
8 slices peeled seedless oranges
2 pounds ground beef
2½ cups crustless soft bread crumbs
2 eggs, lightly beaten
¼ cup minced onions
¼ cup minced celery
½ cup minced green pepper
1½ teaspoons salt
¼ teaspoon pepper
Pinch of powdered allspice
⅔ cup orange juice
1 tablespoon lemon juice

Lightly butter 8 ramekins. Those you plan to freeze may be foil containers. Sprinkle the bottoms and sides equally with the brown sugar, then with the dry mustard. Lay a slice of orange in the center of each ramekin. Combine all the remaining ingredients, mixing thoroughly, and divide into 8 equal parts. Press the mixture into the ramekins.

Freezer portion: Wrap those you are going to freeze in foil or freezer film. Freeze. When solidly frozen, they may be stacked, or gathered into a large plastic bag, and stored up to 6 months.

Serving the unfrozen portion: Bake at 350° for 1 hour. Remove from the oven and stand on a trivet for 10 minutes before turning upside down and unmolding on heated plates.

Serving the freezer portion: Uncover and bake at 425° for 1 hour. Remove from the oven and serve as above.

Variations: Use canned pineapple slices and juice instead of orange, substituting 2 pounds of ground lean pork for the beef.

Substitute 2 pounds of ground cooked ham, using only ⅔ teaspoon of salt, and reducing the baking time for the unfrozen portion to 30 minutes. If the ham ramekins are frozen, thaw them in the refrigerator and bake at 350° for 45 minutes.

Oriental Meat Cake
2 cakes, each serving 4

½ cup minced onions
½ cup slivered celery
2 cloves garlic, minced or put through garlic press
2 tablespoons peanut oil
2 pounds ground beef
½ pound ground lean pork
1 can bean sprouts, drained
1 can water chestnuts, drained and chopped
2 eggs, lightly beaten
2 tablespoons soy sauce
1 teaspoon shaved ginger root (or ½ teaspoon powdered ginger)

Sauté the onions, celery, and garlic in the hot oil for 3 minutes, then combine with all the remaining ingredients. Mix thoroughly. Press into 2 lightly oiled round 1½-quart casseroles or baking dishes (1 for the freezer) and bake at 350° for 1 hour. Tip carefully to pour off the excess oil, if any, and make the following topping:

¼ cup sherry
2 tablespoons brown sugar
1½ teaspoons dry mustard
1 tablespoon soy sauce

Mix these ingredients together until well blended and divide the topping into 2 equal parts, spreading evenly over the 2 cakes.

Freezer portion: Cover with foil, cool, refrigerate, then freeze. Store up to 3 months.

Serving the unfrozen portion: Return to the oven and bake for 20 minutes. Remove to a trivet and let stand for 5 minutes. Cut into wedges.

Serving the frozen portion: Bake, covered with foil, in a 400° oven for 1 hour. Uncover and continue to bake at 350° for 30 minutes. Serve as above.

31.

Lamb Recipes

Barbecued Lamb Chop Dinner in Foil
8 servings

8 large or 16 small lamb chops (shoulder, loin, kidney)
½ cup flour
2 tablespoons oil
2 tablespoons butter
1 large eggplant, peeled and cut into 8 slices
8 small frozen onions
8 small frozen potatoes
8 small firm whole tomatoes, peeled
½ cup diced frozen green peppers
1½ teaspoons salt
½ teaspoon paprika
½ teaspoon marjoram
¼ teaspoon basil or oregano
½ teaspoon crumbled mint leaves
About 1 cup tomato sauce, catchup, or chili sauce

Cut heavy aluminum foil into eight 15- by 15-inch squares. If the foil is not heavy gauge, use double sheets. Trim excess fat from the chops and dredge them in the flour.

Brown the chops on both sides in the hot oil and put each (or 2 small ones) in the center of a foil square. Add 2 tablespoons of butter to the skillet and brown the eggplant slices lightly on both sides. Arrange over the chops the eggplant slices, onions, potatoes, and tomatoes and sprinkle with the diced peppers. Mix the seasonings and herbs together and sprinkle over all. Top with dabs of the tomato sauce, catchup, or chili sauce. Fold the foil over and over to make snug packages.

Freezer portion: Chill in the refrigerator, then freeze. Gather into a plastic bag. Store up to 3 months.

Serving the unfrozen portion: Bake at 350° for 1½ hours, or over barbecue coals for 2 hours. Do not turn.

Serving the freezer portion: Bake unthawed in a 375° oven for 2 hours, or over barbecue coals for 2½ hours. Do not turn.

LAMB STEWS

Armenian Lamb Stew
8 servings, total

4 large bunches parsley (about 3 quarts), chopped
2 bunches scallions (about 16), chopped
6 tablespoons olive oil, heated
4 pounds lean lamb, cubed
1 teaspoon salt
¼ teaspoon black pepper
3 tablespoons lemon juice
2 1-pound cans red kidney beans (or 1 can kidney beans and 1 can garbanzos)

In a large Dutch oven, sauté the parsley and scallions in 3 tablespoons of the hot oil until the parsley is wilted and dark green. In a separate large skillet, brown the lamb cubes in the remaining hot oil and add them to the vegetables. Stir in the salt, pepper, and lemon juice, cover with boiling water, and bring again to a boil over moderate heat. Lower the heat and simmer, covered, for 1½ hours. Add the beans with their juice, stir, and taste for seasonings.

Freezer portion: Remove the amount you wish to freeze to a container. Cool, chill in the refrigerator, then freeze. Store up to 3 months.

Serving the unfrozen portion: Continue to simmer until the meat is fork-tender (about 30 minutes).

Serving the freezer portion: Partially thaw in the refrigerator or at room temperature. Heat in a heavy saucepan over low to moderate heat. When simmering, continue to cook until the meat is fork-tender.

Oven Lamb Stew
8 servings, total

3 pounds lean lamb shoulder cut into 1-inch cubes
4 tablespoons olive oil
1 tablespoon sugar
1 teaspoon salt
¼ teaspoon pepper
3 tablespoons flour
2½ cups any meat or poultry stock, consommé, or bouillon
3 firm tomatoes, peeled and chopped
2 cloves garlic, minced or put through garlic press
¼ teaspoon thyme
1 small bay leaf
16 to 24 tiny white potatoes (or 4 to 6 large potatoes, peeled and quartered)
5 or 6 large carrots, scraped and cut into thick rounds
1 cup diced turnips or parsnips
16 to 24 small white onions, peeled (may be frozen)
1 package frozen peas
1 package frozen cut green beans

Brown the meat on all sides in the oil in a large Dutch oven. When well browned, sprinkle with the sugar and cook over low heat, covered, for 5 minutes. Season with the salt and pepper, sprinkle with the flour, and cook 3 minutes longer, turning the pieces to coat them evenly. Add the stock or other liquid, tomatoes, garlic, thyme, and bay leaf and bring to a boil. Transfer the Dutch oven to a preheated 325° oven and bake for 1 to 1½ hours, until the meat is almost tender. Remove the meat, dividing it between 2 casseroles (1 for the freezer). Strain the sauce and skim off any excess fat. Divide the sauce between the casseroles. Add half the potatoes, carrots, turnips (or parsnips), and onions to each casserole. Cover and bake for 20 minutes at 325°.

Freezer portion: Remove 1 casserole from the oven. Cool, then chill in the refrigerator. Stir in half the frozen peas and beans, cover, wrap or bag, and freeze. Store up to 3 months.

Serving the unfrozen portion: Stir the remaining peas and beans into the second casserole and continue to bake for 20 minutes.

Serving the freezer portion: Partially thaw in the refrigerator or at room temperature. Bake in a 350° oven for 1½ hours.

Lamb and Eggplant Stew
8 servings, total

3 pounds lean lamb stew meat cut into cubes
2 tablespoons olive oil
1 large unpeeled eggplant cut into cubes
1 clove garlic, minced
½ cup chopped onions
6-ounce can tomato paste
2 cups hot stock, consommé, or water
1½ teaspoons salt
¼ teaspoon pepper
¼ teaspoon thyme

Brown the lamb cubes on all sides in the hot oil in a Dutch oven. Remove the meat. In the oil and drippings lightly brown the eggplant cubes, garlic, and onions. Return the meat to the pan, and add the tomato paste, hot liquid, and seasonings. Bring to a boil, cover, lower the heat, and simmer for 1 hour.

Freezer portion: Remove to a container the amount you wish to freeze. Cool, chill in the refrigerator, remove surface fat, then freeze. Store up to 3 months.

Serving the unfrozen portion: Continue to simmer for ½ hour. Serve on hot steamed or boiled rice. Pass bowls of raisins and pine nuts (or Spanish peanuts).

Serving the freezer portion: Partially thaw in the refrigerator or at room temperature. Release the stew in a heavy saucepan and heat slowly. When simmering, cook for ½ hour. Serve as above.

Lamb Marengo *
8 servings, total

3 pounds breast of lamb, trimmed of fat and cut into 1-inch pieces
1 teaspoon salt
¼ teaspoon pepper
4 large onions, peeled and thinly sliced
2 tablespoons butter
2 tablespoons oil
¼ cup flour
3½ cups (1 large can) drained whole peeled tomatoes, coarsely
    cut
1 cup dry white wine
1 cup stock or consommé
1 clove garlic, minced or put through garlic press
3 or 4 sprigs fresh parsley, chopped (or 1 teaspoon parsley flakes)
Frozen sliced mushrooms

Sprinkle the lamb with the salt and pepper and brown with the sliced onions in the hot butter and oil in a Dutch oven. Sprinkle with the flour and stir. Add all the remaining ingredients except the mushrooms. Stir, bring to a boil, lower the heat, cover, and simmer for 45 minutes.

* This recipe may also be made with veal. Simmer for 1 hour.

Freezer portion: Remove to a container the amount you wish to freeze. Cool, chill in the refrigerator, then freeze. Store up to 3 months.

Serving the unfrozen portion: Add 1 package of frozen sliced mushrooms, stir, and simmer for 20 minutes. Serve with boiled potatoes.

Serving the freezer portion: Partially thaw in the refrigerator or at room temperature. Release into a heavy saucepan and heat slowly until simmering. Add 1 package of frozen sliced mushrooms, stir, then continue to simmer for 20 minutes. Serve as above.

Pilaf
8 servings, total

1 pound lean lamb sliced into thin julienne strips
4 tablespoons butter
1 cup finely chopped onions
⅓ cup pine nuts or chopped walnuts or pecans
2 cups uncooked rice
2 or 3 drained whole peeled canned tomatoes, chopped
⅓ cup chopped seedless raisins or uncooked prunes
1 teaspoon salt
1 teaspoon pepper
¼ teaspoon ground sage
¼ teaspoon ground allspice
4 cups boiling bouillon
Chopped fresh parsley or mint

Sauté the lamb strips in the butter in a Dutch oven until well browned. Remove the meat with a slotted spoon and keep it warm. In the same pot sauté the onions until limp. Add the nuts and the uncooked rice and stir over medium heat for 5 minutes. Add the tomatoes, raisins or prunes, seasonings, and bouillon. When the sizzling stops, stir well and cover closely. Cook over very low heat until all the liquid is absorbed and the rice is tender (about 20 minutes for short-grain, 30 for long-grain). Return the lamb strips to the pot and stir thoroughly to distribute.

Freezer portion: Remove the amount you wish to freeze to a casserole. Cover, cool, chill in the refrigerator, then freeze. Store up to 3 months.

Serving the unfrozen portion: Keep hot over low heat. Remove to a pilot light or other warming surface for 10 to 15 minutes before serving. Sprinkle with chopped parsley or mint.

Serving the freezer portion: Partially thaw in the refrigerator or at room temperature. Heat in a 400° oven for 1 hour, or until piping hot. Let stand on a warming surface for 10 to 15 minutes before serving as above.

Curried Lamb
8 servings, total

3 pounds boneless lamb
4 tablespoons flour
1½ teaspoons salt
2 or 3 tablespoons curry powder
⅛ teaspoon ground ginger
Pinch of cayenne
½ cup butter
1 cup chopped onions
1 large clove garlic, minced or put through garlic press
2 tablespoons brown sugar
¼ cup seedless raisins, plumped in water and drained
1 lemon, peeled, seeded, and sliced
2 tablespoons sherry
1 tablespoon Worcestershire sauce
3 cups simmering stock or consommé
Crisp apples, pared, cored, and chopped

Trim the fat from the lamb and cut it into bite-size pieces. Shake them in a paper bag in which you have combined the flour, salt, curry powder, ginger, and cayenne. Coat thoroughly. Melt the butter in a large Dutch oven and sauté the onions and garlic for 3 minutes. Lower the heat, push the onions and garlic aside, and brown the dredged lamb pieces, turning to brown evenly. Sprinkle with the sugar, stir, and add all the remaining ingredients except the apple. Stir well, bring to a boil, lower the heat, and simmer, covered, for 45 minutes.

Freezer portion: Put into containers the amount you wish to freeze. Cool, chill in the refrigerator, then freeze. Store up to 3 months.

Serving the unfrozen portion: Add 1 chopped apple and simmer for 15 minutes. Serve with hot rice and pass any or all of the following: chutney, shredded coconut, chopped nuts, separately grated hard-cooked egg white and yolk, mint or currant jelly.

Serving the freezer portion: Partially thaw in the refrigerator or at room temperature. Release into a heavy saucepan over low heat. When simmering (about 1 hour), add 1 chopped apple and simmer for 15 minutes. Serve as above.

Armenian Meatballs
6 to 8 servings, total

1 cup fine, dry bread crumbs
¾ cup milk
1 cup minced or finely chopped onions
2 pounds ground lean lamb *
1 cup minced fresh parsley
3 or 4 leaves fresh mint, shredded (or 1 teaspoon crumbled mint flakes)
3 egg yolks, beaten
¼ teaspoon garlic powder
1½ teaspoons salt
¼ teaspoon pepper
1½ tablespoons olive oil
2 tablespoons butter
Wine vinegar
Lemon juice
Oregano

* This recipe may also be made with ground beef, ground veal, or a mixture of both.

Soak the bread crumbs in the milk in a large mixing bowl. Stir with a fork until evenly absorbed. Add the onions, meat, parsley, mint, egg yolks, garlic powder, salt, and pepper and mix thoroughly. Shape into small balls and brown slowly on all sides in the heated oil combined with the butter. Remove the meat balls from the skillet with a slotted spoon.

Freezer portion: Put into a container the amount you are going to freeze. Cool, chill in the refrigerator, then freeze. Store up to 3 months.

Serving the unfrozen portion: Add 2 tablespoons of wine vinegar and 2 tablespoons of lemon juice to the skillet, stir, and heat. Return the meat balls and cook over low heat, covered, for 15 to 20 minutes. Serve with sprinklings of oregano.

Serving the freezer portion: Partially thaw in the refrigerator or at room temperature. Make a little sauce by stirring 2 tablespoons of wine vinegar and 2 tablespoons of lemon juice into the hot oil and butter. Heat in a skillet, add the meat balls, cover, and heat through. Serve as above.

RECIPES USING COOKED LAMB

Recipes using leftover cooked lamb may be made—and frozen for storage up to 1 month—the day you decide you've eaten all the Sunday roast you care to.

Leftover cooked lamb may also be sliced, diced, or cubed and frozen for use in recipes to be served when cooked.

Lamb Hash Lyonnaise
4 servings

½ cup minced onions
2 tablespoons butter
1 cup any canned tomato sauce
1 cup leftover lamb gravy
1 tablespoon chopped fresh parsley
½ teaspoon salt

⅛ teaspoon pepper
⅛ teaspoon marjoram, tarragon, dill, thyme, or garlic powder
3 to 4 cups leftover cooked lamb

Sauté the onions in the butter until limp. Add the tomato sauce, gravy, parsley, and seasonings and simmer, covered, for 5 minutes. Put the lamb through the fine blade of a meat grinder and combine with the above mixture. Blend well and transfer to a lightly oiled baking dish. Cover, cool, refrigerate, then freeze. Store up to 1 month.

To serve: Put the dish into a 425° oven for 30 minutes while you make 2 cups of mashed potatoes. Remove the dish, reduce the oven temperature to 350°, top the lamb with the mashed potatoes, sprinkle with about 2 tablespoons of grated Romano, Parmesan, or Cheddar cheese, return to the oven, and bake for 20 minutes. Do not refreeze.

Polish Casserole
4 servings

4 slices bacon
½ cup minced onions
½ pound Kielbasy (Polish sausage), sliced
3½ cups (large can) sauerkraut, drained
1 tablespoon caraway seed
¼ teaspoon paprika
3 to 4 cups diced or minced cooked lamb °

Fry the bacon until crisp, then remove, drain, and crumble. Sauté the onions in the bacon drippings for 3 minutes, push aside, and sauté the sausage slices. Combine all the ingredients, mixing thoroughly, and transfer to a lightly oiled baking dish or casserole. Cover, cool, chill, then freeze. Store up to 1 month.

To serve: Put the covered dish into a 425° oven for 35 to 40 minutes, until piping hot. Serve with boiled or mashed potatoes, if desired. Do not refreeze.

° This recipe may also be made with leftover pork.

Lamb and Vegetable Simmer
4 servings

2 tablespoons minced onions
2 tablespoons butter
2 tablespoons flour
2 cups leftover lamb gravy (or 1 cup gravy, 1 cup tomato sauce)
1 teaspoon salt
¼ teaspoon pepper or paprika
¼ teaspoon mace (or any other favorite herb)
½ teaspoon curry powder
2 to 3 cups diced cooked lamb

Sauté the onions in the butter for 3 minutes, then sprinkle with the flour and stir. Add the gravy and all the seasonings, mix thoroughly, and simmer over low heat for 10 minutes. Add the lamb and stir. Cool, pour into a freezer container, chill in the refrigerator, and freeze. Store up to 1 month.

To serve: Partially thaw by setting the container in a pan of cool to warm water. Release the contents into a heavy saucepan over low heat. When melted and simmering, add 2 cups of shredded lettuce and 1 package of frozen lima beans, peas, cut green beans, or niblet corn. Stir, cover, and simmer for 20 minutes. Serve with rice or noodles. Do not refreeze.

Lamb-Eggplant Parmesan
4 servings

1 fairly large eggplant
1 egg, beaten with 1 tablespoon water
½ cup dry bread crumbs
2 tablespoons olive oil
2 cups any Italian spaghetti sauce
2 cups leftover cooked lamb, sliced or cubed
4 slices Mozzarella cheese
½ cup grated Parmesan cheese

Peel the eggplant and slice into ½-inch rounds or half-rounds, making 8 pieces. Dip into the egg mixture, then into the crumbs, and sauté in the hot oil until brown on both sides. Remove and drain on paper towels.

Spread a little of the spaghetti sauce in the bottom of a lightly oiled baking dish and arrange over it 4 of the eggplant slices. Divide the lamb equally over the eggplant and cover this with about half the sauce. Add a second layer of eggplant slices, cover with the remaining sauce, top with Mozzarella cheese, and sprinkle with grated Parmesan. Cover, cool, chill, and freeze. Store up to 1 month.

To serve: Bake at 400° for 35 to 40 minutes. Brown the topping under the broiler section. Do not refreeze.

32.

Ham and Pork Recipes

HAM

Ham is one of the two meats which are not so kindly treated by the freezer as others. (The other is the delicate organ meat variety.) To tell you the truth, I seldom take the time or trouble to prepare ham recipes for freezer storage, preferring to take it out of the freezer—raw, fresh, or smoked—when needed for an upcoming meal.

As with everything else, there are exceptions. Someone's definition of eternity is "a whole ham and two people," so my exceptions are several recipes using cooked leftover ham. These are the ones given in this book.

For recipes made with frozen whole or portions of ham, simply thaw it completely in the refrigerator and proceed with any standard cookbook directions. On page 304 you will find a way to use smoked ham or pork butts directly from the freezer, without thawing.

If you prefer to freeze cooked leftover ham in bulk for later use in recipes served when completed, wrap it carefully in absolutely airtight packages and remember to use it within 1 month. *Do not refreeze recipes made with frozen leftover cooked ham.*

RECIPES USING COOKED HAM

Risotto
3 or 4 servings

½ cup chopped onions
4 tablespoons butter
3 tablespoons finely diced green peppers
¾ cup uncooked rice
1 to 1½ cups diced cooked leftover ham
½ cup canned tomatoes, drained, or condensed tomato soup
2 cups chicken stock or consommé

In a large skillet, sauté the onions in the butter until limp. Add the green peppers and cook for 3 minutes. Add the uncooked rice and stir over moderate heat until lightly toasted. Add all the remaining ingredients in turn and bring to a boil. Stir once, lower the heat to a simmer, cover, and simmer until almost all the liquid is absorbed.

Let cool, pour into a lightly buttered baking dish, and cover with foil. Chill in the refrigerator, then freeze. Store up to 1 month.

To serve: Partially thaw at room temperature and bake, covered, in a 350° oven for 1 hour.

Danish Ham and Macaroni Casserole
4 servings

8-ounce package elbow macaroni
1½ cups diced cooked leftover ham
2 tablespoons butter
¼ cup grated Cheddar cheese
3 eggs

1 cup milk
Salt and pepper to taste

Boil the macaroni according to the package directions for firmness. Rinse well under running cold water and drain. Sauté the ham in the butter, stirring, for 3 or 4 minutes. Combine the macaroni and ham and stir in the cheese, distributing it well. Beat the eggs with the milk, season lightly with salt and pepper, stir this into the macaroni mixture, and mix thoroughly. Pour into a lightly buttered baking dish, cover, and chill in the refrigerator. Slip the dish into a plastic bag and freeze. Store up to 1 month.

To serve: Unbag and bake, covered, in a 400° oven for 45 minutes.

Ham à La King
3 to 4 servings

1½ cups Average White Sauce (page 19) (or 1 cup *any* condensed cream soup diluted with ½ cup milk or liquid from canned mushrooms)
Yolks of 2 hard-cooked eggs, crumbled
6-ounce can sliced or chopped mushrooms, drained
1 tablespoon minced green peppers
1 tablespoon minced pimiento
1 to 1½ cups diced leftover ham

Heat the sauce or diluted soup to simmering and add all the other ingredients. Stir until heated through, but do not let boil. Cool, pour into a container, chill in the refrigerator, then freeze. Store up to 1 month.

To serve: Set the container in cool to warm water until its contents can be released into the top of a double boiler over simmering water. Heat through without boiling. Serve on toast.

Ham Waffles *
4 servings

To a 4-serving recipe of any packaged waffle mix batter (or your own) add 1 cup of minced leftover ham and stir well. Bake the waffles on your waffle baker until *lightly* browned. Cool, slip-sheet with double thicknesses of freezer film or foil, gather into a freezer bag or waxed carton, and freeze (or freeze first, package later). Store up to 3 months.

To serve: Toast in your pop-up toaster. Put down twice, if necessary. Serve with heated sirup or Mushroom Sauce (page 25).

Ham, Cheese, and Vegetable Pie
4 to 6 servings

1 cup diced leftover ham
1 cup crumbled Cheddar, Swiss, or Gruyère cheese
1 package frozen vegetable (lima beans, green beans, peas, corn niblets)
3 eggs
2 cups milk
½ teaspoon salt
Dash of pepper or paprika
1 recipe pie crust dough (your own, or a package mix)

Combine the ham, cheese, and frozen vegetable (without thawing) and spoon the mixture into a lightly buttered 9-inch pie pan. Beat the eggs with the milk and seasonings and pour over the ham mixture. Top with the rolled-out crust, press with the tines of a fork, and trim. Slip the pie into a plastic bag or waxed pie carton and freeze. Store up to 1 month.

To serve: Let the pie stand at room temperature for 1 hour. Place it on a cooky sheet and put it into a 425° oven

* This recipe may also be made with leftover corned beef or tongue, or with shredded leftover chicken or turkey.

for 10 minutes. Cut slits in the dough, reduce the heat to 350°, and continue baking for 45 minutes.

Spanish Ham Casserole *
4 to 6 servings

2 cups minced or finely diced leftover cooked ham
1 cup any meatless tomato-base spaghetti sauce (your own, or canned)
¼ cup chopped green pepper
¼ cup chopped pimiento
½ teaspoon salt
Dash of pepper
Dash of tabasco sauce
1-pound can red kidney beans, drained (freeze the juice for from-the-freezer soups)
1-pound can garbanzos, drained (freeze the juice for from-the-freezer soups)

Combine the ham, tomato sauce, green pepper, pimiento, and seasonings and simmer, stirring occasionally, for 10 minutes. Add the kidney beans and garbanzos, stir, cover, and cook over low heat for 10 minutes. Cool, pour into a lightly oiled casserole, chill in the refrigerator, then freeze. Store up to 1 month.

To serve: Without thawing, put directly into a 400° oven and heat until piping hot (about 1 hour). Garnish with chopped sweet raw onions and shredded lettuce, or sprinkle with grated yellow cheese.

Ham and Yam Pie
4 to 6 servings

2 cups diced leftover cooked ham
2 teaspoons Worcestershire sauce
Dash of pepper
½ cup orange juice
2 eggs, beaten

* Any leftover meat may be used: beef, lamb, veal, pork. The Spanish call a version of this recipe "Ropa Vieja" ("Old Clothes").

2 cups mashed cooked yams or sweet potatoes
1 tablespoon brown sugar
1 tablespoon butter

Toss the ham with the Worcestershire sauce and pepper, then combine with the orange juice, eggs, and yams or sweet potatoes. Spread the mixture in a lightly buttered pie plate, sprinkle with the sugar, and dot with the butter. Cover the pie plate with freezer film or foil and freeze in a plastic bag or waxed pie carton. Store up to 1 month.

To serve: Bake, uncovered, in a 400° oven for 45 minutes.

PORK

Pork chops should remain in your freezer, well wrapped and raw, until early in the morning of the day you're going to serve them for dinner. Pork roasts should remain there until the day before you're going to bake them. And both should be thawed in their wrappings in the refrigerator in advance of cooking. When fully thawed, cook the pork according to any standard cookbook directions.

On the other hand, many savory recipes using cubed, diced, thin-sliced, shoestring-cut, or ground pork are eminently freezable, and the extra time usually required for preparing them recommends the one-for-the-freezer technique.

The pork used in the following recipes may be fresh from the market or, unless otherwise specified, thawed from the freezer.

Portuguese "Galvanized" Pork Chops (in Vinha d'Alhoes)

Note: If these are to be frozen when marinated, use only chops which were not previously frozen. If you plan to cook them for serving when marinated, you may use thawed, partially thawed, or frozen chops. The marinade may be bottled and preserved in the refrigerator for future use.

Allow 1 large or 2 small center-cut chops per serving. Trim excess fat from the chops and put them in a nonmetallic container that will fit into your refrigerator. Combine the following and pour over them:

Vinha d'Ahloes

1 cup cider vinegar
1 cup wine vinegar
2 cups water
¼ cup sugar
2 teaspoons salt
¼ cup whole mixed pickling spices
3 cloves garlic, minced
¼ teaspoon cumin seed

Refrigerate the container, covered. Stir the marinade and turn the chops once a day for 2 days.

Remove the chops from the marinade, pat them dry with paper towels, and wrap meal-portion amounts in a good freezer wrap. Label and freeze. Store up to 6 months.

To serve: Sauté thawed (or freshly prepared) chops just as you do any pork chops, with or without breading. The Portuguese usually fry them in fine olive oil, but they may also be braised or baked after brief browning.

Marinated Pork Cubes

See the note to the preceding recipe. Use lean pork cut into 1-inch cubes. Marinate in Vinha d'Ahloes as above and freeze in containers. When thawed, sauté slowly in fine mild olive oil until well browned. Sprinkle with oregano and serve with rice.

Chinese Pork Sub Gum
8 servings, total

2 pounds lean pork, cut into 1-inch cubes
¼ cup melted butter plus ⅛ cup peanut oil
½ cup chopped scallions

2 large green peppers, seeds removed, cut into thin strips or dice
¾ pound mushrooms, sliced
1-pound can fancy chop suey vegetables, drained
1 small can bamboo shoots, sliced
1 small can water chestnuts, sliced
2 cups rich chicken stock or broth
3 tablespoons cornstarch
2 tablespoons soy sauce
Salt and pepper to taste

In a large, heavy skillet or Dutch oven brown the pork cubes in the butter-oil mixture. When well browned, cover and cook for 15 minutes. Remove the pork and add to the skillet the scallions, green peppers, and mushrooms. Cook for 3 minutes. Add the chop suey vegetables, bamboo shoots, water chestnuts, chicken stock or broth, and pork and stir. Combine the cornstarch with the soy sauce and add. Bring to a boil, turn the heat as low as possible, and taste for seasonings.

Freezer portion: Stir well and remove the amount you wish to freeze to container(s). Cool, chill in the refrigerator, then freeze. Store up to 3 months.

Serving the unfrozen portion: Continue to simmer, stirring occasionally, for 10 minutes. Serve with heated chow mein noodles and boiled or steamed rice.

Serving the freezer portion: Set the container(s) in cool to warm water until the contents can be released into a heavy pan over direct low heat. When melted, continue to heat, stirring, until thickened and piping hot (about 10 minutes). Serve as above.

Spacesaving suggestion for freezing the entire recipe: Prepare the pork, scallions, green peppers, and mushrooms as above. Stir in 1 cup of stock or broth. Cool, then pour into containers and freeze. *To serve:* Heat the chop suey vegetables, bamboo shoots, and water chestnuts with 1 cup of stock or broth. Add the frozen pork mixture, bring slowly to a boil, reduce the heat, and stir. Combine and add the cornstarch and soy sauce. Stir over low heat until thickened, then continue to cook for 10 minutes. Add salt and pepper if needed.

Chinese Pork with Smoked Oysters
8 servings, total

1½ pounds lean pork
4 tablespoons peanut oil
1 large can (7 ounces) smoked oysters, drained
½ cup diced green celery
½ cup diced sweet onions or scallions
½ pound mushrooms, sliced or diced
1 small can bamboo shoots, sliced
1 small can water chestnuts, sliced or diced
1 cup rich chicken stock or broth
2 tablespoons cornstarch
4 tablespoons soy sauce
1 tablespoon sugar
2 or 3 tablespoons sherry
Salt to taste

Cut the pork into julienne strips about ¼ inch by 2 inches. In a large heavy skillet or Dutch oven sauté the strips in the hot oil for 3 minutes, turning to brown all the sides evenly. Remove the pork from the skillet and combine it with the drained oysters, which have been rinsed briefly under hot running water. In the same skillet sauté the celery, onions or scallions, and mushrooms for 3 minutes. Return the pork-oyster combination, stir, and add the bamboo shoots, water chestnuts, and stock or broth. Combine the cornstarch, soy sauce, sugar, and sherry and add. Simmer over low heat, stirring constantly until thickened. Add salt if necessary. Serve with boiled or steamed rice or Chinese thread noodles cooked according to the package directions.

Freezer portion: Remove the amount to be served to containers. Cool, chill in the refrigerator, then freeze. Store up to 3 months.

Serving the frozen portion: Release into a heavy pan over direct low heat. Serve when piping hot, as above.

Mexican Chili Pork
8 servings, total

1½ cups chopped onions
2 cloves garlic, minced
3 tablespoons bacon grease
3 or 4 tablespoons chili powder
3 pounds lean boneless pork cut into 1-inch cubes
3 cups canned tomatoes
1 teaspoon salt
1 teaspoon oregano
1 teaspoon ground cumin
1 bay leaf
2 cups pitted black olives

In a large heavy skillet or Dutch oven, sauté the onions and garlic in the hot bacon grease until light brown. Sprinkle with the chili powder, stir to blend well, and push aside in the pan. Add the pork to the pan and brown it on all sides. Add all the remaining ingredients and stir to mix thoroughly. Lower the heat and simmer, covered, for 1½ hours. Uncover and stir occasionally.

Freezer portion: Remove the amount you wish to freeze to containers. Cool, chill in the refrigerator, then freeze. Store up to 3 months.

Serving the unfrozen portion: Continue to simmer, covered, for 1 hour. If there appears to be too much liquid, uncover for the final 15 minutes. Serve with rice cooked with saffron or turmeric, or with hot corn-meal mush.

Serving the freezer portion: Thaw slightly. Release into a heavy saucepan and heat slowly. When simmering starts, lower the heat and continue to cook for 1 hour. If there appears to be too little liquid, add a little stock or tomato juice. Serve as above.

Flemish Pork in Beer
8 servings, total

2½ pounds lean boneless pork cut into ½- or 1-inch cubes
3 tablespoons rendered pork fat, or shortening
1 teaspoon salt
¼ teaspoon pepper
16-ounce can or bottle of beer
¼ cup boiling water
1 teaspoon crushed dried rosemary
4 onions, sliced
2 cups vegetable bouillon
10-ounce package frozen Brussels sprouts
1 cup very thinly sliced potatoes
1 cup diced or sliced fresh or frozen carrots
2 tablespoons flour
1 tablespoon water

In a large heavy Dutch oven brown the pork cubes on all sides in the hot fat or shortening. Sprinkle with the salt and pepper, add the beer, water, and rosemary, and simmer, covered, for 45 minutes. Add the sliced onions and simmer for 20 minutes. Add the bouillon, stir, and simmer for 5 minutes.

Freezer portion: With a slotted spoon remove half the pork and onions to freezer container(s) and cover with half the liquid. Cool, chill in the refrigerator, then freeze. Store up to 3 months.

Serving the unfrozen portion: Add the Brussels sprouts, potatoes, and carrots and continue cooking until the vegetables are tender (about 10 to 12 minutes). Make a smooth paste of the flour and water and stir it slowly into the mixture. Simmer until thickened, stirring often.

Serving the freezer portion: Set the container(s) in cool to warm water until the contents can be released into a saucepan. When simmering starts, add the quantities of Brussels sprouts, potatoes, and carrots given above. Cook until the vegetables are tender. Thicken and finish as above.

Indian Pungent Pork Curry
6 servings, total

1 tablespoon curry powder
½ teaspoon ground ginger
1 tablespoon mustard seed
½ teaspoon ground turmeric
⅛ to ¼ teaspoon cayenne pepper
½ cup mild vinegar
¼ cup peanut or other oil
4 onions, sliced or chopped
1 clove garlic, minced
2 pounds lean boneless pork cut into ½ - to ¾ -inch dice
1 cup chicken consommé or bouillon

Combine and blend the curry, ginger, mustard seed, tur-meric, and cayenne. Use a mortar and pestle, if you have one. Blend this combination with the vinegar and oil in an earthenware, enamel, or stainless steel Dutch oven. Add the onions, garlic, and pork dice and let stand for 2 or 3 hours, stirring occasionally to moisten the pork evenly. Add the consommé or bouillon, stir, and cook over medium heat for 30 minutes.

Freezer portion: Remove the amount you wish to freeze to container(s). Cool, chill in the refrigerator, then freeze. Store up to 3 months.

Serving the unfrozen portion: Continue to simmer for 10 minutes. Serve over boiled or steamed rice.

Serving the unfrozen portion: Set container(s) in cool to warm water until the contents can be released into a sauce-pan set over moderate heat. When simmering starts, reduce the heat to low and simmer for 15 minutes. Serve as above.

Pork and Vegetable Casserole
2 casseroles, each serving 4

6 to 8 medium onions, thinly sliced
½ cup vegetable oil

2 pounds boneless lean pork, cut into ½ - or ¾ -inch cubes
5 or 6 medium firm tomatoes, peeled and thickly sliced (about
   ½ inch)
Salt and pepper as directed
2 cups fresh green beans, diagonally cut
2 large carrots, scraped and sliced
4 cups diced green peppers
4 cups peeled, cubed eggplant
1 cup uncooked white rice
1½ cups bouillon

In a large, heavy skillet sauté the onions in the oil until
limp and golden. Remove them with a slotted spoon and
divide between 2 lightly oiled baking dishes (about 12 by 8
by 2 inches). In the same skillet, sauté the pork cubes until
they are browned on all sides. Build up layers in the 2 baking dishes as follows:

In each dish arrange one-fourth of the onions, a layer of
sliced tomatoes, a sprinkling of salt and pepper, one-fourth of
the beans, carrots, peppers, and eggplant. Over these ingredients add the uncooked rice (½ cup for each dish) and the
pork cubes equally divided. Sprinkle with salt and pepper.
Top with the remaining vegetables in the same sequence and
sprinkle with salt and pepper. Swish the bouillon in the skillet to mix with any remaining oil and pour equally over the
2 baking dishes. Cover tightly with foil and bake in a preheated 350° oven for 1½ hours.

Freezer portion: Remove one casserole from the oven to
cool. Chill in the refrigerator, then freeze. Store up to 2
months.

Serving the unfrozen portion: Uncover the casserole and
continue to bake for 35 minutes.

Serving the freezer portion: Put the casserole into a 375°
oven for 1 hour. Remove the foil, reduce the heat to 350°,
and continue to bake for 35 to 40 minutes.

French-Canadian Pork Pie
2 pies, each serving 6

1 cup chopped onions
1 clove garlic, minced
4 tablespoons butter
2 pounds lean boneless pork, ground
1 tablespoon cornstarch
1½ cups chicken stock or bouillon
1 teaspoon salt (½ teaspoon if using bouillon)
½ teaspoon ground black pepper
½ teaspoon ground nutmeg
¼ teaspoon ground mace
½ teaspoon ground sage
½ cup minced fresh celery leaves
½ cup fine bread crumbs
Enough pastry dough for three 1-crust pies (your own, or a mix)
1 egg beaten with 2 tablespoons water

In a large heavy Dutch oven, sauté the onions and garlic in the butter until limp and golden. Add the ground pork, breaking it with a fork and turning until all pinkness disappears and the meat is crumbly (about 10 minutes). Sprinkle with the cornstarch and add all the other ingredients except the bread crumbs, pastry dough, and egg. Stir, bring to a boil, lower the heat, and simmer, uncovered, for 20 minutes. The liquid should be almost entirely evaporated. Cool this mixture, refrigerate, then carefully remove any accumulation of surface fat with a clean paper towel.

Freezer portion: Put half the pork mixture into a 9-inch pie plate. (No bottom crust for this one.) Sprinkle with the bread crumbs and top with rolled-out pastry dough. Brush with half the egg-water mixture. Put into a waxed pie box, slip the box into a plastic bag, and freeze. Store up to 2 months.

Serving the unfrozen pie: Line a 9-inch pie plate with half the remaining pastry, fill with the pork mixture, sprinkle with the bread crumbs, and top with rolled-out pastry.

Brush with the rest of the egg-water mixture, cut steam vents in the pastry, and bake in a preheated 425° oven for 10 minutes. Lower the heat to 350° and bake for 15 minutes, until the pastry is golden brown.

Serving the freezer pie: Put the pie into a preheated 425° oven for 25 minutes. Cut steam vents in the pastry, lower the oven temperature to 350°, and bake until the crust is golden brown (about 30 minutes).

RECIPES USING COOKED PORK

Recipes using leftover pork roast may be frozen and stored up to about 1 month. Or they may be made with frozen leftover pork, to be served when cooked.

Pork (or Beef, or Chicken) Chop Suey or Chow Mein

This is an area of cooking wherein I rely to a great extent on the products packaged by the canners and frozen food companies, feeling no urgency to surround myself with masses of often hard-to-find fresh Chinese vegetables and to chop them interminably. However, I have found that even the best of the commercially available frozen Chinese dishes welcome additions, extenders, and enhancements.

The simplest way to serve a sort of Chinese meal on short notice is to buy a package of frozen chop suey or chow mein and rummage through the freezer for embellishments—those little packages of leftover cooked pork, chicken, beef, or shrimp you tucked away. Tap your supply of frozen or canned mushrooms and your pantry stock of canned water chestnuts, bamboo shoots, duck sauce, soy sauce, and bead molasses. Put them all together, they spell "chop suey." Add fried noodles, you have chow mein. Serve with dry, fluffy rice.

The next simplest way is to add your hoard of leftover cooked meat, poultry, or shellfish (after brief sautéing in hot peanut oil) to a can of fancy Chinese mixed vegetables. Add also some extra mushrooms and toasted almonds and perhaps a little thickening made with cornstarch, soy sauce, and rich chicken stock.

Pozharsky
Substitute cooked ground pork for the veal in the recipe on page 390.

Peppers Stuffed with Pork and Mushrooms
4 servings

4 green peppers
4 tablespoons minced onions
1 clove garlic, minced
2 tablespoons butter
1 cup chopped mushrooms
1 to 1½ cups ground cooked pork
½ teaspoon salt
Dash of pepper
¼ teaspoon ground sage
4 slices American or Cheddar cheese
½ cup water, stock, or tomato juice

Cut the tops from the peppers and remove the seeds and membranes. Discard the stems, but mince the tops. Sauté the minced peppers, onions, and garlic in the butter for 3 minutes. Add the mushrooms and sauté for 2 minutes. Combine these ingredients with the meat and seasonings, mixing thoroughly. Stuff the mixture into pepper shells, top each with a slice of cheese, and put them closely together in a small baking dish. Surround the peppers with the liquid and bake at 350° for 15 minutes. Cool, chill in the refrigerator, wrap the peppers individually in foil, then freeze. Store up to 1 month.

To serve: Thaw for a few hours in the refrigerator. Put the foil-wrapped peppers on a cooky sheet in a preheated 375° oven for 25 to 45 minutes, until piping hot. (Remove the foil for the last 10 minutes of oven time.)

Bigos (Polish Pork Stew)
4 servings

1 pound sauerkraut (fresh or canned)
1½ cups canned tomatoes
1 cup any meat or poultry stock
⅔ cup chopped onions
1 tablespoon rendered bacon, pork, or ham fat
½ pound mushrooms, sliced or chopped
1 firm apple, peeled, cored, and chopped
½ pound Kielbasy (Polish sausage), cut into 1-inch pieces
1 cup diced cooked pork
⅛ teaspoon paprika
Salt to taste
1½ teaspoon sugar
1 tablespoon flour

Drain the sauerkraut and rinse it under running cold water. Combine it in a Dutch oven with the tomatoes and stock, bring to a boil, lower the heat, and let simmer gently. In a large skillet, sauté the onions in the hot fat until limp, add and sauté the mushrooms for 2 minutes, then add the apple and sauté for 1 minute. Add the Kielbasy and pork and cook over low heat for 10 minutes, stirring often. Stir in the seasonings, sugar, and flour and mix thoroughly. Add this mixture to the simmering sauerkraut and tomatoes, stir well, and continue to simmer for 1½ hours, covered. If the mixture appears dry, add a little more stock. Cool, chill in the refrigerator, spoon into a container, then freeze. Store up to 1 month.

To serve: Set the container in a pan of cool to warm water until its contents can be released into the top of a double boiler over simmering water. Allow plenty of time for it to heat through (at least 2 hours). Check the water in the bottom of the double boiler occasionally, adding more if needed. Serve with boiled potatoes or noodles.

33.

Veal Recipes

Veal roasts, chops, and steaks should remain in your freezer, raw, to be thawed for cooking. When fully thawed, cook the meat according to any standard cookbook directions.

Some of the nicest products to come from the frozen meat processors are portion-controlled veal cutlets, sold either plain or breaded. They lend themselves to a number of recipes for the freezer, or from it.

RECIPES USING VEAL

Swiss Veal Steak in Casserole
2 casseroles, each serving 4

½ cup flour
1 teaspoon salt
¼ teaspoon pepper
Two 2-pound veal steaks, cut 1 inch thick
4 tablespoons vegetable oil
4 medium onions, sliced
1 large green pepper, seeds removed, cut sliver-thin in strips
2 cups canned tomatoes
Frozen baby lima beans or peas

Combine the flour, salt, and pepper and pound this mixture into the veal steaks with the edge of a heavy plate. One at a time, sauté the floured steaks in the hot oil in a heavy skillet until well browned on both sides. Remove them to 2 casseroles, 1 for the freezer.

In the same skillet sauté the onions and green peppers for 3 minutes, stirring to coat evenly with oil. Stir in the tomatoes and divide the mixture between the 2 casseroles.

Freezer casserole: Cover, cool, and chill the casserole in the refrigerator. Slip it into a plastic bag and freeze. Store up to 3 months.

Serving the unfrozen casserole: Cover the casserole and bake in a preheated 350° oven for 40 minutes. Uncover, surround the meat with 1 package of frozen lima beans or peas, sprinkle them with a little salt, cover the casserole again, and continue to bake for 1 hour.

Serving the frozen casserole: Thaw at room temperature for 1 hour. Put the covered casserole into a preheated 375° oven for 1 hour. Uncover, surround the meat with 1 package of frozen lima beans or peas, sprinkle lightly with salt, cover, reduce the oven temperature to 350°, and continue to bake for 1 hour.

Hungarian Veal Paprika
8 servings, total

1 medium onion, minced
1 clove garlic, minced
4 tablespoons butter
3 pounds boneless veal cut into 2-inch cubes
1 teaspoon salt
¼ teaspoon pepper
3½ cups simmering veal, chicken, or vegetable stock
4 tablespoons flour
4 tablespoons good Hungarian paprika
Sour cream

In a heavy Dutch oven sauté the onions and garlic in the hot butter for 3 minutes. Sprinkle the veal cubes with the salt and pepper and add to the skillet. Brown on all sides. Add 3 cups of the simmering stock (allow the remaining ½ cup to cool), cover, and simmer gently for 1 hour. Stir the flour and paprika into the cooled ½ cup of stock. Add to the Dutch oven, stirring.

Freezer portion: Remove to container(s) the amount you wish to freeze. Cool, chill in the refrigerator, then freeze. Store up to 3 months.

Serving the unfrozen portion: Simmer for ½ hour longer, until the veal is tender. Stir in ½ cup of sour cream per serving and heat without boiling.

Serving the freezer portion: Set the container(s) in cool to warm water until the contents can be released into a heavy saucepan over very low heat. When simmering, cook until the veal is tender (about 35 to 40 minutes). Add ½ cup of sour cream per serving and heat without boiling.

Traditionally, this is served with potato dumplings, best made just before serving according to any standard cookbook directions.

Veal in Barbecue Sauce
8 servings, total

3 pounds boneless veal cut into 2-inch cubes
2 tablespoons melted shortening
1 teaspoon salt
¼ teaspoon pepper
1 cup chopped onions
½ cup diced celery
½ cup diced green peppers
1½ cups any meatless spaghetti sauce
½ cup tomato catchup
2 tablespoons brown sugar
1 tablespoon Worcestershire sauce
1 or 2 drops tabasco sauce
2 tablespoons prepared table mustard

Brown the veal cubes on all sides in the hot fat in a large skillet or Dutch oven. Sprinkle with the salt and pepper, add all the remaining ingredients, cover, and simmer over low heat for 1½ hours.

Freezer portion: Remove to containers the amount you wish to freeze. Cool, chill in the refrigerator, then freeze. Store up to 3 months.

Serving the unfrozen portion: Continue to simmer for 35 minutes longer, until the veal is tender.

Serving the freezer portion: Partially thaw, then release into a saucepan over low heat. When bubbling, simmer for 35 to 40 minutes, until the veal is tender.

Veal Marengo
8 servings, total

3 pounds boneless veal shoulder cut into 1½-inch cubes
4 tablespoons olive oil
¾ cup minced onions
¼ cup minced shallots (optional)
1 small clove garlic, minced
6-ounce can tomato paste
2 tablespoons flour
1½ cups beef, veal, or chicken stock
1½ cups dry white wine
1 teaspoon salt
¼ teaspoon freshly ground black pepper
Pinch each of basil and thyme
Fresh or frozen small whole white onions
Fresh or frozen whole mushrooms
Butter

In a large, heavy Dutch oven brown the veal cubes on all sides in the hot oil. Add and lightly brown the onions, shallots if desired, and garlic. Stir in the tomato paste and cook for 2 minutes, still stirring. Sprinkle with the flour, stir, add the stock and wine and all seasonings, and mix thoroughly. Cover and simmer for 1 hour.

Freezer portion: Remove to containers the amount you wish to freeze. Cool, chill in the refrigerator, then freeze. Store up to 3 months.

Serving the unfrozen portion: In a separate skillet, sauté 2 small whole white onions and 3 or 4 whole mushrooms per serving in butter and add them to the marengo. Cover and continue to simmer for about 30 minutes, until the veal is tender. Serve with boiled rice or noodles.

Serving the freezer portion: Partially thaw. Heat in a heavy saucepan over very low heat (or use the top of a double boiler over simmering water) until bubbling. In a separate skillet, sauté the whole onions and mushrooms in butter as above and add them. Cover and continue to simmer until the veal is tender. If desired, the recipe may then be transferred to a heated casserole to be kept warm in a low oven until served as above.

Sweet and Sour Veal with Mushrooms
8 servings, total

3 pounds boneless veal, cut into 1-inch cubes
4 cups boiling vegetable stock or water
1 teaspoon salt
1 cup sliced onions
½ cup cut carrots
2 tablespoons chopped fresh parsley (or 2 teaspoons parsley flakes)
1 tablespoon grated lemon rind
1 pound mushrooms, whole or sliced
2 tablespoons butter
2 tablespoons olive oil
1 tablespoon lemon juice
1 tablespoon brown sugar
1 egg yolk, lightly beaten

Without browning, add the veal to the boiling liquid in a large pot along with the salt, onions, carrots, parsley, and lemon rind. When the liquid returns to a boil, lower the heat and simmer, covered, for 1 hour. Use tongs to remove the veal and set aside. Strain the broth and reserve 2 cupfuls. (Freeze the rest as stock.) Sauté the mushrooms in the combined butter and oil in a large skillet. Add the lemon juice, stir, add the brown sugar, and stir until dissolved. Cook for 2 minutes. Add the 2 cups of strained broth, stir, and cook for 5 minutes. Remove from the heat. Beat a few spoonfuls of the liquid into the egg yolk, then add this mixture to the sauce. Return the pot to low heat and stir until slightly thickened.

Freezer portion: Put the amount of veal cubes you wish to freeze into containers, about ⅔ full. Cover with mushrooms and sauce, cool, chill in the refrigerator, and freeze. Store up to 3 months.

Serving the unfrozen portion: Return the remaining veal cubes to the sauce and heat through. Serve with boiled rice or noodles.

Serving the freezer portion: Partially thaw, then heat in the top of a double boiler over simmering water, stirring often as it melts. Do not let it boil. Serve as above.

Veal Stroganoff
8 servings, total

¾ pound mushrooms, sliced
8 tablespoons butter
2 to 2½ pounds boneless veal, cut into small cubes
½ cup minced onions
1 small clove garlic, minced or put through garlic press
5 tablespoons flour
1½ cups veal or chicken stock, or water
1 cup sherry
1 teaspoon Worcestershire sauce
½ teaspoon paprika
Pinch of basil
Salt and pepper to taste
Noodles

Sour cream
Grated Cheddar, Romano, or Parmesan cheese

In a large, heavy Dutch oven, sauté the mushrooms in 4 tablespoons of the butter for 3 minutes, stirring. Drain. Reserve the mushrooms and liquid separately. Melt the remaining 4 tablespoons of butter in the same skillet and brown the veal cubes. Add the onions and garlic and cook over low heat until the veal is no longer pink. Stir in the flour, stock or water, sherry, and reserved buttery mushroom liquid. Cook, stirring constantly, until the liquid boils and thickens. Add the Worcestershire sauce and seasonings, cover, and simmer for 45 minutes. Stir often. Add the sautéed mushrooms and mix thoroughly.

Freezer portion: Pour the amount to be frozen into containers, cool, chill in the refrigerator, and freeze. Store up to 3 months.

Serving the unfrozen portion: Continue to simmer the veal while you cook noodles (¼ pound for each 2 servings) in boiling salted water until tender. Drain and combine with the veal. Add ¼ cup of sour cream for each 2 servings and stir. Transfer to a buttered casserole, sprinkle with grated cheese, and bake at 350° for 30 minutes.

Serving the freezer portion: Partially thaw, then release into the top of a double boiler over simmering water. When melted and hot, combine with the cooked noodles and sour cream as above. Transfer to a buttered casserole, sprinkle with grated cheese, and bake at 375° for 40 minutes.

Hungarian Veal and Mushroom Rolls
8 servings (2 rolls per serving)

1½ pounds mushrooms
¼ pound plus 4 tablespoons butter
4 tablespoons flour
1 teaspoon salt
½ teaspoon freshly ground black pepper
16 very thin veal cutlets

¼ cup minced onions
¼ cup chopped fresh parsley
4 tablespoons vegetable oil
2 tablespoons freshly ground Hungarian paprika
Heavy sweet or sour cream

Chop or grind the mushrooms, stems and all, until very fine. In a large, heavy skillet sauté them in ¼ pound of the butter over very low heat, covered, until the mushrooms are limp and a quantity of liquid forms in the pan. Sprinkle with the flour, salt, and pepper, stir, and continue to cook over low heat until the mixture is pastelike in consistency. "Butter" the thin veal cutlets with this mixture and top each with combined minced onions and parsley (about a teaspoonful for each cutlet). Roll and tie the cutlets. Combine the remaining 4 tablespoons of butter with the oil in the mushroom skillet and brown the rolls, turning frequently. Sprinkle with the paprika as they brown.

Freezer portion: Remove and cool the number you wish to freeze. Wrap them in a single layer in foil, chill in the refrigerator, then freeze. Store up to 1 month.

Serving the unfrozen portion: Add ¼ cup of sweet or sour cream per serving to the skillet. Cover and simmer, but do not boil, for ten minutes, turning occasionally. Serve with buttered noodles or rice.

Serving the freezer portion: Heat the foil-covered rolls in a 350° oven for 35 minutes. Remove the foil, transfer the rolls to a skillet with about 1 tablespoon of butter per roll, and cook, covered, over very low heat until piping hot. Add ¼ cup of sweet or sour cream per serving and simmer as above.

Veal Parmigiana
8 servings, total

8 large, thin Italian-style veal cutlets (about 2 pounds)
3 eggs beaten with 1 teaspoon salt and ¼ teaspoon pepper
About 1½ cups fine bread crumbs

¼ cup grated Parmesan cheese
4 tablespoons olive oil
3 cups thick, well-garlicked Italian spaghetti sauce (your own,
   or canned)
12 ounces to 1 pound mozzarella cheese, thinly sliced

If the cutlets are not quite thin enough, flatten them with
a mallet. Dip them first into the seasoned egg, then into the
bread crumbs combined with the grated cheese. Refrigerate
on a platter, layers separated with waxed paper, for at least
1 hour. Sauté the chilled cutlets in the hot oil, turning from
time to time, until golden brown on each side. Spoon about
half the spaghetti sauce into the bottoms of 2 or more shallow baking dishes. Put the browned cutlets close together
over this sauce, cover with the remaining sauce, and top
with the cheese slices.

Freezer portion: Cool the amount you plan to freeze in
the baking dish(es) covered closely with foil. Chill in the refrigerator, slip into a plastic bag, and freeze. Store up to 3
months.

Serving the unfrozen portion: Put the baking dish into a
350° oven and bake for 30 to 40 minutes, until the sauce
bubbles and the mozzarella melts. If desired, brown under
the broiler. Pass extra grated cheese.

Serving the freezer portion: Partially thaw at room temperature for 1 hour. Put the uncovered baking dish in a 350°
oven for 45 to 50 minutes, until the sauce bubbles and the
mozzarella melts. Brown and serve as above.

Easy Veal Parmigiana
4 servings, total

1 clove garlic, quartered
2 tablespoons olive oil
4 frozen breaded portion-controlled veal cutlets (about 1 pound),
   thawed
1½ cups thick, well-seasoned Italian tomato sauce (your own
   or canned)

½ pound mozzarella cheese, thinly sliced
Grated Parmesan cheese

Lightly brown the garlic in the hot oil, stirring to flavor the oil evenly. Discard the garlic. Brown the breaded veal cutlets on both sides. Spoon about half the sauce into the bottom of a shallow baking dish, add the cutlets, cover them with the remaining sauce, and top with the sliced cheese. Bake in a 350° oven about 30 minutes. Pass grated cheese.

Serve, or freeze up to 1 month. *To serve after freezer storage:* Heat in a moderate oven until the cheese melts and the sauce bubbles. Serve as above.

Stuffed Veal Birds Cacciatore
8 servings (2 per serving)

12 chicken livers
3 tablespoons butter
3 slices prosciutto (Italian ham)
3 or 4 sprigs parsley
⅛ teaspoon sage, basil, or oregano
½ teaspoon salt
¼ teaspoon pepper
16 very thin (Italian-style) veal cutlets (about 2 pounds)
1 clove garlic, quartered
2 tablespoons olive oil
2 teaspoons flour
1½ cups Marsala (or sherry) wine
Italian or French bread
Chicken or veal stock

In a large skillet, sauté the chicken livers in the butter until cooked through but not well done (about 5 minutes), turning once. Put the livers, ham, and parsley through a grinder (using the small blade) or chop fine. Add and blend in the seasonings. Spread the cutlets with this mixture, dividing it evenly. Roll the veal and tie the rolls with string. Brown the garlic in the hot oil, then discard the garlic. Add the rolls and brown well on all sides over low heat. Sprinkle with the flour, add the wine to the skillet, and continue to cook over low heat, uncovered, until almost all the wine is evaporated. Spoon the liquid over the veal rolls as they brown.

Freezer portion: Remove the rolls you plan to freeze. Let them cool, then wrap in meal-sized portions in foil. Chill in the refrigerator and freeze. Store up to 1 month.

Serving the unfrozen portion: Toast thin slices of bread (2 slices per serving). Put the toast onto a platter and top with veal rolls. Add ¼ cup of stock per serving to the skillet, stir and swirl over moderate heat for 1 minute, and pour the liquid over the veal.

Serving the freezer portion: Heat foil-covered rolls in a 350° oven for 40 minutes. For each 2 rolls, combine and heat in a small saucepan 1 teaspoon of butter, 1 tablespoon of stock or bouillon, 1 tablespoon of Marsala or sherry. Toast Italian or French bread as above, unfoil the rolls and put them onto the toast, and pour the sauce over them.

RECIPES USING COOKED VEAL

Recipes using leftover veal roast may be frozen and stored up to about 1 month. Or they may be made with frozen leftover veal, to be served when cooked.

Peppers Stuffed with Veal and Mushrooms
Substitute ground cooked veal for the pork in the recipe on page 376.

Veal and Frozen Spinach Casserole
4 servings

2 10-ounce packages frozen creamed spinach
½ teaspoon onion salt
Thinly sliced leftover cooked veal roast
1 cup (or 8-ounce can) mushroom, chicken, or brown gravy

½ cup fine bread crumbs
2 teaspoons butter
2 tablespoons grated Cheddar, Romano, or Parmesan cheese

Without cooking or thawing the frozen spinach, put it into the bottom of a lightly buttered casserole, sprinkle with the onion salt, arrange the veal slices over it, smother with the cold gravy, cover with the bread crumbs, dot with the butter, and top with the grated cheese. Cover with foil, slip into a plastic bag, and freeze immediately.

To serve: Bake at 350° for 1 hour, until the spinach is cooked and the topping brown.

Note: A smaller recipe can be prepared to serve 2. Just divide all the ingredients in half.

Curried Veal
4 servings

2 cups diced leftover cooked veal
4 tablespoons butter
1 cup chopped onions
1 tablespoon curry powder
¼ teaspoon powdered ginger
1 tablespoon flour
1 cup veal or chicken stock
1 tablespoon lemon juice
¼ cup seedless raisins, plumped in water and drained

Brown the veal briefly in 2 tablespoons of the butter, then put the meat into a freezer container. Add the remaining 2 tablespoons of butter to the skillet and, when hot, sauté the onions over low heat until they are limp. Sprinkle with the curry powder, ginger, and flour, stirring well. Add the stock, stir, and bring to a boil. Remove from the heat and stir in the lemon juice and raisins. Let the sauce cool, then pour over the veal in the container. Chill in the refrigerator and freeze. Store up to 1 month.

To serve: Thaw until the contents can be released into

the top of a double boiler over simmering water, to melt and heat. When completely thawed and simmering, peel, core, and chop 1 firm apple and add. Stir and cook for 1 or 2 minutes. When piping hot, serve with boiled rice.

Pozharsky
4 servings

Although this recipe is given for leftover cooked veal, it is worth cooking veal especially for it. It is one of the recipes for which I use frozen portion-controlled unbreaded veal cutlets, letting them thaw sufficiently to pan-fry until cooked through, then putting them through the meat grinder.

4 slices crustless white bread
About ½ cup milk
2 cups chopped or ground cooked veal
½ cup minced onions
2 tablespoons butter
Salt and pepper to taste
1 egg, lightly stirred with a fork
1 egg, beaten with 2 tablespoons water
⅔ cup or more fine bread crumbs

Soak the bread in the milk, squeeze almost dry, and combine with the veal. Sauté the onions in the butter over very low heat, covered, until soft and limp. Add them to the meat along with salt, pepper, and the stirred egg. Mix thoroughly and form into 8 somewhat flattened cutlets, round or oval. Dip the cutlets into the beaten egg, then into the bread crumbs, coating them well. Lift them carefully and refrigerate in a single layer on wax paper. Wrap serving portions in foil, or pack them in a freezer box, and freeze. Store up to 1 month.

To serve: Thaw the cutlets. Heat butter (1 tablespoon per cutlet) and fry until brown on both sides. Remove them to a warm platter or individual plates. Add to the pan butter a few tablespoons of stock, broth, or bouillon, bring to a boil, and pour over the cutlets. If desired, serve with a topping of sautéed sliced mushrooms or a thick mushroom sauce.

34.

Meat or Poultry Pies

Any of your favorite stews, boneless fricassees—even some ground meat recipes—can easily become dressier if they are converted into pies. For freezer storage, I find them more satisfactory when made without bottom crusts, which may become soggy.

Meat or Poultry Pies for the Freezer

Cook the stew or other appropriate recipe according to cookbook directions (this book, or an old standby). Add *fresh* vegetables for the last 5 minutes of cooking time. Cool, then refrigerate the stew. Add *frozen* vegetables after the stew has been thoroughly chilled in the refrigerator, after first removing congealed fat, if any, from the surface. Stir to distribute the ingredients evenly. Spoon into a lightly buttered freezer casserole, baking dish, or pie plate. Choose for the purpose a dish which the stew will fill to the top.

Pastry Crust: Make your own recipe or use a mix and roll the dough to a thickness of ¼ inch, stretching it so that it is about ½ inch wider than the dish all around. Beat an egg with a tablespoon of water and brush some of this mixture around the top rim of the dish. Cover the filling loosely with dough and seal the edges firmly by pressing with the tines of a dinner fork. Brush the remaining egg mixture over the top of the dough, taking care not to pierce it. Trim excess dough from the edges of the rim.

Biscuit Topping: Make your own baking powder biscuit recipe or use a mix. Put the dough onto a floured board and, after kneading, roll out to a thickness of ½ inch. Cut into rounds with a small biscuit cutter. Arrange unbaked biscuits on top of the stew and brush them with melted butter.

Mashed Potato Topping: Use leftover or newly made mashed white or sweet potatoes. Mix well by beating with 2 or 3 tablespoons of melted butter, a little cream or milk (orange juice is nice with mashed sweet potatoes), beaten egg, salt and pepper to taste, and any additions you like— chopped parsley or chives, poppy or caraway seeds, a pinch of a favorite herb, grated cheese. Let the potato mixture cool, then use a spoon or an icing tube to swirl the topping over the stew. Dribble melted butter over your design.

To freeze: The best containers I know for pies with fragile toppings are the waxed boxes you get when you buy frozen pies. Slide your pie into such a box, close it, and slip it into a plastic bag. Store in the freezer up to 1 month, in a spot where it won't get bumped.

To serve: Partially thaw at room temperature. Unbox and put the pie onto a cooky sheet. If topped with pastry dough, cut a few slits.

Bake pies with pastry topping at 450° for 15 minutes, reduce the heat to 350° and bake for 30 to 45 minutes, depending on size. Bake pies with biscuit or potato topping at 400° for 40 to 45 minutes.

35.

Vegetables

Bless the frozen food processors. Not only do they save you time, work, and uncertainty, but they also provide you with packaged vegetables fresher than any others available—unless, of course, you harvest your own or buy them directly from the farmer who grows them.

With very few exceptions, I rarely freeze a cooked vegetable recipe. After brief blanching, I freeze farm produce for use in recipes which will be served when cooked. The exceptions are Eggplant Parmigiana, Stuffed Whole Onions, and, around Thanksgiving time, Candied Sweet Potatoes. Aside from these exceptions, the recipes in this section will be *from* the freezer, not for it, using many of the commercial frozen vegetables neatly and compactly packaged for freezer storage.

VEGETABLE RECIPES FOR THE FREEZER

Eggplant Parmigiana
8 servings, total

1 very large or 2 smaller eggplant (8 or more slices)
2 or 3 eggs beaten with 2 tablespoons water
1½ cups fine bread crumbs (best made in a blender from stale
    Italian bread)
1 teaspoon salt
¼ teaspoon pepper
¼ cup grated Romano or Parmesan cheese
4 tablespoons olive oil
3 cups any Italian sauce (your own or canned)
1 teaspoon oregano
1 pound mozzarella cheese, thinly sliced

Peel the eggplant and slice into ½-inch rounds. Dip the slices first into the eggs, then into the crumbs mixed with the salt, pepper, and grated cheese. Refrigerate on wax paper for at least 1 hour. In a large, heavy skillet sauté a few slices at a time in the hot oil until lightly browned on one side. Turn with a wide spatula and brown the other side. Remove as they are browned to drain on paper towels. Spread about 1 cup of the sauce over the bottoms of 2 shallow baking dishes (1 for the freezer). Arrange the eggplant over the sauce, sprinkle with the oregano, cover with the remaining sauce, and top with the sliced mozzarella.

Freezer portion: Cover the dish with foil, chill in the refrigerator, slip into a plastic bag, and freeze. Store up to 1 month.

Serving the unfrozen portion: Bake, uncovered, in a 350° oven for 25 to 30 minutes. Brown the topping under the broiler section. Pass more grated cheese.

Serving the freezer portion: Unbag, uncover, and bake at 375° for 35 to 40 minutes. Brown and serve as above.

Baked Stuffed Onions
8 servings, total

16 large, whole yellow onions of equal size
4 cups moist bread stuffing (page 413), or packaged stuffing
1 cup hot stock or consommé

Without peeling the onions, drop them into a quantity of boiling water and simmer for 2 minutes. Drain and, when cool enough to handle, slip the skins off. Lightly butter 2 casseroles or baking dishes, spread some of the stuffing over the bottoms, stand the onions upright and fairly close together, and top with the remaining stuffing. Bake at 350° for 1 hour, basting occasionally with the hot stock or consommé.

Freezer portion: Remove and cool the casserole you plan to freeze. Chill in the refrigerator, cover with foil, slip into a plastic bag, and freeze. Store up to 1 month.

Serving the unfrozen portion: Continue to bake for about 35 to 40 minutes longer, until the onions are tender.

Serving the freezer portion: Let stand at room temperature. Unbag and uncover and bake at 350° for 1 hour or longer, until the onions are tender.

Candied Sweet Potatoes
8 servings, total

8 large sweet potatoes or equivalent of smaller ones
1½ teaspoons salt
½ teaspoon pepper
1 cup dark brown sugar
4 tablespoons orange juice
1 teaspoon grated orange rind
4 tablespoons butter

Without peeling the potatoes, bring them to a boil in a large pot of water and cook for 15 to 20 minutes. They should not be fully cooked. Peel and slice them either as rounds or in lengthwise slices about ½ inch thick. Arrange them in 2 lightly buttered shallow baking dishes (1 for the freezer), sprinkle with the equally divided salt, pepper, sugar, orange juice, and rind. Dot them with the butter.

Freezer portion: Cool, then refrigerate the portion you plan to freeze. Cover with foil, slip into a plastic bag, and freeze. Store up to 1 month.

Serving the unfrozen portion: Bake at 375°, uncovered, for 20 minutes. Turn the potatoes with a spatula and bake for 10 minutes. Spoon the drippings over them.

Serving the freezer portion: Let stand at room temperature for 1 hour. Bake, covered, for 15 minutes at 400°. Reduce the temperature to 350°, uncover, and continue to bake for 30 minutes. Turn the potatoes with a spatula and bake for 10 minutes. Spoon the drippings over them.

VEGETABLE RECIPES FROM THE FREEZER

Artichoke Hearts and Mushrooms en Brochette
8 brochettes

2 packages frozen artichoke hearts
Medium to large fresh mushroom caps (as many as artichoke hearts)
¼ cup butter
Salt, pepper, nutmeg
3 tablespoons olive oil
1 clove garlic, cut in half

Cook the artichoke hearts according to the package directions. Drain well. Peel the mushroom caps. Sauté both vegetables in the hot butter in a large, heavy skillet for 3 minutes, turning often. Remove carefully with a slotted spoon and thread alternately on 8 skewers. Sprinkle lightly with salt, pepper, and nutmeg on all sides. Add the olive oil to the skillet and heat. Sauté the garlic for 3 minutes, then discard it. Roll the brochettes in the oil and broil over coals or

under the broiler for 5 minutes, turning frequently. Serve
piping hot.

Artichoke Hearts Alicia
8 servings

2 packages frozen artichoke hearts
¼ cup fine olive oil
¼ cup lemon juice
1 large clove garlic, minced or put through garlic press
1 tablespoon minced parsley
1 tablespoon minced onion
½ teaspoon salt
¼ teaspoon black pepper
Pinch or two of oregano
2 tablespoons crumbled Roquefort, bleu, or Gorgonzola cheese

Cook the artichoke hearts according to the package directions and drain well. Combine all the remaining ingredients
in a jar with a tight-fitting lid, close the jar, and shake vigorously. Pour this marinade over the artichokes in a bowl and
toss with 2 wooden spoons to coat evenly. Cover the bowl
and refrigerate for at least 4 hours, stirring occasionally.
These are delicious served as a toothpick appetizer in advance of an Italian meal.

Baked Asparagus Tips au Gratin
4 servings

2 packages frozen asparagus tips
4 pieces toasted white bread, cut diagonally
1 cup light-colored gravy or sauce (chicken, mushroom, Hollan-
    daise, etc.
½ cup fine bread crumbs
½ cup grated Cheddar or Swiss cheese
2 tablespoons butter

Cook the asparagus tips according to the package directions and drain well. Arrange them on the toast in a shallow
casserole. Cover with the sauce. Sprinkle with the bread

crumbs combined with the grated cheese and top with dots of the butter. Bake at 400° until the topping is browned.

French Fried Asparagus Spears
4 servings

2 packages frozen asparagus spears
2 eggs, lightly beaten
1 cup fine bread or cracker crumbs
Deep fat for frying

Drop the asparagus spears into a 2-quart saucepan half-filled with boiling salted water. As soon as they separate, remove them and drain well on paper towels. They should not be cooked. Dip the spears first into the beaten egg, then roll them in the crumbs. Refrigerate for 1 hour. Drop them, a few at a time, into hot deep fat (375°) and fry until well browned. Serve with Hollandaise Sauce (page 29) or Hot Mayonnaise Sauce (page 22).

Baked Beans, Chinese
6 to 8 servings

2 packages frozen cut green or yellow beans
1-pound can Chinese bean sprouts, washed and drained
1 small can water chestnuts, chopped
¼ cup minced onion
1 tablespoon peanut oil
¾ cup chicken stock or consommé
3 tablespoons soy sauce
1 tablespoon cornstarch
¼ cup cold water

Cook the beans according to the package directions and drain well. Combine them in a casserole with the bean sprouts and water chestnuts. Sauté the onions in the oil until limp and stir into the bean mixture. Combine the stock or consommé with the soy sauce in a small saucepan. Mix the cornstarch with the cold water and add to the saucepan.

Stir over low heat until the mixture thickens. Pour the sauce over the beans and bake, covered, at 350° for 20 minutes. This may be served as is, or with a topping of crisp chow mein noodles.

Fried Green Beans, Chinese
4 to 6 servings

2 packages frozen julienne green beans
3 tablespoons peanut oil
1 teaspoon salt

Drop the beans into boiling salted water until they can be separated. Do not cook fully. Drain well—first in a colander, then on paper towels. Heat the oil in a skillet, add the beans, and stir over fairly high heat until crisp and tender (about 5 to 7 minutes). Sprinkle with the salt before serving.

Italian Cut Beans Alicia
4 to 6 servings

2 packages frozen Italian cut beans
1 clove garlic, put through garlic press or minced
½ teaspoon oregano or basil
3 tablespoons fine olive oil
2 cups Italian spaghetti sauce (your own or canned)

Cook the beans according to the package directions and drain well. Sauté the garlic and oregano or basil in the hot olive oil until the garlic is golden brown. Add the spaghetti sauce, stir, and simmer for 5 minutes. Toss the beans in the sauce.

Sherried Lima Beans with Mushrooms
4 to 6 servings

1 package frozen large Fordhook lima beans
2 packages frozen sliced mushrooms

4 tablespoons butter
2 tablespoons flour
1 cup rich chicken stock or consommé
½ teaspoon salt
⅛ teaspoon pepper
2 tablespoons sherry
⅔ cup fine bread crumbs
Butter

Cook the lima beans according to the package directions and drain well. Sauté the frozen mushrooms in the butter according to the package directions and remove them from the skillet with a slotted spoon. Add the flour to the skillet, stir until blended with the butter and mushroom liquid, then stir in the stock or consommé and seasonings. Cook over low heat until slightly thickened. Stir in the sherry. Combine the beans and mushrooms in a lightly oiled casserole, cover with the sauce, sprinkle with the bread crumbs, and dot with butter. Bake in a 350° oven for 10 minutes. If desired, brown the topping under the broiler.

Buttery Lima Bean Bake
4 to 6 servings

2 packages frozen baby lima beans
¾ cup butter
1 tablespoon dry mustard
½ cup brown sugar
1 teaspoon salt
1 tablespoon dark molasses
1 cup sour cream

Drop the lima beans into a 2-quart saucepan of boiling salted water until they separate. Do not cook. Drain them well and put them into a casserole. While they are still hot, stir in the butter by the teaspoonful, mixing well. Combine the mustard, brown sugar, and salt and sprinkle over the beans. With a wooden spoon, gently stir in the molasses and finally the sour cream, mixing thoroughly. Cover and bake at 350° for 1 hour.

Sweet and Sour Beets
4 to 6 servings

2 packages frozen whole tiny or sliced beets
½ cup sugar
1 tablespoon cornstarch
½ teaspoon salt
¼ teaspoon ground cloves
½ cup wine vinegar or dry red wine
3 tablespoons butter
1 tablespoon cranberry-orange relish

Cook the beets according to the package directions and drain well. Combine in the top of a double boiler all the dry ingredients and the vinegar or wine. Stir and cook over direct but very low heat until thickened and almost clear. Add the drained beets, tossing them in the sauce with a wooden spoon, and set the pan over simmering water. Heat for 20 minutes. Just before serving, stir in the butter and relish.

Broccoli Amandine
4 to 6 servings

2 packages frozen broccoli spears
½ cup melted butter
2 tablespoons lemon juice
¼ cup toasted almond slivers

Cook the broccoli according to the package directions and drain well. Arrange on a serving platter and cover with the melted butter mixed with the lemon juice. Top with the toasted almond slivers.

Broccoli Alicia
4 to 6 servings

2 packages frozen chopped broccoli
2 cloves garlic, minced
¼ cup fine olive oil

Salt and pepper to taste
¼ cup grated Romano or Parmesan cheese

Cook the broccoli for 3 minutes less than the package directs and drain well. Sauté the garlic in the hot oil only until light gold. Add and sauté the broccoli briefly, stirring, until tender. Season to taste and sprinkle with the cheese.

Brussels Sprouts in Creamed Chicken Sauce
6 to 8 servings

2 packages frozen Brussels sprouts
2 tablespoons minced onion
4 tablespoons butter
3 tablespoons flour
1½ cups rich chicken stock or consommé
½ cup light cream
Salt to taste
⅛ teaspoon white pepper
Pinch of nutmeg
1 tablespoon minced parsley

Cook the Brussels sprouts according to the package directions, drain well, and keep warm. In a saucepan, sauté the onions in the butter until limp. Stir in the flour, blend well, and cook over low heat until the mixture is lightly browned. Slowly stir in the stock or consommé, cream, and seasonings and continue to stir over low heat until smooth and thickened. Stir in the parsley and pour over the Brussels sprouts.

Brussels Sprouts in Cheese and Celery Sauce
6 to 8 servings

2 packages frozen Brussels sprouts
1½ cups chopped green celery
3 cups boiling salted water
4 tablespoons butter
4 tablespoons flour
½ cup light cream
Celery salt and pepper to taste

Pinch of nutmeg
½ cup grated Cheddar or Swiss cheese

Cook the Brussels sprouts according to the package directions, drain, and put them into a shallow baking dish. Cook the chopped celery in the rapidly boiling salted water until just tender but not soft. Drain, reserving both the celery and the liquid. In the top of a double boiler over simmering water, heat the butter, stir in the flour, and mix well. Add the cream, 1½ cups of the celery water, and the seasonings, stirring constantly. Simmer until smooth and thickened. Combine the sauce with the reserved celery, pour it over the Brussels sprouts, sprinkle with the grated cheese, and brown under the broiler.

Whole Baby Carrots with Ginger Glaze
6 to 8 servings

2 packages frozen whole baby carrots
3 tablespoons butter
2 tablespoons sugar
½ teaspoon salt
½ teaspoon cinnamon
1½ tablespoons finely minced preserved ginger

Cook the carrots for 2 minutes less than the package directs and drain. In a large, heavy skillet, melt the butter over low heat. Stir in the sugar, salt, and cinnamon, raise the heat to moderate, add the ginger, and stir for 1 minute. Add the partially cooked carrots, cover the skillet, and cook over low heat for 5 minutes. Raise the cover occasionally and turn the carrots to glaze them evenly. If they seem to be sticking to the pan, add ¼ cup of boiling water and stir.

Cut Carrots Glazed with Pineapple
6 to 8 servings

2 packages frozen cut carrots
1 cup crushed pineapple, drained
½ cup firmly packed dark brown sugar

Cook the carrots according to the package directions and drain well. Add the crushed pineapple and sugar to the carrots and stir constantly over moderate heat until the carrots are well glazed.

Diced Carrots and Mushrooms au Gratin
6 to 8 servings

2 packages frozen diced carrots
1 package frozen sliced mushrooms
2 tablespoons butter
1 cup Heavy White Sauce (page 19)
½ cup fine bread crumbs
½ cup grated Cheddar, Swiss, Romano, or Parmesan cheese

Cook the carrots according to the package directions and drain. Sauté the mushrooms in the butter according to the package directions. Combine the carrots and mushrooms with the white sauce, add the mushroom drippings, and pour into a lightly buttered casserole. Sprinkle with the bread crumbs, top with the grated cheese, and bake at 400° for 10 minutes.

Cauliflower Amandine
6 to 8 servings

8-ounce container frozen stockpiled sauce (Cheese, Mornay, Curry, etc.)
2 packages frozen cauliflower
½ cup toasted slivered almonds

Release the sauce into the top of a double boiler over simmering water and heat until smooth. Cook the cauliflower according to the package directions and drain. Serve covered with the hot sauce topped with the toasted almonds.

Batter-Fried Cauliflower
6 to 8 servings

2 packages frozen cauliflower
⅛ teaspoon white pepper

1 teaspoon lemon juice
1 cup fritter batter (see Index)
Deep hot fat

Cook the cauliflower in well-salted water 2 minutes less than the package directs. Drain well, dry on paper towels, then sprinkle with the pepper and lemon juice. Dip into the fritter batter, coating well, and fry in deep hot fat until well browned. Drain on paper towels. Serve as is, or with any heated light sauce from your freezer stockpile.

Corn Bake
6 to 8 servings

2 packages frozen niblet-style corn
½ cup water
½ cup milk
1 cup frozen diced green peppers
4 tablespoons butter
3 tablespoons flour
1 teaspoon salt
½ teaspoon dry mustard
1 egg, beaten
2 tablespoons chopped pimiento
About ¾ cup dry bread crumbs
½ cup grated Cheddar cheese

Simmer, but do not boil, the frozen corn in the combined water and milk until just tender, but not soft. Drain, reserving the liquid. In a heavy saucepan, sauté the diced peppers in 2 tablespoons of the butter for 3 minutes. Sprinkle with the flour and salt, stir to blend, add the reserved corn liquid, mustard, beaten egg, and pimiento. Heat to simmering but do not boil. Combine with the corn and pour into a lightly buttered casserole. Sprinkle with the bread crumbs, dot with the remaining butter, and top with the grated cheese. Bake at 350° for 30 minutes. Brown under the broiler.

Corn Creole
6 to 8 servings

2 packages frozen niblet-style corn
½ cup frozen chopped onions
½ cup frozen diced green peppers
4 tablespoons butter
1½ cups drained canned tomatoes
1 teaspoon salt
¼ teaspoon pepper

Drop the corn into 2 or 3 cups of rapidly boiling salted water until the kernels separate. Do not cook. Drain thoroughly. In a large, heavy skillet or Dutch oven, sauté the corn, onions, and green peppers in the butter, stirring constantly, until tender (about 5 minutes). Add the tomatoes and seasonings, stir, then simmer until piping hot.

Easy Frozen Eggplant Sticks Parmigiana
4 servings

2 packages frozen breaded eggplant sticks
2 tablespoons olive oil
1½ cups any Italian spaghetti sauce (your own, or canned)
½ pound mozzarella cheese, thinly sliced
Grated Parmesan cheese

Sauté the frozen eggplant sticks in the hot olive oil until well browned on all sides. Spoon ½ cup of the spaghetti sauce into the bottom of a small baking dish, cover with the eggplant, and top with the remaining sauce, sliced mozzarella, and Parmesan cheese. Bake at 350° until the cheese melts. Brown under the broiler.

Parsnips
Substitute frozen parsnips for the carrots in the recipes for glazed carrots, page 404.

Sweet and Sour Parsnips
6 to 8 servings

2 packages frozen sliced parsnips
¼ cup butter
1 tablespoon minced fresh parsley
2 tablespoons lemon juice
1 tablespoon brown sugar
Salt and pepper to taste

Drop the parsnips into boiling salted water and remove when the slices separate. Do not cook. Drain well—first in a colander, then on paper towels. Sauté them in the butter over low to moderate heat, turning from time to time, until tender (about 8 to 10 minutes). Sprinkle with the parsley, lemon juice, sugar, and seasonings, cover, and simmer over very low heat until the sugar melts. These are very good served with a garnish of crumbled crisply fried bacon.

Peas
Peas were among the first vegetables to be successfully frozen as a commercial product and the first to gain consumer acceptance. By now, peas have been combined by the frozen food industry with so many other vegetables and sauces that no recipes come to mind which are not already in the store cabinets.

Potatoes
Freeze leftover mashed potatoes, white or sweet, in containers. To serve, thaw until they can be released into the top of a double boiler over simmering water. When soft and hot, stir in additional butter and cream. Or freeze them, mixed with a little flour, beaten egg, and grated cheese, as croquettes, to be sautéed in butter or fried in deep fat as needed. Store no longer than 1 month.

Spinach Siciliani
6 to 8 servings

2 packages frozen leaf spinach
2 clove garlic, minced or put through garlic press
2 tablespoons olive oil
3 or 4 anchovy fillets, chopped
1 teaspoon lemon juice

Cook the spinach for 2 minutes less than the package directs and drain well. Press excess moisture from the leaves with the back of a spoon. Let stand in a colander over paper towels to drain further. Sauté the garlic in the hot olive oil for 3 minutes. Add and sauté the spinach, stirring with a fork, for 3 minutes. Stir in the chopped anchovies and serve sprinkled with the lemon juice.

Spinach and Three-Cheese Casserole
6 to 8 servings

2 packages frozen chopped spinach
8-ounce package cream cheese, softened
¼ pound butter, softened
½ teaspoon salt
⅛ teaspoon pepper
2 or 3 hard-cooked eggs, sliced
1 cup Cheese Sauce (page 21)
1 cup fine bread crumbs
2 tablespoons grated Romano or Parmesan cheese

Cook the spinach according to the package directions, drain well, and mix with the softened cream cheese and 4 tablespoons of the butter. Stir in the salt and pepper and spread in a lightly buttered 2-quart casserole. Top with the sliced eggs. Pour over this the sauce and top with the bread crumbs tossed with the grated cheese and the remaining butter, melted. Bake at 350° for 20 minutes and brown the topping under the broiler.

Squash Crisp
6 to 8 servings

2 packages frozen cooked yellow squash
4 tablespoons butter
2 tablespoons flour
2 eggs, beaten
1 teaspoon dry mustard
⅔ teaspoon salt
⅛ teaspoon pepper
1½ tablespoons brown sugar
1 cup crushed corn or rice flakes

Heat the squash in the top of a double boiler over simmering water until thawed. Stir in 2 tablespoons of the butter and, when this is melted, add the flour, eggs, mustard, salt, pepper, and 1 tablespoon of the sugar. Mix thoroughly and transfer to a buttered shallow baking dish (or use two 9-inch pie plates). Melt the remaining butter and add it to the crushed flakes with the remaining sugar, mixing well. Sprinkle this mixture over the squash and bake at 350° for 30 minutes.

Squash Griddle Cakes
6 to 8 servings

2 packages frozen cooked yellow squash
½ cup fine bread crumbs
½ cup ground nutmeats (any kind)
1 whole egg, stirred with a fork
¼ cup minced onion (optional)
4 tablespoons butter
1 tablespoon brown sugar

Heat the squash in the top of a double boiler over simmering water until soft. Add all the remaining ingredients, stirring until the butter melts and the mixture is well blended. Drop by the spoonful onto a hot lightly buttered griddle and bake on both sides.

Baked Zucchini
6 to 8 servings

2 packages frozen zucchini
½ cup sour cream
2 tablespoons butter, well softened
⅔ teaspoon salt
¼ teaspoon paprika
4 tablespoons grated Cheddar cheese
2 egg yolks, beaten
2 tablespoons minced scallions or chives
½ cup fine bread crumbs

Cook the zucchini 2 minutes less than the package directs and drain well. Combine the sour cream, butter, seasonings, and 2 tablespoons of the cheese and stir in the top of a double boiler over simmering water until the cheese melts and the mixture is smoothly blended. Remove from the heat and stir in the egg yolks and scallions or chives. Combine the zucchini and sauce in a casserole, cover with the bread crumbs, dot with additional butter, and top with the remaining cheese. Bake at 350° for 30 minutes, then brown the topping under the broiler.

36.

Stuffings for Poultry, Meat, or Fish

Each of the recipes given here will yield about 2 cups of stuffing. They may be prepared as needed, or they may be prepared for storage in the freezer for use within 6 months. If 1 cup or less of a stuffing is required for an immediate meal, why not make the entire amount and freeze the rest in a small plastic bag or container? *To freeze:* Cool, chill in the refrigerator, and pack, labeling as to ingredients. *To use after freezer storage:* Thaw in the refrigerator.

Simple Bread Stuffing

2 cups soft bread crumbs
½ teaspoon salt
⅛ teaspoon ground black pepper
1 small onion, grated
¼ cup melted butter
4 tablespoons liquid (stock, milk, bouillon)

Combine all the dry ingredients and moisten with the melted butter and liquid. Toss lightly with a fork. Pack loosely.

Seasoned Bread Stuffing

2 cups soft bread crumbs
½ cup finely chopped celery
¼ cup minced onions
2 tablespoons minced parsley
1 egg, beaten well with ¼ teaspoon salt
⅛ teaspoon paprika
½ teaspoon any favorite herb (basil, marjoram, dill, thyme, sage, tarragon)
2 tablespoons drained chopped capers
Enough melted butter, milk, stock, or bouillon to make a moist stuffing

Combine all the ingredients, blending well.

Rice Stuffing

Substitute 2½ cups of cooked rice for the soft bread crumbs in either of the 2 preceding recipes.

Mushroom Stuffing

½ pound mushrooms, sliced
3 tablespoons butter
1 tablespoon minced onion
1 cup soft bread crumbs
1 tablespoon minced parsley
½ teaspoon salt
⅛ teaspoon ground black pepper
3 tablespoons stock, milk, or bouillon

Sauté the mushrooms in the butter for 2 minutes. Combine the mushrooms and drippings with all the other ingredients and mix thoroughly.

Almond-Shallot Stuffing

6 small shallots, minced
4 tablespoons butter
2 tablespoons minced parsley

⅛ teaspoon ground black pepper
⅛ teaspoon ground nutmeg
1½ cups fine bread crumbs
¾ cup blanched almonds, preferably ground (or finely chopped)
2 egg yolks beaten with ½ teaspoon salt
¼ cup rich bouquet wine (medium sherry, Madeira, Marsala)

Sauté the shallots in the butter until light gold. Combine with all the other ingredients and mix thoroughly.

Oyster Stuffing

1 cup (about a dozen) plump oysters with liquor (see note under following recipe)
¼ cup melted butter
1½ cups soft bread crumbs
⅛ teaspoon ground black pepper
1 tablespoon lemon juice
1 tablespoon minced parsley
Grating lemon peel
Grating whole nutmeg (or pinch of ground nutmeg)

It is not necessary to cook the oysters, but they may be easier to chop if they are frizzled briefly in their own liquor (which reserve) until their edges curl slightly. Chop them. Combine all the other ingredients, and add the chopped oysters with enough of the reserved liquor to moisten the stuffing. Taste for salt (oysters have their own) and add some if necessary.

Shrimp, Crab-Meat, or Lobster Stuffing

2 tablespoons butter
2 tablespoons flour
½ cup stock, milk, or consommé
½ teaspoon salt
Dash of pepper
1 tablespoon lemon juice
1 cup chopped cooked shrimp, crab meat, or lobster *

* If you are going to freeze part or all of this stuffing, do not use sea food that is or has been frozen. Frozen sea food may, of course, be used for immediate serving. Thaw it sufficiently to chop.

½ cup chopped mushrooms
1 cup soft bread crumbs

Melt the butter, blend in the flour, add the liquid, and stir over low heat until smooth and thick. Add the seasonings and lemon juice, sea food, and chopped mushrooms and mix well. Toss the mixture with the bread crumbs until well distributed.

37.

Dessert Stockpiling

You can meet heavy dessert demands, family or social, by using your freezer with canny foresight.

Stockpiling is made seductively easy, of course, by the food industries which provide a wide variety of frozen desserts to store ready to serve when thawed, heated, or baked —or, in many cases, ready to eat. Children believe that home freezers are really vending machines designed to supply instant ice cream.

Another stockpile method is to double up when you follow any favorite recipe from a well-thumbed cookbook or file. Serve one and put the spare in cold storage. No special freezer techniques are required, and desserts that aren't served frozen need only be thawed.

Using freezer space creatively for dessert stockpiling can be achieved by other means, too. One strategy is the large-quantity recipe. Another puts into compact space important components of many diversified desserts:

The largest sheet cakes your oven will accommodate.

Stacks of layers composed at leisure from time to time in your kitchen from scratch or from a box, or several made at one time. After space-economical freezer storage these can be matched or mixed for cakes as lofty in dimension as you please, with fillings and frostings made fresh or chosen from your stockpile supply.

Bottom crusts and pastry shells awaiting fulfillment as pies, tarts, and puffs according to menu requirements.

Preformed pie fillings prepared during the seasons of fresh fruits or berries.

A collection of crepes, those fashionable little thinner-than-pancake delicacies. Made with sugar, crepes become chic desserts when thawed and rolled around sweet fillings or flamed in liqueurs. (Made without sugar, they lend themselves to a number of high-style party entrees for brunch, lunch, or supper.)

FREEZING LARGE-QUANTITY DESSERT RECIPES

The recipes given in generous proportions can be fully prepared for dividing into serving requirements sized to family or company meals. They can also be frozen in bulk in anticipation of a children's party or as your contribution to a church or community supper.

For short-term storage, oven desserts to be served to a large gathering may be frozen in the pans in which they are baked, after they are cooled and covered with foil or freezer film. (Longer storage is possible, but can you spare the pans or the freezer space?)

For freezer storage of quantity recipes divided into meal-proportioned home desserts, make it a thrifty habit to wash and save the foil pie plates, cake pans, and deeper casse-role-type dishes in which so many commercially frozen foods are sold. Foil ware can also be purchased, as can metal-rimmed paper pie plates.

Flatten and save also waxed pie and cake cartons and bake-shop boxes for crush protection in the freezer.

A supply of large plastic bags is recommended.

If you plan to freeze iced or frosted layer cakes, plastic cake boxes are a good investment. They provide the required moisture-vapor protection, can be stacked in the freezer, and require no overwrap.

In general, it is not wise to freeze layer cakes with soft fillings which may tend to soak the layers soggily at home freezer temperatures. However, freezer space and kitchen time can be saved by separately freezing the fillings as well as frostings or icings. Use pint and quart plastic or waxboard containers for these and be sure to remove them from the freezer *to the refrigerator* at least 16 hours before attempting to spread them on still-frozen or thawed layers.

SHEET CAKES

The sheet cake is a versatile form for short-term freezing of cake to serve a crowd, or to cut into family sizes for longer stockpiling.

Baked in a special sheet cake pan (16½ by 24½ by 1 inch), it can be frozen plain or creatively and appropriately decorated for a special occasion. It can be cut in half for an enormous layer cake, into quarters for 2 large ones. In addition, the large sheet can be frozen cut and packaged in serving portions of a size determined by family appetites, putting at your disposal a variety of spur-of-the-moment desserts when topped with fruits, garnished with whipped cream or pudding sauce, or spread with frosting.

To freeze a frosted or decorated sheet cake: Invert a second sheet pan over it before wrapping in freezer paper.

To thaw: Let stand at room temperature, wrapped, for 1 hour.

RECIPES FOR SHEET CAKES

Applesauce Cake
1 large cake pan sheet, 16½" x 24½" x 1" (40 to 50 servings)

1 cup shortening
3½ cups brown sugar
6 eggs
3 cups applesauce, your own or canned
5 cups sifted cake flour
2 teaspoons cinnamon
1 teaspoon ground cloves
2 teaspoons ground nutmeg
2 teaspoons baking soda
1½ teaspoons salt
½ cup buttermilk
3 cups raisins

Cream the shortening and sugar. Add the eggs one at a time, beating until light. Blend in the applesauce. Sift 4¾ cups of the flour with the spices, soda, and salt and add these dry ingredients alternately with the buttermilk to the applesauce mixture. Blend well. Toss the raisins in the reserved ¼ cup of flour and stir into the batter.

Pour into a greased sheet cake pan and bake at 350° for 30 minutes.

When cool, wrap and freeze, or remove from the pan and cut into your choice of sizes before wrapping and freezing.

Suggested icing: Any of the cream frostings on page 424.

Banana Cake
1 large sheet cake pan, 16½" x 24½" x 1" (40 to 50 servings)

1½ cups shortening
4½ cups sugar

1 tablespoon vanilla
6 eggs
2½ cups banana pulp
7 cups sifted cake flour
1 tablespoon baking powder
1 teaspoon baking soda
1½ teaspoons salt
1½ cups buttermilk

Cream the shortening, sugar, and vanilla. Add the eggs one at a time, beating constantly. Add the banana pulp and continue beating. Sift together the flour, baking powder, soda, and salt and add this alternately with the buttermilk. Blend thoroughly. Pour into a greased sheet cake pan and bake at 325° for 1 hour.

When cool, wrap and freeze, or remove from the pan and cut into your choice of sizes before wrapping and freezing.

Suggested topping: Sliced bananas and whipped cream

Chocolate Cake
1 large sheet cake pan, 16½" x 24½" x 1" (40 to 50 servings)

1½ cups shortening
3½ cups sugar
4 teaspoons vanilla
8 eggs
8 ounces melted chocolate (1 cup)
1 cup boiling water
5¼ cups cake flour
1 tablespoon baking powder
1 tablespoon baking soda
1 tablespoon salt
2 cups milk

Cream the shortening, sugar, and vanilla. Add the eggs two at a time, beating well after each addition. Add the melted chocolate and blend well. Add the boiling water and mix well. Sift the dry ingredients together and add them alternately with the milk. Mix thoroughly and pour into a greased sheet cake pan. Bake at 350° for 50 minutes.

When cool, wrap and freeze, or remove from the pan and cut into your choice of sizes before wrapping and freezing.

Suggested toppings: Chocolate Cream Cheese Frosting or Vanilla Cream Frosting (page 424)

Spice Cake

1 large sheet cake pan, 16½" x 24½" x 1" (40 to 50 servings)

2 cups shortening
4 cups sugar
7 eggs
7 cups sifted cake flour
2 tablespoons baking powder
1 teaspoon salt
2 teaspoons ground ginger
1 tablespoon cinnamon
1 teaspoon ground cloves
1 teaspoon ground nutmeg
1 cup molasses
2½ cups cold coffee

Cream the shortening and sugar until light and fluffy. Add the eggs one at a time, beating after each addition. Sift together the flour, baking powder, salt, and spices and add these ingredients alternately with the combined molasses and cold coffee. Blend until smooth. Pour into a greased sheet cake pan and bake at 375° for 30 minutes.

When cool, wrap and freeze, or remove from the pan and cut into your choice of sizes before wrapping and freezing.

Suggested topping: Lemon Cream Frosting (page 424) sprinkled with chopped nuts

White Cake

1 large sheet cake pan, 16½" x 24½" x 1" (40 to 50 servings)

1¾ cups shortening
4½ cups sugar
1⅓ tablespoons vanilla
9½ cups sifted cake flour
3⅔ tablespoons baking powder
2 teaspoons salt
3½ cups milk
12 to 14 egg whites (1½ cups)

Cream the shortening, sugar, and vanilla until light and fluffy. Sift together the flour, baking powder, and salt and add these ingredients alternately with the milk to the creamed mixture, blending after each addition. Slowly pour in the unbeaten egg whites, mixing at medium speed until well blended. Pour into a greased sheet cake pan and bake at 350° for 35 minutes.

When cool, wrap and freeze, or remove from the pan and cut into your choice of sizes before wrapping and freezing.

Suggested toppings: Any icing or frosting; soft pudding; sliced fruit or berries with whipped cream

QUANTITY RECIPES FOR SHEET CAKE FROSTINGS

The recipes which follow are correlated with the preceding sheet cakes, as each will frost one 16½ x 24½ by 1 inch sheet.

However, a large quantity may be made the day you fill and frost a family-size layer cake. Satisfy present requirements, and freeze the rest in pint or quart containers or in cup-size amounts.

To freeze: Cool the freezer portion by standing the mixing bowl in very cold water to half its depth. Cover the bowl with film or wax paper. When cool, spoon into containers. Cover, label clearly, and refrigerate for 1 hour or more. Store in the freezer when thoroughly chilled.

To use: Remove the container from the freezer to the refrigerator at least 16 hours before spreading between or on the layers.

Apricot Frosting
Frosts 1 sheet cake

¾ pound dried apricots *
5 cups boiling water
1 cup butter or margarine
3½ pounds powdered sugar
¼ cup lemon juice
Milk or cream as needed

Cover the apricots with the boiling water and boil for 30 minutes. Force through a sieve or Foley mill, or buzz at low speed in a blender until smoothly puréed. Combine the purée with the butter or margarine, and cream thoroughly. Add the sugar gradually, beating constantly. Add the lemon juice and, if needed, enough milk or cream to make a spreadable consistency.

Chocolate Cream Frosting
Frosts 1 sheet cake

¾ cup butter or margarine
2 pounds confectioners' sugar
1 cup dry cocoa
½ cup hot milk

* Fresh or canned apricots may be used for the purée. If fresh, boil 1 pound of peeled, pitted, sliced apricots for 3 or 4 minutes in 1½ cups of water before puréeing. If canned, use a large can of peeled halves and purée without cooking.

Fresh berries of your choice may also be used. About 1 quart of berries yields 1 cup of purée.

¼ teaspoon salt
1 tablespoon vanilla

Cream the butter or margarine until light and fluffy. Combine the sugar and cocoa and sift together. Add this mixture to the creamed butter alternately with the hot milk, beating well. Blend in the salt and vanilla and beat until light and fluffy.

Lemon Cream Frosting
Omit the cocoa and substitute 3 tablespoons of lemon juice for the vanilla.

Orange Cream Frosting
Omit the cocoa, substitute 3 tablespoons of orange juice for the vanilla, and add ½ teaspoon grated orange rind.

Vanilla Cream Frosting
Omit the cocoa and use 2 tablespoons of vanilla.

Chocolate Cream Cheese Frosting
Frosts 1 sheet cake

¾ cup (two 3-ounce packages) cream cheese
¼ cup milk
3½ cups powdered sugar
½ cup (4 ounces) chocolate, melted
⅛ teaspoon salt

Beat the cream cheese until soft, then gradually beat in the milk. Add the powdered sugar slowly, continuing to beat. Add the chocolate and salt and beat until smooth.

COTTAGE CHEESE CAKE

Any cream-cheese cake can be frozen. *Any* one. So every time you make your luscious recipe, make 2.

More economical cheese cakes to make in quantity to regale a crowd or stockpile for family meals can be composed with cream-style, small-curd cottage cheese, with a graham cracker crust. The cottage cheese is made finer in texture by forcing it through a food mill or the finest blade of your food grinder.

Graham Cracker Crust

2½ pounds graham crackers
½ pound sugar
2 tablespoons cinnamon
1 cup flour
1½ pounds melted butter or margarine

Grind the graham crackers or crush them by rolling between sheets of wax paper until fine. Put the crumbs into a large mixing bowl. In a separate bowl mix together the sugar, cinnamon, and flour and blend these ingredients thoroughly with the graham cracker crumbs. Add the melted butter or margarine and mix thoroughly.

Press the mixture into the bottoms and sides of 2 large baking pans (approximately 10″ x 18″ x 2½″), or 8 foil cake pans, or 1 large foil cake pan and as many smaller ones as you have crumbs for.

Cottage Cheese Cake I
40 to 50 servings, total

4½ pounds cream-style cottage cheese (forced through food mill, or ground)
1¾ cups flour
4⅔ cups sugar
2 teaspoons salt
18 eggs, separated
4½ cups milk
2 tablespoons vanilla

Mix the cottage cheese and flour together thoroughly. Combine 3⅔ cups of the sugar with the salt and add to the

cheese mixture, blending well. Beat the egg yolks well and
add. Mix thoroughly. Add the milk and vanilla and mix
well. Beat the egg whites with the remaining cup of sugar
and fold lightly into the cheese mixture. Pour into crumb-
lined cake pans and bake at 350° for 1 hour.

Cottage Cheese Cake II
40 to 50 servings, total

½ cup flour
4¼ cups sugar
4 pounds cream-style cottage cheese (forced through food mill,
    or ground)
16 eggs, separated
1 cup melted butter or margarine
1⅔ tablespoons vanilla
1 teaspoon salt
1 quart whipping cream

Sift the flour and sugar together and add to the cottage
cheese. Mix thoroughly. Beat the egg yolks until thick and
add with the melted butter or margarine and vanilla. Add
the salt to the egg whites and beat briskly until stiff but
moist. Fold into the cheese mixture. Whip the cream thoroughly and fold in. Pour into crumb-lined cake pans and
bake at 350° for 1 hour and 10 minutes.

To freeze cottage cheese cake: Cool slightly, cover with
foil, and chill thoroughly in the refrigerator. Wrap large
pans in freezer paper, and slip small ones into waxed cartons. Freeze.

To serve: Let stand at room temperature (about 1½
hours for small cakes, 2 to 3 hours for larger ones).

EASY AS PIE

Browse through the frozen food cabinets in stores and
you'll conclude—correctly—that pies of all kinds can be

frozen. If you long for a freezer full of pies of all kinds, you will arrive at your goal by preparing 2 or more of your favorites instead of 1 and freezing the extras either unbaked or fully baked.

To freeze unbaked double-crust pies: Make the pies as usual with your own pastry or a prepared mix. Do not bake when filled and topped with a crust, and do not cut vent slits. Cover the freezer-bound pie with foil or film and freeze. When solidly frozen, slip the pie into a carton and store it in the freezer up to 4 months.

To serve unbaked double-crust pie: Unwrap and put the pie into a preheated 450° oven. Wait until the top crust is pliable (about 10 minutes) before cutting vent slits. Bake at 450° for 15 minutes, reduce the heat to 375°, and continue baking another 40–50 minutes, until the crust is golden.

To freeze baked double-crust pies: Make crusts and fillings and bake according to cookbook directions—or your own experience. Cool thoroughly. Wrap in film or foil and freeze. When solidly frozen, slip the pies into cartons and store up to 6 months.

To freeze open-face pies: Make and bake pie shells as usual, and fill as usual. When cool, refrigerate until chilled. When cold, cover lightly with wax paper and lift carefully into the freezer, making sure that the filling remains level. When solidly frozen, remove the wax paper and cover the pies with film or foil. Slip into cartons and return to the freezer. Store up to 6 months for fruit, berry, or pumpkin pies, up to 3 months for cream or custard fillings.

To serve frozen baked pies:

Served cold: Thaw the pie in its wraps at room temperature. Depending on the filling, this will take from 1 to 4 hours.

Served warm: Unwrap and put the still-frozen pie into a preheated 300° oven for 35 to 45 minutes.

To be topped with meringue: Two hours before serving, remove the pie from the freezer and stand at room temperature for 1 hour. Make and pile the meringue on the pie at the end of 1 hour and bake in a preheated 325° oven for 15 minutes. Let stand again at room temperature no longer than 1 hour before serving.

Cream or custard pies: Remove the pie from the freezer in time to thaw in the refrigerator 6 to 8 hours before serving. Add whipped toppings, if any, just before serving.

PIE PASTRY, PLURAL

With pastry in the freezer, you can produce one pie or several without having to go through the dough preparation.

Pastry may be frozen unbaked in flat circles (these are easier to store in the freezer).

If you prefer, and have the freezer space, bottom crusts can be fitted into foil or metal-rimmed paper pie plates and frozen, with the top-crust pastry flattened into a smaller circle, frozen on wax paper, then wrapped in film and nested in the shell. Both are frozen unbaked. Thus paired, the plate can be slipped into a carton. The crusts must be removed from the freezer in time for the top circle to thaw for further rolling (1 hour).

On the day you decide to stockpile pastry, there is nothing to prevent you from proceeding to the triumphant finale and completing as many pies as you wish before freezing them either unbaked or baked (page 427). Store the rest of the pastry unbaked as circles or shells. In addition, some of the pastry may be earmarked for tarts or little individual pies by making smaller circles sized to muffin tins or to your hoard of small foil pans donated by the frozen food industry.

Plain Pastry

For 16 single-crust or 8 double-crust 9-inch pies

Use a very large mixing bowl or a curved-bottom clean dishpan that will fit into your refrigerator.

2 pounds solid chilled shortening (lard or half-lard/half-butter, if you like, for flakier pastry)
4 pounds sifted all-purpose flour
2⅓ tablespoons salt
About 2⅔ cups ice water

Cut the shortening lightly into the flour combined with the salt until it is meal-like in texture. Add the ice water a little at a time, distributing it evenly and adding only enough to make the dough hold together in a ball.

Divide the ball into 2 parts, one a little larger than the other, and refrigerate both parts, lightly covered, for any amount of time you can spare—from 10 minutes to 10 hours.

At your leisure, before you start rolling the dough, upend your favorite, oftenest-used pie plate on a piece of heavy wax paper and cut a circle that is 1 inch larger all around (top crust). Cut a second pattern that is 2 inches larger than the first one (bottom crust).

Next, cut thirty-two 12-inch lengths of either foil or slick-sided freezer paper that is 12 inches wide. If you are using freezer paper, make 14 "sets" by putting 2 pieces back to back, slick side outward for both. These are for slip-sheeting the dough circles for easier removal and separation.

When you are ready to form the pastry circles, remove the bottom-crust dough from the refrigerator and divide it into 8 equal parts. Using the larger wax paper pattern, roll each part to the size of the pattern. Put the first pastry circle onto a single piece of foil (or the slick side of freezer paper) and top it with a foil or paper "set." Continue to roll and slip-sheet, making sure that you stack the paper edges evenly.

When all are done, lift the stack carefully and slip it into a waxed carton. Label the carton "Plain pastry, bottom crusts." Put the carton flat in the freezer.

Repeat the entire process with the remaining top-crust dough. Put these circles in a second, correctly labeled carton.

To bake a pie: Remove 1 top and 1 bottom crust from the stored carton. Let them stand at room temperature for 1 hour. Line a pie plate with a bottom crust, fill it with the pie mixture, and top with pastry. Bake according to cookbook directions for the specific pie.

Sweet Pastry
For 16 single-crust or 8 double-crust 9-inch pies

2 tablespoons salt
½ cup powdered sugar
3¾ pounds cake flour
2 pounds chilled solid shortening (lard or half-lard/half-butter, if you like, for flakier pastry)
About 1½ cups ice water

Sift together the salt, sugar, and flour. Cut the shortening lightly into this mixture and refrigerate it for 1 hour. Add the ice water slowly, mixing lightly until the dough holds together in a ball. Divide the ball into 2 parts, one a little larger than the other, and refrigerate again until you are ready to roll into circles. See the preceeding recipe for plain pastry. Follow the directions for handling, packaging, freezing, and using. If desired, top-crust circles may be cut into strips for lattice pies.

PIE FILLINGS AD LIB.

Keep your family's pie-consumption statistics in mind when fresh fruits and berries are in abundant low-cost supply. Freeze these bounties in quart containers, prepared according to instructions given in many method books on home freezing, including mine. One quart, one pie. To make a pie after freezer storage, thaw the container in the refrigerator and follow standard recipe directions to bake it as usual, double-crust or topless.

However, in May, June, and July berries reach their peak. Except for cultivated crops, they are often free for the picking and even the cultivated varieties are irresistibly low in price. They may be frozen in containers as above, of course, but they may also be frozen as preformed fillings and compactly stored to bring spring and summer succulence to winter tables.

Making and Freezing Preformed Berry Pie Fillings
Fillings for five 9-inch pies

Note: The following recipe uses a greater amount of cornstarch than is ordinarily required for pies that are baked and served without freezing.

8 quarts berries (blackberries, blueberries, raspberries, straw-
    berries)
2 to 2½ pounds sugar (the lesser amount for sweet berries)
2 cups cornstarch
¼ to ½ cup lemon juice (the lesser amount for tart berries)

Pick over, wash, and (if necessary) hull the berries. Mash half of them. Cut or slice the remaining half of *strawberries* only; leave other varieties whole. Mix the sugar and cornstarch together and blend well with the mashed berries. Cook for 5 minutes over moderate heat, stirring to prevent sticking, until the sugar is melted and the mash is thick. Stir in the lemon juice and remove from the heat. When cool to lukewarm, add the reserved berries and mix well.

While the filling cools further, line 5 pie plates with heavy foil, pressing it smoothly across the bottoms and sides of the pans and allowing it to extend about 6 inches beyond the rims. Fill the lined pans with the berry mixture. Put the pans flat in the freezer. When the filling is solidly frozen, remove the pans from the freezer and double-fold the foil down until it hugs the filling. Upend the pie plates to release the discs and press the foil tightly all around. Slip the packages into a plastic bag with an identifying label and freeze. Store up to 6 months.

When you're ready for a fresh berry pie, the freezer is ready for you.

Line a pan with pastry (newly made or thawed from the freezer), unwrap the filling, and lower it into the pastry shell. Cover it with a crust, if desired. If topped, cut vent slits. Either way, bake the pie for 1 hour in a preheated 400° oven. Open-faced pies may be garnished with a whipped topping when baked and cool.

DESSERT CREPES

Not only because they take up so little freezer space, but also because they elicit flattering, eye-widening appreciation, crepes are a delight to stockpile for company desserts.

Crepe batter is simple to make, and crepe cooking is not difficult. It requires only confidence and a deft wrist.

Batter for Dessert Crepes
4 dozen

2¼ cups presifted all-purpose flour
½ cup sugar
⅛ teaspoon salt
6 eggs
3 cups milk
2 tablespoons melted butter
1 tablespoon grated orange rind
2 teaspoons grated lemon rind
2 tablespoons brandy, if desired
Melted butter for pan

Resift the flour with the sugar and salt into a large mixing bowl. Beat the eggs until light and add the milk to them gradually, beating after each addition. Add the egg mixture to the sifted ingredients and stir until smooth. Add the melted butter, grated rinds, and brandy if desired, and stir. The batter will be very thin, as it should be—of a consistency to coat a spoon without bunching. It may be used immediately, or it may be refrigerated up to a week. If refrigerated, pour the batter into a tall pitcher, float a few drops of milk over the top to prevent crusting, and seal the top of the pitcher with film or foil.

To cook crepes: Have ready a ⅛-cup measure, or a spoon holding 2 tablespoonfuls; a thin rubber spatula; and a length of paper toweling, or a long clean cloth.

Heat a crepe pan (a 5- or 6-inch Teflon frying pan is recommended) until a drop of water bounces in it. Use a pastry brush to coat the bottom and sides of the pan with melted butter. Pour in a measure (2 tablespoons) of batter. Working quickly, swirl the pan to spread the batter evenly over the bottom, and cook until lightly browned. Lift an edge carefully with a rubber spatula to check. Turn the crepe and brown the second side. When cooked, flip the crepe onto the toweling or cloth to cool.

Continue this process until as many as you need are cooked. (At Poor Richard's Buttery in Provincetown, the crepe chef manages to keep 3 pans going at once. It's a challenge, but I'm satisfied with one at a time.) If time runs out, refrigerate the batter.

To freeze crepes: When you have finished 8 crepes (dessert servings for 4 people) or more, package them in one of the following ways:

1. Slip-sheet the crepes with double thicknesses of freezer film or foil, then wrap groups of 8 in freezer paper.

2. "By the yard": Center 8 crepes an inch apart on 12-inch foil, then fold both sides of the foil toward the middle. Make a compact package by folding the covered crepes over each other, accordion style.

Freeze, then pack several packages together in a labeled tub container or carton. Store in the freezer up to 6 months.

To finish a crepe dessert: Remove as many as are needed from the freezer and thaw at room temperature, wrapped, until they are pliable (from 45 minutes to 1 hour).

Choose from the recipes to follow or invent some of your own—anything goes.

When the crepes are fully thawed, brush them lightly with melted sweet butter.

Crepes Ambrosia
Serves 4

8 buttered crepes
1 large sweet orange, peeled, with all membranes removed
1 peeled banana
¾ cup shredded coconut
¼ cup orange juice
2 tablespoons melted sweet butter
2 tablespoons confectioners' sugar
2 tablespoons (or more) Cointreau, kirsch, or other liqueur

Slice the fruit thinly, cutting the orange slices in quarters. Alternate the fruit sufficiently off-center of the crepes to permit you to fold them in half. Sprinkle the fruit with the coconut. Fold the crepes and lift them carefully to a buttered chafing dish, electric frypan, or serving skillet. Pour the orange juice around them. Brush them with the melted butter, cover the cooking vessel, and heat until warm. Sprinkle with the sugar and liqueur and flame the liqueur at the table.

Crepes Poor Richard
Serves 8

1 package any instant or cooked vanilla pudding (or 3 cups of your own)
1 teaspoon almond flavoring
16 buttered crepes

½ cup almond paste
1 can mandarin sections
¼ cup melted butter
2 jiggers (or more) cognac

Make the pudding according to the package directions (or your recipe), and add the almond flavoring. Spoon an equal amount of pudding off-center of each crepe. For each, roll 1 tablespoon of the almond paste like a thin Tootsie Roll and center the rolls on the pudding. Top with a layer of mandarin sections. Fold or roll the crepes and put them into a shallow serving casserole. Brush them with the melted butter, add the mandarin juice to the pan, and heat in a 400° oven until warm (about 5 minutes). Pour the cognac over the crepes, light it, and bring it flaming to the table.

Crepes Suèdes

In other words, Swedish pancakes. We have on many happy occasions made an entire meal by heaping stacks of warm crepes on a heated platter flanked by a large Lazy Susan holding bowls of all kinds of garnishes from caviar and sour cream to lingonberries for do-it-yourself composition. For a dessert course, perhaps just the lingonberries and a selection of jams, jellies, and marmalades—with or without powdered sugar, whipped topping, and a selection of fruity liqueurs.

Crepes Suzette
Serves 4

½ cup butter
4 tablespoons confectioners' sugar
¼ cup orange juice
1 tablespoon lemon juice
2 teaspoons grated rind or orange marmalade
8 buttered crepes, folded twice into triangles
1 jigger each, curaçao and kirsch
2 jiggers cognac

Stir the butter, sugar, juices, and rind or marmalade together in a chafing dish over hot water until they are well blended and smooth. Add the folded crepes, turning them over and over until well coated on both sides. Let them warm in the sauce. Pour the liquors into the chafing dish, light them, and spoon the flaming liquid over the crepes. Serve when the flames subside.

Other suggestions for dessert crepes: Canned, fresh, or thawed fruit (apricots, peaches) thinly sliced, rolled in the crepes, then flamed in a fruit liqueur.

Sliced strawberries, rolled in buttered crepes with whipped cream, flamed in liqueur, and topped with whipped cream.

Honey mixed with chopped nuts folded or rolled in crepes and flamed in cognac.

38.

Life of the Party

Apart from an open bar and twice as many ice cubes as I think necessary, my recipe for a large party is plenty of attractive and, usually, filling food, whether the gathering is met to celebrate cocktails from 5:00 to 7:00 or to while away the late evening hours.

The food served on these occasions may be a mélange of tidbits in a variety of shapes, sizes, and tastes, or casseroles in chafing dishes or over improvised warmers.

It doesn't always follow that the biggest parties are given by owners of the biggest freezers, but even the refrigerator top, cleared for action, can help you keep your cool when you plan your merrymaking. Do the fussy work on the day or days you can wear sneakers, and prepare freezable fixings ready to serve when thawed or heated.

If an attempt were made here to include an encyclopedic collection of all the dips, dunks, spreads, canapés, sandwiches, chafing dish concoctions, platter palatables, toothpick hors d'oeuvres, and finger foods that are appropriately festive—and freezable—the words you are reading now would appear on page 1 of Volume II.

Any party food within reason can be prepared beforehand and entrusted to the freezer for short-term storage. The standard exceptions are deviled eggs and fresh-vegetable salads. To these exceptions I add open-faced canapés, although you needn't. Just remember to butter the toast, bread, and crackers before you add the toppings, to prevent sogginess. If the canapés are to be served cold, thaw them unwrapped, but covered, at room temperature for 1 hour. If they are to be served hot, unwrap and set them on cooky sheets in a preheated 350° oven for about 10 minutes.

My chief reason for omitting open-faced canapés from my party list is sheer laziness. They take an unconscionable time to compose, freeze in a single layer, gather into boxes (slip-sheeting between layers), and overwrap to guard against the intrusion of moisture.

In the canapé department pinwheel and ribbon sandwiches (pages 441–443) are every bit as effective, if effect is what you're after. They are simpler to make and more compactly stored in the freezer.

For a big bash at which a variety of dishes both hot and cold are served buffet style, see the Index to locate recipes for the suggestions listed below. On the buffet table one dinner portion will serve from six to a dozen nibblers when combined with other selections. Pattern your offerings to a regional theme, or mix them up for a mingling of international flavors.

BUFFET TABLE SUGGESTIONS (SEE INDEX)

Dips and Spreads

For a variety of subtle flavors, make any of the salad dressings listed and mix them separately with heavy sour cream for a dip or with softened cream cheese for a spread. Freeze in marked containers.

To serve: Remove the containers to the refrigerator for at

least 8 hours. Stir if necessary. Spoon the dips into serving
bowls. Shape the spreads into flattened loaves, ovals, or
fancy figures. Decorate with appropriate garnishes—sliced
stuffed olives, pimientos, sliced hard-cooked eggs, red or
black caviar, capers, nuts, chopped onions, grated cheese.

Salad Dressings

Basic Italian
Caper
Chutney
Creamy Roquefort, Bleu, or Tangy Cheese
Curry
Horse-radish
Remoulade

Spicy All-Purpose Dunk

For cold shrimp, finger vegetables, cocktail frankfurters, etc.

1 quart		*2 quarts*
3 medium	onions, chopped	4 or 5 large
1 clove	garlic, minced	2 cloves
1 cup	oil (preferably peanut)	2 cups
¼ pound	butter	½ pound
1 large can	whole Italian tomatoes	2 large cans
6-ounce can	tomato paste	10-ounce can
1 teaspoon	rosemary	1½ teaspoons
1 small	bay leaf	1 large
1 pint	dry red wine	1 quart
¼ cup	capers, drained	½ cup

Over very low heat, covered, sauté the onions and garlic
in the combined oil and butter until the onions are very soft
(20 to 30 minutes). Add the tomatoes, tomato paste, rosemary, bay leaf, and wine. Stir well and simmer for 40 minutes. Stir in the capers, add salt only if necessary, and simmer 30 minutes longer. Remove from the heat, stir well, cool
at room temperature, then chill in the refrigerator. When

thoroughly chilled, stir again and pour into containers sized for your party. Freeze.

To serve: Thaw overnight in the refrigerator, or for 3 hours at room temperature. Release into a dunk bowl and stir briskly.

This recipe may also be used as a hot sauce for toothpick meat balls. Release into a heavy saucepan and heat through slowly, stirring from time to time.

Salads for the Buffet Table
Any recipe on pages 105 through 127.

Chafing Dish Casseroles
See the Index for recipes, as listed below. Follow the directions for Freezer Portion.

Casserole Pronto
Chicken à la King *
Chicken Creole
Chicken Marengo
Chicken Stroganoff
Chili Con Carne (with Beans)
Coquilles St. Jacques Provençal *
Crab Meat Creole
Crab Meat Florentine
Crab Meat Newburg *
Deviled Crab Meat *
Deviled Lobster *
Deviled Oyster Casserole
Kedgeree
Kima (East Indian)
Lobster Cantonese
Moussaka

Picadillo, Key West *
Piquant Lobster
Scalloped Oyster Casserole
Scallops à la Newburg *
Shrimp Creole
Shrimp Jambalaya
Shrimp Marinara
Shrimp Sub Gum (Har Ding), Chinese
Sweet and Sour Shrimp, Chinese Style
Shrimp with Lobster Sauce * (Boston or Chinese Style)
Stuffed Cabbage Leaves Hargood House

* Recipes marked with an asterisk are excellent fillings for Crepes. Mince or dice all ingredients and follow the directions for making Dessert Crepes but *omit the sugar.* Serve the Crepes with an appropriate sauce.

Finger and Toothpick Hors d'Oeuvres

See the Index for recipes, as listed below. Roll the mixture into marble-sized balls. Follow the directions for Freezer Portion.

Chinese Sweet and Pungent Meatballs
Crab Meat Croquettes
Curried Meatballs
Fish Balls
Gefüllte Fish Balls
Italian Meatballs I
Matzoth Balls
Russian Meatballs Stroganoff
Batter-fried Shrimp
Batter-fried Chicken Wings, Chinese Style
Artichoke Hearts Alicia

Meat Loaves

Served hot or cold, sliced meat loaves are fine buffet table fare. Make any favorite recipe, or choose from those in the Index. Shape into long, thin loaves about the size and shape of cocktail rye bread. Bake the loaves side by side in a large roasting pan for one hour at 325°. Wrap individually in foil, refrigerate, and freeze when chilled.

To serve cold: Thaw overnight in the refrigerator, wrapped.

To serve hot: Put the foil-wrapped loaves into a 350° oven for 35 to 45 minutes.

Pinwheel Sandwiches

Use unsliced day-old white bread. Remove the crusts with a sharp knife, forming an even "brick," then cut the brick lengthwise into 6 or 7 even slices. With a rolling pin, roll the slices lightly from one end to the other. This makes them easier to handle and provides more compact pinwheels.

Spread each slice with softened butter—plain, or flavored with anchovy paste, mustard, horse-radish, lemon juice, soft cheese, onion juice, etc. Next, spread the slices with various fillings of your choice. These may be purchased in tubs or jars or blended with your own loving hands, and they may be any easily spread cheese, meat, or sea-food product. Along one outer edge put a central motif—red or black caviar, chopped green or ripe olives, pimentos, capers, etc. Starting at the central motif end, roll the bread tightly like a jelly roll and wrap it closely in freezer film or foil. Freeze. When solidly frozen, gather the rolls in freezer boxes or bags.

To serve: Thaw in the refrigerator for 1 hour, or at room temperature for 20 minutes. Unwrap. Slice into rounds with a very sharp knife and arrange on trays or platters. If the pinwheels are not to be set out immediately, keep them in a cool place covered with wax paper or film. They will be ready to eat about 30 minutes after they are sliced.

Ribbon Sandwiches

Choose unsliced loaves of various kinds of bread that are approximately equal in size—cheese, rye, pumpernickel, white, whole wheat, pastel-tinted. Let the bread "stale" in a dry place for a day, or refrigerate in wraps for several hours. Remove the crusts with a sharp knife, forming even "bricks." Cut each brick lengthwise into 6 even slices.

Spread the slices with softened butter on one side. Spread the first slice with your choice of filling and top with a second slice of a different bread variety, butter side down. Spread the second slice first with butter and then with a different filling. Top with bread of a different color, butter side down. Butter this slice and spread with a different filling. Continue alternating until the height is about half that of a normal loaf. Be sure that the top and bottom slices are unbuttered bread. Wrap the loaf in freezer foil and refrigerate for several hours. Open the foil, set the loaf on a cutting board, and slice it down *the long way only* to yield 6 or 7 striped pieces. Wrap each piece individually in freezer film, re-form the slices into a compact loaf, wrap the loaf in foil, and freeze.

To serve: Thaw in the refrigerator for 2 hours or at room temperature for 30 minutes. Unwrap the long slices and cut them across the grain into fingers about ¾ inch wide. They are ready to eat.

39.

Thawing and Heating Frozen Recipes

In discussions about home freezing, a frequently asked question is, "How long does frozen food take to thaw?" What the inquirer usually means, however, is "How long before I can eat or serve it?"

Any frozen food will start to *thaw* as soon as it is placed in a temperature higher than the temperature to which it has been accustomed in freezer storage. The length of time required is influenced by a number of conditions: the size of the package, the material of the wrap or container, the proportion of liquids to solids, and the surrounding temperature of the refrigerator or room in which the thawing takes place.

For example, a couple of raw veal or pork chops or a 1-pound steak will thaw in the refrigerator in 4 to 6 hours, and at room temperature in 2 to 4 hours. A large turkey or roast, on the other hand, may require up to 8 hours a pound in the refrigerator, up to 5 at room temperature.

Foods normally served raw (as fruits) or cold (as desserts and breadstuffs) also thaw at varying times. Fruits usually require up to 8 hours in the refrigerator before they are ready to be served.

Desserts, depending on their composition, are edible anywhere between 1 hour and 4 hours.

Dry baked goods need only stand in their wraps at room temperature for 30 minutes to 1 hour—unless you care to put them into a moderate oven, when they will be warm in less than 15 minutes.

Because this is a cookbook, however, we are more concerned with *heating times* for frozen recipes which are put into the freezer either wholly or partially cooked for later serving.

Heating times also depend on a number of variable conditions as cited above. Explicit range and oven temperatures —and heating times—are given with each recipe's instructions for "Serving the freezer portion" throughout this book.

While there can be no all-inclusive rule about methods for heating food which has been cooked and then frozen, my personal preference is for heating most recipes directly from the frozen state whenever possible, or thawing only briefly before heating. This method not only provides a fresher, just-cooked taste; it also protects a recipe's texture and nutritive value.

For the most part, food frozen in containers or wraps which can be emptied directly into cooking vessels over heat or simmering water will reach serving temperature more rapidly than food frozen in casseroles to be heated in the oven. Casseroles—unless they are metal, or, if ceramic or glass, manufactured to withstand extremes of heat after cold —may be allowed to stand at room temperature up to 1 hour only (unless otherwise specified in recipe directions) before being put into the oven. The food won't thaw to its detriment, and the risk of a cracked casserole is minimized.

Like everybody else, I sometimes feel my life will be easier if a recipe is thawed either completely or at least partially, to hasten the heating time. At those times I break my own rules and write myself a memo to take the container or casserole out of the freezer and put it into the refrigerator before going to bed the night before the food is going to be served.

And, like everybody else, I forget. To shorten the time before dinner, when necessary or desirable, I set a freezer container in warm, not hot, water to the depth of the food it contains until the contents can be released into its cooking vessel.

A casserole recipe will heat faster by improvising a double boiler. Set the casserole into a larger vessel containing cold water and set the larger vessel over moderate heat for 1 hour before placing the casserole in the oven. Taste and touch will tell you when it's ready to be served.

Index

NOTES

NOTES

NOTES

NOTES

NOTES

NOTES

NOTES

NOTES

NOTES

NOTES

NOTES

NOTES